The Psychology Major

Career Options and Strategies for Success

Sixth Edition

R. Eric Landrum
Boise State University

Stephen F. Davis
Morningside College

Pearson

Portfolio Manager: *Tanimaa Mehra*
Content Producer: *Sugandh Juneja*
Portfolio Manager Assistant: *Anna Austin*
Product Marketer: *Christopher Brown*
Art/Designer: *SPi Global*
Full-Service Vendor: *SPi Global*
Full-Service Project Manager: *Gopinath Balaraman, SPi Global*
Compositor: *SPi Global*
Printer/Binder: *LSC Communications, Inc.*
Cover Printer: *LSC Communications, Inc.*
Cover Design: *Lumina Datamatics, Inc.*
Cover Art: art4all/Shutterstock

Library of Congress Cataloging-in-Publication Data

Names: Landrum, R. Eric, author. | Davis, Stephen F., author.
Title: The psychology major : career options and strategies for success / R. Eric Landrum, Boise State University, Stephen F. Davis, Morningside College.
Description: Sixth edition. | Hoboken, NJ : Pearson Education, [2019]
Identifiers: LCCN 2019019249 | ISBN 9780135705100 (print)
Subjects: LCSH: Psychology--Vocational guidance.
Classification: LCC BF76 .L36 2020 | DDC 150.23/73--dc23
LC record available at https://lccn.loc.gov/2019019249

1 2019

Pearson

Rental Edition
ISBN-10: 0-13-570510-X
ISBN-13: 978-0-13-570510-0
Instructor's Review Copy
ISBN-10: 0-13-516159-2
ISBN-13: 978-0-13-516159-3

Brief Contents

Contents

Preface

These feel like turbulent times. And we don't think it really matters when you are reading this, or when we are writing this. It feels turbulent, whether you are thinking about your future, thinking about the economy, thinking about politics (whatever your beliefs are). As a scientist, having data we can trust, have current, up-to-date information is comforting; however, we still have to use our own judgment, leverage our critical thinking skills, and draw our own conclusions, but thinking like a scientist—that is, thinking like a psychological scientist—definitely has its advantages in times of turmoil.

No matter where you are in your undergraduate career, whether you are in the exploration stage, the career pursuit stage, the skill development stage—or you are hovering over some of these stages simultaneously—we have written and revised this book to be practical and inspirational. Our goal for this sixth edition continues to be to provide strategies for success that will allow students to achieve their career goals, whatever they may be. Also, we wanted to provide some fundamental tips and advice that can be useful to all students, but especially useful for psychology majors. Honestly, this book is all about you, and promoting your academic health and career exploration—It is always a pleasure to get a chance to update our work, and here's what new to this edition:

- In our previous edition, not every chapter had an end-of-chapter exercise. In this 6th edition of *The Psychology Major*, every chapter has two end-of-chapter exercises.
- In the previous edition, some chapters contained the personal Success Story feature, others did not. In this 6th edition, every chapter contains a Success Story, and all the Success Stories throughout the entire book are all new.
- When we revised the book previously from the 4th edition to the 5th edition in 2014, of course we updated the information through the references cited, adding 85 new citations at that time; for this upgrade from the 5th edition to the 6th edition, we are adding 166 new citations to the book.
- We have added an entirely new chapter on Student Self-Care (Chapter 11). The toll on a college student's physical and mental health is real, and we believe that it is pertinent to address these issues in a text that is focused on strategies for success for all psychology majors. It seems prudent to provide some evidence-informed advice on self-care.

We are indeed thankful to so many of our colleagues who adopt this book for their courses and tell us about it when we see them at conferences. With the continuing growth in the popularity of psychology, a chance to update the resources and statistics is always welcome. Also, a revision gives us a chance to continue to add to our collective knowledge base about these topics, hopefully making this book more valuable to the students and to our colleagues.

Our basic approach to writing this book was to provide immediately useful and helpful information to students majoring in psychology or thinking about majoring in psychology. The approach of this book is applied—to provide students with practical, timely, up-to-date information that helps them. This text standardizes and catalogs much of the practical advice that professors often give to students on a one-to-one basis—this book does not replace that interaction, but it helps to supplement it. We encourage students to "get their hands dirty" by engaging with the content by completing both of the exercises at the end of each chapter. We hope that students will be inspired by the Success Story (all new) that is presented in every chapter. We hope this will be a one-stop shop for advice about the psychology major, discipline, job market, and employment strategies. We provide tips on how to do well in all classes, how to find research ideas and use PsycINFO and Web of Science, and how to write papers in APA format. Also, the book contains up-to-date career information that faculty might not normally have at their fingertips, including the latest salary figures for a number of psychology-related jobs and occupations. Other benefits include the coverage of ethics for undergraduate students, sections on self-reflection, and an overview of disciplines related to psychology. These features are important perspectives that may not often be shared with the new or prospective psychology major.

We hope this book might be one of the first books that an undergraduate student keeps for his or her own professional library. Specifically, this book makes a good supplemental text for research methods/experimental psychology courses, any capstone course, introductory courses, careers courses, etc. The unique mix and coverage of topics makes this text useful in a variety of teaching situations. Quite frankly, because of the wide variety of topics covered and expert advice offered, we believe that these are some of the key reasons why this volume has thrived for 20 years, and now is presented to you in a 6th edition.

Projects such as this one do not occur in a vacuum. We would like to thank all the many talented individuals and teams at Pearson for seeing the value and potential in a sixth edition of the book. We also want to thank our colleagues who have helped shape the direction of this sixth edition—whether through formal reviews, e-mails, conversations at conferences, etc.—you have greatly helped confirm the value and necessity of such a book. We would like to thank the following reviewers: Douglas Engwall, *Central Connecticut State University*; Erinn Green, *Wilmington College*; Katherine Hooper, *University of North Florida*; Andrea Lassiter, *Minnesota State University, Mankato*; Greg Loviscky, *Penn State*; Mary Anne Taylor, *Clemson University*; and Patti Tolar, *University of Houston & UH-Downtown*.

Finally, we dedicate this book to our students—past, present, and future—our students are *the* reason we wrote the book, and it continues to be our honor and privilege to teach and profess in a manner that positively influences others' lives. Thank *you* for allowing *us* to maximize the opportunity.

R.E.L. & S.F.D.

Chapter 1
Why College?

Learning Objectives

1.1 Explain how college demand has changed over time

1.2 Describe the benefits of a college education

1.3 Identify the basic skills and competencies most useful in the labor force

1.4 Determine the personal and social benefits of a liberal arts education

1.5 Relate college education to financial status

1.6 Compare job and educational alternatives to college

There is a disconnect, a churn, a feeling of anxiety that seems pervasive in higher education today. The sources of this discontent are complex, and they contribute to the complicated answer of "why college?" There are still positive perceptions about the need for college and how a bachelor's degree can facilitate success in the workplace. In a poll conducted in 2013, 70% of American adults indicated that a college education is 'very important;' in 1970, 36% of American adults answered 'very important' (Newport & Busteed, 2013). So, the good news is that a college degree is still viewed positively. But in other news:

- Major industries are reporting an inability to grow and compete. In one instance, 49% having unfilled job openings, translating to 37% of companies unable to take on new business (U.S. Chamber of Commerce Foundation, 2017).
- In a report on the skills gap between what companies need and value and what new graduates possess, one example cited is that 96% of chief academic officers believed that their own U.S. institutions were 'very effective' or 'somewhat effective' at preparing students for the workforce, whereas 11% of business leaders strongly agree (Gallup, 2017).
- Of employed U.S. adults with a bachelor's degree, only 26% strongly agree that their education is relevant to their work and their daily life. Why does this matter? Because relevance is a positive predictor of value and quality (of the education received), and relevance is related to well-being (Strada Education Network and Gallup, 2018).
- "The old rules of thumb no longer apply. Go to college. Get good grades. Get a degree. Get a job. This is great advice that has served many generations well. However, these simple principles are no longer enough in today's more complex world. The relationship between education after high school and jobs has become trickier are harder to navigate" (Carnevale et al., 2017, p. 1).

The mixed messages are abundant. A college education is still thought to be very important but might not be enough to get a good job. Colleges and universities think they are doing a great job with their new graduates, but some employers of those graduates do not seem to agree. The ease of gaining employment a generation ago with a college degree appears to no longer exist today. It does appear that the collegiate terrain is more challenging in the present day—let the advice we provide throughout this book be your added advantage to success. Combined, your authors have over half a century of experience in higher education, and you will see throughout this text that we cite current research as often as possible to give you the best possible advice for making informed decisions about your future.

The Popularity of College and Why Attend College?

1.1 Explain how college demand has changed over time

Overall, the demand for a college education continues to grow, despite any recent rising levels of anxiety or churn (Carnevale et al., 2017). There are a number of indicators that demonstrate this growth; see Table 1.1 for a comparison of changes in a 65-year span (National Center for Education Statistics, 2017a).

You can see for yourself the tremendous growth over time—and we have not even started to address growth within the psychology major. With all of the competition in college, it is interesting to note the most popular reasons that students report going to college. In a study commissioned by the New American Education Policy Program, the top reasons for prospective students to indicate they want to go to college (a combination of the percentage "very important" and percentage "important" responses) were (a) to improve my employment opportunities (91%), (b) to make more money (90%), (c) to get a good job (89%), (d) to learn more about a favorite topic or area of interest (85%), (e) to become a better person (81%), (f) to improve my self-confidence (76%), and (g) to learn more about the world (74%) (Fishman, 2015).

We wrote this book to help you make the most of your undergraduate education to maximize your opportunities for future success, whatever that route may be. With this number of people attending and completing college, how will you stand out? Given that you know what is important to you as you start college, how will you carry that forward and achieve your goals? If you follow our advice, you will know what to do to work toward achieving your goals and to stand out from the crowd.

Table 1.1 Historical Changes in U.S. Higher Education, 1949–1950 to 2014–2015

	1949–1950	2014–2015
Number of Institutions	1,851	4,627
Total Number of Faculties	246,722	1,551,000
Total Enrollment Fall Semester	2,444,900	20,207,369
Number of Bachelor's Degrees Conferred	432,058	1,894,934
Number of Master's Degrees Conferred	58,183	758,708
Number of Doctoral Degrees Conferred	6,420	178,547

SOURCE: National Center for Education Statistics. (2017a). Historical summary of faculty, enrollment, degrees conferred, and finances in degree-granting postsecondary institutions: Selected years, 1869-70 through 2014-15 [Table 301.20]. *Digest of Education Statistics*. Washington, DC: U.S. Department of Education. Retrieved from https://nces.ed.gov/programs/digest/d16/tables/dt16_301.10.asp?current=yes

Broad Benefits of College Beyond a Paycheck

1.2 Describe the benefits of a college education

There are clear reasons why so many Americans pursue a college education; they not only acquire knowledge and skills that augment lifelong learning but also these undergraduate experiences usually lead to employment opportunities and enhanced income. The details of these directly tangible benefits to a college education are presented later in this chapter. However, it is important to realize that there are broader beneficial effects accompanying a college education beyond a paycheck.

Based on data accumulated in 2012, Torstel (2015) calculated the benefits of having a bachelor's degree (with no additional graduate training) as compared to individuals who graduated from high school but never attended college. See Table 1.2 for the benefits (Torstel, 2015, pp. 1–2):

Of course, the types of studies that lead to these conclusions are correlational studies, meaning that these are not cause-and-effect conclusions. That is, going to college is not a guarantee of the outcomes presented in Table 1.2. However, when studied over

Table 1.2 Broad Earnings Benefits of College Completion Compared to High School Completion

- Annual earnings are about $32,000 (134%) higher. Moreover, there is no evidence that the college earnings premium is declining. Indeed, it has been increasing.
- Lifetime earnings are, conservatively, about $625,000 (114%) greater in present discounted value (using a 3%-real interest rate and taking forgone earnings while in college into account).
- The incidence of poverty is 3.5 times lower.
- The likelihood of having health insurance through employment is 47% higher. Annual additional compensation in the form of employer contributions for health insurance is $1,400 (74% greater).
- The likelihood of having a retirement plan through employment is 72% greater. Retirement income is 2.4 times higher.
- Job safety is greater. The incidence of receiving workers' compensation is 2.4 times lower.
- Measures of occupational prestige are significantly higher.
- The probability of being employed is 24% higher.
- The likelihood of being unemployed is 2.2 times lower.
- The likelihood of being out of the labor force (neither employed nor unemployed) is 74% less.
- Age at retirement is higher. The probability of being retired between the ages 62 and 69 is about 25% lower.
- The likelihood of reporting health to be very good or excellent is 44% greater.
- The likelihood of being a regular smoker is 3.9 times lower. The incidence of obesity and heavy drinking are significantly lower. The likelihood of exercising, having a healthy diet, wearing seat belts, and seeking preventative medical care are significantly higher.
- The incidence of a disability making it difficult to live independently is 3.6 times lower.
- Life expectancy at age 25 is seven years longer (for those having at least some college compared to those never having gone to college).
- Asset income is 4.9 times greater ($1,900 more per year).
- The likelihood of not having a bank account is 8.1 times lower. Reliance on expensive forms of banking and credit is significantly lower.
- The probability of being in prison or jail is 4.9 times lower.
- The probability of being married is 21% higher and the probability of being divorced or separated is 61% lower.
- The likelihood of being happy is significantly higher.

SOURCE: Trostel, P. (2015, October 14). It's not just the money: The benefits of college education to individuals and to society. *Lumina Issue Papers*. Indianapolis, IN: Lumina Foundation. Retrieved from https://www.luminafoundation.org/files/resources/its-not-just-the-money.pdf

Table 1.3 Broad Societal Benefits of College Completion Compared to High School Completion

- Although the evidence is not completely conclusive, the positive effect on the aggregate earnings of others appears to be roughly similar to the effect on own earnings.
- Lifetime taxes are, conservatively, $273,000 (215%) greater in present discounted value (using a 3%-real interest rate and taking into account forgone taxes while in college). That is, college graduates contribute hundreds of thousands of dollars more toward government services and social insurance programs.
- Lifetime government expenditures are about $81,000 (39%) lower in present value. College graduates rely much less on other taxpayers.
- The lifetime total fiscal effect is roughly $355,000 in present value.
- Crime is significantly lower.
- Volunteering is 2.3 times more likely. The estimated value of volunteer labor is 4.1 times ($1,300 annually) greater.
- Employment in the nonprofit sector is twice as likely. The estimated value of the implicit wage contribution to nonprofits is 8.7 times ($1,500 annually) greater.
- Annual cash donations to charities are $900 (3.4 times) higher.
- Total philanthropic contributions (i.e., the value of volunteer labor plus the value of the implicit contribution to nonprofits plus cash donations) are $3,600 (4.7 times) higher.
- Voting and political involvement are significantly higher.
- Participation in school, community, service, civic and religious organizations is substantially (1.9 times) higher. Leadership in these organizations is particularly (3.2 times) greater.
- Community involvement is significantly greater. For example, attendance at community meetings is 2.6 times greater.
- Neighborhood interactions and trust are significantly higher.

SOURCE: Trostel, P. (2015, October 14). It's not just the money: The benefits of college education to individuals and to society. *Lumina Issue Papers*. Indianapolis, IN: Lumina Foundation. Retrieved from https://www.luminafoundation.org/files/resources/its-not-just-the-money.pdf

time and with large samples, college attendance is associated with these outcomes, especially when compared to individuals with a high school diploma.

This similar methodology was also used to calculate the collective benefits of college to society. The same types of comparisons are made between college graduates (without further graduate school education) and high school graduates with regard to the statements in Table 1.3 (Torstel, 2015, pp. 2–3).

The broad benefits to society are truly impressive, which makes the stakes even higher for the individual college student. Let's turn our attention to the individual student, examining in more detail those desired skills and competencies necessary for success in the workforce.

Desired Skills and Competencies

1.3 Identify the basic skills and competencies most useful in the labor force

College graduates need to be ready for a variety of work situations and experiences. Chen (2004) reported that the average college graduate will have eight different jobs that will require work in three different professions or occupations. What types of skills and abilities will lead to success during a lifetime of work and career change? First, we should be clear on how we depict skills, and what is the difference between skills and competencies? Are competencies and badges (mini-certifications awarded based on pre-established assessment criteria; not the same as a course, typically less than what you would consider as a "minor") the same? In very recent history, the higher education landscape has become more interesting and more confusing with the options available to students.

There are numerous ways to depict skills and their organizational frameworks, but one that we find particularly useful is from Burrus et al. (2013) and their work regarding the Occupational Information Network (O*NET). Their organizational scheme is presented in Table 1.4.

Table 1.4 An Organizational Framework for 21st-Century Skills

Category	Skill
Analytic skills	Critical thinking Problem solving Decision making Research and inquiry
Interpersonal skills	Communication Collaboration Leadership and responsibility
Ability to execute	Initiative and self-direction Productivity
Information processing	Information literacy Media/information and communication technology Digital citizenship information and communication technology operations and concepts
Capacity for change	Creativity/innovation Adaptive learning/learning to learn Flexibility
Living in the world	Citizenship/civic literacy Life and career Personal and social responsibility
Core subjects/21st-century themes	Mastery of core academic subjects Global awareness Financial, economic, business, and entrepreneurial literacy Health literacy Environmental literacy

SOURCE: Burrus, J., Jackson, T., Xi, N., & Steinberg, J. (2013, November). *Identifying the most important 21st century workforce competencies: An analysis of the Occupational Information Network (O*NET).* Research Report ETS R-13-21. Princeton, NJ: Educational Testing Service. Retrieved from https://www.ets.org/Media/Research/pdf/RR-13-21.pdf

In a survey of Chief Executive Officers (CEOs) and other business leaders, the Committee for Economic Development of the Conference Board (2015) reported on essential competencies necessary for being hired, those competencies in shortest supply, and the combination—that is, competencies that are both essential and in short supply. We'll have much more to say about skills throughout this book, but to preview, the top five most essential competencies reported by individuals in this survey sample were (1) problem solving, (2) ability to work with others of diverse backgrounds, (3) critical thinking, (4) teamwork/collaboration, and (5) oral communication. The top five competencies reported as the 'hardest to hire' (starting with the hardest) were (1) quantitative ability/numeracy; (2) creativity/innovation; (3) Science, Technology, Engineering, and Mathematics (STEM) skills; (4) critical thinking; and (5) written communication. When asked about the combination of factors, CEOs and business leaders reported that critical thinking and problem-solving skills were both essential and the hardest to hire.

Of course, psychology majors can and do achieve many of these skills throughout their undergraduate careers, whether they intend to enter the workforce directly or pursue additional education in some postgraduate capacity. However, more options are becoming available to students at some colleges and universities in the form of credentialing, certificates, and badges (Horn, 2015). In addition to the major and the minor that appears on the institutional transcript, some institutions are implementing programs—sometimes called competency-based education or competency-based learning—where micro-credentials or badges can be earned "along the way" of earning the undergraduate degree. These badges can be independent of coursework or in parallel with coursework, depending on the design of the competency-based program. When done well, these badges and certificates are backed by valid assessment strategies that provide support to the claim that the badge holder has achieved a particular skill level in a particular area, such as information literacy, oral communication, global awareness, and so forth. Colleges and universities that meaningfully engage in badging and credentialing programs can provide their students an added advantage for their launch into the workplace. These advantages can be useful even for students who may not even graduate from their institution.

The Civic, Liberal Arts Value of a College Education

1.4 Determine the personal and social benefits of a liberal arts education

Your college education is not all about the accumulation of skills and abilities to get you a job. There are larger goals of an undergraduate education. All colleges and universities attempt to produce better-educated citizens who are capable of using higher order critical thinking skills.

> One of the major characteristics of a liberal or liberal arts education is that it is not focused on a specific career, but aims instead to provide an environment both within the curriculum and outside it that helps students to learn how to think, how to be creative, how to be flexible, how to get on with others—and how to go on learning for the rest of their lives. (Chen, 2004, p. 2)

Long ago, Newman (1852) communicated this idea quite well (see Table 1.5).

The Financial Value of a College Education

1.5 Relate college education to financial status

We have already explored many of the reasons for coming to college, whether it is to obtain a good job, to improve yourself, to become a better citizen, to gain critical thinking skills, or to master the covert curriculum. These are all appropriate motivations, but so is the motivation to improve your financial standing. Money is not everything in life, but it sure helps. We would be remiss if we did not address this important issue.

In later chapters of this book, we discuss the specifics of what you can earn with the various degrees in psychology, including specialty areas. For now, let's focus on the general benefit of staying in college. How much more money can you expect to make with a college degree compared to a high school diploma? Is there much financial advantage to

Table 1.5 The Aim of a University Education

If then a practical end must be assigned to a University course, I say it is that of training good members of society. Its art is the art of social life, and its end is fitness for the world. It neither confines its views to particular professions on one hand, nor creates heroes or inspires genius on the other. Works indeed of genius fall under no art; heroic minds come under no rule; a University is not a birthplace of poets or of immortal authors, of founders of schools, leaders of colonies, or conquerors of nations. It does not promise a generation of Aristotles or Newtons, of Napoleons or Washingtons, of Raphaels or Shakespeares, though such miracles it has before now contained within its precincts. Nor is it content on the other hand with forming the critic or the experimentalist, the economist or the engineer, although such too it includes within its scope. But a university training is the great ordinary means to a great but ordinary end; it aims at raising the intellectual tone of society, at cultivating the public mind, at purifying the national taste, at supplying true principles to popular enthusiasm and fixed aims to popular aspiration, at giving enlargement and sobriety to the ideas of the age, at facilitating the exercise of political power, and refining the intercourse of private life. It is the education which gives a [person] a clear, conscious view of their own opinions and judgments, a truth in developing them, an eloquence in expressing them, and a force in urging them.

SOURCE: Newman (1852).

Table 1.6 Estimates of Average Annual Earnings and Median Lifetime Earnings for Full-Time, Year-Round Workers by Educational Attainment

Educational Attainment	Average Annual Earnings[1]	Median Lifetime Earnings[2]
Doctoral degree	$ 99,697	$3,525,000
Professional degree[3]	$125,019	$4,159,000
Master's degree	$ 70,856	$2,834,000
Bachelor's degree	$ 58,613	$2,422,000
Associate's degree	$ 39,506	$1,813,000
Some college	$ 32,555	$1,632,000
High school graduate or GED	$ 31,283	$1,371,000
Less than 9th grade	$ 21,023	$ 936,000

[1]U.S. Census Bureau.

[2]Julian (2012).

[3]Professional degrees include M.D. (physician), J.D. (lawyer), D.D.S. (dentist), and D.V.M. (veterinarian).

getting a master's degree compared to a bachelor's degree? These types of questions are answered in Table 1.6. We should note that although the findings presented in this table generally are correct, your results may vary—that is, reality is more complicated than the rows and columns of the table. Carnevale et al. (2011), in examining previous iterations of median lifetime earnings data, offered the following four cogent observations:

Rule 1: Degree level matters, and on average, people with more education make more money than those with less education.

Rule 2: Occupations can trump degree levels, meaning that people with less education can sometimes outlearn people with more education, typically because of occupational differences.

Rule 3: Although occupation can sometimes trump education, degree level achieved still matters most within individual occupations (e.g., an accountant with more education will make more than an accountant with less education).

Rule 4: Race, ethnicity, and gender are wild cards that can trump everything else when trying to develop general statements about determining career-based earnings.

Again, it is important to reiterate that financial reasons alone should not dictate your life decisions—do you really want to be quite miserable while making a good income? However, these data are useful as one component of your decision-making process. Also, if you are in the middle of your sophomore year in college and having a hard time staying motivated, the information in Table 1.6 might be helpful. For instance, you might think about getting your associate's degree (an intermediate degree that can typically be earned in two years) if you are too burned out to finish the bachelor's degree. And remember, there are over 4,600 colleges and universities in the United States—if you drop out and then decide to drop back in, there will be opportunities to do so.

We would encourage you, with our strongest possible advice, to finish what you start. There are financial benefits to completing your education, but as you read earlier, there are health-related benefits, child-rearing benefits, societal benefits, etc. You might be surprised at the percentages of college students who actually end up earning their bachelor's degree. After four years, 38.9% complete a bachelor's degree; after five years, 56.4%; and after six years, 61.2% (DeAngelo et al., 2011). To the extent possible in your life, finish what you start!

Success Stories

Keri Kytola
Wilson College

After completing many years of higher education, I have just started my career as an Assistant Professor of Psychology at a small liberal arts school. Although my educational journey has not been easy, it has been well worth it because I have met a lot of intelligent, inspiring people and learned many important lessons along the way. One lesson that I learned early on, but only recently embraced is that you should never underestimate yourself or give up simply because you believe you cannot achieve a goal. Like many students about to graduate from high school, that goal for me was going to college. However, as a female from a low income background with limited family support, I struggled with low self-esteem and thus had little confidence in my ability to succeed in college due to the financial, academic, and social demands. The fact that I was going to be a first-generation college student made me even more uncertain about being able to meet those demands. Shortly after I decided to go to college (i.e., I applied to prestigious institutions all over the country that I had never heard of), it became clear that achieving my goal would be much more daunting than I imagined when I repeatedly got rejected by the schools I had hoped to attend. Once everything was said and done (i.e., I was turned down by every school I applied to due to my less-than-satisfactory performance in high school) and the dust settled (i.e., I stopped panicking about my future), I re-evaluated my expectations and my goal (i.e., I got a close friend to mentor me). During this re-evaluation process, I learned that I could attend a local community college for one year and then transfer to a neighboring four-year university to finish my Bachelor's degree. Ten years to the day later, choosing to attend community college early on in my academic career turned out to be invaluable for several reasons. First, I got to experience college-level courses on a much smaller scale in terms of class size. This aspect afforded me the opportunity to develop personal relationships with my professors and classmates prior to attending a larger university where it is often more difficult to set oneself apart. Additionally, this small but diverse population exposed me to students from many different backgrounds, age groups, and cultures. As a result, I got to know many non-traditional students who were also first-generation college students. Building these relationships helped me feel more connected to and supported by fellow students who faced similar struggles. Through these experiences, I gained the much needed confidence and momentum I needed to transfer to a four-year university. With the ongoing help of many close friends and mentors, I finally achieved my goal of becoming the first person in my family to graduate from college three years after transferring. That accomplishment was monumental and only served to further boost my confidence! Unbeknownst to my 18-year old self, my new and improved goal was to go to graduate school to earn a doctorate. Just like my undergraduate experience, the graduate application process was grueling and the five-year long training was difficult for me. But, despite the obstacles, completing my Ph.D. was tremendously rewarding because I not only got to delve more deeply into the vast field of psychology, but I also discovered my passion for teaching others about psychology. As a college professor and mentor, it is my hope that I can serve as a source of support for other underrepresented students throughout their academic endeavors so they, too, can achieve their goals.

Oh, You Don't Have to go to College . . .

1.6 Compare job and educational alternatives to college

Better pay typically comes with more education. However, to be fair, if pay is your primary consideration, we should point out that you can have a top-paying job without a bachelor's degree at all. From recent research, Lozon (2018) reported on research from CareerBuilder regarding the top-paying jobs without the need for a college degree. See Table 1.7 for the job titles, hourly wages, and approximate annual salaries.

Not only are these salaries attractive but also many of these jobs are in high demand now. As of this writing, there were 700,000 electrician jobs available, 400,000 plumber, pipefitter, or steamfitter jobs available, and 700,000 computer user support specialist jobs available (Lozon, 2018).

It is important to note that, for most, if not all of the jobs listed in Table 1.7, additional education and training are necessary, and in many cases, certification and/or some type of licensing. So although you may not need "college" to be successful, you will likely need additional training and education for the rest of your life to be successful in whatever pursuit you choose.

We believe it is important to point out one additional opportunity that may be viable for many individuals: military service. There are so many options available, which involve training that can lead to excellent civilian jobs, training that can lead to lifelong careers in the military, enlistment programs that can pay for college, and more. An education and training for your future can come in many forms, and the military route may be an excellent choice for some. If interested, you can start to explore this path at https://www.todaysmilitary.com.

Table 1.7 Highest-Paying Jobs Not Requiring a College Degree

Job Title	Hourly Wage	Approximate Annual Salary
Electrician	$26.33	$52,660
Plumbers, pipefitters, steamfitters	$25.76	$51,520
Computer user support specialists	$25.50	$51,000
Industrial machine mechanics	$24.87	$49,740
Surgical technologists	$22.68	$45,360
Heating, air-conditioning, and refrigeration mechanics and installers	$22.39	$44,780
Chefs and head cooks	$21.54	$43,080
Fitness trainers and aerobics instructors	$20.23	$40,460
Medical records and health information technicians	$19.96	$39,920
Self-enrichment education teachers	$19.91	$39.820

NOTE: Approximate annual salary was based on an estimated 2000-hour work year multiplied by the hourly wage.

SOURCE: Lozon, V. (2018, June 30). Didn't graduate college? Here are the highest-paying jobs. *clickondetroit.com*. Retrieved from https://www.clickondetroit.com/money/jobs/didnt-graduate-college-here-are-the-highest-paying-jobs-without-needing-a-college-degree

As we conclude this chapter, we hope you can see that we want to be fair with the data. We want to present all possible options, and evidence-based whenever possible. There are plenty of good answers to the question "why college," but college is not the answer for all. You have to decide if you are going to make the most of the opportunities and experiences. With regard to majoring in psychology, the remainder of this book is devoted to providing advice and support on just how to make the most of your undergraduate career.

Exercise 1.1 Potential Challenges to Staying in College

We assume that you are reading this book because you are already in college. However, you should know that a great many students start college but never finish. Even though this first chapter (and the rest of this book) will make persuasive arguments for continuing your college education, some students do drop out. Researchers studying college student adjustment (e.g., Klein & Pierce, 2009) use different methods and scales to attempt to measure adjustment to college. Once such scale, the College Adjustment Scales (Anton & Reed, 1991), has different factors or subscales by which scores are recorded. In the table below are the subscale titles—just for your own self-reflection, think a bit about how much each of these categories might be a threat for you to stay in college or not. Remember that you are not actually completing the College Adjustment Scales, but this is just an exercise to help you proactively think about possible threats in your own college environment. Being familiar with the items on this list may alert you to positive situations to pursue and negative situations to avoid.

	The Level of Potential Threat for Dropping Out of School				
Area	**Not at all**	**Slightly**	**Somewhat**	**Moderately**	**Absolutely could be**
Academic problems	O	O	O	O	O
Anxiety	O	O	O	O	O
Interpersonal problems	O	O	O	O	O
Depression	O	O	O	O	O
Career problems	O	O	O	O	O
Suicidal ideation	O	O	O	O	O
Substance abuse	O	O	O	O	O
Self-esteem problems	O	O	O	O	O
Family problems	O	O	O	O	O

Knowing about these factors may help you to anticipate negative situations and increase your chances for success during your undergraduate education. Be sure to take advantage of the counseling services available on your campus.

Exercise 1.2 The College Success Checklist

In 2014, Purdue University and the Gallup Organization began a collaboration supported in part by the Lumina Foundation to study more than 30,000 college graduates (i.e., alumni) across the United States (Gallup, Inc. 2014). Each year, they collect survey data and issue reports based on the analyzed data.

One of the reports from the data analysis is from Busteed (2017) about the methods to make college a success. What is intriguing about these recommendations is that they come from college graduates, who can reflect on their own workforce experiences and what was and was not relevant to their college experience. Scan the checklist below for advice from tens of thousands of alumni on the ways to make college a success.

√	Advice for Making the Most of College
	Get a postsecondary credential or degree. But don't feel like you need to do this until you have a clear or somewhat clear idea of your goals. Think about career and life goals first, then think about majors and fields of study.
	Do not pursue a bachelor's degree by default. Associate degree holders are more likely to strongly agree that they have their ideal job than bachelor's degree holders, and you can always stack more degrees later if you need them.
	Don't take on more than $25,000 in total student loan debt.
	Question the value of attending prestigious, highly selective, and high-priced colleges and universities. "College is much more about what you make of it—how you take advantage of your education—than the type of institution you attend" (Busteed, 2017, para 5).
	As much as you can, pick professors, not courses. Seek out professors who have the reputation for being the amazing teachers and mentors.
	Speaking of mentors, invest in a mentor. Spend time finding a mentor who will invest in you, and invest yourself in that professional relationship.
	When possible, have a job or internship that gives you the opportunity to apply what you are leaning in the classroom—make the classroom to real-work connections.
	Purposely take one or more courses that are long-term projects, requiring a semester/quarter or more to complete.
	Do not pad your resume with a bunch of extracurricular activities where you did not do much; rather, take a deep dive and become involved in one or two (leadership opportunities are even better).

SOURCES: Gallup, Inc. (2014). *Great jobs, great lives: The 2014 Gallup-Purdue Index Report: A study of more than 30,000 college graduates across the U.S.* Washington, DC: Author. Retrieved from https://www.luminafoundation.org/files/resources/galluppurdueindex-report-2014.pdf.; Busteed, B. (2017, June 6). 5 ways to make college a success. Gallup, Inc. Retrieved from https://news.gallup.com/opinion/gallup/211796/ways-college-success.aspx

Of course, there is no "right" or "wrong" score from this checklist, but it is meant to be thought-provoking. We recommend that you revisit this checklist at least once a year, or better yet, and the beginning and end of every semester/quarter/term, just to check to make sure you are on track with your overall, ultimate goals.

Chapter 2
Why Psychology?

Learning Objectives

2.1 Describe the diversity of psychology degrees

2.2 Summarize current trends in psychology majors

2.3 Evaluate your psychology-related skills

2.4 Identify traits common to effective mentoring and advising

2.5 Explain the benefits of majoring in psychology

At the undergraduate level, many students select psychology as a major because of their interest in becoming a psychologist. If you study this book carefully, talk to students majoring in psychology, and listen to your psychology professors, you will quickly understand that you will not be qualified to be a psychologist at the conclusion of your undergraduate training. It is best to think of your undergraduate education in psychology as learning about psychology, not learning "to do" psychology. McGovern et al. (1991, p. 600) made this point clear when they stated that "a liberal arts education in general, and the study of psychology in particular, is a preparation for lifelong learning, thinking, and action; it emphasizes specialized and general knowledge and skills." A quality undergraduate education in psychology should prepare you to be a citizen and a critical thinker—the professional functioning of a psychologist comes after specialized work and training at the graduate level.

Even though the bachelor's degree in psychology is not a professional degree, it is still a good choice to produce a well-rounded, well-educated citizen and person. You may have heard of the notion of reading literacy or information literacy? McGovern et al. (2010) formulated and articulated the notion of psychological literacy, and the characteristics of a psychologically literate person include:

- having a well-defined vocabulary and basic knowledge of the critical subject matter in psychology;
- valuing the intellectual challenges required to use scientific thinking and the disciplined analysis of information to evaluate alternative courses of action;
- taking a creative and amiable skeptic approach to problem solving;
- applying psychological principles to personal, social, and organizational issues at work, relationships, and the broader community;
- acting ethically;
- being competent in using and evaluating information and technology;
- communicating effectively in different modes and with many different audiences;
- recognizing, understanding, and fostering respect for diversity; and
- being insightful and reflective about one's own and others' behavior and mental processes (p. 11).

Completing a rigorous program of undergraduate coursework while majoring in psychology should put graduates well on their way to achieving psychological literacy.

And before someone tries to tell you that you cannot make any money with a bachelor's degree in psychology, let's just pre-empt that notion right now. There are a few different perspectives for looking at salaries, income, and employment in general. The National Association of Colleges and Employers (NACE) published a report in 2015 that reported on the first destinations of the graduations of the Class of 2014. For those majoring in psychology, here is what they reported:

- Percentage standard employment full time: 36.7%
- Percentage continuing education: 25.9%
- Percentage without an income: 22.3%
- Mean starting salary: $33,210

This is the reality based on these data. It is difficult to know for those reporting no income if they were actually seeking an income or not. Obviously, these are topics that matter to many, and it should not be surprising that these are topics studied by many. Carnevale and Cheah (2015) in their own national study through Georgetown University's Center on Education and the Workforce studied over a three-year span both unemployment rates and median earning by major. They also made comparisons of recent college graduates versus experienced college graduates and young graduate degree holders and experienced graduate degree holders. These data are presented in Table 2.1.

Areas of Specialization Within Psychology

2.1 Describe the diversity of psychology degrees

The skills and abilities that a student can attain with a psychology major are impressive. These skills and abilities help explain, in part, the growing popularity of this major. Students seem to be initially attracted to psychology by courses in the areas of abnormal psychology, personality developmental psychology, and social psychology. Students are also attracted to the major because of the applicability of the subject matter—human behavior. For instance, although some students enter college declaring psychology as their major, often psychology departments see increases in the number of majors following completion of the introductory/general psychology course. Introductory psychology can be a challenging course, and many departments have very talented instructors teaching the course. Talented instructors can make interesting subject matter come alive—perhaps another reason for the popularity of psychology.

Table 2.1 Psychology Graduates Unemployment and Median Earnings, Early and With Experience

	Year	Recent College Graduate	Experienced College Graduate	Young Graduate Degree Recipient	Experienced Graduate Degree Recipient
Unemployment	2009–2010	7.6%	6.0%	3.9%	3.3%
	2010–2011	9.2%	6.9%	3.9%	3.5%
	2011–2012	9.3%	6.3%	3.9%	3.3%
Median Earnings	2009–2010	$32,000	$52,000	$53,000	$71,000
	2010–2011	$32,000	$54,000	$52,000	$69,000
	2011–2012	$31,000	$53,000	$50,000	$68,000

SOURCE: Carnevale, A. P., & Cheah, B. (2015). From hard times to better times: College majors, unemployment, and earnings. Center on Education and the Workforce. Washington, DC: Georgetown University. Retrieved from https://cew.georgetown.edu/wp-content/uploads/HardTimes2015-Report.pdf

Success Stories

Amanda West

I grew up on a municipal airport in a middle class family. My father was the caretaker of the airport and my mother operated a bakery out of the home. I remember having a happy childhood, using the airplane hangars as my personal roller skating rink, and learning how to drive on the runways.

I was a bright child who did well in school, and had a publication by the time I was 15. Somewhere around that time my brother was charged with murder and my parents started having problems. The stress and the money were too much to bear and they divorced not long after the charge, and I began to get bullied by the family of the victim. It was then that I started spiraling out of control.

I quit school halfway through my senior year and by the time I was 18 I had my first child. Shortly after that, I was married and by the time I was 21, I had my second child. I was happy as a mother of two wonderful children, but my husband began doing opiates and it wasn't long after that I was doing them too. By the time I was 26, I had a full-blown habit and struggled to get clean.

I was in and out of rehab for years. During that process, I thought that becoming a counselor may be the right career path for me, and my love of psychology began to bloom. I separated from my husband at 32 because I knew that it was the only way to get clean, and tried to make a new life for my children and myself.

I slept on my mother's floor for about 9 months, wearing my children's clothes because I left everything behind. I was 33 when I received the call that would change my life. My husband had been found dead after an overdose.

Suddenly, I was alone. With no skills to speak of other than bartending, I decided that I would get my GED and go to college. I was a non-traditional first-generation student and I was terrified, but as it turned out, I was an excellent student. I graduated from community college in 2013, and went on to double major in psychology and gerontology at the Missouri State University while working two jobs and caring for my two teenagers. I finally felt like I was worth something.

In my final semester as I was preparing to take the GRE and apply for doctorate programs, my father was diagnosed with dementia and I became his legal guardian. It was a stressful time and I had to put off my dreams of a Ph.D., but my dad was worth it. I continued to work in the restaurant business while I finished school, and that is where I was offered a job by the CEO of a local center for independent living. I landed the job, got published in a scholarly journal, and then graduated cum laude all within a couple of months, and I finally realized my full potential.

Today I am the Assistive Technology Coordinator at the third largest center for independent living in the state, an Americans with Disabilities Act Coordinator, and a member of the board of directors for another nonprofit organization. I apply the knowledge that I gained in the psychology program on a daily basis, whether I am working with someone with aphasia, dementia, PTSD, or depression and anxiety due to aging or acquiring a new disability. My hard work has paid off, and now I have a profession of helping others.

In the introductory course, students are introduced to the various areas and specializations in psychology; the options are staggering. As a psychology major, you will receive a good grounding in the basics of psychology, taking courses that emphasize the development of skills and abilities (e.g., research methods and statistics) while also accumulating a knowledge base (e.g., developmental psychology, social psychology, and history and systems). Even if you recently completed an introductory course, it is hard to remember all the options. To our knowledge, there is no "official" list of the major areas of psychology; we compiled our list from a number of sources. Within most of these areas, there are opportunities to specialize even further—more on this later in this chapter. Technically speaking, though, the American Psychological Association (APA) recognizes only four "specialties"—clinical, counseling, school, and industrial/organizational psychology (APA, 2007). All the remaining areas are considered subfields or areas of concentration. For the sake of clarity, however, we will call the specializations with psychology "areas." Typically, you will not specialize in a particular area at the undergraduate level, although there are a handful of institutions in the United States where a student can earn a specialized undergraduate degree in psychology. Your area of specialization becomes much more important if you elect to attend graduate school. In fact, if you decide to pursue a graduate degree in psychology, not only will you probably specialize in one of the areas presented but also your degree may also come from a program that specializes even further.

For a sense of those different levels of specialization, Table 2.2 presents a listing of master's degrees and/or doctoral degrees that can be earned in psychology programs in the United States—these broad categories were gleaned from the index of the helpful book to those with an interest in graduate school titled *Graduate Study in Psychology* (American Psychological Association [APA], 2018). Note that the number in parentheses following each area indicates the number of schools offering that specialty area as of July 2018.

At this point, it is not necessary to know exactly which area of psychology you want to study—what is important is that you begin to understand the vast opportunities and diversity of specializations that psychology has to offer. With all of the choices available, you may ask, "Where do I begin selecting courses as a psychology major, and what can I do with a bachelor's degree?" Those questions sound like ones that you might ask of your academic advisor or your mentor—more on these important roles later in this chapter.

Table 2.2 APA Areas of Specialization for Master's and Doctoral Degree Psychology Programs

Applied Behavior Analysis (60)	Human Development and Family Studies (12)
Behavioral Psychology (58)	Human Factors (25)
Biological Psychology (30)	Humanistic Psychology (4)
Child and Adolescent Psychology (67)	Industrial/Organizational Psychology (150)
Clinical Psychology (367)	Marriage and Family Therapy (33)
Cognitive Psychology (152)	Mental Health Counseling (71)
Community Counseling (9)	Multicultural Psychology (17)
Community Psychology (30)	Neuropsychology (27)
Comparative Psychology (1)	Neuroscience (114)
Consulting Psychology (16)	Other (10)
Counseling Psychology (133)	Personality Psychology (30)
Developmental Psychology (143)	Physiological Psychology (11)
Educational Psychology (75)	Primary Care Psychology (1)
Environmental Psychology (2)	Psychoanalytic Psychology (2)
Experimental Psychology (Applied) (50)	Psycholinguistics (5)
Experimental Psychology (General) (133)	Psychopharmacology (3)
Family Psychology (9)	Quantitative Psychology (63)
Forensic Psychology (37)	Rehabilitation Psychology (6)
Gender Psychology (3)	School Counseling (45)
General Psychology (Theory, History, and Philosophy) (41)	School Psychology (187)
Geropsychology (8)	Social Psychology (130)
Health Psychology (66)	Sport Psychology (3)

SOURCE: American Psychological Association. (2018). *Graduate study in psychology 2018*. [Online]. Washington, DC: Author: Retrieved from http://gradstudy.apa.org/index.cfm?action=browseprogram

Who Majors in Psychology?

2.2 Summarize current trends in psychology majors

Psychology continues to be an extremely popular choice, both for students enrolled in its courses and psychology majors. Currently, psychology is a very popular major. At the time of this writing with the latest data available (2015–2016) from the National Center for Education Statistics (2017a), the top four degree-granting majors in the United States are business (371,694 graduates), health professions and related programs (228,896 graduates), social sciences and history (161,230 graduates), and psychology (117,440 graduates). To be fair, those three "majors" ahead of psychology are an amalgamation of multiple majors under one cluster. If majors were "counted" on an individual basis, it is likely that psychology is the most popular major in the nation (if the metric were number of bachelor's degrees earned).

The number of students choosing to major in psychology has grown over time and is likely to continue growing. There have been over 70,000 bachelor's degrees in psychology awarded every year since 1994–1995 (Snyder & Dillow, 2011). To graphically see the historical trend in the awarding of bachelor's degrees in psychology, see Figure 2.1. How do the other graduation statistics stack up? In 2015–2016, 10,603 students received an associate's degree in psychology (National Center for Education Statistics, 2017b), 27,645 students received master's degrees in psychology, and 6,532 students received doctorates in psychology (National Center for Education Statistics, 2017c).

One of the recurring themes to think about as you read this book is this: What will you do, as an undergraduate, to make yourself competitive with 117,000+ graduates in psychology each year? It doesn't matter if you go the workforce psychology route or the graduate school route—the competition will be fierce for premium opportunities. Assuming the continued popularity of psychology as witnessed in Figure 2.1 over the past 65 years, there will only be more competition for the best opportunities as time goes on. Multiple sections of this book are dedicated to alerting you to the opportunities available now and preparing you to maximize those opportunities now. We also focus on skills and abilities that you can develop while you are still an undergraduate.

Figure 2.1 U.S. Psychology Bachelor's Degrees by Gender, 1950–2016

SOURCE: National Center for Education Statistics. (2017c). Degrees in psychology conferred by postsecondary institutions, by level of degree and sex of student: Selected years, 1949–1950 through 2015–2016 [Table 325.80]. *Digest of Education Statistics*. Washington, DC: U.S. Department of Education. Retrieved from https://nces.ed.gov/programs/digest/d17/tables/dt17_325.80.asp

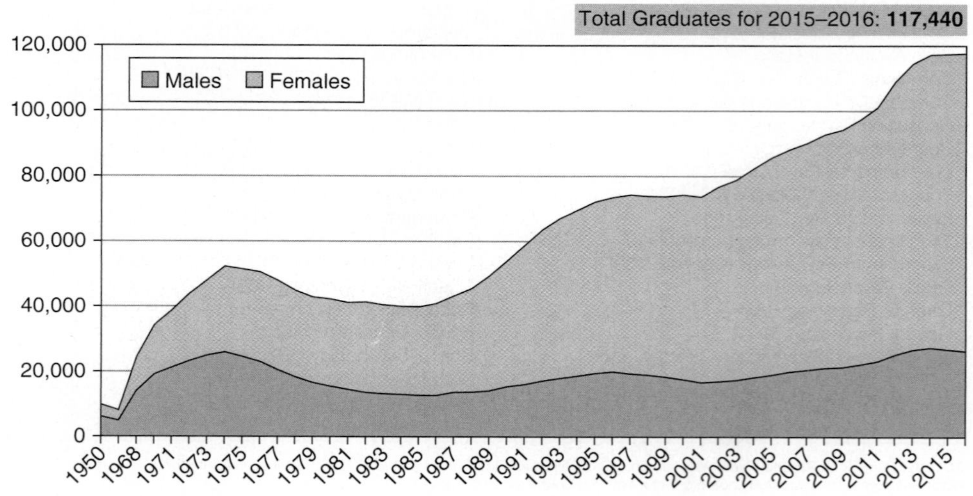

Desirable Skills and Abilities for the Psychology Major

2.3 Evaluate your psychology-related skills

So, what are those skills, abilities, and traits that employers want you to acquire en route to your baccalaureate degree (with a special emphasis on a bachelor's degree in psychology)? Although there are many good lists available, see Table 2.3 for transferable skills with examples.

What is the benefit of knowing this information? As you pursue your undergraduate career, try to arrange your curriculum choices to give yourself the opportunity to acquire as many of these skills and abilities as possible. You will not be able to master every one of them—at least not during your undergraduate years, and you certainly cannot master complex skills in a single course. These are skills and abilities you aspire to acquire—design your undergraduate coursework so that, as you complete the coursework, you acquire proficiency in many of the above-mentioned areas. Also remember that these skills and abilities can be gained in extracurricular activities such as club involvement, internship opportunities, at the job(s) you already have, and so on. Realize, however, that some of these items are more "teachable" or "learnable" than others. With the right coursework and variety of experiences, a teacher can improve your computational/statistical ability, but a teacher is less able to influence traits such as your personality. Advisors and mentors can help you seek those opportunities to

Table 2.3 A Listing of Transferable Skills, with Examples

Skills	Examples
Resourceful	Ability to locate hard-to-find information; handle difficult situations; or secure scarce resources.
Detail Oriented	Acute attention to minutia results in excellent follow-through on all projects and assignments.
Good Writer	Ability to prepare proposals, e-mails, speeches, newsletters, direct mail, letters, advertising copy, website content, and interoffice memos.
Excellent Communicator	Ability to interact with clients, coworkers, and managers in a meaningful way while maintaining a professional demeanor and keeping conflicts at a minimum.
Articulate	Ability to get a point across effectively and interact with clients, coworkers, and managers in a professional manner.
Enthusiastic	Maintains a positive attitude toward challenges and obstacles. Ability to keep a team motivated.
Action Oriented	Determined to complete projects and assignments on time. Ability to focus on the task at hand and get the job done. Always ready to work.
Process Oriented	Avoids mistakes by carefully considering each project from all angles before starting any project. Meticulous planning results in very few unexpected delays and problems.
Strategic Thinker	Ability to prioritize effectively; separate issues into relevant "buckets"; anticipate potential challenges; and easily identify the most critical aspects of any project.
Organized	Reduces anxiety in the workplace due to ability to locate resources quickly and easily. Ability to develop new company processes in a methodical and well-thought-out manner that others can follow.
Excellent Public Speaker and Presenter	Exudes confidence in front of large groups and does not get rattled easily. Able to think on one's feet and stay focused on the subject matter. Ability to explain complex material in an easy to understand manner. Good teacher.
Good Listener	Ability to observe and read others. Quick to understand what someone is saying and able to follow directions.

SOURCE: Brown and Zefo (2007), reprinted with permission.

become more well-rounded and to be competitive whether your goal is to enter the workforce or to go to graduate school and then enter the workforce.

This list of skills and abilities is impressive. As an undergraduate, it would be difficult to achieve all of those skills and abilities to any significant level of proficiency. So, which ones are the *most* important? If you have to choose certain skills and abilities to concentrate on, what should they be? First, you want to honestly evaluate your current strengths and weaknesses and seek out opportunities to improve on your weaknesses. We sometimes tell students: You need to have good oral communication skills before you leave this university. Where and with whom do you want to hone this skill—with professors, where the absolute worst thing that can happen in a supportive environment is that you get one bad grade; or on the job, where a bad performance might cost you your job, your security, your home, and your car. College is a place that provides a safety net for you to explore your strengths and weaknesses. College is the place to improve what you are not good at—not the place to avoid your weaknesses altogether. Students who fear math courses often take the minimum number of credits required when they should be working to strengthen their math skills. A similar pattern often occurs with writing. If you have difficulty in writing, or are not confident in your writing ability, the last thing you need to do is avoid all courses that involve writing. You might be able to graduate that way ("Cs get degrees"), but you may not be very employable.

The Importance of Advising and Mentoring

2.4 Identify traits common to effective mentoring and advising

At some universities, advising is divided into categories: academic advising and career advising. Academic advising focuses on the curricular demands of the major and addresses such issues as course scheduling and availability, student success in academic courses, meeting prerequisites, and graduation requirements. Career advising emphasizes the student's short- and long-term goals and takes the form of multiple discussions between the student and advisor over the course of an academic career. It is during these career-advising sessions that much of the information provided in this book would be imparted. For example, questions about employment opportunities with a bachelor's degree and graduate school options are often discussed during career advising. Advising provides faculty members with valuable teaching moments (Foushee, 2008), such as correcting misperceptions about psychology, helping develop realistic career goals, enhancing your strengths, and getting to know the real you. We'll provide you with plenty of resources about the psychology major and thinking deeply about these issues will help you prepare for meetings with your academic advisor.

Academic and career advising-based decisions are ultimately your responsibility; the institution shares some responsibility in providing accurate information about academic and career choices, satisfaction with the major, progress toward the degree, and interest in the profession. It is hard to imagine a psychology department in any college or university where you will not be able to find someone to help you—the key may be in finding out *whom* to ask. At times, you may be surprised by the reactions of your advisor(s); he or she has your best interests at heart. That is, if your best option is to withdraw from school, your advisor will probably not try to talk you out of it. In making that big a decision, however, an advisor may suggest that you seek additional input, such as from trusted friends, a career center, counseling center, and so on. If you are thinking about pursuing an online graduate program, consult your advisor! If you are miserable as a psychology major, why remain in the major? As academics, we should have your best interests in mind—we want you to be successful and satisfied with your college experience. Many students fail to take advantage of the advising opportunities afforded to them—be sure that you are not one of those students.

Researchers are now beginning to study the different types of advising styles that departments offer, and student preferences for those styles. Vespia et al. (2018) developed measures to study student preferences. To see the types of distinctions drawn by students seeking advising, see Table 2.4.

The role of the mentor has long been acknowledged as important at the graduate student level, but there is increasing emphasis on mentoring for undergraduate-level students. Not only is effective mentoring good for you, but it's good for faculty members as well. Effective mentoring helps faculty become better teachers, leads to better productivity with student collaborators, and creates an environment that promotes student involvement (Schultz, 2001). As a student, when you are thinking about selecting/choosing a mentor, think about these dimensions (adapted from Johnson et al., 2015): (1) look for a faculty member willing to invest time in you outside of class time; (2) a good mentor will naturally provide informal academic and career advising; (3) mentors provide strong encouragement and emotional support, and ultimately you should feel better about the institution because of your mentoring relationship; (4) when you share segments of your career dreams with your mentor, good mentors pick up on that and help you explore your dreams, rather than steering you in a pre-determined direction; and (5) mentors will likely slip into parenting roles from time to time—not because of any immaturity but because they care about you and wish to share advice that they think would be beneficial.

Is a mentor the same as an advisor? Not necessarily. They could be the same person, or not. The mentor is more of a long-term guide who helps you to succeed and fulfill your goals. Your mentor might very well also be your academic advisor. However, you might have one faculty member to be an academic advisor and another to be your mentor. There are some advantages to this approach. First, you would gain multiple perspectives on issues relevant to you. Second, it would allow you to build important relationships with multiple faculties. Third, it would allow you to cultivate relationships with professionals that might lead to letters of recommendation, which will be

Table 2.4 Examples of Direct and Nondirective Advising Styles

Direct Advising Style	Nondirective Advising Style
Gives direct advice on what I should do	Helps me explore options with no direct advice
Tells me which skills I should improve	Helps me explore which skills I want to improve
Tells me what requirements I have left to fill for graduation	Allows me to determine for myself what requirements I have left to fill for graduation
Tells me what career goals are realistic for me	Asks me about identifying realistic career goals for myself
Recommends which internships I should apply to	Helps me evaluate the pros and cons of different internship choices
Explains what the implications of the current economy are to me	Encourages me to discuss the implications of the current economy
Notices my strengths and tells me which careers I should explore for employment	Notices my strengths and helps me explore how they could apply to different professional fields
Will directly teach me how to write a resume	Discusses different methods I can take to approach resume writing
Tells me step-by-step what to do to search for a job	Explores different options with me to approach job searching
Prescribes a course of action for me to obtain my goals	Helps me consider all the different options available to reach my goals

SOURCE: Vespia, K. M., Freis, S. D., & Arrowood, R. M. (2018). Faculty and career advising: Challenges, opportunities, and outcome assessment. *Teaching of Psychology*, *45*, 24–31. doi:10.1177.0098628317744962

important for pursuing either a good job or graduate school. You can begin to see how important a mentor can be in your professional development.

Here's one last attempt to convince you of the importance of the connections you make as an undergraduate. In the Gallup-Purdue national study of 30,000 college alumni that we introduced in Chapter 1 (Gallup, Inc. 2014), when analyzing the most salient predictors of college preparing alumni for life, the top predictors (called the "big six") are the items when respondents can *strongly agree* to the following items (Seymour & Lopez, 2015, para. 2):

- I had at least one professor at [my institution] who made me excited about learning.
- My professors at [my institution] cared about me as a person.
- I had a mentor who encouraged me to pursue my goals and dreams.
- I worked on a project that took a semester or more to complete.
- I had an internship or job that allowed me to apply what I was learning in the classroom.
- I was extremely active in extracurricular activities and organizations while I attended [my institution].

As you can see from the alumni data, judging their own success after college, mentoring, connections, and activity outside the classroom were key. We will focus on how to succeed at all of these activities throughout this text.

Why the Psychology Major is a Good Choice

2.5 Explain the benefits of majoring in psychology

Completion of a rigorous undergraduate program in psychology affords students with a host of developed and honed skills that they can apply to the psychology workforce (with a bachelor's degree) or to graduate school (for a master's degree or a doctorate). Successful graduates of undergraduate psychology leave their undergraduate program with many of these skills and abilities:

- Scientific literacy in reading and writing as well as psychological literacy
- Strong analytical skills and statistical/computer familiarity
- Interpersonal awareness and self-monitoring/management skills
- Communication skills and the ability to work in groups
- Problem-solving and information-finding skills
- Critical thinking and higher order analysis capabilities
- Research and measurement skills

More than likely, the opportunities to acquire these skills exist in your psychology department. Some of these skills will be honed and sharpened in the classroom and by performing class-related tasks, but others are better learned outside the classroom from experiences gained as a research assistant, during internship, or as a teaching assistant. This book is designed for one primary purpose—to help you get the most out of your undergraduate psychology major experience. If *you* don't take advantage of the opportunities that surround you, someone else will.

Exercise 2.1 Psychology Survey

Below is a survey that addresses many of the topics in this book. Before reading any further, complete this survey now, and at the end of the book (or the end of the course), and you can revisit this survey and see if there have been any changes. Select the response that best represents your current opinion.

	Strongly Disagree	Moderately Disagree	Neutral	Moderately Agree	Strongly Agree
I feel prepared for any type of bachelor's level job	O	O	O	O	O
I know how to apply for graduate programs in psychology	O	O	O	O	O
I will be able to work in a psychology-related job	O	O	O	O	O
I understand the course requirements for the psychology major	O	O	O	O	O
I am familiar with bachelor's level jobs	O	O	O	O	O
I am ready to apply for graduate school	O	O	O	O	O
I understand the course requirements for the psychology minor	O	O	O	O	O
I know about my psychology-related options outside of the classroom	O	O	O	O	O
I am committed to majoring in psychology	O	O	O	O	O
I know how to find information on the Internet	O	O	O	O	O
I understand the importance of math and science	O	O	O	O	O
I know how to use PsycINFO	O	O	O	O	O
I know the study skills needed for success in college	O	O	O	O	O
I am familiar with the type of careers alumni have attained	O	O	O	O	O
I understand the ethical implications of studying and doing psychological research	O	O	O	O	O
Letters of recommendation are important	O	O	O	O	O
I understand which disciplines are related to psychology	O	O	O	O	O
After this course, I think I will still be majoring in psychology	O	O	O	O	O
I want a psychology-related career	O	O	O	O	O
Which term best reflects your current feelings about majoring in psychology? (Circle one)	Very negative	Somewhat negative	Uncertain	Somewhat positive	Very Positive

SOURCE: Dillinger and Landrum (2002).

Exercise 2.2 Employable Skills Self-Efficacy Survey

Please indicate your level of agreement with the following statements using the options provided below.

1	2	3	4	5	6
Strongly Disagree	**Disagree**	**Somewhat Disagree**	**Somewhat Agree**	**Agree**	**Strongly Agree**

Score	Statement
	1. I feel comfortable working in group settings.
	2. I would rather be the person who gets to lead a group project.
	3. People easily understand what I mean when I am talking to them.
	4. I struggle to manipulate numbers in a spreadsheet.
	5. Writing is not a strong skill for me.
	6. I can easily think of ways for testing my research questions.
	7. I prefer not to volunteer for more than I have to already do.
	8. I can persuasively present my ideas through my writing.
	9. My mind seems to go blank when I have to speak in front of a group of people.
	10. I have difficulty delegating when working in groups.
	11. I feel uncomfortable in professional settings.
	12. I have trouble evaluating the quality of information I get from publications.
	13. I struggle to gather the information from reliable sources.
	14. People often misunderstand my point when reading my writing.
	15. I have difficulty planning a project from start to finish.
	16. I typically remember all information I read.
	17. Others sometimes believe that I can be somewhat unreliable in meeting deadlines.
	18. My mind tends to wander when someone is verbally telling me what needs to be done.
	19. It is easy for me to follow written directions.
	20. I can easily use software to create tables and graphs to effectively display information.
	21. I am eager to learn new information.
	22. When I have multiple projects, I can easily set priorities.
	23. I do what it takes to finish a project even if I do not find it enjoyable.
	24. I often have difficulty verbally expressing my thoughts to others.
	25. I can easily fit into any group work setting.
	26. It is easy for me to use the scientific approach when solving problems.
	27. Professional writing is easy for me.
	28. I am easily overwhelmed by data.
	29. It is difficult for me to remember information I only hear.
	30. I am confident whenever I need to a lead a group project.
	31. I know where to find relevant information from good sources when I need it.
	32. It is easy for me to find the information that I need using search engines such as Google.
	33. It is easy for me to follow verbal directions.
	34. I am an effective leader in group settings.
	35. I usually understand information that I read.
	36. I like having opportunities to improve my leadership skills.
	37. I am comfortable learning to use new technology when working on a project.
	38. I am not sure what it means to dress "professionally."
	39. I typically comprehend information that someone tells me verbally.
	40. It is easy for me to integrate information from a wide of variety of sources.
	41. I struggle to manage my time.

Score	Statement
	42. I rarely procrastinate when working on projects.
	43. I prefer to work alone on projects.
	44. It is easy for me to use data when making decisions.
	45. I have trouble working in groups successfully.
	46. I struggle with being self-motivated in my work.
	47. I have the analytical skills to work with data.
	48. I often feel lost when trying to read professional publications.
	49. I can persuasively present my ideas in talking with others.
	50. I think I do some of my best work in group settings.
	51. I can easily organize information into a database.

SCORING KEY

NOTE: "r" indicates the item rating should first be reverse-coded. This means there will be a subtraction problem, in this case 7 – x. If your original answer was a 5, and the key indicates "reverse score" with the letter r, then the score you will use for the calculation will be 7 – 5 = 2. Use the value 2 in your calculation of the subscores and overall scores.

Subscore Area	Score	Scoring Method
Collaboration Skills		
Working in Groups Skills Subscore		Take mean of Items 1, 25, 43r, 45r, and 50
Leadership Skills Subscore		Take mean of Items 2, 10, 30, 34, and 36
Overall Collaboration Skills Score		Take mean of working in groups skills and leadership skills items
Professional Development Skills		
Self-Management Skills Subscore		Take mean of Items 21, 22, 41r, and 42
Professional Skills Subscore		Take mean of Items 7r, 11r, 15r, 17r, 23, 38r, and 46r
Technology Skills Subscore		Take mean of Items 4r, 20, 32, 37, and 51
Overall Professional Development Skills Score		Take mean of working in self-management skills, professional skills, and technology skills items
Analytical Inquiry Skills		
Research Skills Subscore		Take mean of Items 6, 26, 28r, 44, and 47
Information Literacy Skills Subscore		Take mean of Items 12r, 13r, 31, and 40
Overall Analytical Inquiry Skills Score		Take mean of research skills and information literacy skills items
Communication Skills		
Writing Skills Subscore		Take mean of 5r, 8, 14r, and 27
Speaking Skills Subscore		Take mean of Items 3, 9r, 24r, and 49
Reading Skills Subscore		Take mean of Items 16, 19, 35, and 48r
Listening Skills Subscore		Take mean of Items 18r, 29r, 33, and 39
Overall Communication Skills Score		Take mean of writing skills, speaking skills, reading, and listening skills items

SOURCE: Ciarocco, N. J., & Strohmetz, D. B. (2017). The Employable Skills Self-Efficacy Survey: An assessment of and resource for fostering skill development. *Office of Teaching Resources in Psychology*, Society for the Teaching of Psychology. Retrieved from http://teachpsych.org/page-1603066

Chapter 3

Careers with a Bachelor's Degree in Psychology

Learning Objectives

3.1 Outline the major goals of an undergraduate curriculum in psychology

3.2 Summarize employment expectations for psychology majors

3.3 Describe job market experiences for a person with a psychology bachelor's degree

3.4 Explain how students can prepare for challenges in transitioning to a workplace

As a psychology major, you have a complex future ahead, no matter what your educational or employment path. What do we mean? After you earn your bachelor's degree in psychology, even if you choose not to attend graduate school in psychology (or some other field), there will be more education in your future. This "education" may not be the type of formal education that leads to a degree, but you will receive training and keep learning for the rest of your life. These graduates who seek to transition into careers with their bachelor's degrees are referred to as psychology workforce graduates. Some psychology bachelor's degree recipients elect to continue their formal education, perhaps in a graduate school program in psychology, or in medical school, law school, a social work program, and so on. However, their ultimate goal is also entry into the workplace, and they too will also be lifelong learners, receiving more training. Thus, there are (at least) two tiers or two tracks, workforce psychology graduates and graduate school-bound students. This chapter is about the options you have as a psychology workforce graduate. You may be surprised at the opportunities that are available, but you also need to recognize the challenges and limitations.

The Undergraduate Curriculum

3.1 Outline the major goals of an undergraduate curriculum in psychology

As you think about selecting a particular college or university, or as you ponder the decision you have already made, how much did the curriculum (the courses required and recommended by the psychology department and the university) influence your decision? Although the overall reputation of the institution probably influenced your decision, your choice of psychology as a major was probably not made on the basis of a particular course offered by the department. Of course, you should pay attention to the curriculum at your own institution, but know that educators do study these issues from a national perspective (Dunn, Cautin, & Gurung, 2011; Norcross et al., 2016), and there have even been suggestions that there should be a "common core" across all of psychology (Dunn et al., 2010). Sometimes scholars take a deep dive and examine how prevalent a course is within the discipline, such as Psychological Measurement (Dahlman & Geisinger, 2015) or even an opportunity such as service learning (Bringle et al., 2016; Simon, 2017). Recently, there has been a great amount of interest and multiple calls for internationalization of the undergraduate psychology curriculum (Bikos et al., 2013; Gross, Abrams, & Enns, 2016; Jessop & Adams, 2016; Lutsky, 2016; Takooshian et al., 2016).

Learning goals and outcomes of psychology majors receive serious consideration by psychology educators. An American Psychological Association (APA) Board of Educational Affairs Task Force on Psychology Major Competencies was formed in 2012 to begin work on updating the first iteration of the *APA Guidelines for the Undergraduate Psychology Major,* which was published in 2007 (APA, 2007). This update, known as *Guidelines 2.0,* was published in 2013 (APA, 2013). To give you a sense of *Guidelines 2.0* and the learning goals intended for every psychology major, see Table 3.1.

Table 3.1 Superstructure of the APA Guidelines for the Undergraduate Psychology Major, Version 2.0

Goal 1: Knowledge Base in Psychology
Students should demonstrate fundamental knowledge and comprehension of the major concepts, theoretical perspectives, historical trends, and empirical findings to discuss how psychological principles apply to behavioral phenomena. Students completing foundation courses should demonstrate breadth of their knowledge and application of psychological ideas to simple problems; students completing a baccalaureate degree should show depth in their knowledge and application of psychological concepts and frameworks to problems of greater complexity.

1.1 Describe key concepts, principles, and overarching themes in psychology.
1.2 Develop a working knowledge of psychology's content domains.
1.3 Describe applications of psychology.

Goal 2: Scientific Inquiry and Critical Thinking
The skills in this domain involve the development of scientific reasoning and problem solving, including effective research methods. Students completing foundation level courses should learn basic skills and concepts in interpreting behavior, studying research, and applying research design principles to drawing conclusions about psychological phenomena; students completing a baccalaureate degree should focus on theory use as well as designing and executing research plans.

2.1 Use scientific reasoning to interpret psychological phenomena.
2.2 Demonstrate psychology information literacy.
2.3 Engage in innovative and integrative thinking and problem solving.
2.4 Interpret, design, and conduct basic psychological research.
2.5 Incorporate sociocultural factors in scientific inquiry.

Goal 3: Ethical and Social Responsibility in a Diverse World
The skills in this domain involve the development of ethically and socially responsible behaviors for professional and personal settings in a landscape that involves increasing diversity. Students completing foundation-level courses should become familiar with the formal regulations that govern professional ethics in psychology and begin to embrace the values that will contribute to positive outcomes in work settings and in building a society responsive to multicultural and global concerns. Students completing a baccalaureate degree should have more direct opportunities to demonstrate adherence to professional values that will help them optimize their contributions and work effectively, even with those who do not share their heritage and traditions. This domain also promotes the adoption of personal and professional values that can strengthen community relationships and contributions.

3.1 Apply ethical standards to evaluate psychological science and practice.
3.2 Build and enhance interpersonal relationships.
3.3 Adopt values that build community at local, national, and global levels.

Goal 4: Communication
Students should demonstrate competence in writing and in oral and interpersonal communication skills. Students completing foundation-level courses should be able to write a cogent scientific argument, present information using a scientific approach, engage in discussion of psychological concepts, explain the ideas of others, and express their own ideas with clarity. Students completing a baccalaureate degree should produce a research study or other psychological project, explain scientific results, and present information to a professional audience. They should also develop flexible interpersonal approaches that optimize information exchange and relationship development.

4.1 Demonstrate effective writing for different purposes.
4.2 Exhibit effective presentation skills for different purposes.
4.3 Interact effectively with others.

(continued)

Table 3.1 Superstructure of the APA Guidelines for the Undergraduate Psychology Major, Version 2.0 *(continued)*

Goal 5. Professional Development The emphasis in this goal is on application of psychology specific content and skills, effective self-reflection, project management skills, teamwork skills, and career preparation. Foundation-level outcomes concentrate on the development. The skills in this goal at the baccalaureate level refer to abilities that sharpen student readiness for postbaccalaureate employment, graduate school, or professional school. These skills can be developed and refined both in traditional academic settings and in extracurricular involvement. In addition, career professionals can be enlisted to support occupational planning and pursuit. This emerging emphasis should not be construed as obligating psychology programs to obtain employment for their graduates but instead as encouraging programs to optimize the competitiveness of their graduates for securing places in the workforce.
5.1 Apply psychological content and skills to career goals.
5.2 Exhibit self-efficacy and self-regulation.
5.3 Refine project-management skills.
5.4 Enhance teamwork capacity.
5.5 Develop meaningful professional direction for life after graduation.

SOURCE: American Psychological Association (2013). *APA Guidelines for the Undergraduate Psychology Major, Version 2.0*. Washington, DC. Author. Retrieved from http://www.apa.org/ed/precollege/undergrad/index.aspx

As you can see, this is an impressive list! Given a thoughtful curriculum, by the time you have completed your undergraduate education you should be improving in all of these areas.

What Employers Want, and What They Pay

3.2 Summarize employment expectations for psychology majors

Researchers continue to study those job skills that employers who hire bachelor's degree psychology majors value. The skills presented in Chapter 1 (Table 1.4) provide an excellent overview for the types of skills your future employers may be seeking (Burrus et al., 2013). Faculty members often write about the skills psychology majors should possess, and Kuther (2013) created an excellent list of skills and abilities, including:

- critical thinking skills;
- problem-solving skills;
- oral communication skills, written communication skills, and interpersonal skills;
- the ability to locate, organize, and evaluate information from multiple sources;
- an appreciation of diversity and individual differences;
- the potential for continued learning and professional development;
- innovation and creativity; and
- an ability to apply knowledge and skills in a real-world setting.

It is important for students and faculty alike to understand the importance of both knowledge and skills; faculty members need to strive to design curricular experiences that allow students to practice the acquisition of such skills.

O'Hare and McGuiness (2004) offer a macro-level, organizational view of the *types* of skills and abilities that psychology majors should possess. One category of skills is known as *thinking skills* and includes such items as interpreting and evaluating information, testing and formulating hypotheses, analysis, information gathering and handling, evaluation, using research methodology, referencing, writing, and so on. A second category is labeled *self-management skills* and includes items such as time management, self-discipline, presentation skills and public speaking, self-confidence, responsibility, and self-assessment. The third category of skills is *corporate management skills*. These skills involve managing people and resources, negotiation, adaptability, networking, leadership, teamwork, assertiveness, etc. This organizational scheme may also be helpful as you think about what you want to achieve during your undergraduate career.

Another way to approach the topic of "what employers want" is to address what employers do not want. First, there is classic (and good) advice such as that offered by Brown and Zefo in Table 3.2 here.

In a research study that is a bit dated now, but still quite relevant, Phil Gardner at the Collegiate Employment Research Institute at Michigan State University surveyed a national network of employers and asked about the factors that influence the firing of new college hires. Think about that. You have just graduated with your bachelor's degree, and you land your first job (congratulations!). Want to keep that job? According to Gardner (2007), the reasons below are the top six reasons new collegiate hires are fired:

- Unethical behavior (28%)
- Lack of motivation/work ethic (18%)
- Inappropriate use of technology (14%)
- Failure to follow instructions (9%)
- Late for work (8%)
- Missing assignment deadlines (7%)

The last four items on this list are behaviors that can be practiced in and out of the classroom with educators, mentors, and advisors who care about you and hold you to high standards—value those individuals. The first two items—unethical behavior and lack of motivation/work ethic—well, as an undergraduate, it's up to you to acquire and retain a standard of ethical behavior and high motivation/great work ethic.

In Chapter 1, we mentioned the overall value of a bachelor's degree. But what about a bachelor's degree in psychology? Like so much else related to majoring in psychology, the answers are complicated and sometimes hard to come by. The National Association of Colleges and Employers (NACE) conducts an annual salary survey, including starting salary offers. The average starting salary for psychology workforce graduates for the Class of 2017 was $34,664; for the Class of 2016, the average starting salary was $35,587 (NACE, 2017).

Another organization, Payscale, tracks psychology workforce salaries differently. Rather than average starting salary, you can extract median salaries based on years' experience (mean and median are different measures of central tendency or typical score). At the time of this writing, here are the salary data being reported for Bachelor of Arts (BA) holders of psychology degrees (remember, median salary by years' experience): less than 1 year: $40,146 and 1–4 years: $47,314 (Payscale, 2018).

Desjardins (2018) reported the starting median salary for psychology major graduates as $35,900, and, interestingly, 10 years later, the median mid-career salary is $60,400. Desjardins warns to be careful with the $35,900 cited as the median starting salary

Table 3.2 Ten Mistakes to Avoid at Work

Not asking for help.
Trying to show up your boss.
Not showing up on time.
Not learning from your co-workers.
Being afraid to make mistakes.
Not admitting you've made a mistake.
Not being able to handle feedback.
Having a bad attitude.
Engaging in office gossip.
Not understanding generational differences.

SOURCE: Brown, A., & Zefo, B. (2007). *Grad to great*. Chicago, IL: Dalidaze Press.

because that was the median starting salary 10 years ago. The 68.2% rate of growth in salary over 10 years is a promising indicator, however.

A fourth perspective comes from the Digest of Education Statistics (2017) reporting the median annual earnings of 25- to 29-year-old bachelor's degree recipients in psychology in 2016 was $40,100 (and the unemployment rate was 2.9%). As you can see, we cannot provide you with a definitive answer about what a starting salary will be for an individual with a bachelor's degree in psychology. It's not that your results may vary, it's that your results will vary. The estimates provided here differ based on mean versus median, the size of the sample, starting salary versus first year in job versus 25- to 29-year-olds, and many other factors. As it turns out, methodology matters, which you undoubtedly will learn about in a research methods/experimental design course (yes, part of that curriculum).

As in most professions, you will most likely start at the bottom and have to work your way up in an organization. So, although these salary figures may be a bit disappointing (or not), remember that these are starting mean or median salaries. Of course these starting salaries will vary by region of the country, job demands, experience, etc. Again, your results will vary.

We have mentioned the importance of the curriculum, and later in the book, we will return to curricular and related extracurricular activities, opportunities like serving as a research assistant, teaching assistant, internships, participating as a member of a Psychology Club, Psi Beta chapter, or Psi Chi chapter. Extracurricular activities can help you hone skills and abilities that complement your classroom knowledge and skills.

Careers With a Bachelor's Degree

3.3 Describe job market experiences for a person with a psychology bachelor's degree

You may be surprised to discover the variety of opportunities available to you with a bachelor's degree in psychology. Some faculties present this career path as a bleak alternative (as compared with going to graduate school); the majority of psychology graduates *do not pursue* graduate training in psychology. However, we do want to be realistic about the opportunities. You will *not* be able to be a practicing psychologist without an advanced degree in psychology. With your bachelor's degree, you can obtain jobs directly related to psychology (usually in a support-staff type of role) and other jobs that are not related directly to psychology but benefit from one's knowledge about human behavior. The general label now used in the field for this group is "psychology workforce graduates" or the "psychology workforce," rather than the "individuals with a bachelor's degree in psychology but who did not go to graduate school." If you stop to think about it, there are very few, if any, jobs or careers that do not involve or would not benefit from a greater understanding of human behavior.

Before we dig into the details, it's worth a brief look into the research into what makes our work meaningful. As you can imagine, that simple sounding question has complex answers. Allan (2018) summarized much of the research in this area. First, when Americans are asked what makes their work meaningful, about 70% state helping others, with the next highest response (16%) being contributing to the greater good. The perception that your work is helping others is called *task significance*; researchers have demonstrated strong positive correlations between meaningful work perceptions and task significance perceptions. Allan (2018) concludes, based on some of his own work and that of others, that contributing to the welfare of others is a central tenet of meaningful work. Helping others is a prosocial behavior, and the emerging profile about meaningful work is that it is an important component of a meaningful life and may even inoculate us against some of the harmful effects of stress. Thus, seeking out a bachelor's degree that can lead you to meaningful work and task significance is worthy of your time, effort, and serious self-reflection.

What can you do with a bachelor's degree in psychology? What are the careers related to psychology that are available to the bachelor's-level psychology major? Previous editions of this book have provided a list of "potential careers with a bachelor's degree in psychology." And we could certainly keep providing this list. And the list can be helpful at times in brainstorming; our colleague and friend Drew Appleby created an online version (teachpsych.org/Resources/Documents/otrp/resources/appleby15students.docx) that has substantive links and resources to 258 careers (Appleby, 2015). However, the challenge is this—many of the job/occupations/careers on such lists are only attainable with an education greater than a bachelor's degree. Many of those occupations are obtainable with less than a bachelor's degree, or individuals with a bachelor's degree compete with individuals who have more (or who have less) than a bachelor's degree. And here is the real bottom-line message of all—with your bachelor's degree in psychology, you will be qualified for a high number of jobs, but your degree does not uniquely qualify you for any particular job (Landrum, 2018). That is, your bachelor's degree in psychology does not make you a lock for a job compared to someone with a bachelor's degree in sociology or a bachelor's degree in criminal justice, for instance.

To drive this point home, let's consider the occupation of probation officer. In O*NET (more on this later), the formal job title is "Probation Officers and Correctional Treatment Specialists." The general job description is to "Provide social services to assist in rehabilitation of law offenders in custody or on probation or parole." Make recommendations for actions involving formulation of rehabilitation plan and treatment of offenders, including conditional release and education and employment stipulations" (O*NET, 2018, para. 2). When examining education level required, here is an example of the complexity alluded to earlier. Although 86% of the individuals in the O*NET database have bachelor's degrees, 7% have some college but no degree (meaning that a high school diploma is likely their highest level of education completed) and 7% have a master's degree. Of those 86% holding a bachelor's degree, the O*NET database does not indicate what percentage of those individuals have a degree in psychology, criminal justice, social work, English, mathematics, and so on. This is an example of the blessing and the curse of the psychology major: the skill set is broad enough to widely appeal to a high number of potential jobs and occupations (258 according to Appleby), but so many other undergraduate majors prepare their students in the liberal arts tradition as well, qualifying those students for many if not most of the same jobs.

Career Options, Job Descriptions, and O*NET

Mentioned previously, O*NET stands for Occupational Information Network, which is a comprehensive database of work attributes and job characteristics. O*NET incorporates much of the information that was formerly available from the *Dictionary of Occupational Titles* (which is no longer published). Quite simply, O*NET is an amazing tool that anyone with Internet access (http://www.onetcenter.org) can use. Covering over 1,000 occupations, O*NET provides detailed information about each job, including knowledge, skills, and abilities needed, interests, general work activities, and a work context. It also provides links to salary information.

All occupations are organized using O*NET-SOC codes (SOC stands for standard occupational classification). This system is well designed and user-friendly, and a great deal of detail is available. You can examine not only the tasks of a job but also the knowledge required, skills necessary, abilities used, typical work activities, the context of work, training expected and general interest of those in the job, work styles, work values, related occupations, and a link to wage information!

Success Stories

Todd Walter
D'Youville College

Two things were certain to me as I completed high school – I excelled in math and I was expected to go to college. I am the first member of my family to go to college and throughout my youth my family reminded me of how fortunate I was to have such an opportunity because of money they had saved up to help me do so. When I arrived at Niagara University as a freshman math major I assumed I would fulfill my family destiny and figure out my career along the way. Unfortunately, I quickly found myself feeling uninspired, lacking direction, and had a less than stellar GPA to show for it.

After withdrawing from Calculus III in the middle of my sophomore year, I took the leap to major in Psychology. I had recently earned a C in General Psychology, but I found the subject so much more appealing and I connected with the Psychology faculty in ways that I hadn't with others. I would go on to achieve a 4.0 GPA in nearly all of my remaining semesters and with the mentorship of my wonderful professors at Niagara, I would present my senior honors thesis at a national conference!

Despite my relative meteoric rise during the second half of my undergraduate studies, I found myself feeling as though I was outside looking in regarding a career in psychology. As I neared graduation I recognized that I wanted to pursue a career in either counseling or clinical psychology. However, I did not strategically pursue graduate school admission. For starters, I wanted to stay close to my hometown in upstate New York. And if I were to go out of town, I chose to apply to only a few doctoral programs – all of which (unknowingly to me at the time) were among the most competitive to be admitted to in the nation. Suffice to say, I was not accepted to any of the doctoral programs I applied to. My pursuit of a professional career in psychology seemed stymied. Near my undergraduate graduation, one of my professors, Dr. Timothy Osberg suggested that I apply to a terminal masters program. He told me that such a program could enable me to further my research experience, and demonstrate that I could complete graduate level study. He told me that it might not be going through the "front door" in terms of direct entry into doctoral study, but a masters degree could ultimately be a "side door" entrance to fulfilling my aspiration to become a psychologist.

Following his advice, I successfully completed my masters degree at SUNY Buffalo, strategically applied to approximately a several doctoral programs varying in competitiveness and with faculty whose clinical and research interests mirrored my own, and was successfully offered admission to many of them! Ultimately, I proudly completed my doctoral studies in Counseling Psychology at the University of Florida, subsequently moved back to upstate New York, and secured a faculty position at D'Youville College. Despite the uncertainty, adversity, and self-doubts of my initial pursuits as a college student, I have found a career that I love and spend my days sharing my passion for psychology through educating and mentoring students like me!

To continue with the example started previously, here is a visual depiction of what the display would look like (as of July 2018) for probation officers (technically, Probation Officers and Correctional Treatment Specialists).

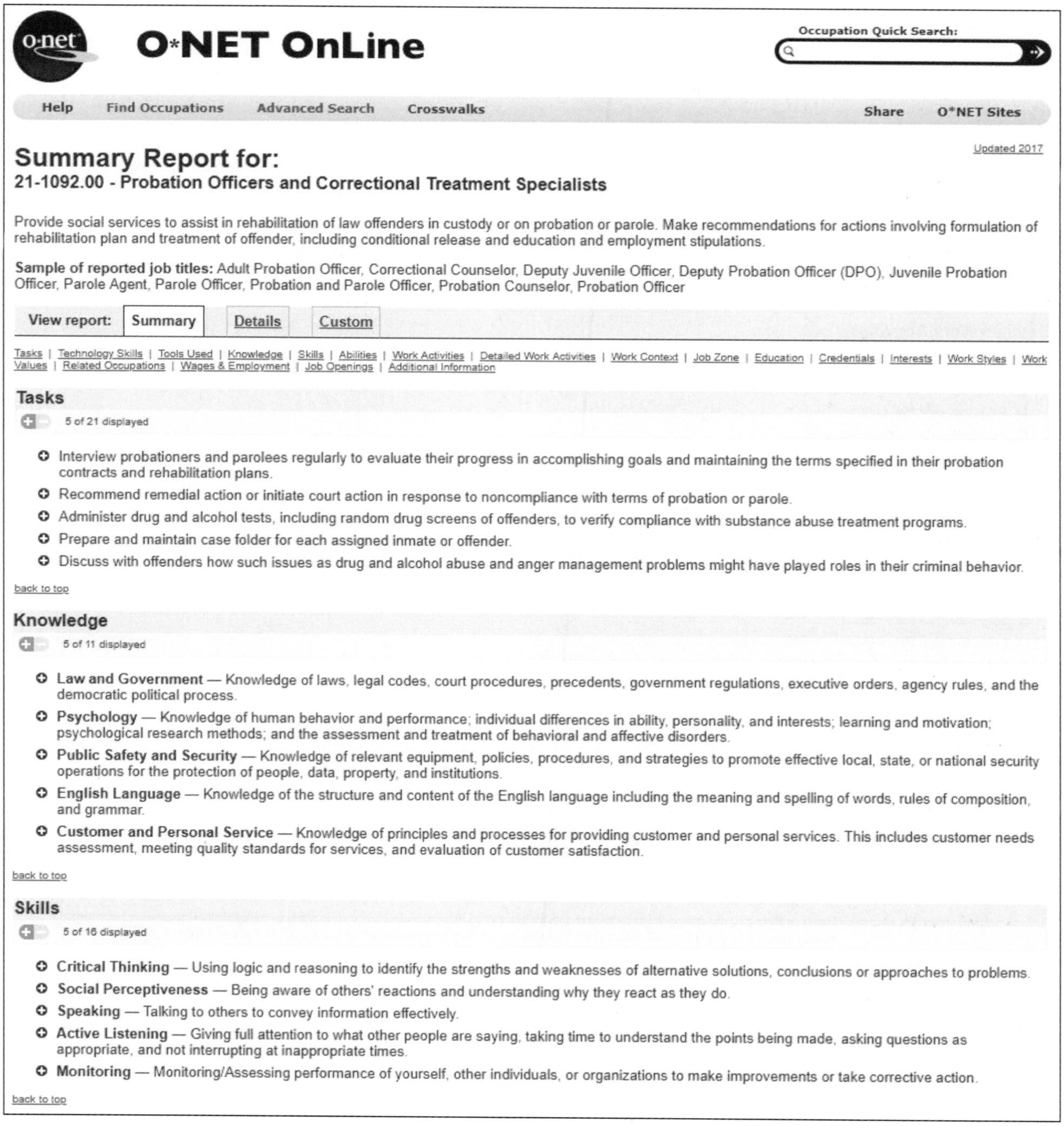

O*NET OnLine

Occupation Quick Search:

Help | Find Occupations | Advanced Search | Crosswalks | Share | O*NET Sites

Updated 2017

Summary Report for:
21-1092.00 - Probation Officers and Correctional Treatment Specialists

Provide social services to assist in rehabilitation of law offenders in custody or on probation or parole. Make recommendations for actions involving formulation of rehabilitation plan and treatment of offender, including conditional release and education and employment stipulations.

Sample of reported job titles: Adult Probation Officer, Correctional Counselor, Deputy Juvenile Officer, Deputy Probation Officer (DPO), Juvenile Probation Officer, Parole Agent, Parole Officer, Probation and Parole Officer, Probation Counselor, Probation Officer

View report: Summary | Details | Custom

Tasks | Technology Skills | Tools Used | Knowledge | Skills | Abilities | Work Activities | Detailed Work Activities | Work Context | Job Zone | Education | Credentials | Interests | Work Styles | Work Values | Related Occupations | Wages & Employment | Job Openings | Additional Information

Tasks
5 of 21 displayed

- Interview probationers and parolees regularly to evaluate their progress in accomplishing goals and maintaining the terms specified in their probation contracts and rehabilitation plans.
- Recommend remedial action or initiate court action in response to noncompliance with terms of probation or parole.
- Administer drug and alcohol tests, including random drug screens of offenders, to verify compliance with substance abuse treatment programs.
- Prepare and maintain case folder for each assigned inmate or offender.
- Discuss with offenders how such issues as drug and alcohol abuse and anger management problems might have played roles in their criminal behavior.

back to top

Knowledge
5 of 11 displayed

- **Law and Government** — Knowledge of laws, legal codes, court procedures, precedents, government regulations, executive orders, agency rules, and the democratic political process.
- **Psychology** — Knowledge of human behavior and performance; individual differences in ability, personality, and interests; learning and motivation; psychological research methods; and the assessment and treatment of behavioral and affective disorders.
- **Public Safety and Security** — Knowledge of relevant equipment, policies, procedures, and strategies to promote effective local, state, or national security operations for the protection of people, data, property, and institutions.
- **English Language** — Knowledge of the structure and content of the English language including the meaning and spelling of words, rules of composition, and grammar.
- **Customer and Personal Service** — Knowledge of principles and processes for providing customer and personal services. This includes customer needs assessment, meeting quality standards for services, and evaluation of customer satisfaction.

back to top

Skills
5 of 16 displayed

- **Critical Thinking** — Using logic and reasoning to identify the strengths and weaknesses of alternative solutions, conclusions or approaches to problems.
- **Social Perceptiveness** — Being aware of others' reactions and understanding why they react as they do.
- **Speaking** — Talking to others to convey information effectively.
- **Active Listening** — Giving full attention to what other people are saying, taking time to understand the points being made, asking questions as appropriate, and not interrupting at inappropriate times.
- **Monitoring** — Monitoring/Assessing performance of yourself, other individuals, or organizations to make improvements or take corrective action.

back to top

Abilities

5 of 11 displayed

- **Problem Sensitivity** — The ability to tell when something is wrong or is likely to go wrong. It does not involve solving the problem, only recognizing there is a problem.
- **Oral Comprehension** — The ability to listen to and understand information and ideas presented through spoken words and sentences.
- **Oral Expression** — The ability to communicate information and ideas in speaking so others will understand.
- **Inductive Reasoning** — The ability to combine pieces of information to form general rules or conclusions (includes finding a relationship among seemingly unrelated events).
- **Speech Recognition** — The ability to identify and understand the speech of another person.

back to top

Work Activities

5 of 25 displayed

- **Getting Information** — Observing, receiving, and otherwise obtaining information from all relevant sources.
- **Documenting/Recording Information** — Entering, transcribing, recording, storing, or maintaining information in written or electronic/magnetic form.
- **Interacting With Computers** — Using computers and computer systems (including hardware and software) to program, write software, set up functions, enter data, or process information.
- **Making Decisions and Solving Problems** — Analyzing information and evaluating results to choose the best solution and solve problems.
- **Communicating with Supervisors, Peers, or Subordinates** — Providing information to supervisors, co-workers, and subordinates by telephone, in written form, e-mail, or in person.

back to top

Detailed Work Activities

5 of 15 displayed

- Interview clients to gather information about their backgrounds, needs, or progress.
- Recommend legal actions.
- Administer drug screening tests.
- Investigate legal issues.
- Counsel clients or patients with substance abuse issues.

back to top

Work Context

5 of 23 displayed

- **Contact With Others** — 89% responded "Constant contact with others."
- **Telephone** — 89% responded "Every day."
- **Face-to-Face Discussions** — 84% responded "Every day."
- **Indoors, Environmentally Controlled** — 90% responded "Every day."
- **Electronic Mail** — 81% responded "Every day."

back to top

Job Zone

Title	Job Zone Four: Considerable Preparation Needed
Education	Most of these occupations require a four-year bachelor's degree, but some do not.
Related Experience	A considerable amount of work-related skill, knowledge, or experience is needed for these occupations. For example, an accountant must complete four years of college and work for several years in accounting to be considered qualified.
Job Training	Employees in these occupations usually need several years of work-related experience, on-the-job training, and/or vocational training.
Job Zone Examples	Many of these occupations involve coordinating, supervising, managing, or training others. Examples include accountants, sales managers, database administrators, graphic designers, chemists, art directors, and cost estimators.
SVP Range	(7.0 to < 8.0)

back to top

Education

Percentage of Respondents	Education Level Required
86	Bachelor's degree
7	Some college, no degree
7	Master's degree

back to top

Credentials

Find Training | Find Certifications | Find Licenses

back to top

Interests

All 3 displayed

Interest code: **SEC** Want to discover your interests? Take the O*NET Interest Profiler at My Next Move.

- **Social** — Social occupations frequently involve working with, communicating with, and teaching people. These occupations often involve helping or providing service to others.
- **Enterprising** — Enterprising occupations frequently involve starting up and carrying out projects. These occupations can involve leading people and making many decisions. Sometimes they require risk taking and often deal with business.
- **Conventional** — Conventional occupations frequently involve following set procedures and routines. These occupations can include working with data and details more than with ideas. Usually there is a clear line of authority to follow.

back to top

Work Styles

5 of 16 displayed

- **Integrity** — Job requires being honest and ethical.
- **Self Control** — Job requires maintaining composure, keeping emotions in check, controlling anger, and avoiding aggressive behavior, even in very difficult situations.
- **Stress Tolerance** — Job requires accepting criticism and dealing calmly and effectively with high stress situations.
- **Dependability** — Job requires being reliable, responsible, and dependable, and fulfilling obligations.
- **Attention to Detail** — Job requires being careful about detail and thorough in completing work tasks.

back to top

Work Values

All 3 displayed

- **Support** — Occupations that satisfy this work value offer supportive management that stands behind employees. Corresponding needs are Company Policies, Supervision: Human Relations and Supervision: Technical.
- **Relationships** — Occupations that satisfy this work value allow employees to provide service to others and work with co-workers in a friendly non-competitive environment. Corresponding needs are Co-workers, Moral Values and Social Service.
- **Working Conditions** — Occupations that satisfy this work value offer job security and good working conditions. Corresponding needs are Activity, Compensation, Independence, Security, Variety and Working Conditions.

back to top

Related Occupations

5 of 9 displayed

21-1012.00	Educational, Guidance, School, and Vocational Counselors
21-1021.00	Child, Family, and School Social Workers — Bright Outlook
21-1093.00	Social and Human Service Assistants
23-1022.00	Arbitrators, Mediators, and Conciliators — Green
25-2031.00	Secondary School Teachers, Except Special and Career/Technical Education

back to top

Wages & Employment Trends

Median wages (2017)	$24.71 hourly, $51,410 annual
State wages	Local Salary Info
Employment (2016)	91,000 employees
Projected growth (2016-2026)	Average (5% to 9%)
Projected job openings (2016-2026)	8,300
State trends	Employment Trends
Top industries (2016)	Government

Source: Bureau of Labor Statistics 2017 wage data and 2016-2026 employment projections. "Projected growth" represents the estimated change in total employment over the projections period (2016-2026). "Projected job openings" represent openings due to growth and replacement.

back to top

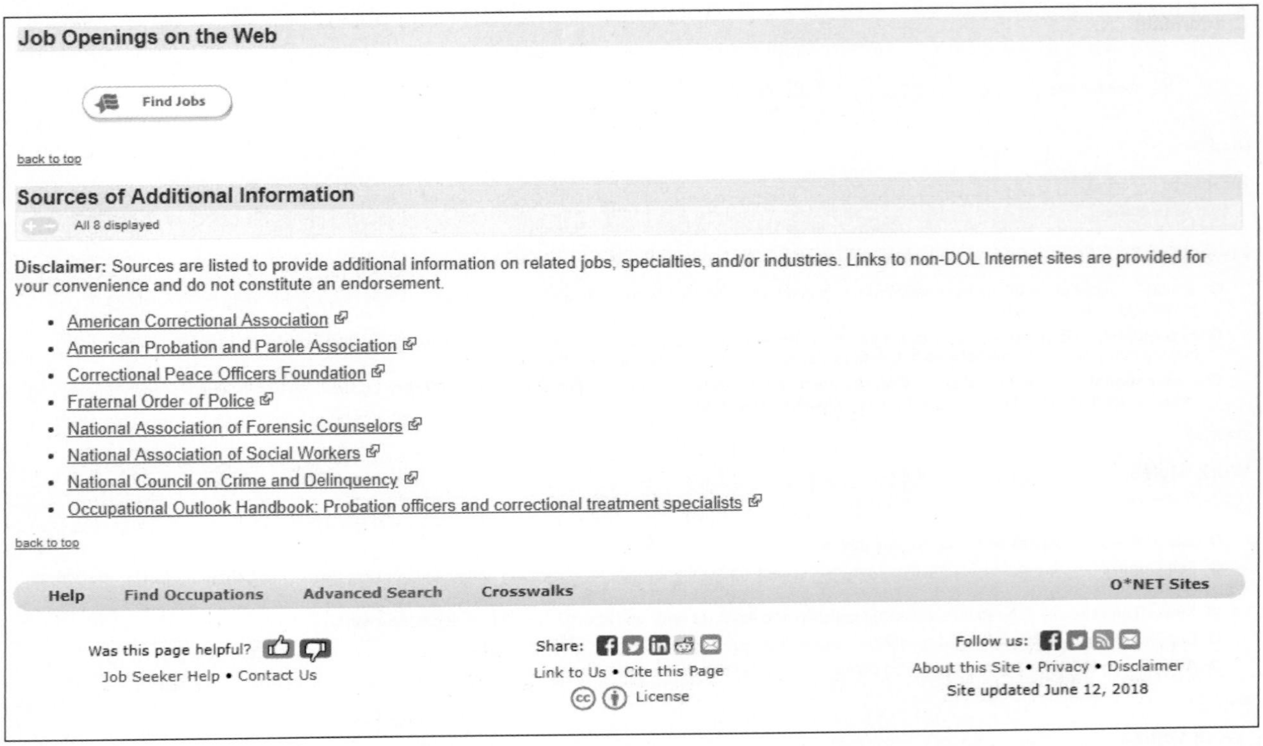

Becoming a Freshman Again

3.4 Explain how students can prepare for challenges in transitioning to a workplace

At the beginning of this chapter, we alluded to the challenges in making the transition from college to the world of work. In the next chapter, we will explore the strategies you can use to land a good job with a bachelor's degree. But for now, it's worth considering the challenges. Hettich (2004) studied this issue of transitions (as well as others; Murphy et al., 2010) and not only identified the parameters but also offered tips on how to deal with the challenge of becoming a freshman again in the workplace.

The challenges are numerous! In thinking about how to prepare for this transition, Hettich (2004, pp. 8–9) provided concrete advice on strategies you can pursue while still an undergraduate student. His suggestions include:

- Complete courses that focus directly on specific organizational aspects of the workplace, such as management, leadership, communication and group skills, organizational behavior, the sociology of organizations, career planning, and human resources.
- Enroll in workshops, seminars, or courses that focus on self-development, leadership, conflict management, team building, interpersonal communication, time management, stress management, and similar professional skills.
- Join clubs, sports, and campus organizations where collaboration, teamwork, conflict, communication, and leadership are practiced as constructive tools.
- Complete internships and perform volunteer work.

- Collect evidence of curricular and cocurricular achievements, including papers, projects, awards, and performance evaluations, and organize them in an electronic portfolio that monitors personal progress and serves as a tool in job searches.
- Recognize that grades, test scores, and GPAs are often skewed predictors of intelligence in the workplace.
- Remember that teachers cannot give students all the answers because we do not know them.

Writing about adult workers in workplace transitions, Goodman, Schlossberg, and Anderson (2006) addressed dimensions of career maturity or career adaptability. In fact, the theme of resiliency emerges because of the multiple jobs and career changes that adults will likely face during their lifetimes. The specific dimensions of this ability to adapt may include (a) work values and work salience, (b) autonomy or sense of agency, (c) planfulness or future perspective, (d) exploration and establishment, (e) information, (f) decision-making, and (g) reflection on experience (p. 158).

There are multiple opportunities for success in the workplace, but there are matching challenges as well. We hope this chapter has alerted you to some of the opportunities; Chapter 4 provides strategies for how to pursue the career you want. If financial considerations are your primary objective, many areas of psychology may not satisfy your needs. Serious career exploration and an understanding of your own value system will help you find a suitable career match. A recent study by Strapp et al. (2018) helps highlight just how much psychology majors struggle with career expectations and understanding future opportunities. When psychology majors (mostly juniors and seniors) were asked to name a career for which they were currently preparing, they had difficulty doing so—20% left the item blank or wrote "do not know," and seniors were as undecided as freshmen. When students did select careers, the trend was to overestimate the amount of education needed; this is troubling because career attainment may be lessened or advising resources could be inadequate. These psychology students exhibited high variability with regard to accurately understanding job salaries as well, which is understandable given the difficulty of obtaining these data.

Other chapters of this book also help you to find where your "niche" might be after you complete your formal education. Our suggestion—be as honest as you can with yourself from the start, and you may have less grief in the long run. You are employable with a bachelor's degree in psychology! Combs (2000, p. 14) bluntly summarized the relationship between selecting your major and getting a good job: "No matter what you major in, if you can't answer the phone, make a presentation, do a spreadsheet, or write a business letter, nobody needs you."

Exercise 3.1 Self-Reflections about My Undergraduate Experience

Regardless of your year in your undergraduate program, the survey below is intended to provide a prompt or cue for you to reflect on your experiences to date. There are no right or wrong answers. After thinking about your responses, if you are disappointed with your academic advising experiences, research experiences, or level of personal growth to date, make an action plan for improvement, with specific steps to be taken. If you are satisfied with one or more of these areas, be sure to give credit where credit is due, and that includes yourself for the good work you have invested in you!

Please be sure to leave blank/skip any items that do not apply to you. Remember, there are no correct answers. Please answer honestly with the goal of prompting deep self-reflection about each of the three areas below.

	Strongly Disagree	Disagree	Neutral	Agree	Strongly Agree
Perceptions of Academic Advisors and Peer Advisors					
Has sufficient knowledge of psychology/institutional policies, processes, and requirements to provide me with accurate and useful information	O	O	O	O	O
Is available during scheduled hours or schedules alternative times	O	O	O	O	O
Advises on immediate academic problems	O	O	O	O	O
Is well informed about campus support services, and refers me to other sources of information and assistance when such referral better suits my needs	O	O	O	O	O
Respects my feelings and concerns	O	O	O	O	O
Is helpful and effective	O	O	O	O	O
Overall, I am pleased with advising	O	O	O	O	O
Perceptions of Research Experience in Psychology					
Applying the ethical principles psychologists follow	O	O	O	O	O
Learning the relations among psychology, the physical sciences, and the social sciences	O	O	O	O	O
Developing the ability to read and evaluate research in psychology	O	O	O	O	O
Heightening my self-understanding	O	O	O	O	O
Developing self-reliance and independence	O	O	O	O	O
Showing sensitivity, tolerance, and respect for others	O	O	O	O	O
Understanding the ways in which psychology and society interact	O	O	O	O	O
Contributions to Personal Growth					
Cooperation with others	O	O	O	O	O
Defining and solving problems	O	O	O	O	O
Making logical inferences based on assumptions	O	O	O	O	O
Developing self-reliance	O	O	O	O	O
Tolerating other points of view	O	O	O	O	O
Applying scientific methods and principles	O	O	O	O	O
Using the computer for word processing	O	O	O	O	O
Exercising initiative	O	O	O	O	O
Developing persistence	O	O	O	O	O
Learning independently	O	O	O	O	O
Writing effectively	O	O	O	O	O
Thinking creatively	O	O	O	O	O
Selecting personal goals	O	O	O	O	O
Data analysis applications on the computer	O	O	O	O	O
Leadership skills	O	O	O	O	O
Understanding and applying mathematics to daily life	O	O	O	O	O
Learning new computing programs and applications	O	O	O	O	O

SOURCE: Adapted from Nelson, E. S., & Johnson, K. A. (1997). A senior exit survey and its implications for advising and related services. *Teaching of Psychology, 24*, 101–105.

Exercise 3.2 Does the Label Matter? Job, Occupation, Career, or Calling?

You may have heard the statement that over the typical work career, a college graduate will have eight different jobs requiring work in three different professions or occupations (Chen, 2004). Well, what does that mean, really, and what's the difference between a job and an occupation? Have you ever heard of someone saying they have a "calling"—how do you get one of those? Using the table below, explore what you think the differences for each of these terms might be.

For the table, check the boxes for each statement which you believe is part of the definition of the term listed at the top of the column. Although there may be precisely right or wrong answers, the point of this exercise is for you to explore what these different terms mean and to be aware that in certain contexts, the differences may be meaningful, and in other contexts, the differences may be trivial. You will have to extract clues from each context to know which situation is which. After filling in the table, you can read a little about similarities and differences between a career and a calling from Sittser (2004).

	Check the box if the statement is part of the definition of the term			
	Job	**Occupation**	**Calling**	**Career**
Provides power and status	☐	☐	☐	☐
Serves the needs, welfare, and interests of the larger society	☐	☐	☐	☐
Demand time, energy, and loyalty	☐	☐	☐	☐
Means of earning a living	☐	☐	☐	☐
Requiring special training, followed as one's lifework	☐	☐	☐	☐
A spiritual vision for how to use time, energy, and abilities to serve the world	☐	☐	☐	☐
Path or progress though life or history	☐	☐	☐	☐
Line of work performed to earn an income	☐	☐	☐	☐
Involves some kind of socially useful work	☐	☐	☐	☐
Formal education is required	☐	☐	☐	☐
A strong inner urge to follow, such as a vocation	☐	☐	☐	☐
Anything a person is expected or obliged to do	☐	☐	☐	☐
Part of our identity, waiting to be discovered and expressed	☐	☐	☐	☐

Chapter 4

Pursuing Bachelor's-Level Options

Learning Objectives

4.1 Summarize the general skills and connections useful for a job search

4.2 Create a superior resume

4.3 Explain how to secure a strong letter of recommendation for a job

4.4 Practice strategies for successful interviewing

4.5 Put an unsuccessful job search in context

4.6 Identify traits associated with workplace value

If you are reading the chapters in order, you know something about the opportunities afforded to you by your undergraduate education. You also know that a college-to-career transition may be more difficult than expected. You know that most undergraduate psychology majors do *not* go to graduate school, but they become workforce psychology graduates. This chapter is dedicated to providing you with tips and ideas on how to facilitate your job search. Here, you will find tips on preparing your resume, interviewing skills and potential questions, and strategies for securing strong letters of recommendation. We did not design these materials to provide comprehensive information on every job application situation—there are plenty of good resources available, both in print, at your Career Center on your campus, and on the Internet. In fact, there are entire books based on each of the topics addressed in this chapter.

Before we jump into the details, let's recap once again why the psychology major is such a great choice and provide some of the reasons why workforce psychology graduates succeed (Halonen & Dunn, 2018, p. 43); see Table 4.1.

Table 4.1 Advantages for Workforce Psychology Graduates

- Describe and predict individual and group behavior
- Use data to support arguments
- Evaluate behavioral claims accurately
- Synthesize information from diverse sources
- Recognize problematic behaviors
- Interpret data and graphs accurately
- Demonstrate capacity to adapt to change
- Operate in informal and formal channels of organizations
- Exhibit persistence
- Communicate effectively in oral and written forms

Table 4.1 Advantages for Workforce Psychology Graduates *(Continued)*

• Carry out projects with limited information or experience
• Manage difficult or stressful environments
• Work well in teams that comprise diverse membership
• Generate trust through personal integrity
• Write reports following directions and using appropriate conventions

SOURCE: Halonen, J. S., & Dunn, D. S. (2018). Embedding career issues in advanced psychology major courses. *Teaching of Psychology*, *45*, 41–49. doi:10.1177/0098628317744967

Alright then—now, how to find the opportunities to put the knowledge, skills, and abilities to good use.

The Complexity of Finding a Job

4.1 Summarize the general skills and connections useful for a job search

At first glance, the job search may seem overwhelming. There are many components to the job search, each with its own level of importance and each having consequences if not satisfactorily completed. In this chapter, we lead you step-by-step through the basics needed for the job application process. It is likely that the job search skill will become a practiced skill because college graduates are predicted to have eight different jobs during their lifetime and will require work in three different professions or occupations (Chen, 2004). As an undergraduate, you can start to build toward your future career searches. You can start a resume now. You can participate in activities that not only help you build a resume but also help you build mentoring relationships that can lead to strong letters of recommendation. You can also take classes and participate in class projects that help build interpersonal skills (highly valued by employers, by the way) that will lead to success in interviews. What do we mean by interpersonal skills? Yancey et al. (2003) articulated a cogent list of interpersonal competencies: (a) effectively translating and conveying information, (b) being able to accurately interpret other people's emotions, (c) being sensitive to other people's feelings, (d) calmly arriving at resolutions to conflict, (e) avoiding gossip, and (f) being polite. Focus on developing and honing these interpersonal skills, and you'll be well on your way to success.

The Internet is certainly one of your primary tools in the job search process, and Strauss (2017) advises on how to leverage this tool to your advantage. Learn about companies and job openings through websites such as LinkedIn and Glassdoor, but do not forget about other job posting sites, such as:

- Indeed.com
- Monster.com
- Careerbuilder.com
- ZipRecruiter.com
- SimplyHired.com
- MightyRecruiter.com

Be sure to tap into connections that you might already have, and they include connections that you have through social media (Strauss, 2017). Former employers, family connections, and others can be extremely helpful in getting your "foot-in-the-door." Internships often lead to possible job opportunities after graduation; you get a look at how it would be to work in that environment, and the employer gets a sneak peek at your work habits, skill, and potential. It is also important to remember that you are not going to get the perfect job with the perfect salary the first time you apply. You need to be patient as you build your own set of skills and abilities, establish your track record, hone your work ethic, and develop your work history.

Success Stories

Mark Ostach

It all started in 2001. As a student at Albion College, I was buying items on eBay with student loan money and feeling depressed when checking my ex-girlfriend's Myspace page. I quickly realized that my online habits had a negative effect on my mental and emotional health. Thus began my journey into advocating for digital wellness. But let me back up for a moment . . .

I was born in 1981—the same year that Justin Timberlake and Brittany Spears were born. Although I can't quite dance like them, I was born musically inclined. As a child, I had big plans to become famous and began writing songs at an early age. When I came to Albion College, I declared a music major. However, after taking a class on Traditional Chinese Medicine, I knew I wanted to work with the mind body connection. In addition to my class on Traditional Chinese Medicine, I also had taken the History of Psychology. I immediately changed my major to Psychology.

After graduating, I enrolled in massage therapy school. I was interested in workplace wellness and wanted to bring massage into Metro Detroit businesses as a means of stress reduction. However, that plan quickly faded when my best friend since grade school asked me to help him start a technology company. I left massage school and spent the next decade compulsively checking my email while running a 30-person software development company in Detroit. I also enrolled into a master's program in Information Systems Management.

While navigating my 20s as a serial entrepreneur, I noticed more people confiding in me how their online habits were having a negative effect on their emotional and mental health. I saw an opportunity to help.

At 26 years old, I spent my life savings on creating an online plugin that allowed people to manage their time and mood online (see more at www.markostach.com/about/). Unfortunately, the software I developed only worked on the desktop. By the time it was ready to launch, the Smartphone craze had swept the nation, turning my million-dollar idea to an expensive mistake. However, as I reflect on this time in my life, I realize I gained invaluable life experience and credibility in the space now (?) known as the Psychology of Technology.

As I pivoted away from my own software business, I began speaking about ways to become digitally fit. To me, a healthy digital life meant fostering relationships where true human connection can be had with the people you love most. It means to root your sense of identity into something deeper than your LinkedIn network and higher than your best score on Candy Crush.

For the past 10 years, I've had the opportunity to speak around the country on digital wellness. Highlights include a TEDx talk, large conferences, and a host of organizations who've hired me to educate their teams on ways to create boundaries with their digital devices to help reduce stress and burnout. I've even had the chance to come back to Albion College to share this message with students!

Preparing Your Resume, with Samples

4.2 Create a superior resume

Because there are many resume preparation books on the market and websites dedicated to this process, we will provide some general tips and ideas to help you prepare a superior resume. A resume should answer two important questions for a potential employer: (1) what can you do for me (answered in career objectives) and (2) why should you be considered for this job (answered in educational history and work experience; La Sierra University, 2000).

Lore (1997) suggests two general sections of the resume. In the first section, make the claims and assertions about your abilities, qualities, and achievements. In the second section, present the evidence in support of the statements you made in the first section. Within these two sections, you will have multiple parts of the resume. Some of these parts (Coxford, 1998) should include the sections given in Table 4.2.

If you have just received your bachelor's degree in psychology, you may have a relatively short resume. That's OK—take that opportunity to go into some detail about the experiences you have had. Table 4.3 contains a list of action verbs you can use to accurately describe the types of duties and responsibilities you held as an undergraduate (and before, if applicable). A number of resources are available that provide tips on resume preparation. Taken from CareerMosaic (1997) and JobWeb (2001), Table 4.4 (p. 43) offers some of the most common resume tips. These are the basics that must be mastered prior to sending out your resume to anyone.

Some of these suggestions are based on the practice of companies that scan resumes; you do not want to do anything on paper that will make it more difficult for companies to read scanned copies of your resume. In fact, if you really want to be prepared, scan a copy of your resume yourself and then print the file on your computer. Can you read all of the print? Is the font readable, or too small? Making sure your scanned resume is readable would demonstrate an impressive level of attention to detail to any employer. It is the obligation of the person sending the resume to make sure that his or her computer system/program is compatible with that of the company (generally speaking, Microsoft Word is the dominant word processor today—avoid Google Docs or Open Office files). If the company cannot open a resume on the first try, there typically will not be a second try. That first impressive happens quickly, varying from a 10-second window (Toorrenburg, Oostrom, & Pollet, 2015) to a 25-second window (Borysek, 2011).

In telling your own professional story, Landrum (2015) offers three tips specifically regarding the preparation of your resume. First, make sure your resume is completely accurate—be fair with the data. If you have not yet graduated, make sure your current resume has an "anticipated" or "expected" graduation date. If you have a manuscript that you are planning to submit for publication but you have not yet submitted the manuscript, be fair with that information too. Second, and this has been already mentioned, think about the convenience of the reader during resume preparation. Use keywords to organize sections of your resume. Start subsections of job descriptions with action verbs

Table 4.2 Potential Resume Sections

Name, address, city, state, phone number, and e-mail address where you can be reached
Position objective statement and summary of qualifications
Employment and education history, including professional training and affiliations
Military service history (if applicable)
Licenses and certificates (if applicable)
Knowledge of foreign languages
Publications and professional presentations
Special accomplishments
Statement that references and work sample are available upon request

Table 4.3 Action Verbs

accelerated	automated	consolidated	drafted	framed	investigated	oriented	received
acclimated	avail	constructed	earned	fulfilled	invited	originated	recommended
accompanied	awarded	consulted	eased	functioned	involved	overhauled	reconciled
accomplished	balanced	contracted	edited	furnished	isolated	oversaw	recorded
achieved	bargained	contrasted	effected	gained	issued	paid	recovered
acquired	borrowed	contributed	elected	gathered	joined	participated	recruited
acted	bought	contrived	eliminated	gauged	judged	passed	rectified
activated	broadened	controlled	employed	gave	launched	patterned	redesigned
actuated	budgeted	converted	enabled	generated	lectured	penalized	reduced
adapted	built	convinced	encouraged	governed	led	perceived	referred
added	calculated	coordinated	endorsed	graded	lightened	performed	refined
addressed	canvassed	corrected	enforced	granted	liquidated	permitted	regained
adhered	capitalized	corresponded	engaged	greeted	litigated	persuaded	regulated
adjusted	captured	counseled	engineered	grouped	lobbied	phased out	rehabilitated
administered	carried out	counted	enhanced	guided	localized	pinpointed	reinforced
admitted	cast	created	enlarged	handled	located	pioneered	reinstated
adopted	catalogued	critiqued	enriched	headed	maintained	placed	rejected
advanced	centralized	cultivated	entered	hired	managed	planned	related
advertised	challenged	cut	entertained	hosted	mapped	polled	remedied
advised	chaired	debugged	established	identified	marketed	prepared	remodeled
advocated	changed	decentralized	estimated	illustrated	maximized	presented	renegotiated
affected	channeled	decided	evaluated	illuminated	measured	preserved	reorganized
aided	charted	decreased	examined	implemented	mediated	presided	replaced
aired	checked	deferred	exceeded	improved	merchandised	prevented	repaired
allocated	chose	defined	exchanged	improvised	merged	priced	reported
altered	circulated	delegated	executed	inaugurated	met	printed	represented
amended	clarified	delivered	exempted	indoctrinated	minimized	prioritized	requested
amplified	classified	demonstrated	exercised	increased	modeled	probed	researched
analyzed	cleared	depreciated	expanded	incurred	moderated	processed	resolved
answered	closed	described	expedited	induced	modernized	procured	responded
anticipated	co-authored	designated	explained	influenced	modified	produced	restored
appointed	cold called	designed	exposed	informed	monitored	profiled	restructured
appraised	collaborated	determined	extended	initiated	motivated	programmed	resulted
approached	collected	developed	extracted	innovated	moved	projected	retained
approved	combined	devised	extrapolated	inquired	multiplied	promoted	retrieved
arbitrated	commissioned	devoted	facilitated	inspected	named	prompted	revamped
arranged	committed	diagrammed	familiarized	inspired	narrated	proposed	revealed
ascertained	communicated	directed	fashioned	installed	negotiated	proved	reversed
asked	compared	disclosed	fielded	instigated	noticed	provided	reviewed
assembled	compiled	discounted	figured	instilled	nurtured	publicized	revised
assigned	completed	discovered	financed	instituted	observed	published	revitalized
assumed	complied	dispatched	fit	instructed	obtained	purchased	rewarded
assessed	composed	displayed	focused	insured	offered	pursued	routed
assisted	computed	dissembled	forecasted	interfaced	offset	quantified	safeguarded
attained	conceived	distinguished	formalized	interpreted	opened	quoted	salvaged
attracted	conceptualized	distributed	formed	interviewed	operated	raised	saved
audited	concluded	diversified	formulated	introduced	operationalized	ranked	scheduled
augmented	condensed	divested	fortified	invented	orchestrated	rated	screened
authored	conducted	documented	found	inventoried	ordered	reacted	secured

Table 4.3 Action Verbs *(Continued)*

authorized	conferred	doubled	founded	invested	organized	read	simplified
sold	standardized	substantiated	synchronized	tightened	traveled	utilized	won
solved	steered	substituted	synthesized	took	treated	validated	worked
spearheaded	stimulated	suggested	systematized	traced	tripled	valued	wrote
specified	strategized	summarized	tabulated	traded	uncovered	verified	
speculated	streamlined	superseded	tailored	trained	undertook	viewed	
spoke	strengthened	supervised	targeted	transacted	unified	visited	
spread	stressed	supplied	taught	transferred	united	weighed	
stabilized	structured	supported	terminated	transformed	updated	welcomed	
staffed	studied	surpassed	tested	translated	upgraded	widened	
staged	submitted	surveyed	testified	transported	used	witnessed	

SOURCE: TMP Worldwide (1998).

(see Table 4.3 for many examples). Include white space in your resume layout and do not use too many different combinations of fonts, boldface, italics, and such—it will look too busy and too cluttered. Third, your resume is a work sample; be sure it shows off your best professionalism. If you have conference presentations to list on your resume, be sure to list them in the closest approximation to APA format as possible (although probably not using double-spacing). Make sure there are absolutely no typographical errors, and use a professional-sounding email address, even if you have to get a new one specifically for the job application process. If you need help with this process, remember that network available to you—peers, advisors, mentors, a Career Center on campus, parents, and family friends—be sure to utilize all of the options available to maximize your opportunities. To help describe those opportunities on your resume, action verbs help focus on the actions you take to achieve the goals and tasks of the organization—see Table 4.3 for plenty of examples of action verbs.

On the following pages, you will find some sample resumes from undergraduate psychology majors (Figures 4.1 and 4.2). Note that the identities of the actual persons have not been changed, but the contact information has been made "fake." These are both very good examples of resumes of senior-level psychology majors.

Table 4.4 Resume Preparation Tips

- Make the first impression count. A good resume may get you to the next stage of the process. A poor resume may stop you from going anywhere.
- Keep your resume current. Make sure it has your new phone number, e-mail address, etc.
- Make sure others proofread your resume before you show it to potential employers. Typographical and grammatical errors are **unacceptable**. Mistakes in your resume will cost you the opportunity to advance in the employment process.
- Have your resume reviewed and critiqued by a career counselor, and also have your mentor in psychology review your resume for you.
- Run a spell check and grammar check on your computer before showing your resume to anyone.
- Find a competent friend (an English major would be handy here) to do a grammar review of your resume.
- Then ask another friend to proofread it. The more sets of eyes that examine your resume, the better.
- Be concise—try to limit yourself to 1–2 pages. If the employer sets a page limit, follow it exactly.
- Use white or off-white paper, use standard size, 8.5″ × 11″ paper, and print on one side of the paper, using a font size between 10 and 14 points.
- Use a nondecorative font (like Arial or Times New Roman), choose one font, and stick to it.
- Avoid italics, script, and underlined words.
- Don't use horizontal or vertical lines, or shading.
- Don't fold or staple your resume; if you must mail it, mail it in a large envelope.
- Electronic resumes have different formatting demands. Many websites can assist you in the process of preparing a web-friendly resume. It probably is worth noting that it is your responsibility to make sure that the company's equipment is compatible when sending an electronic resume.

Figure 4.1 Resume Sample 1 from Kinsey Bolinder

KINSEY BOLINDER

123 Oak Street | Fairfax, VA 22033 | (208) 555-1212 | kinseybolinder@fake-email.com

EDUCATION

Boise State University, Boise, ID — May 2016

Bachelor of Science, Psychology

- Cumulative GPA: 3.38

PROFESSIONAL EXPERIENCE

ROCS Staffing, Herndon, VA — October 2017-Current

Recruiter

- Screen resumes to find strongest candidates for various positions
- Conduct phone and in-person interviews with candidates
- Coordinate interviews for candidates with clients' hiring managers
- Perform reference and background checks
- Complete new hire paperwork, including Form I-9

*Out of state helping care for family member with medical issues — February 2017-July 2017

Kaseya, McLean, VA — September 2016-January 2017

Administrative Assistant (Temporary Position)

- Managed high volume email account for Accounting and Billing Department
- Practiced excellent customer service while corresponding with customers via email and phone
- Planned company events including happy hours, employee farewells, and holiday party
- Kept inventory of office and kitchen supplies and created shipment orders as needed
- Cleaned and organized data

St. Alphonsus Regional Medical Center, Boise, ID — November 2015-August 2016

Administrative Specialist

- Developed a system to deliver Important Message from Medicare letters, resulting in the delivery rate increasing to 99% in just two months—a new record high for the department
- Communicate discharge appeal rights to patients and their families
- Worked closely with nursing staff, case managers, and social workers
- Coordinated monthly meetings to review policies and procedures

STARR Family Behavioral Health, Boise, ID — April 2014-August 2015

Lead Receptionist

- Managed schedules for multiple clinicians in two office locations
- Audited client and employee files for Medicaid compliance
- Processed incoming client referrals
- Verified insurance eligibility and benefits

Figure 4.1 *(Continued)*

KINSEY BOLINDER

123 Oak Street | Fairfax, VA 22033 | (208) 555-1212 | kinseybolinder@fake-email.com

RESEARCH EXPERIENCE

Boise State University, Boise, ID August 2015-May 2016

Research Assistant for Dr. Eric Landrum

- Designed and administered a research project assessing critical thinking skills in psychology undergraduate students
- Reviewed previous literature on the topic
- Created assessment and rubric to score participants
- Analyzed and interpreted statistical data using SPSS
- Wrote and submitted an APA style research paper to the Rocky Mountain Psychological Association and presented a poster at their annual convention

VOLUNTEER EXPERIENCE

Boise State University Alumni Association, Washington, DC Metro Area March 2017-Current

Idaho Conservation League, Boise, ID August 2015-August 2016

Conservation Voters for Idaho, Boise, ID August 2015-November 2015

Figure 4.2 Resume Sample 2 from Mallory Haynes

Mallory Haynes

malloryhaynes@trulyfakeaddress.com

Education:
Boise State University, Boise, ID,
Bachelor of Science Psychology
Minor: Family Studies

Professional Experience:
College of Western Idaho, *CNA Program,* Boise, ID 11/2014-02/2015

- Participated in and completed CNA course
- Completed 32 clinical hours at Kindred of Nampa
- Passed state CNA state exams

Boise State University, *Research Assistant,* Boise, ID 08/2013-04/1014

- Research assistant under mentorship of Dr. Eric Landrum
- Analyzing research related to projected job outcomes for Psychology majors, developed and implemented research to help Psychology majors find jobs after graduation, used SPSS to analyze data, set up meetings to prioritize, coordinate, and implement future research

Boise State University, *Research Assistant,* Boise, ID 04/2012-12/13

- Research assistant under mentorship of Dr. Mary Pritchard
- Analyzing research books and topics related to disordered eating habits, bi-weekly meetings to discuss, prioritize, and coordinate research, used SPSS to evaluate data, developed and implemented disordered eating prevention-based program to college students

Work Experience:
Lucky 13, *Counter Clerk and Bartender,* Boise, ID 09/2011-05/2015

- Greet customer, pour drinks, take food orders, maintain positive work environment in a busy restaurant

Chigbrow & Ryan, *Assembly,* Boise, ID 02/2015-04/2015

- In charge of filing, preparing taxes and assembling taxes at tax firm
- Enter information into Excel

Caregiver, *In-Home-Caregiver,* McCall, ID 03/2011-09/2011

- Full- time Caregiver for adult, male patient
- 40 hours per week, full-time caregiver for 85-year-old male with dementia. Providing companionship, daily feeding, bed transfers, daily hygiene, bathroom assistance, changing diapers

Aspen Market, *Assistant Manager,* McCall, ID 01/1993 - 2007

- Assisted with running convenient store, customer service, putting out freight, stocking merchandise, and daily cleaning of convenient store and Laundromat
- Dealing with a wide range of responsibilities including: banking, diverse range of customers, answering phones, and renting videos

Figure 4.2 *(Continued)*

Stone Security/ADT, *Office Manager*, Seattle, WA 5/2007-9/2007

- Responsible for running sales office
- Customer service, answered phones, managed sales associates and their clients, in charge of reviewing ADT Alarm contracts, scheduled alarm system installations, faxed, charged credit cards, prepared documents in Word and Microsoft XP

Portneuf Medical Center, *Assistant Teacher*, Pocatello, ID 11/2006-5/2007

- Responsible for caring for infants in hospital setting
- Social skills, great communicator with parents and multitasking

Computer Skills:

- Statistical software program: SPSS
- Microsoft Word
- Excel
- Photoshop
- Lightroom

Volunteer Service:

Allies Linked for the Prevention of HIV and AIDS (a.l.p.h.a) Volunteer/Service Learning- 02/2012- May 2012- Worked front desk at the Testing Center. Greeted clients, scheduled HIV, Gonorrhea, and Chlamydia tests, answer incoming phone calls.

Baby Steps Volunteer/Service Learning- 08/2011- 08/2013
Greet clients, help fill out point booklets, help maintain office, answer questions, provide support

Catholic Charities of Idaho/Service Learning- 08/2011-12/ 2011
Worked front desk answering phone calls, greeted and welcomed customers. Worked with refugee population and assisted with helping to teach English

Boys and Girls Club Volunteer/Service Learning- 2010
Help supervise after school program for the children that attended Boys and Girls club

Oregon Health and Sciences Dorenbercher Children's Hospital-
Float Volunteer on Pediatric Oncology/Hematology and Pediatric Intensive Care Unit. I worked alongside Child Life Therapists and with kids and their families to make their hospital experience as good as possible by using good communication, compassion, and empathy.

References:

Joni Stright, *Director of Business Operations St. Luke's,* Phone: 208-555-0317
Dr. Eric Landrum, *PhD, Boise State University*, Phone: 208-555-1993
Megan Stright, *MSW St. Luke's Boise*, Phone: 208-555-0304
Chelsea Olson, PAC, *Snake River Dermatology*, Phone: 208-555-1681

Letters of Recommendation, Samples

4.3 Explain how to secure a strong letter of recommendation for a job

In many job application situations, you may be asked for one or more letters of recommendation (and letters of recommendation are more typical requirement for graduate school applications, see Chapter 6). Plous (1998a) suggests that you should ask for recommendations from people who (a) have worked closely with you; (b) have known you long enough to know you fairly well; (c) have some expertise; (d) hold senior-level positions and are well known, if possible (e.g., department chair); (e) have a positive opinion of you and your abilities; and (f) have a warm and supportive personal style. When you ask a faculty member or other professional for a letter of recommendation, ask for a *strong* letter of recommendation. Most faculty members would rather not write a letter than write a weak letter of recommendation. How do you ask for a strong letter—just like that—"Would you be willing to write me a strong letter of recommendation?"

Plous (1998a) also recommends that you give your letter writers plenty of lead time, at least 3 or 4 weeks. Then, about one week before the deadline, give your letter writer a gentle reminder about the upcoming due date for the letter of recommendation. You will want to provide your letter writers with a complete packet of materials—this packet needs to be well organized in order for all the letters to get where they need to go and get there on time. Table 4.5 includes some of the items you might be asked to provide.

How do you secure those strong letters of recommendation? You must be more than a good book student. Being involved outside of the classroom gives you well-rounded experiences; it also gives your letter writers something to write about. Future chapters highlight many of the ways you can become involved in your psychology education outside of the classroom. Table 4.6 from Appleby (1998) lists, in order of importance, ideas on how to secure a **strong** letter of recommendation.

When faculty members are asked to write a strong letter of recommendation, and the student is a strong student, the letter is easy (and often a pleasure) to write. However, when faculty members are pressed to write for a student who is not so strong, what is not said in the letter may be as important as what is said. Figure 4.3 (see pp. 49–50)

Table 4.5 Typical Items Needed by Letter of Recommendation Writers

- Access to unofficial transcripts, list of classes taken with letter writer, and grades earned
- Due dates for letters/references
- Updated resume or curriculum vitae (CV)
- Link/URL to online forms to be completed/paper forms to be completed and mailed
- Personal statement (if applicable and available)

Table 4.6 Strategies for Securing a Strong Letter of Recommendation

Deal effectively with a variety of people
Display appropriate interpersonal skills
Listen carefully and accurately
Show initiative and persistence
Exhibit effective time management
Hold high ethical standards and expect the same of others
Handle conflict successfully
Speak articulately and persuasively
Work productively as a member of a team
Plan and carry out projects successfully
Think logically and creatively
Remain open-minded during controversies
Identify and actualize personal potential
Write clearly and precisely
Adapt to organizational rules and procedures
Comprehend and retain key points from written materials
Gather and organize information from multiple sources

Figure 4.3 Sample Letter of Recommendation

BOISE STATE UNIVERSITY

College of Social Sciences and Public Affairs

1910 University Drive Boise, Idaho 83725-1715

Department of Psychology

phone 208-426-1207
fax 208-426-4386

May 24, 2003

Tiffany Christensen, Director
Distance Education and Extended Studies
The University of Montana
32 Campus Drive
Missoula, MT 59812

Dear Tiffany,

I have been asked by Sean Adams to write a letter of recommendation in support of his application for your recently advertised position "Distance Education Coordinator." It is my pleasure to provide my support and this letter on Sean's behalf.

I have known Sean for a little over a year. Although he has not taken any courses from me, he served as one of my research assistants for the past year. He graduated with his bachelor's degree in psychology from Boise State earlier this month. Through these interactions I know Sean fairly well.

Quite frankly, I think he is a good match for the job requirements. As a research assistant, Sean often worked independently, balancing multiple tasks. His first project with me was to revise a previously rejected manuscript for publication in a scholarly journal. With Sean's assistance, we revised the manuscript and it has now been accepted for publication. His next project involved a major extension of the first one, involving working with adolescents to determine typical caffeine consumption along with their behavioral preferences while consuming caffeine. Sean diligently worked with multiple members of the community to establish a mechanism for collecting caffeine consumption data from high school students. When the approvals did not come in time to finish the project, Sean quickly shifted gears and studied college students. This quick thinking and ability to adapt allowed him to make a presentation at the Midwestern Psychological Association meeting in Chicago earlier this month. I have to say that it is unusual for an undergraduate to work hard enough to have both conference presentation and publication credits so early in an academic career. Even

Figure 4.3 *(Continued)*

Letter of Recommendation for Sean Adams
May 24, 2003
Page 2

more impressively, he has also accomplished this while working with another psychology professor as well!

I am confident that Sean has the analytical and problem-solving skills necessary for this position. He has a bona fide passion for education, and he will thrive with the opportunity to help distance education students achieve their educational goals. I think that Sean currently possesses all of the skills necessary to achieve in this job. His interpersonal skills are superb, and he is pleasant to work with. He's just that good!

If I can provide any additional information about Sean, please contact me directly. **I recommend Sean Adams for the Distance Education Coordinator position with my highest recommendation and without reservation.**

Sincerely,

R. Eric Landrum, Ph.D.
Professor
Department of Psychology

Phone: (208) 426-1993 Fax: (208) 426-4386 Email: elandru@boisestate.edu

shows a sample of an actual letter the first author has written. The names and other identifying factors have been changed. The details in this letter make it valuable to those requesting the letter. Would you like this type of letter written about you?

Interview Skills, Questions, and Knockout Factors

4.4 Practice strategies for successful interviewing

So you have written your resume, the resume did its job, and now you have landed that valuable interview. Before the interview, you need to do your homework—learn as much as you can about the company and about the job. What should you know about your potential employer? Appleby (1998) suggests that you should know about the relative size and potential growth of the industry, the product line or services, information about management personnel and the headquarters, the competition, and recent items in the news. Also, you should know about training policies, relocation policies, price of stock (if applicable), typical career paths, and potential new markets, products, or services. Table 4.7 lists ideas on attending interviews suggested by the United States Department of Labor (1991).

DeLuca (1997) suggests that before an interview, use this pre-interview checklist: (a) name and title of the person you are meeting, with correct spelling; (b) exact address and location of the organization, including accurate directions (and account for time-of-day traffic too); (c) research notes regarding the organization and the position you are interested in; (d) a list of points that you want to make; (e) any questions remaining to be answered about the position; (f) your employment and educational history in case you are asked to complete an application on the spot; and (g) your business card and a recent copy of your resume. Being prepared for the interview helps you to show your seriousness about the position you are applying for.

What type of questions might you be asked during an interview? Table 4.8 lists a sampling of the type of questions that interviewees have been asked. It's a good idea to do a mock interview with someone and think about your answers to these questions, and do the mock interview "dressed up" in the clothing you will wear for the real interview. Have your practice interviewer ask you some surprise questions. Often, the type of answers you can come up with "on the fly" impresses your potential employer as to how you can handle yourself in pressure situations, such as a job interview. Think about these questions when prepping for an interview from Budnick and Barber (2018, p. 39).

Table 4.7 Tips for Successful Interviewing

- Dress for the interview and the job—don't overdress, don't look too informal.
- Always go to the interview alone.
- Find common ground with the employer, and if possible, with the interviewer.
- Express your interest in the job and the company based on the homework you did prior to the interview.
- Allow the interviewer to direct the conversation.
- Answer questions in a clear and positive manner.
- Speak positively of former employers or colleagues, no matter what.
- Let the employer lead the conversation toward salary and benefits—try not to focus your interest on these issues (at least not during the initial interview).
- When discussing salary, be flexible.
- If the employer doesn't offer you a job or say when you'll hear about their decision, ask about when you can call to follow up.

Table 4.8 Sample Questions You Might Be Asked in an Interview

- Tell me about yourself. How do you think a friend who knows you well would describe you? How do you work under pressure?
- What are your greatest strengths and weaknesses? Describe a time when your work was criticized. How did you handle the criticism? What is success to you?
- How has your college experience prepared you for this job? Which subjects did you like best? The least? What was your GPA? Do you think your GPA is a good reflection of your academic achievement?
- Give me an example of a time when you faced a major problem. How did you solve it? How would you handle a project deadline that was given to you at the last minute? Tell me about a time what you failed at a task. How did you handle it?
- What salary are you expecting? Will $_______ be OK with you? How much are you hoping to earn if we offer you this position?

SOURCE: Budnick, C. J., & Barber, L. K. (2018). Developing and enhancing students' job search skills and motivation: An online job search intervention training module. *Society for the Teaching of Psychology*. Office of Teaching Resources in Psychology. Retrieved from https://teachpsych.org/page-1603066

Also, you need to be ready with questions of your own (Table 4.9). Remember, although you are being interviewed by the organization, you are interviewing them as well! You need to determine if this position is a good match or fit for you. Having your own interview questions prepared in advance will indicate your level of interest to the employer and help promote a balanced interview.

What if the interview does not pan out? In a survey, executives were asked what they think is the most common mistake applicants make during job interviews: little or no knowledge of the company (44%), unprepared to discuss career plans (23%), limited enthusiasm (16%), lack of eye contact (5%), and unprepared to discuss skills/experience (3%; Lindgren, 2003). Think of each interview as a practice trial toward the next opportunity. If you can identify certain reasons why the interview did not go well, work on those problems—for example, do not ask during the initial interview "what about vacation time?" In some cases, you can contact the interviewer and ask for constructive feedback about the interview process: Was it the way that you handled yourself during the interview, or was it qualifications and experience?

For an interesting perspective, think about the employer's decision about whether or not to hire the individual being interviewed. Jeff Bezos, the now-famous head of Amazon.com, has become renowned for implementing a "3-question test" for new Amazon employees (Montag, 2018)—that is, after an interview, if the person in human resources wants to hire the person he/she just interviewed, the interviewer should ask herself/himself the following three questions:

1. Will you admire this person?
2. Will this person raise the average level of effectiveness of the group they're entering?
3. Along what dimension might this person be a superstar?

Table 4.9 Sample Questions to Ask Potential Employers

What are your organization's current major challenges?
May I have a copy of a current organizational chart, employee handbook, or other relevant publications?
Was this job posted internally?
Do you feel I have the characteristics necessary to be hired and to advance in this organization?
What do you feel are the most important aspects of this position?
Who will make the final hiring decision?
When will you have to make a hiring decision?
How long have you worked here?
What do you like about this organization?
Would this position lead to other job openings?
Can I get a tour of the facility?
How does the organization regard its employees?
How many applicants have applied for this job?
How long do you think it will take until you make a decision?

SOURCE: DeLuca, M. J. (1997). *Best answers to the 201 most frequently asked interview questions*. New York: McGraw-Hill.

As you are preparing to be the interviewee, think about these three dimensions. How might you help the interviewer answer these questions, thinking of you in a positive light? And if they cannot answer these positively thinking about you specifically, is that job a good match and fit for you then? Food for thought.

What if You are Not Initially Successful in Your Job Search?

4.5 Put an unsuccessful job search in context

This could happen. You could follow all of the advice in this chapter and throughout this book, and you might not get the job you want. Whose fault is that? It's not about fault, but it's about a host of factors. For instance, the success of the economy drives a large part of hiring decisions. If you happen to graduate with your bachelor's degree in psychology at a time when the economy is not doing so well, it might take some time to find the job that you want. In this type of situation, it might be best to take a job related to what you want and continue to build your skills and abilities, therefore building your resume. Also, it's hard sometimes for graduates to realize the size of the market and the competition. Although you might be competing with your classmates for some of the local jobs, the competition is even fiercer than that. Remember, there are over 117,000 graduates with bachelor's degrees in psychology every year. You are competing with many of them for the best jobs. You are also competing with some of last year's grads for those good jobs, and next year a new batch of graduates will be competing for your job. If you follow much of the advice offered throughout this book and by your faculty members, we sincerely believe that you will put yourself in an advantageous position to get the best jobs available.

If you have the opportunity, try to obtain feedback from employers about the status of your application. What was it that prevented you from getting the job you wanted? Was it poorly prepared materials? Was it nervousness at the interview? Was it a lack of match or fit with the organization? If you can obtain some feedback, it might give you some insight on how to proceed and how to minimize or eliminate any weaknesses. Whatever the feedback, try to assess its accuracy. Outside help would be good here. Discuss these issues with your faculty mentor or other trusted, respected individuals. The disappointment of rejection may cloud your objective evaluation of the critiques offered; an external opinion can help. After you have determined any actual weaknesses, then work to resolve them. It might mean taking a workshop or class. It might mean consulting with a career coach on how to better prepare and submit your materials. Be willing to invest in you—it will be the best investment you ever make!

It may be difficult to obtain this information from larger corporations; however, if you interviewed with someone, your interviewer would be a good first contact to receive feedback about your unsuccessful application. Additionally, pursuing this type of information, although not the most pleasant of tasks, will impress upon the company how serious you were about your job application and how serious you are about self-improvement. Inquiries such as yours might be remembered when future opportunities arise with that organization.

Finally, be persistent. Invest in yourself and expect to reap benefits. Be persistent in your acquisition of the type of position you want and be persistent in self-improvement. It is important to be intelligent, personable, motivated, etc.—but if you are not persistent in pursuing your goals, all the rest may be for naught.

You Got the Job, Now How to Keep it (Or Not Lose It)

4.6 Identify traits associated with workplace value

We know, we know, you are just trying to get through undergraduate schooling, and you may not be worried about getting or keeping a job (yet). However, you would be surprised at how what is valued in school is also valued in the workplace. Gardner (2007) asked employers of new college hires (not just psychology majors) about the reasons that a new employee is fired. We have already mentioned data in Chapter 2, but Gardner (2007) also asked in this same study about factors that lead to promotions and new assignments for new college hires. The top reasons employers reported for promoting new hires were as follows:

1. Taking initiative (accepting responsibility above and beyond, volunteering for additional work, and self-motivated—16%)
2. Self-management (setting priorities, time management, handling stress, ability to handle change, and flexibility—13%)
3. Personal attributes (friendliness, dependability, patience, flexibility, reliability, and respecting diversity—9%)
4. Commitment (positive attitude, work ethic, enthusiasm, and dedication—9%)
5. Leadership (building consensus, developing management skills, and recognizing the need to develop people—8%)
6. Show and tell (presenting own ideas persuasively in written and oral forms—7%)
7. Technical competency (understand core area of study, technical skills, mastery of current position, and high competence—7%)

What is interesting about this list is that it appears that the same characteristics that your future employers want are the characteristics your college professors want too!

Simply put, college is the place to practice for the future. In college, the stakes are relatively low, and the safety net is there to catch you if you fall. Practice the "what to do" list and avoid the "what not to do" list, and you should be right on target to get the job you want.

Exercise 4.1 What Kind of Perfectionist Are You?

This chapter outlines a number of important documents that students will prepare over the course of their undergraduate careers. Making them as accurate as possible is of course desirable, but you want to avoid the potential paralysis that could occur by expecting every document to be completely perfect in every way.

According to Slaney, Rice, Mobley, Ashby, and Trippi as described by Laber-Warren (2009), healthy perfectionists are energetic, effective, and enjoy success. However, unhealthy perfectionists doubt whether they can meet their own goals, are usually unsatisfied with their own achievements, and are motivated by fear of failure.

Answer the survey items below, then use the scoring key to obtain two scores—your tendency to set ambitious goals ("standards") and your own sense of whether or not you are meeting those goals ("discrepancy" or inner critic).

	Strongly Disagree	Disagree	Slightly Disagree	Neither Disagree or Agree	Slightly Agree	Agree	Strongly Agree
1. I have high standards for my performance at work or at school.	O	O	O	O	O	O	O
2. I often feel frustrated because I can't meet my goals.	O	O	O	O	O	O	O
3. If you don't expect much out of yourself, you will never succeed.	O	O	O	O	O	O	O
4. My best just never seems to be good enough for me.	O	O	O	O	O	O	O
5. I have high expectations for myself.	O	O	O	O	O	O	O
6. I rarely live up to my high standards.	O	O	O	O	O	O	O
7. Doing my best never seems to be enough.	O	O	O	O	O	O	O
8. I set very high standards for myself.	O	O	O	O	O	O	O
9. I am never satisfied with my accomplishments.	O	O	O	O	O	O	O
10. I expect the best from myself.	O	O	O	O	O	O	O
11. I often worry about not measuring up to my own expectations.	O	O	O	O	O	O	O
12. My performance rarely measures up to my own standards.	O	O	O	O	O	O	O
13. I am not satisfied even when I know I have done my best.	O	O	O	O	O	O	O
14. I try to do my best at everything I do.	O	O	O	O	O	O	O
15. I am seldom able to meet my own high standards of performance.	O	O	O	O	O	O	O
16. I am hardly ever satisfied with my performance.	O	O	O	O	O	O	O
17. I hardly ever feel that what I've done is good enough.	O	O	O	O	O	O	O
18. I have a strong need to strive for excellence.	O	O	O	O	O	O	O
19. I often feel disappointment after completing a task because I know I could have done better.	O	O	O	O	O	O	O

For the instructions below, use this scoring scheme:

Strongly disagree = 1

Disagree = 2

Slightly disagree = 3

Neither disagree or agree = 4

Slightly agree = 5

Agree = 6

Strongly agree = 7

Add the answers to Items 1, 3, 5, 8, 10, 14, and 18. Write the answer here →	Standards
Add the answers to Items 2, 4, 6, 7, 9, 11, 12, 13, 15, 16, 17, and 19. Write the answer here →	Discrepancy

According to the authors, if you scored 42 or more on the Standards and less than 42 on Discrepancy, you may be what is described as a healthy perfectionist. If you scored 42 or more on Standards and 42 or more on Discrepancy, your perfectionism is likely making you sad at times. If you scored less than 42 on Standards, the authors state that it is highly likely that you also scored less than 42 on Discrepancy, meaning that you are a non-perfectionist—their example being Homer Simpson.

SOURCE: Laber-Warren, E. (2009). What kind of perfectionist are you? *Scientific American Mind*, July/August, 50. Retrieved from https://www.scientificamerican.com/article/can-you-be-too-perfect/

Exercise 4.2 Resume Self-Reflection Survey

If you have not created a resume, or perhaps it has been some time since you updated your resume, it can be a daunting task. We suggest that you take the short 8-item survey below to help orient yourself to the task. There are no correct answers, but the questions might help prompt you to think about specific strategies you can use as you create and update your resume—a task that you will presumably need to do the remainder of your professional work life.

	Strongly Disagree	Disagree	Neutral	Agree	Strongly Agree
1. I have the knowledge and skills necessary to create a professional and effective resume.	O	O	O	O	O
2. I have an effective resume that will attract company recruiters in my desired career field who want to interview me.	O	O	O	O	O
3. I need further guidance and instruction to help me design and develop an effective resume.	O	O	O	O	O
4. Effective resume writing is very easy for me.	O	O	O	O	O
5. I do not know how to build a resume that stands out from other resumes.	O	O	O	O	O
6. My current resume will obtain all the interviews I will need to be selected for a position in my desired career field.	O	O	O	O	O
7. I struggle with creating and writing an effective resume.	O	O	O	O	O
8. I have a good understanding about how the job application works.	O	O	O	O	O

SOURCE: Hunt, I., Taylor, R., & Oberman, W. (2017). Advisory board engagement: Assisting undergraduates with resume development. *Journal of Education for Business*, 92, 288–295. doi:10.1080/08832323.2017.1362680

Chapter 5
Career Options with a Master's Degree or Doctoral Degree

Learning Objectives

- **5.1** Explain the role of graduate training in psychology jobs
- **5.2** Compare types of graduate training
- **5.3** Identify typical settings for graduate-level psychology jobs
- **5.4** Relate job possibilities to a psychology master's degree
- **5.5** Describe the current state of Ph.D.-related psychology jobs
- **5.6** Interpret demographic data about psychology degree-holders
- **5.7** Define postdoctoral study

You may decide that your interest in psychology is going to take you beyond the bachelor's degree in psychology. You overhear some of the juniors and seniors in the psychology department talk about graduate school. You hear some of your classmates talking about all the time they spend studying for the Graduate Record Examination (GRE), and you do not even know what the GRE is. All you want to do is help people. Why do you need to go to graduate school to be able to do this? In this chapter, we tackle what your career options are with graduate training, and in Chapter 6 we provide an overview on the process of applying to and getting accepted into graduate school.

Why Graduate Training?

5.1 Explain the role of graduate training in psychology jobs

If you want to be a psychologist, psychology is one of those professions for which an additional professional degree is required to practice the craft. This requirement is similar to the additional training that you need to become a physician or lawyer. You do not get your M.D. (medical doctor degree for physician) or J.D. (juris doctor for lawyer) after completing your bachelor's degree. This situation is unlike other undergraduate majors, such as teacher education, accountancy, nursing, or engineering—for which a bachelor's degree (and usually some type of licensing or certification, often included as part of one's undergraduate instruction) is adequate preparation for employment. Even before we discuss the occupational opportunities available and the entire graduate school admissions process, there is much to think about when considering the graduate school question. First, here is some background about who graduates presented in Table 5.1 from 2015 to 2016 (2017c). Information from this chapter will update you about what you can do with a graduate degree in psychology, and information from Chapter 6 will help you with information about the application and admissions process.

Let's consider the admissions process for a moment and think about big broad themes. To give you an overall sense of the process in the United States, consider the report by Michalski, Cope, and Fowler (2017). In a survey filled out completely by 477 Departments of Psychology that appear in the annual *Graduate Study in Psychology* volume, Table 5.2 displays the data for these schools. However, it is important to remember that there are graduate programs in psychology that are not listed in the Graduate Study in Psychology volume. Furthermore, many psychology graduates are interested in pursuing postbaccalaureate educational opportunities, but not in a psychology graduate program. Our advice—don't get carried away by these data; your results may vary.

The emphasis on graduate training in psychology exists because of the skills and abilities required to function as a professional psychologist. Although some of these skills and abilities are addressed in your undergraduate education, the idea is that you master skills in the process of obtaining a more advanced degree (such as a master's degree or a doctorate). Shen (2010) advised graduate students to continue to improve their marketability during graduate school and to focus on developing a broad perspective, continuing to network with others, seek out applied experiences, and gain as much leadership experience as you can. These are similar goals to what you should accomplish as an undergraduate student, but in graduate school, the goal would be to take each up a notch—become proficient, not just knowledgeable. The Bureau of Labor Statistics (2012) nicely summarized the skills desired in professional psychologists:

- ***Analytical skills.*** Analytical skills are important when performing psychological research. Psychologists must be able to examine the information they collect and draw logical conclusions from them.
- ***Communication skills.*** Psychologists must have strong communications skills because they spend much of their time listening to and speaking with patients.
- ***Observational skills.*** Psychologists study attitude and behavior. They must be able to watch people and understand the possible meanings of people's facial expressions, body positions, actions, and interactions.

Table 5.1 Psychology Degrees Conferred by Gender, 2015–2016

	Bachelor's Degree	Master's Degree	Doctoral Degree
Women	91,161 (77.6%)	22,074 (79.8%)	4,874 (74.6%)
Men	26,279 (22.4%)	5,571 (20.2%)	1,658 (25.4%)
TOTAL	117,440	27,645	6,532

NOTE: Percentages apply to column totals.

Table 5.2 Graduate Admissions Data from 2015 to 2016 *Graduate Study in Psychology*

	Master's Degree Programs	Doctoral Programs
Number of Applications	24,357	69,233
Number of Applicants Accepted	11,754	9,057
Acceptance Rate	48.3%	13.1%

SOURCE: Michalski, D. S., Cope, C., & Fowler, G. A. (2017, December). Summary report: Admissions, applications, and acceptances. *Education Directorate*. American Psychological Association. Retrieved from https://www.apa.org/education/grad/survey-data/2018-admissions-applications.pdf

- ***Patience.*** Because research or treatment of patients may take a long time, psychologists must be able to demonstrate patience. They also must be patient when dealing with people who have mental or behavioral disorders.
- ***People skills.*** Psychologists study people and help people. They must be able to work well with their clients, patients, and other medical professionals.
- ***Problem-solving skills.*** Psychologists need problem-solving skills to find treatments or solutions for mental and behavioral problems.
- ***Trustworthiness.*** Patients must be able to trust their psychologists. Psychologists also must keep patients' problems in confidence, and patients must be able to trust psychologists' expertise in treating sensitive problems.

As you can start to understand, graduate school is a major commitment not only to your own education, but also to the discipline of psychology. If you have decided that graduate school is for you (and more on that topic in Chapter 6), then you will have to think about the type of training you want and the type of degree to earn. Both of these decisions go hand in hand. Thus, if it were literally possible, you'd need to process the information from this chapter and Chapter 6 simultaneously, because choices made on one end of the spectrum effect the other end of the spectrum.

Types of Graduate Training and Graduate Degrees

5.2 Compare types of graduate training

In psychology, there are basically three broad career paths or models that most graduate school students pursue: the *scientist model*, the *practitioner model*, or the *scientist-practitioner model*. Under the scientist model (sometimes called the research model), graduate students receive training in a specific content area, as well as intense instruction in research methods statistics, and those methods of basic and applied research that further our understanding of human behavior. The trainee under the scientist model typically has a research emphasis, advancing our knowledge of human behavior. In the scientist model, the graduate receives a Ph.D. (doctor of philosophy).

In the scientist-practitioner model, the graduate student receives similar rigorous training in the creation and comprehension of scientific information but receives additional training in the helping professions. Thus, the student in the scientist-practitioner model typically has the goal of becoming a therapist (or a psychologist, in the strict licensing sense of the word). This person is trained in various therapeutic theories, conducts therapy under supervision, and completes an internship prior to receiving a Ph.D. This approach to training is called the Boulder model, named after a conference held in Boulder, Colorado, in 1949. This conference formalized the approach of equal weight given to the development of both research skills and clinical skills. Thus, clinical psychologists trained in the scientist-practitioner model are prepared for work in both academia and practice (Norcross & Castle, 2002). In fact, those "in-the-know" in such programs will often talk about items such as "small s, big P"—meaning that a particular program has a larger emphasis on the (p)ractitioner side and a smaller emphasis on the (s)cience side.

The newest of these three career paths is the practitioner model. In the practitioner model, there is less emphasis on the science side of psychology, but there is additional training on the practitioner side. In this model, the person is trained to become a full-time practitioner. In this program, the graduate receives a Psy.D. (doctor of psychology). Training in a Psy.D. program is modeled after other professional degrees (M.D., J.D.) in that it is oriented toward being a practitioner in the field rather than the researcher (Keith-Spiegel, 1991). This approach to training is called the Vail model, named after a conference held in Vail, Colorado, in 1973. The general notion that emerged from this conference was that psychological knowledge had developed far enough that an explicitly professional degree was possible (similar to professional degrees in law, medicine, and dentistry). Also, it was proposed that different degrees be used to distinguish between the practitioner role (Psy.D.—doctor of psychology) and the scientist role (Ph.D.—doctor of philosophy). Clinical psychologists trained in this later approach focused primarily on clinical practice and less on scientific research. The Vail model also broadened where practitioner-modeled training could be delivered—those settings include a psychology department at a university, in a university-affiliated psychology school, and in an independent, freestanding psychology school (not affiliated with a university; Norcross & Castle, 2002). APA (1997) provides this summary of degree options:

> The Ph.D., then, is usually the degree granted by university-based psychology departments that train in the research or scientist-practitioner models, although some professional programs award the Ph.D. as well. The Psy.D. is usually granted by a university-based or freestanding professional school of psychology that trains with the professional model. The Ed.D. is a psychology Ph.D. that is granted by a university-based education department, as opposed to a psychology department, and, like the Ph.D., reflects either the research or the scientist-practitioner model.

If you are confident that your future is in becoming a practitioner, then it is a safe bet to consider a Psy.D. program. There are fewer Psy.D. training programs available than Ph.D training programs, and they tend to be more expensive compared to Ph.D. training programs. Norcross and Castle (2002) succinctly summarized the difference between the two training approaches: "Boulder programs aspire to train producers of research; Vail programs train consumers of research" (p. 23).

It is important to note that the American Psychological Association (APA) accredits some Ph.D. and Psy.D. degrees, as well as some predoctoral and postdoctoral programs. Accreditation asserts that a graduate program operates under certain practice and training principles that are believed to be beneficial to the training of future psychologists. Accreditation does not guarantee that you will have a good experience in the program, and many good graduate programs are not accredited. Accreditation is APA's seal of approval. APA does not accredit undergraduate degree programs. The doctoral degree is recognized by APA as the credential for psychologists and the entry-level degree for the profession. Many jobs, as well as licenses to practice, require a doctorate. Terminal programs are those intended to prepare a person for a specific occupation that requires only a master's degree for entry-level employment. Choosing between the master's degree and the doctorate? The master's option is less daunting because it requires a smaller investment of both time and money, and it affords the flexibility of part-time study in some cases. The master's degree offers a testing ground if a person is not completely sure that the doctoral degree is appropriate; sometimes faculty advisors refer to a master's degree program as a "stepping-stone" to future opportunities. If, as a master's degree student, you think you might eventually go on further for a doctorate, here are some suggestions that you can pursue while still earning your doctorate that should enhance your ability to gain admission into a doctoral program (APA, 1997):

- Get as much research experience as possible.
- Establish good relationships with professors, who can later support your doctoral ambitions.
- Get the broadest training possible and get a good foundation in core subjects.
- Maintain good grades.
- Obtain practical experiences in the areas on which you wish to concentrate.

In essence, this is exactly the type of advice we would give an undergraduate psychology major wishing success in the workforce (see Chapters 3 and 4).

Sample Job Descriptions, Work Locations of Graduate Degree Recipients

5.3 Identify typical settings for graduate-level psychology jobs

Educational attainment of a graduate degree in psychology allows a great deal of flexibility for employment settings. Moreover, as careers change and evolve, the basic skills acquired through graduate education allow for adaptation to new work environments. To appreciate the diversity of potential work environments, see Table 5.3.

Owing to the more specialized training at the graduate levels, there are actually fewer formal job descriptions available from O*NET (see Chapter 3 for more on this impressive resource). However, the skills and abilities attained through graduate training give these individuals a greater range of employment options.

Occupational Opportunities with the Master's Degree

5.4 Relate job possibilities to a psychology master's degree

In this section, we discuss the options and opportunities you will have with a master's degree (M.A. or M.S.). Some of the areas that we will cover include the outlook for the future of these positions, perceptions of the future, actual employment figures, different work settings, and relative salaries. The diversity of opportunities with a graduate degree is reflective of the diversity in psychology.

According to APA (2017e), based on 2015 data, there were 604,200 individuals in the United States with a master's degree in psychology. The most common job titles are counselors (20%), psychologists (13%), social workers (5%), and other mid-level managers. It was determined that 24% of the master's degree holders were not in the labor force, 2% were unemployed, and 74% were employed. Cumulatively they reported 71 different job occupations; 87% believed that their jobs are related to psychology, with 69% believing their jobs are closely related to psychology. The primary work activities indicated are professional service (49%), teaching (10%), research (6%), management (24%), and sales and marketing (4%). When placed in the sector of the economy, breakdown for master's degree holders is self-employed (16%), educational institution (32%), private for-profit (21%), private non-profit (18%), and government (12%) (APA, 2017e).

The differences between a master's-level psychologist and a master's-level counselor are subtle. Master's-level psychologists probably received their education in a department of psychology, and although their degree is from a psychology department, they may call themselves a counselor depending on the state rules and regulations concerning the title. (For instance, in some states "psychologist" is a legally protected term, often reserved for persons with a Ph.D. or Psy.D. who have also passed a licensing examination.) Master's-level counselors may or may not have received their degree from a psychology department; they may have earned the degree in a counseling department, guidance department, educational psychology department, etc. In many states, the term "counselor" is not legally protected; hence in some situations almost anyone can advertise as a counselor.

How much do master's-level counselors and psychologists earn? In a research study of a random sample of new master's degree recipients, the median starting salary was $45,000 (the mean was $45,546) (Doran, Kraha, Marks, Ameen, & El-Ghoroury, 2016). The most recent data available are presented in Table 5.4. Remember, these are

Table 5.3 Sample Work Settings for Psychology Master's Degree and Doctoral Degree Recipients

University settings	
	Psychology department
	Education department
	Business department
	Other academic department
	Administrative office
	Research center or institute
Four-year colleges	
	Psychology department
	Education department
	Other academic department
	Administrative office
	Research center or institute
Medical school	
	Psychiatry
	Department other than psychiatry
Other academic settings	
	Two-year college
	University-affiliated professional school for health services other than medical
	Professional school of psychology, independent
Schools and other educational settings	
	Elementary-Secondary school
	School system district office
	Other educational setting
Independent practice	
	Individual private practice
	Group practice
	Primary care group practice
Hospital	
	Public general hospital
	Private general hospital
	Public psychiatric hospital
	Not for-profit private psychiatric hospital
	VA medical center
	For-profit private psychiatric hospital
	Military hospital
	Nursing home
Other human service	
	University/college counseling center
	Outpatient clinic
	Counseling/guidance center
	Specialized health service
	Other human service setting
	Rehabilitation facility
	Primary care office/community health center
Managed care	
	CMHC
	HMO
	Other managed care
Business/government and other	
	Self-employed, not practice
	Consulting firm
	Private research organization or lab
	Government research organization or lab
	Business-industry
	Independent consultant
	Criminal justice system
	Military service
	Federal government
	State government
	Local government
	Other nonprofit organization
	Other noneducational, nonservice

SOURCE: Michalski, D., Kohout, J., Wicherski, M., & Hart, B. (2011, May). 2009 Doctorate employment survey. *Center for Workforce Studies*. American Psychological Association. Retrieved from http://www.apa.org/workforce/publications/09-doc-empl/report.pdf

Success Stories

Brittany Butler

At the age of 17, I was a parentless youth in foster care. I had lost my mother to congestive heart failure at 16 and my father to a fatal highway accident at 13. Raised in Baton Rouge, Louisiana, I came from a low-income, two-parent household and was the middle child of seven offspring. My parents were high school graduates; neither had the opportunity to pursue higher education. As a parentless teen, I graduated from high school with honors and was accepted into several colleges. After sharing my story with others, I was provided a way to attend my top choice, Spelman College.

In addition to having a passion for psychology when I started college, I was also interested in law. In the second semester of my first year, I took a national government course and joined the Morehouse-Spelman Pre-Law Society. I formed a deep interest in law and asked myself, 'Why not pursue two fields I have interests for at once?' Upon returning to Spelman for my sophomore year, I declared as a psychology major on the pre-law track and I could not be more proud that I did.

During the next years of my undergraduate studies, I was determined to prepare myself for a career in law following graduation. I joined student organizations geared toward my discipline and pre-law studies, such as the Spelman College Mock Trial Team, the Psi Chi International Honor Society, and the Beta Kappa Chi Scientific Honor Society. I mapped out a study plan that would intertwine all the materials learned from psychology and law courses as a focal point that would enhance my skill set, mindset, and agency to change the world as a Spelman woman. At the peak of my senior year, however, I no longer felt passionate about pursuing a career in law following graduation. I was more passionate about national advocacy work for young people in the foster care system. From personal experiences in foster care and researching the tough challenges young adults undergo when transitioning from foster care, I grew more passionate about increasing awareness on this social issue. Acknowledging the challenges of youth aging out of foster care, I wanted to help prevent someone else from having the same experience, thus leading to my path in social work.

Without parental and extended family support, getting through college was a challenge. As a full-time student, I worked part-time to support myself and provide for my siblings. However, my college experience was an incredible success. During my undergraduate study at Spelman College, I worked diligently in the discipline of psychology. By taking courses including lab courses and sociocultural electives, I expanded skills that will enable me to understand material taught throughout the social work curriculum. Along with these courses, I participated in internships, volunteer opportunities, and practicum experiences in efforts to develop interpersonal skills and competencies required for entry into graduate school. I served as a tutor and mentor to high school students residing in distressed neighborhoods, I volunteered abroad, and I acquired independent research experience at a local hospital

(continued)

> in Atlanta. The adversity I have endured has motivated me to achieve post-secondary success and find my true passion in child advocacy. After being accepted to every graduate program to which I applied, I am now attending Columbia University's Masters of Social Work program.
>
> I know in my heart my parents are proud of all of what I have accomplished so far. They have motivated me to end the generational curses that have affected my family and start a legacy that my parents never had the opportunity to pursue. A legacy that will make them proud. A legacy that I created in honor of my parents. This would be the greatest gift I could have given them.

average starting salaries. By the way, we searched for more updated information about starting salaries with a master's degree, and we could not find any source that is more comprehensive and more up-to-date than what is presented here.

Master's-level counselors and psychologists help people in a number of ways, such as evaluating their interests, abilities, and disabilities, and dealing with personal, social, academic, and career problems. You should know that there are related disciplines that also address some of these similar issues—included in this category are professions such as college and student affairs workers, teachers, personnel workers and managers, human services workers, social workers, psychiatric nurses, clergy members, occupational therapists, and others (Occupational Outlook Handbook [OOH], 1998). In fact, Walsh (2006) highlighted an alternative master's degree program for psychology majors by presenting information about master's in social work programs, master's degrees in allied health professions (like occupational therapy and physical therapy), master's programs in marriage and family, and master's programs in student affairs. There are a variety of options available for helping those who need help; more on this topic is presented in the later chapters of this book.

Occupational Opportunities with a Doctoral Degree

5.5 Describe the current state of Ph.D.-related psychology jobs

The doctoral degree in psychology (e.g., Ph.D. or Psy.D.) is generally required for employment as a licensed clinical or counseling psychologist. (Some states have limited licensure for master's-level psychologists, so you need to check local laws carefully.) In 2015, there were 207,100 individuals in the United States with a psychology doctoral degree; 15% were not in the labor force, 1% were unemployed, and 83% were employed. By far the most common occupational title was psychologists (41%), followed by postsecondary teachers: psychology (9%) (APA, 2017e). Of this group, 96% believed that their job is related to psychology, and 84% believe that their job is closely related to psychology.

From this same study (APA, 2017e), psychology doctorates (Ph.D. and Psy.D. holders) report their primary work activities as professional service (47%), teaching (16%), research (18%), management (14%), and sales and marketing (3%). Regarding the job sector within which they work, the data are self-employed (30%), educational institution (33%), private for-profit (15%), private non-profit (11%), and government (12%). Overall, there were 59 different occupational categories represented. This type of result speaks to the diversity of employment opportunities and the value of the skills attained by the completion of the doctoral degree. Although the doctorate is more difficult to obtain, persons who obtain it provide themselves with more opportunities for employment in a variety of settings.

What about the salaries for doctoral-level psychologists? In a survey of early career psychologists in collaboration with APA, Doran et al. (2016) randomly sampled new members and conducted a salary survey, and the results are presented in Table 5.4.

Let's Try to See the Big Picture

5.6 Interpret demographic data about psychology degree-holders

If you are reading this book in a linear fashion, you have now read about your options with a bachelor's degree (Chapter 3) and with a master's degree and a doctoral degree (this chapter). This is not an either/or proposition. Many students earn their bachelor's degree, enter the psychology workforce, and decide later they want to go back to school. Some stay in the workforce because they find a great job and turn it into a career, or perhaps even a calling. The path really is not linear, and to be fair with the data, it is often not linear.

The graphic below was prepared by American Psychological Association's Center for Workforce Studies (2017). It is based on a snapshot of the United States in 2015 of individuals under age 76 who received a bachelor's degree in psychology. This is an interactive tool, so when you get the chance, you should really use a computer monitor and hover over the pathways using this URL: http://www.apa.org/workforce/data-tools/degrees-pathways.aspx

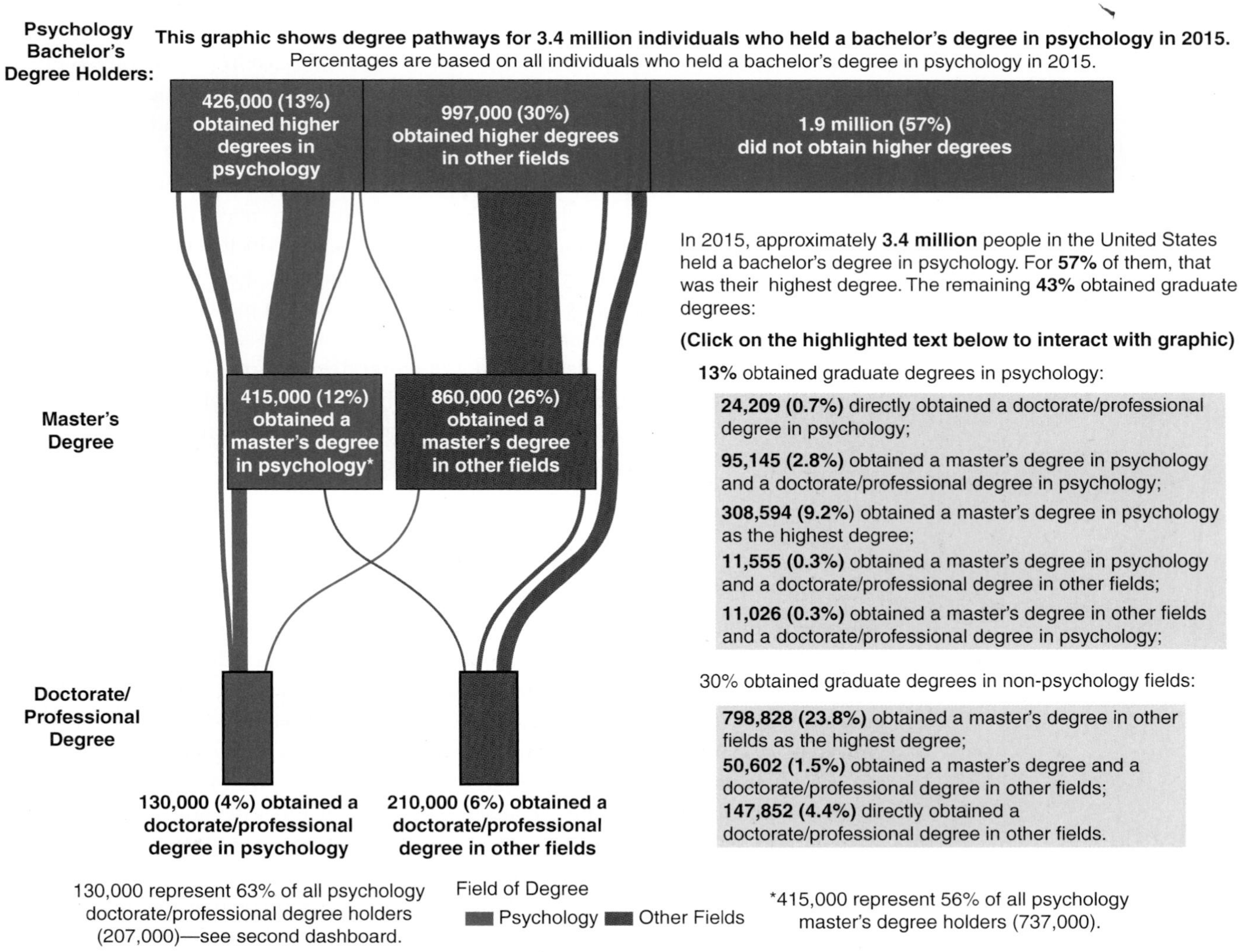
Psychology Bachelor's Degree Holders:
This graphic shows degree pathways for 3.4 million individuals who held a bachelor's degree in psychology in 2015.
Percentages are based on all individuals who held a bachelor's degree in psychology in 2015.
426,000 (13%) obtained higher degrees in psychology
997,000 (30%) obtained higher degrees in other fields
1.9 million (57%) did not obtain higher degrees
Master's Degree
415,000 (12%) obtained a master's degree in psychology*
860,000 (26%) obtained a master's degree in other fields
Doctorate/ Professional Degree
130,000 (4%) obtained a doctorate/professional degree in psychology
210,000 (6%) obtained a doctorate/professional degree in other fields
130,000 represent 63% of all psychology doctorate/professional degree holders (207,000)—see second dashboard.
Field of Degree
Psychology
Other Fields
*415,000 represent 56% of all psychology master's degree holders (737,000).

In 2015, approximately **3.4 million** people in the United States held a bachelor's degree in psychology. For **57%** of them, that was their highest degree. The remaining **43%** obtained graduate degrees:

(Click on the highlighted text below to interact with graphic)

13% obtained graduate degrees in psychology:

24,209 (0.7%) directly obtained a doctorate/professional degree in psychology;

95,145 (2.8%) obtained a master's degree in psychology and a doctorate/professional degree in psychology;

308,594 (9.2%) obtained a master's degree in psychology as the highest degree;

11,555 (0.3%) obtained a master's degree in psychology and a doctorate/professional degree in other fields;

11,026 (0.3%) obtained a master's degree in other fields and a doctorate/professional degree in psychology;

30% obtained graduate degrees in non-psychology fields:

798,828 (23.8%) obtained a master's degree in other fields as the highest degree;

50,602 (1.5%) obtained a master's degree and a doctorate/professional degree in other fields;

147,852 (4.4%) directly obtained a doctorate/professional degree in other fields.

Table 5.4 First-Year (Starting) Salaries for Early Career (Doctoral) Psychologists

	Minimum Starting Salary Reported	Median Starting Salary	Maximum Starting Salary Reported
Degree obtained			
Ph.D.	$24,000	$63,000	$140,000
Psy.D.	$10,000	$60,000	$130,000
Health-service provider subfields			
Counseling	$24,000	$56,000	$130,000
Clinical	$10,000	$65,000	$130,000
Clinical neuropsychology	$36,000	$72,500	$125,000
School	$35,000	$60,000	$110,000
Health	$24,000	$57,500	$96,000
Forensic	$27,000	$50,000	$60,000
Research and other subfields			
Industrial/Organizational	$43,000	$65,000	$120,000
Social	$42,000	$63,000	$100,000
Educational	$30,000	$60,000	$100,000
Developmental	$37,000	$55,000	$75,000
General	$12,000	$40,000	$50,000

SOURCES: Doran, J. M., Kraha, A., Marks, L. R., Ameen, E. J., & El-Ghoroury, N. H. (2016). Graduate debt in psychology: A quantitative analysis. *Training and Education in Professional Psychology*, *10*, 3–13. doi:10.1037/tep0000112

Lu, S. (2016, April). Median salaries for new psychologists are static. *gradPSYCH Magazine*, *14*(2), 22. Retrieved from http://www.apa.org/gradpsych/2016/04/salaries.aspx

In 2015, 3.4 million Americans held a bachelor's degree in psychology, with no higher degree; these are workforce psychology graduates. This graphic helps explain the complicated pathways of the remaining 43% of psychology graduates who do pursue some sort of postbaccalaureate education. Thirty percent (30%) earn a master's degree in a field other than psychology, and the remaining 13%—these individuals acquire more education in psychology. Out of this remaining "slice" if you will—13%—almost all earn a master's degree and then some also earn a doctorate, but a small portion just earn the doctorate (as you can see from the diagram, it is complicated). So, out of the 3.4 million psychology graduates in 2015, 12% have a master's degree, and 4% have a doctoral degree, but some of those individuals are the same people—that is—a person can have a master's degree and a doctoral degree. The Center for Workforce Studies (APA, 2017e) is to be commended for showing the complexity of the data in this fashion, because it is indeed a complex set of pathways leading to careers.

What Is a Postdoc?

5.7 Define postdoctoral study

You might think that after having completed your doctorate, you are done with your formal education. For some, that is not the case. The term "postdoc" is short for postdoctorate or postdoctoral study. Technically, it means just what it implies—additional education post (after) receiving the doctorate. Postdoctoral study is fairly common for clinical psychology students, but students from other areas of psychology also pursue the postdoctorate. In fact, in the 2009 survey of new doctorates (Michalski et al., 2011), 47% of recipients were pursuing or had completed postdoctoral study. In this same, the common reasons reported for completing postdoctoral study included improving employability, complementing research knowledge and skills, to prepare for a licensing exam, or to obtain specialized clinical training. By the way, no degree is associated with the postdoc (thus, no "Ph.D." or other letters attached to this additional education).

Are postdocs just for clinical psychology students? Not at all. According to Walfish (2001), a postdoc can set the stage nicely for the next steps of a research career. Postdocs can be grant funded, work as part of a research team, and receive valuable mentoring from a senior-level faculty member. At this point in your undergraduate career, you do not need to worry about a postdoc. We just wanted you to know what it is and why it exists. The bottom line is this—to become a psychologist, you will need additional training beyond the bachelor's degree. How much additional training may depend on the area of psychology you want to specialize in and the type of employment settings in which you will work. You do not need to think about all the combinations and permutations available right now—that will all work itself out in time. For now, try to follow the suggestions in this book for what you can do *as an undergraduate* to maximize your opportunities for success. It's OK to think about the future and plan accordingly, but do not lose sight of the present and succeeding in the here and now, else that future planning may be for naught.

Exercise 5.1 Is Graduate School Right for You?

As you can imagine, the decision to attend graduate school, whether it be in psychology or not or for a master's degree or a doctoral degree—the decision is momentous. To help shape your thinking and reflection about this decision, we have crafted the yes/no checklist below to start your thinking about "is graduate school right for you?"

Part I

✓ Yes	✗ No	Item
✓		Am I willing to go the extra mile to gain a wide range of skills **now** (as an undergraduate student) and as a graduate student?
✓		Am I willing to do that without being paid to do it?
	✓	Am I intrinsically motivated?
✓		Do I like being a student? Do I really, really like it?
✓		Am I able to work independently?
	✓	Am I a good time and stress manager?
✓		How well do I take criticism?
✓		Can I live with the feeling that I may not be able to accomplish all that I am expected to accomplish?
✓		Do I have some "street smarts" or practical intelligence?
✓		Am I willing to live without some of the luxuries of life for a while?

Part II

✓ Yes	✗ No	Item
✓		Is graduate school really an option for me?
	✓	Am I postponing some tough decisions by going to graduate school?
	✓	Have I done some hands-on reality testing?
✓		Do I need an advanced degree to work in my desired field or would a bachelor's degree do?
	✓	Have I compared my expectations of what graduate school will do for me compared to what it has done for alumni of the program I am considering?
	✓	Have I talked with people in my field to explore what I might be doing after graduate school?
✓		Am I excited by the idea of studying the particular field I have in mind?

There is not a scoring key for these yes/no items. If you answered them honestly, look back at your answers and see if you notice any patterns. Are you interested in graduate school and ready to apply now? Are you interested in graduate school but perhaps not ready now? Or perhaps are you intrigued by the idea of graduate school but not thrilled about more "school" after completing your undergraduate degree. Hopefully your reflections about the questions and your answers will bring you some clarity.

SOURCES: Part I: Giordano (2004). Part II: DeGalan and Lambert (1995).

Exercise 5.2 Is Graduate School Right for You, Revisited

This is not an error. It's an important decision—that is, deciding whether or not to go to graduate school. In light of that, here we present another inventory, the Unvalidated Graduate School Potential Test, developed by Fretz and Stang (1988); note that Keith-Spiegel (1991) adapted this instrument using very similar items but a different scaling and scoring system.

Instructions. Your answers to the following 22 yes–no questions will give you a good idea of your potential for success in graduate school, as determined by your current values and level of motivation. Answer each question honestly and truthfully. This is not a standardized or validated test, and its items are so transparent that anyone can fake them. Unless you are completely honest with yourself, the results will be of no value.

Check one ✔		
Yes	**No**	**Item**
		1. Does the idea of living at near-poverty level for 2 to 7 years while studying most of the time repulse you?
		2. Do you enjoy writing term papers?
		3. Does the idea of making verbal presentations of academic material in front of a group bother you?
		4. Do you enjoy reading psychology books even if they are not assigned?
		5. Do you put off studying for tests or writing papers as long as possible?
		6. Do you often give up desirable social opportunities in order to study?
		7. Do you want to earn a high salary when you finish graduate school?
		8. Do you like to study?
		9. Do you have trouble concentrating on your studies for hours at a time?
		10. Do you occasionally read recent issues of psychology journals?
		11. Do you dislike library research?
		12. Do you have a drive to enter the profession of psychology?
		13. Are there many other careers (besides being a psychologist) that you would like to pursue?
		14. Do you intend to work full-time at a career?
		15. Are you sick of school right now?
		16. Are your grades mostly As and Bs?
		17. Have any of your teachers ever suggested that you go to graduate school?
		18. Did you do well (i.e., receive an A or a B) in statistics?
		19. Do you feel a Ph.D. is desirable primarily because of the social status it gives to those who hold it?
		20. Do you like doing research?
		21. Do you dislike competing with other students?
		22. Can you carry out projects and study without direction from anyone else?

Scoring the test:

- Give yourself one point for each "yes" you marked for Items 2, 4, 6, 8, 10, 12, 14, 16, 17, 18, 20, and 22.
- Give yourself one point for each "no" you marked for Items 1, 3, 5, 7, 9, 11, 13, 15, 19, and 21.

Total your points. Your score can range from 0 to 22. The higher your score, the greater your graduate school potential.

The test should also make you aware of some of the issues that are often relevant to the successful completion of graduate school.

SOURCE: Fretz, B. R., & Stang, D. J. (1988). *Preparing for graduate study in psychology: Not for seniors only!* Washington, DC: American Psychological Association.

Chapter 6
The Graduate Admissions Process

Learning Objectives

6.1 Compare graduate admissions rates by degree and subfield

6.2 Describe the general skills and procedures required in applying to graduate school

6.3 Identify application elements most valuable to graduate admissions committees

6.4 Describe the ways graduate committees interpret grades, transcripts, and GRE scores

6.5 Explain how to earn a strong letter of recommendation for graduate applications

6.6 Outline the elements of a strong personal statement

6.7 Create a curriculum vita

6.8 Evaluate graduate programs for their individual fit

6.9 Summarize followup strategies for unsuccessful applications to graduate school

The message is clear about the benefits of receiving a master's degree or a doctorate. These advanced degrees prepare you for a career as a professional—they afford you greater job opportunities and flexibility, as well as enhanced salary benefits. So, you want to earn your master's degree or doctorate in psychology—how do you get started? This chapter is dedicated to providing an overview of the details of the graduate school application process. You will need to have some clear ideas about your short-term and long-term goals before you can start the graduate school search process in a meaningful manner, however.

Before you start down this long and winding road, we encourage you to seek out information from a variety of sources about your graduate education options. There are numerous support materials and information sources for students intending to apply to graduate school in psychology. In this chapter, we provide a beneficial overview of the entire process. However, you should know that there are entire books devoted to the topic (Privitera, 2015) and a free 12-part video series from the American Psychological Association (APA) on preparing and applying for graduate school in psychology (Norcross & Hogan, n.d.). Although not usually psychology specific, there are entire books on creating a curriculum vitae, writing a personal statement, and so on.

The Popularity and Competitiveness of Graduate Admissions

6.1 Compare graduate admissions rates by degree and subfield

In general, psychology is a popular choice at the undergraduate level. As you already know, each year over 117,000 students in the United States graduate with a bachelor's degree in psychology. Graduate education is quite popular, with continued increases in both master's degrees and doctorates awarded. We know from the data presented in Chapter 5 (APA, 2017e) that in the year 2015, 13% of all individuals with a bachelor's degree in psychology had or were seeking either a master's degree or doctoral degree in psychology. However, it is also important to remember that students with undergraduate degrees in disciplines other than psychology also seek graduate training in psychology. The graphic depicted in Figure 6.1 here from the Center for Workforce Studies (APA, 2017f) shows the various pipelines into psychology graduate education (read from the bottom up).

Figure 6.1 This Graphic Shows Degree Pathways for 207,000 Individuals Who Held a Doctorate/Professional Degree in Psychology in 2015

SOURCE: American Psychological Association. (2017f). *Careers in psychology*. [Interactive data tool]. Retrieved from http://www.apa.org/workforce/data-tools/careers-psychology.aspx

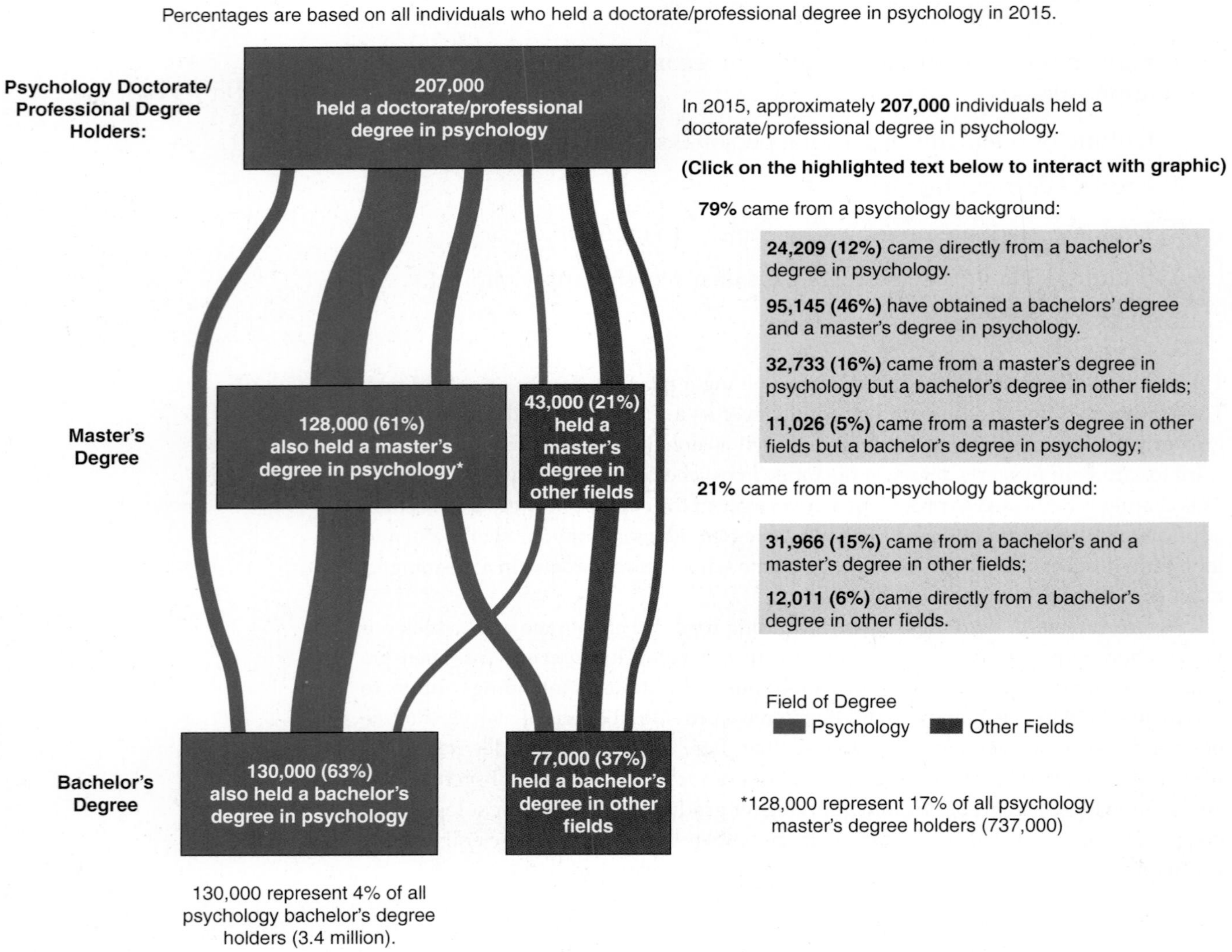
Percentages are based on all individuals who held a doctorate/professional degree in psychology in 2015.
Psychology Doctorate/ Professional Degree Holders:
207,000 held a doctorate/professional degree in psychology
Master's Degree
128,000 (61%) also held a master's degree in psychology*
43,000 (21%) held a master's degree in other fields
Bachelor's Degree
130,000 (63%) also held a bachelor's degree in psychology
77,000 (37%) held a bachelor's degree in other fields
130,000 represent 4% of all psychology bachelor's degree holders (3.4 million).
In 2015, approximately 207,000 individuals held a doctorate/professional degree in psychology.
(Click on the highlighted text below to interact with graphic)
79% came from a psychology background:
24,209 (12%) came directly from a bachelor's degree in psychology.
95,145 (46%) have obtained a bachelors' degree and a master's degree in psychology.
32,733 (16%) came from a master's degree in psychology but a bachelor's degree in other fields;
11,026 (5%) came from a master's degree in other fields but a bachelor's degree in psychology;
21% came from a non-psychology background:
31,966 (15%) came from a bachelor's and a master's degree in other fields;
12,011 (6%) came directly from a bachelor's degree in other fields.
Field of Degree
Psychology
Other Fields
*128,000 represent 17% of all psychology master's degree holders (737,000)

Table 6.1 Applications, Acceptances, and Acceptance Rates in U.S. Graduate Psychology Programs, 2015–2016

	U.S. Doctoral Programs	U.S. Master's Programs
Number of applications	69,233	24,357
Number of acceptances	9,057	11,745
Acceptance rate	13.1%	48.3%
Number of programs	885	470

SOURCE: Michalski, D. S., Cope, C., & Fowler, G. A. (2017). Graduate study in psychology 2018: Summary report: Admissions, applications, and acceptances. *Education Directorate*. American Psychological Association. Retrieved from http://www.apa.org/education/grad/survey-data/2018-admissions-applications.pdf

Thus, there is competition from your psychology major cohort as well as from the outside. This level of competition should not dissuade you from applying to graduate school, but you need to know what you are getting yourself into. What is popular currently? How many applications are received in specialty areas of psychology? The tables that follow help us present some of the data to answer these questions.

The information in Table 6.1 provides an overall snapshot of master's degree and doctoral degree pursuits in psychology in the United States. You can see that applying to doctoral programs is more popular (more applications) than applying to master's programs, and entrance to doctoral programs is more competitive (a lower acceptance rate). These are factors that you should take into consideration if you are thinking about applying to graduate school (the exercises at the end of Chapter 5, and some closing thoughts at the end of this chapter may also help you think about that decision).

But not all of the subfields in psychology are created equal. Some of the subfields in psychology are more popular and more competitive. For those details, see Table 6.2.

Table 6.2 Applications, Acceptances, and Overall Acceptance Rates by Degree Type and Broad Subfield in Psychology

	Master's Degrees				Doctoral Degrees			
	N programs	Applications	Acceptances	Acceptance Rate	N programs	Applications	Acceptances	Acceptance Rate
Clinical psychology	57	3085	970	31.4%	231	39,781	4806	12.1%
Cognitive psychology	10	281	105	37.4%	110	4518	539	11.9%
Counseling psychology	92	6874	3902	56.8%	66	5191	592	11.4%
Developmental psychology	19	452	233	51.5%	96	2919	434	14.9%
Experimental psychology	81	3668	1619	44.1%	42	2388	268	12.1%
Industrial/ Organizational psychology	61	3237	1238	38.2%	47	2826	362	12.8%
Neuroscience	6	188	123	65.4%	71	2570	365	10.3%
School psychology	57	2106	1166	55.4%	48	1768	553	31.3%
Social psychology	14	375	102	27.2%	98	5156	409	7.9%
Other applied psychology	57	2842	1473	51.8%	70	1482	317	21.4%
Other psychology	16	1249	823	65.9%	6	634	492	77.6%
Total	470	24,357	11,754	48.3%	885	69,233	9057	13.1%

It is worth noting that for both of these tables presented, they come from the Graduate Study in Psychology book. This is an excellent book published by the American Psychological Association each year. As with any data collection effort, however, there are limitations. First, the data reported in the book are self-reports by the graduate departments of psychology, and then aggregated by researchers at APA for reports such as Michalski et al. (2017). Sometimes, departments don't keep their data updated as they should. Second, not every Department of Psychology offering a master's or doctorate in the United States is listed in the book. Third, there are many departments in the nation offering master's degrees and doctorates that are of interest to psychology graduates, but they are not in a Department of Psychology—thus, they would not be represented in this book. The bottom line is that the data presented is a decent snapshot, but it's a limited sample at best, and your options are likely much more diverse than you think.

Overview: The Application Process

6.2 Describe the general skills and procedures required in applying to graduate school

Before we jump into the details of the process, an overview is in order. Buskist (2002) provided a thoughtful overview of the graduate application process in his seven tips for preparing a successful graduate school application: (a) be planful; (b) develop competencies as an undergraduate; (c) settle on a specialty area; (d) involve yourself in undergraduate research; (e) do homework on potential graduate schools; (f) identify possible major professors (who would be good for potential mentors and future letter of recommendation writers); and (g) write an outstanding letter of intent. Unlike your undergraduate studies, you will specialize in your graduate training (although there are some generalist graduate programs and degrees). When you first start thinking about graduate school, you'll need to be thinking about a lot of decisions at the same time—what specialty area you are interested in, what level of education do you need/want to pursue, how will your academic record support what you want to do next, where are you willing to relocate to pursue these educational goals, how much debt are you willing to incur to further your education, and so on. There are many decisions to make. Over the course of this chapter, we'll try to give you a glimpse of the process.

Narrowing Your Program List

An excellent guide to finding information about graduate programs in psychology in the United States is the annual *Graduate Study in Psychology* published by the American Psychological Association. Note that this book is published (or updated) each year; when it's your time to pursue this option, make sure you obtain the most recent edition; if you prefer, you can purchase electronic access and search the book like a database. But remember, there are more departments that offer degrees than which are listed in the book. This resource is a great start, but for a comprehensive approach you will need to do more. The 2000 edition of *Graduate Study in Psychology* contained the following suggestions about how to narrow your list of schools:

- Apply to a range of programs, with most offering you a reasonable chance at acceptance. It takes too much time, effort, and money to apply to programs at which you have no reasonable chance of acceptance.
- When possible, apply to programs that offer the degree that you ultimately want to obtain.
- Apply to programs that offer the specialty in which you would like to eventually gain employment. It is difficult to change your major emphasis or area "midstream" in your graduate education.

- Apply to programs that match your interests and your experience. Know who the faculty members are, do your homework, and apply to programs where you believe you will be a good "fit."
- Be informed about the issues related to career opportunities of your chosen area of psychology. Although your graduate program is responsible for your educational opportunities, you are responsible for your employment opportunities.

Understanding the Application Process

The second area of expertise that you will have to develop in this endeavor is a good working knowledge of the application process. The advice we provide includes the following: (a) access departmental websites to determine the application details, departmental information, and financial aid information (if necessary) and (b) prepare the materials required by most applications (in addition to determining the application fee). The typical items to be included in your application are a letter of intent/autobiographical statement/personal statement, letters of recommendation and transcripts/grades, GRE scores forwarded directly from the Educational Testing Service (ETS), a curriculum vitae (CV) or resume (see more below), and a cover letter/e-mail. For some programs, after the first portion of the application process is complete, graduate departments may ask qualified candidates to interview, either in person or electronically (by telephone/Skype/Zoom/GoToMeeting).

We mentioned curriculum vita above—what is the difference between a curriculum vita (commonly called a vita) and a resume? A vita is an academic document that chronicles your accomplishments and achievements related to the discipline. A resume is more of a work history and advertisement of your skills and abilities. In general, a resume needs to be short, one to two pages, whereas a long vita means a long list of accomplishments. More on these two documents can be found later in this chapter—you can also find more information about the student CV and another example in Landrum (2005). A guide to vita preparation and sample vitae of undergraduate students is also presented later in this chapter.

Diehl and Sullivan (1998) also offered additional suggestions to make the graduate school application process turn out in your favor. For example, if appropriate, you might send electronic copies of your written work as writing samples, such as an impressive term paper from an upper division psychology course, or your work from a senior thesis, internship, independent study, or directed research project. After you have sent off your packet of application materials, make sure that the department received *everything*. It is *your* responsibility to make sure that letters of recommendation and transcripts are received. Appropriately timed telephone calls or e-mails can save an application. An incomplete application package is an easy excuse for a graduate admissions committee to *not* review your materials. Note that, sometimes, a graduate application might not even make it past the administrative assistant's desk. Many graduate programs are serious about minimum GPAs and GRE scores; the remainder of the packet may be for naught if these initial hurdles are not adequately completed.

Be sure to fill out all web forms completely. Regarding your letter of recommendation, you will be asked to electronically sign documents—be sure to be thorough and complete, because when the faculty member completes their portion, they cannot complete your portion. Watch for more tips about the application process throughout this chapter.

Patience

The third component in this overview of the process is patience. Sometimes, patience is the hardest part. The process typically works like this: You will usually be notified of your acceptance or rejection before April 15—sometimes earlier, and sometimes later (if you are on a wait list); however, you should receive some feedback by April 15. Then, you accept or reject an offer, in writing, by or on April 15; if you decide to attend, it's good to have that decision behind you. If you decide not to attend, the school can go to the next person on the wait list and make that person an offer. Although you may need some time to make your decision, it is not appropriate to delay this decision after April 15. In the remainder of this chapter, we examine the details of navigating through this process and finish up with some of the keys to being a successful applicant and a successful graduate student.

What Is Important to Graduate Admissions Committees?

6.3 Identify application elements most valuable to graduate admissions committees

What can you do to make your application more competitive? What do graduate admissions committees look for? How do they make these decisions about whom to admit into their program or whom to reject from their program? A number of researchers, over time, have answered this question in a number of published books and research articles (Cashin & Landrum, 1991; Keith-Spiegel, 1991; Keith-Spiegel & Wiederman, 2000; Landrum & Clark, 2005; Landrum et al., 1994; Schoeneman & Schoeneman, 2006; Walfish & Turner, 2006). What consistently emerged over time are what came to be known as the big five:

- Grade point average (GPA)
- Graduate Record Examination (GRE) scores
- Letters of recommendation
- Autobiographical statement/letter of intent/personal statement
- Research experience

Of course, other materials are required in graduate school admissions, but these five variables were consistently identified as the most important factors in decision making by graduate school admissions committees. Other factors come into play, perhaps as tie-breakers, such as an on-campus interview, whether the applicant has a master's degree or is coming directly from a bachelor's degree program, and so on.

In 2018, Littleford, Buxton, Bucher, Simon-Dack, and Yang published a study where they surveyed 221 doctoral program admissions committees regarding what committee members rate as important in admissions decisions. In addition to drawing overall conclusions about the relative importance of admissions criteria, Littleford et al. (2018) parsed the institutional responses into these categories: clinical Ph.D., counseling Ph.D., Psy.D., research subfields, and practice subfields. As is typically the case, the pattern of results can become complex and nuanced depending on specialty area desired and degree sought. However, the credentials rated to be the most important in overall doctoral admissions were:

- personal statement;
- letters of recommendation;
- interview;
- undergraduate GPA;
- student-mentor research match ("match and fit"); and
- GRE scores

Littleford et al. (2018) also identified the next tier, or second level of credentials—you might think of these as potential tie-breakers if two applicants were equally qualified on the six items listed above:

- Graduate GPA (if available)
- Curriculum vita
- Research assistant experience
- Independent research project
- Research publications

It is interesting to compare the updated data to the classic "big five." Does this mean that research experience is now less important than it once was? We would argue not at all. It is through working with a faculty member on a research project that you can learn about the discipline of psychology and learn how to think like a psychologist. When you do this in an outside-of-classroom experience (more about this in Chapter 7), you get to know your research mentor. This will likely lead to an improved letter of recommendation, meaningful material for you to write about in your personal statement, and high grades in your research-based courses, helping your GPA. Plus, it is easy to directly see the value of the research experience in the secondary selection/tie-breaker criteria. Given the tens of thousands of applicants to graduate institutions in psychology in the United States annually, there are so many good students applying that yes, these "tie-breaker" credentials will most certainly be employed in many cases.

The type of research provided by Littleford et al. (2018) is invaluable in providing an overview to the importance of criteria in the graduate admissions process. However, this is no substitute for the research you will need to do about the individuals' schools and programs you are interested in. As mentioned previously, a great starting point for this is the annual *Graduate Study in Psychology* book. In Figure 6.2, we present a series of screenshots from the online version of *GSP* which presents the details about the graduate programming available at the University of Washington in Seattle. Another attractive feature of *GSP* is that all of the tables for all of the schools are formatted in the same way, so if you want to compare data across schools, this is relatively easy to do.

Your graduate school application package is likely to be complex; one reason for this is that each school's application requirements will be different. There is no uniform method of applying to graduate schools, and as an applicant, you need to follow the rules set by each school. The graduate school application is not the place to ad-lib and do it your own way—that strategy is likely to backfire. What might be in your application package? Keith-Spiegel and Wiederman (2000) generated a fairly comprehensive list (see Table 6.3). There is research on what not to do for the graduate school application process; what Appleby and Appleby (2006) call "kisses of death" (KODs). They identified five different areas of harm: damaging personal statements, harmful letters of recommendation, lack of program information, poor writing skills, and misfired attempts to impress. These researchers concluded that many KODs can be avoided by improvements to advising and better mentoring of students.

In the rest of this chapter, we will address some of the key components of this application process (see Table 6.3), by examining (a) grades, transcripts, and the GRE; (b) letters of recommendation with faculty examples; (c) the personal statement with student examples; (d) a student's version of a vita; (e) the importance of research experience; and (f) the importance of match or fit with your graduate programs of interest.

Figure 6.2 Online version of Graduate School in Psychology about Graduate Programming

Washington, University of

Washington, University of
Department of Psychology
Arts & Sciences
Box 351525
Seattle, WA 98195-1525
Telephone: (206) 543-8687
E-mail: mizumori@uw.edu
Web: http://www.psych.uw.edu/

Chairperson: Sheri J.Y. Mizumori, Ph.D.

Orientation, Objectives, and Emphasis of Department:

The program is committed to research-oriented scientific psychology. No degree programs are available in counseling or humanistic psychology. The clinical program emphasizes both clinical and research competencies and has areas of specialization in child clinical, and subspecialties in behavioral medicine, health psychology, and community psychology. Diversity science and quantitative psychology minors are now available to students in our program.

Programs and Degrees Offered:

Program	Degree	Application Deadline	Applications Received	Accepted	Enroll (PT)	Total Enrolled (PT)	Degrees Awarded in 2015-2016	Mdn. Yrs to Complete Degree	Dismissed/Withdrew
Animal Behavior	PhD	December 1 (Fall)	9	0	0 (0)	9 (0)	2	6.12	0
Clinical Psychology	PhD	December 1 (Fall)	580	7	7 (0)	49 (8)	9	6.75	0
Cognition and Perception	PhD	December 1 (Fall)	56	5	2 (0)	16 (2)	2	6.87	0
Developmental Psychology	PhD	December 1 (Fall)	59	3	1 (0)	6 (0)	2	5.75	0
Behavioral Neuroscience	PhD	December 1 (Fall)	29	6	4 (0)	12 (0)	1	4.75	0
Social and Personality Psychology	PhD	December 1 (Fall)	114	3	1 (0)	9 (2)	2	6.12	0
Quantitative Psychology	PhD	December 1 (Fall)	18	1	0 (0)	0 (0)	0	0	0

Figure 6.2 *(Continued)*

Internships/Practica:

A variety of local and national predoctoral internships are available in clinical psychology.

Admissions:

Entries appear in the following order: required test or GPA, minimum score (if required)/median score of students entering in 2016-17.

Program	Degree	GRE-V	GRE-Q	GRE-Writing	GRE Subject	UGrad GPA	Last 2 years GPA	Psychology GPA	Master's GPA
Animal Behavior	PhD								
Clinical Psychology	PhD					NA/3.8			
Cognition and Perception	PhD								
Developmental Psychology	PhD								
Behavioral Neuroscience	PhD								
Social and Personality Psychology	PhD								
Quantitative Psychology	PhD								

Admissions Requirements:

Degree	GRE-General	GRE-Subject	Letters of Rec	Research/Personal Statement	Writing Sample	CV/Resume	Interview
Doctoral	Required	Optional	3	Required	None	Optional	Required

Criterion	Level of importance
GRE Scores	High
Research Experience	High
Work Experience	Medium
Clinically Related Public Service	Low
GPA	Medium
Letters of Recommendation	High
Interview	High
Statement of Goals and Objectives	High
Undergraduate Psychology Preparation	Medium

Please note if these criteria vary for different programs : Individual areas evaluate applications differently, but all require a strong background in research and/or statistics.

For additional information on admission requirements, visit
http://www.psych.uw.edu/psych.php?p=137

(continued)

Figure 6.2 *(Continued)*

Department Demographics:

	Male (PT)	Female (PT)	Total	African-American/Black (PT)	Hispanic/Latino (PT)	Asian/Pacific Islander (PT)	American Indian/Alaska Native (PT)	Caucasian/White (PT)	Unknown	Multiethnic (PT)	ADA (PT)	Int (P
Students	31 (3)	70 (9)	101	6 (0)	10 (0)	18 (3)	1 (0)	64 (8)	0 (0)	2 (1)	0 (0)	8 (0)

Financial Information/Assistance:

Tuition for Full-Time Study:

Doctoral:

State residents: per academic year $16,266.00.
Nonstate residents: per academic year $28,314.00.

For more information on tuition costs, visit: http://opb.washington.edu/content/tuition-fees. Tuition is subject to change.

Financial Assistance:

	Teaching Assistantship (% Receiving)	Teaching Assistantship Remission	Research Assistantship (% Receiving)	Research Assistantship Remission	Fellowship (% Receiving)	Fellowship Remission
First year Student	$21,546.00 (NA)	Full	$21,546.00 (NA)	Full	NA (NA)	NA
Advanced Student	$23,148.00 (NA)	Full	$23,148.00 (NA)	Full	NA (NA)	NA

Table 6.3 Potential Components of a Graduate School Application Package

- Curriculum vita or resume
- Biographical statement (sometimes called personal statement, autobiographical statement, letter of intent), including a statement of your interests and career goals
- Overall grade point average (GPA), GPA in psychology, verified by an official copy of your transcripts
- List of relevant courses you have completed in the major, and a timetable for those courses not yet completed but planned for the future
- GRE scores
- Letters of recommendation sent by you or directly to the school by the referees as directed, application fee (if applicable)
- Cover letter, if necessary

SOURCES: American Psychological Association (1997); Osborne (1996).

Grades, Transcripts, and the GRE

6.4 Describe the ways graduate committees interpret grades, transcripts, and GRE scores

Your grades in college serve as one of the major factors for graduate school admissions committees. Although programs vary, as a general rule most graduate programs are going to have a minimum GPA cutoff of 3.0; many programs have higher minimum requirements. The best sources of information about these requirements come from *Graduate Study in Psychology*, and from institutions' websites. Although exceptions are occasionally made about the minimum cutoff, they must be accompanied by an explanation about why an exception to the rule is warranted. Given that more students want to attend graduate school than graduate school slots are available, universities can be (and must be) selective in choosing those students who have the best potential to be successful graduates of their program. A low GPA, without any accompanying information, is a predictor of your future performance. A 'C' grade or average work is not acceptable in most graduate programs. If you are striving for admission into a graduate program, and a 3.0 is probably the minimum requirement, think about this—*every C that you earn as an undergraduate hurts your chances for admission to graduate school* because every C (and of course, even lower grades) pulls your GPA down below 3.0.

Your transcript is an important record of your academic accomplishments, it speaks volumes about your potential as a future graduate student. Landrum (2003) examined the effect of student withdrawals (Ws) on the transcript and its effect on graduate admissions. Based on the responses of 139 graduate admissions directors, he found (a) graduate admissions committees carefully examine transcripts; this is typically done by two faculty members; (b) graduate admissions committees highly value transcripts, and either a low GPA or low GRE score may trigger a closer examination of transcripts; and (c) one withdrawal on the transcript does not seem to be a problem. Two withdrawals is probably not a problem, except for a small number of schools. For some schools, withdrawals in particular courses (such as Statistics or Research Methods) are more detrimental than withdrawals in other courses. Your transcript is one of your credentials that you will need for future opportunities—be sure your transcripts tell the story you want. We encourage you to consult with faculty mentors and academic advisors when considering the effects of withdrawals on future prospects.

Another significant component of graduate admissions at many schools is the Graduate Record Examination (GRE), a series of tests administered nationally by the Educational Testing Service. The GRE is administered via computer, and you take the GRE in authorized test centers located throughout the nation (and literally the world). You schedule the computer-based test at your convenience; another benefit is that you know your unofficial test scores prior to leaving the test center. Scores from the GRE are believed to represent one's verbal reasoning, quantitative reasoning, and analytical writing skills. Graduate admissions committees often care about verbal and quantitative GRE scores because they are useful predictors of performance of some of the key tasks of graduate school, namely writing and statistical ability—similar skills you will be acquiring and practicing as an undergraduate psychology major. In addition, a subject test is available in psychology, and some graduate schools may require psychology subject test scores. See Table 6.4 for examples of the types of analytical writing tasks used.

Table 6.4 Sample Questions from the GRE Analytical Writing Section

Sample Issue Task: Present Your Perspective on an Issue	
Directions: Write a response in which you discuss the extent to which you agree or disagree with the claim. In developing and supporting your position, be sure to address the most compelling reasons or examples that could be used to challenge your position.	Sample: "The best way for a society to prepare its young people for leadership in government, industry, or other fields is by instilling in them a sense of cooperation, not competition."
Sample Argument Task: Discuss How Well Reasoned You Find This Argument	
Directions: Write a response in which you discuss what questions would need to be answered in order to decide whether the recommendation and the argument on which it is based are reasonable. Be sure to explain how the answers to these questions would help to evaluate the recommendation.	Sample: "The following is taken from a memo from the advertising director of the Super Screen Movie Production Company: According to a recent report from our marketing department, during the past year, fewer people attended Super Screen-produced movies than in any other year. And yet the percentage of positive reviews by movie reviewers about specific Super Screen movies actually increased during the past year. Clearly, the contents of these reviews are not reaching enough of our prospective viewers. Thus, the problem lies not with the quality of our movies but with the public's lack of awareness that movies of good quality are available. Super Screen should therefore allocate a greater share of its budget next year to reaching the public through advertising."

SOURCE: Copyright 2012 Educational Testing Service, www.ets.org.

Prior to 2011, the verbal and quantitative measures were scored on a scale from 200 points to 800 points; the scores on each of the subscales now range from 130 to 170 in one-point increments (ETS, 2012). It should be noted that many disciplines require potential graduate students to take the GRE general test, not just psychology-bound graduate students; other disciplines also have specialized subject area tests.

It is important for you to make sure that you even need to take the GRE for your graduate school pursuits. Many graduate programs in psychology do not require the GRE for admission into their programs. Some students, for whatever reasons, do not believe that they test well, and they may even "shop" for graduate programs not requiring the GRE so as to avoid that additional hurdle in the arduous graduate admissions process. We recommend that you talk to multiple faculty members, advisors, and of course a faculty mentor to strategize your options about how to best pursue your postbaccalaureate goals.

Letters of Recommendation, with Faculty Examples

6.5 Explain how to earn a strong letter of recommendation for graduate applications

Your letters of recommendation serve as a key component of your graduate admissions package. Letters of recommendation are interesting and somewhat different from the GPA or your GRE scores. Although other people certainly have some degree of influence over GRE and GPA, your professors and supervisors have direct influence over the letters of recommendation given. You are going to need to choose people who know your professional development, skills, and abilities and know them *well*. For a faculty member to get to know you this well, you are going to have to get involved outside of the classroom and spend quality time with them. It takes more than being a good book student to get superb letters of recommendation. In fact, you will realize that you have to *interact personally* with faculty members for them to recognize your talents to the degree that it benefits you in a letter of recommendation.

If you are a student in one class with a faculty member, do the bare minimum work, never speak up in class, and never have a conversation with the faculty member outside of class, then that faculty member will have a difficult time writing a strong letter of recommendation for you. Whom should you ask? Keith-Spiegel and Wiederman (2000) found that the best sources for letters are from (a) a mentor with whom the applicant has done considerable work, (b) an applicant's professor who is also well known and highly respected, (c) an employer on a job related to the applicant's professional goals, and (d) the department chair.

Letters of recommendation are sometimes stressful for both the student and the letter writer. For more tips on how to solicit strong letters of recommendation, see the exercise at the end of this chapter. Students often wonder about their letters of recommendation. When applying to graduate school, one of the forms will likely ask the students if they want to waive their access to their application file (including letters of recommendation). If you do not waive your right, you will get to see your application file if you are accepted into that graduate program.

Faculty members differ on their practices of releasing letters to students. For very good students with very good letters, faculty may be inclined to give the student a copy of the letter. Other faculty members never release letters to students, no matter how good the letter (or the student). A direct conversation with the faculty member can resolve any of these concerns. Also, do not assume that the lack of access means a bad letter—faculty may be following their own personal policy, or even a departmental or university policy. To take some mystery out of the process, we include a sample letter of recommendation for a student applying to graduate school (see Figure 6.3). Think about the types of things YOU need to do to garner strong letters of recommendation.

Figure 6.3 Sample Letters of Recommendation for Graduate School Applicants

BOISE STATE UNIVERSITY
College of Social Sciences and Public Affairs
Department of Psychology
1910 University Drive Boise, Idaho 83725-1715
phone 208-426-1207
fax 208-426-4386

December 3, 1999

Graduate Admissions Committee
Interdisciplinary Program in Development Psychology
University of Nevada-Reno
Reno, NV 89557

Dear Colleagues,

I have been asked by Julie Fendon for a letter of recommendation in support of her application to your graduate program in social psychology. It is my pleasure to provide this letter and my support for Julie.

I have known Julie for about a year. She has been a student in a few of my classes, the most recent of which was PSYC 321 Research Methods. Since my interactions with her have been fairly limited, I must admit that I do not know her very well.

Julie has been a good student in my classes. I do think that she possesses the ability to be successful in graduate school. It is hard for me to address other skills and abilities because I have not observed her in other situations, such as serving as a research assistant or completing an internship. I think she is a dedicated and bright student who would do well and also benefit highly from continuing her higher education.

I recommend Julie Fendon to you and your graduate program without reservation.

Sincerely,

R. Eric Landrum, Ph.D.
Professor
Department of Psychology

Phone: (208) 426-1993 Fax: (208) 426-4386 Email: elandru@boisestate.edu

(continued)

Figure 6.3 *(Continued)*

BOISE STATE UNIVERSITY
College of Social Sciences and Public Affairs
Department of Psychology
1910 University Drive Boise, Idaho 83725-1715
phone 208-426-1207
fax 208-426-4386

February 28, 2003

Graduate Admissions Committee
Department of Psychology
Idaho State University
Pocatello, ID 83209-8112

Dear Colleagues,

I have been asked by Kevin Howardlock to write a letter of recommendation in support of his application to your graduate program in psychology. It is my pleasure to provide this letter and my support for Kevin.

I have known Kevin for almost one year. He was my student in PSYC 295 Statistical Methods, PSYC 120 Introduction to the Psychology Major course, and PSYC 321 Research Methods course. In addition, I invited him to serve as a teaching assistant for my PSYC 295 Statistical Methods course for Spring 2003. Through these interactions in and out of class, I feel that I know Kevin very well. I think this is remarkable in itself, because I don't usually get to know my students that well in that short a time frame. That begins to tell you Kevin's story.

I think Kevin is probably one of the most motivated, talented, and self-directed students I have encountered in many years. I have enjoyed getting to know Kevin because he has a mature attitude about his education. He takes every opportunity seriously, and maximizes every possible moment. On many occasions I have had the chance to talk to Kevin about his graduate school plans and career aspirations. Not only will he be successful in graduate school, but he will thrive in whatever program is lucky enough to get him. He is very personable, and easy to talk to. I have enjoyed my numerous conversations with him.

I have seen his class performance and his work ethic firsthand in the courses that he has taken from me. For instance, after completing Research Methods, Kevin took his manuscript and modified it for submission to the 2003 Rocky Mountain Psychological Association meeting in Denver (we

Figure 6.3 *(Continued)*

Letter of Recommendation for Kevin Howardlock
February 28, 2003
Page 2

just heard earlier this week that it was accepted!). Although I make that opportunity available to all my Methods students, very few are willing to go the extra mile and see the opportunity available to them. With some careful planning on his part, he used his project in my class as a pilot project for a senior thesis that he plans to complete with a colleague of mine in the spring. Kevin thinks about everything. He plans in advance. He sees the relationship between the classroom and his future; he recognizes the opportunities available to him as an undergraduate, and he maximizes those opportunities to full potential. When Kevin approached me about being a teaching assistant for Statistics, I jumped at the chance because I knew it would be a good experience for him, and that he would be a great teaching assistant for our students. I wish that Kevin had a bit more time at Boise State; I would have invited him to serve as a Research Assistant with me, and I am confident that our collaborations would have been extremely fruitful. He knows how to get things done, and done well.

The skills and abilities that I have observed in Kevin will serve him well in graduate school. His persistence, strong self-motivation, clear career goals, and pure talent will help him to succeed in graduate school and beyond. He is the type of student that will instantly emerge as a natural leader, even among the talented graduate students he will be joining. He will be a credit to our profession, and I look forward to having him as a professional colleague. He's simply that good.

If you think I can be of any additional assistance, please contact me directly. **I recommend Kevin Howardlock to you with my highest recommendation and without reservation.**

Sincerely,

R. Eric Landrum, Ph.D.
Professor
Department of Psychology

Phone: (208) 426-1993 Fax: (208) 426-4386 Email: elandru@boisestate.edu

The Personal Statement, with Student Examples

6.6 Outline the elements of a strong personal statement

Although the letters of recommendation communicate the faculty members' perspectives about you, you also have the opportunity to present yourself. Most graduate programs require applicants to submit something called a personal statement (or statement of intent, or autobiographical statement, or letter of intent). It allows you to provide valuable background information about yourself, and it also provides the graduate admissions committee with a writing sample. The requirements for completing this task are about as varied as most graduate programs—there is not a uniform method or procedure to follow. Hence, you need to make sure that you completely satisfy the requirements of *each* school when you are preparing your personal statement. For a nonrandom sample of personal statement instructions, see Table 6.5. If you note the variability, you will see that the same statement could not possibly satisfy the different instructions.

There are a growing number of sources for advice on preparing a personal statement. For instance, Bottoms and Nysse (1999) suggest that the major sections of your personal statement should be previous research experience, current research interests, other relevant experience, and career goals. Additional tips for preparing your personal statement are presented in Table 6.6. Keith-Spiegel and Wiederman (2000) found that in the personal statement instructions that they examined, 13 themes emerged. One point to be stressed—*do not write a single one-size-fits-all letter for all schools.* Do your homework, and give the committee the answers it wants, not a generic statement that vaguely addresses the school's information needs.

Table 6.5 Sample Instructions for a Personal Statement

1. Include a one- to two-page statement describing your plans for graduate study and professional career in psychology—University of Wyoming

2. The statement of purpose should be 500–600 words (clinical: 900 words) in length and should contain a description of relevant work/research/volunteer activities, outline future professional goals, and state your expectations of the graduate school experience—Arizona State University

3. A letter of intent describing your clinical and research interests, educational and professional goals, faculty whom you might be interested in working with, factors that you would want the admissions committee to consider in evaluating your application that are not evident from other materials, and some background information describing how you became interested in these areas—University of Nevada–Las Vegas

4. On this or a separate page(s), please provide a clear, concise one- to two-page essay summarizing your background in psychology (or related field), career objectives, research experience, research interests, and why you are applying to Montana State University's M.S. program in Applied Psychology. Please be sure to read and sign the signature page at the end of this document—Montana State University

5. Clinical program: Your autobiographical sketch should answer the following questions:
   - What is the source of your interest in psychology?
   - Why do you want to pursue graduate studies in clinical rather than another area of psychology?
   - Why do you want a clinical Ph.D. rather than a Psy.D. degree?
   - Why are you applying to the University of Colorado?
   - Which two (2) research mentors have you selected at the University of Colorado and why?
   - What has been your previous research experience? Provide letter(s) of recommendation from your research supervisor(s) with their phone number(s).
   - What has been your previous practical experience, paid or volunteer? Provide a letter of recommendation from your clinical supervisor.

   All other programs: Your autobiographical sketch should address the following items, numbering your answers as listed below:
   - Describe your previous research experience.
   - Why do you wish to pursue graduate studies in your chosen area of specialization?
   - Why are you applying to the University of Colorado?
   - Which two (2) research mentors have you selected at the UC and why?—University of Colorado

6. Please prepare approximately two to three pages of typewritten, double-spaced autobiographical material which will be considered confidential. If available include a copy of your vita and e-mail address. (Please be aware that the review committees may contain graduate student representatives.) Indicate the source of your interest in psychology and the reasons why you wish to pursue graduate studies in your chosen area of specialization. If you have had practical experience (work or volunteer) in psychology, please describe it. If you have been in other areas of academic study or employment, discuss your change. When and how was your attention directed to our graduate program? Indicate how the specific features of our training program would facilitate your professional goals, and indicate which faculty's research interests represent a match with your own training goals. What are your career plans? What would you ultimately like to do?—University of Denver

SOURCE: Landrum, R. E. (2004). New odds for graduate admissions in psychology. *Eye on Psi Chi*, *8*(3), 20–21, 32.

Table 6.6 Tips for Preparing Your Personal Statement

- Allow yourself ample time to write, revise, edit, and proofread.
- Be willing to write as many drafts as are necessary to produce a unified, coherent essay.
- Attend to the instructions carefully and discover what the program is most interested in knowing about you.
- Personal details included in the statement must seem relevant to your ability to be a successful graduate student.
- Follow the instructions to the letter, adhere to length limitations, and answer everything that is asked.
- Do not repeat information that is already in your application, such as your GRE scores or your GPA.
- Use the essay as an opportunity to highlight your uniqueness and your strengths.
- Describe yourself honestly and realistically, acknowledging your weak points (if requested) and stress your good points without exaggerating. Try to connect these good points to your aspirations in psychology.
- Demonstrate that you have taken the time to familiarize yourself with the program. Emphasize the match between your goals and those of the program.
- Reveal characteristics of your "self" that reflect maturity, adaptability, and motivation.
- Use formal language and a serious tone; avoid slang, clichés, and colloquialisms. Pay attention to spelling and grammar. Mistakes here seriously detract from your overall statement.
- Avoid jargon. It is more important to use the right word than the complex word.
- Be careful in using superlative language, such as all, every, always, and never.
- Read your essay out loud to help find trouble spots.
- Have someone else help edit and proofread your work.
- Convey a convincing portrayal of your abilities to succeed in this school's graduate program.

SOURCES: American Psychological Association (1997); Osborne (1996).

One final note on this topic—be sure to answer the questions exactly. Graduate admissions committee members will actually read your personal statement, so make sure that you answer the questions that you are asked. Answer completely and concisely. To help visualize this process, see Figure 6.4 which contains a sample personal statement from a former student who successfully entered graduate school.

Figure 6.4 Sample Personal Statements

Sample #1

The field of psychology has always been very interesting to me. It all began with an Introduction of Psychology class when I was a junior in high school. In that class, I was introduced to human development, human assessment, and psychological disorders. I recall thinking that psychology can serve a purpose, especially in the aspect of counseling people and helping them with their problems and concerns. It turned out to be one of my favorite classes of high school.

Unfortunately, I reentered college late starting up again when I was 27 years old. When I had decided to go back to college, I chose the field of psychology as my major. This choice was influenced by my previous experiences that I had while I was a junior in high school. Also, many people had told me that I had a talent for listening to them, and helping them solve their issues and concerns. I thought that becoming a psychologist would be an excellent way to help others, and was something that I could be happy with as a career.

My interest and knowledge of psychology really grew as I continued my studies as an undergraduate. I was amazed at all the fields of study that psychology had to offer. Even though there were so many to choose from, I always knew that I wanted to become a therapist so I would be able to help others with their needs. Also, research has become a large part of my life. Part of my research was to develop and distribute a survey in the community where I currently live. Through this research I was able to see the benefits of statistics in telling my group what people liked and disliked about their community. As it turns out, the local government used the results of the study to see what was needed for improvements in the community. Another research project that I was involved in was an analysis of what graduate schools valued as important for graduate admissions. What I learned from that experience was what schools I would like to attend, and what they required for admission. This research is in review now for publishing, and it is my hope that others may benefit from my work on the project. Through it all, I have come to love psychology, and I want to be able to use research and the skills learned from psychology to create a better world for others and myself.

To continue on with my studies, I have chosen to pursue a Ph.D. in Counseling Psychology. I really feel that a Ph.D. in Counseling Psychology will give me the skills and the knowledge to

(continued)

Figure 6.4 *(Continued)*

become a source of help for many people. With the research experience that I will gain, it is my great desire to publish my research through textbooks and novels that can be available to the public. I am also interested in the ability to teach at the university level. I feel that the Ph.D. program offered by the New Mexico State University can provide all of these.

I can see that the program at New Mexico State University can provide many opportunities for me. I am especially interested in the focus of cultural diversity in our society. I lived in Spain for two years, and am fluent in Spanish. Therefore, I am very interested in working with Dr. Luis A. Vázquez in his bilingual counseling. I feel that I could be a great service to my community if I had bilingual skills in counseling. It is my concern that there are many Spanish-American people that do not receive the help they need due to a language barrier. Along the same lines, I am interested in working with Dr. Rod J. Merta due to his expertise in addictions and multicultural counseling. Some of the research conducted by Dr. Charles H. Huber on family and marriage holds great interest for me. The family is the cornerstone of society. I am very interested in working with younger people. Therefore, I would be interested in working with Dr. Peggy Kaczmarek in her study of child and adolescent therapy. Any and all of these professors would be great mentors for my goals as a professional.

It is easy to see that New Mexico State University has much to offer for a Ph.D. in Counseling Psychology. I am very impressed with the focus of research that the professors are conducting. I feel that the university holds the goals that I am looking for. My favorite is rule #13 which states, "Students will be expected to integrate the roles of psychologist, counselor, and researcher, to assess their own strengths and weaknesses, and to remain open and committed to both personal and professional growth." I strongly feel that this says it all. I know that I can be a great asset to New Mexico State University. Thank you.

Sample #2

To Whom It May Concern:

I believe psychology is intended to help individuals through careful examination of human behavior, cognition, and neurological development. The development of the field yields two important branches, psychotherapy and research. I believe the two branches rely heavily upon one another. The research branch investigates the nature of human behavior, tests theories, and provides a vast knowledge base from which new ideas can grow. The psychotherapy branch provides an outlet for the application of theories and reciprocates new ideas to be tested and investigated by researchers. The concept of a scientist-practitioner is the primary reason why I want to study clinical psychology. The combination of the two paths yields a great ability in improving mental health and further expanding the field of psychology. The flexibility of applied research, psychotherapy, and assessment has drawn me to the field of clinical psychology. Through my experiences as an undergraduate student I have come to appreciate the intensity and skill in conducting clinical services and research.

As I started my college education career I knew I wanted to join the field of psychology. I performed well as a student in high school and continued to do well into college. Unfortunately, during my first year and a half in school I never heard of any opportunities to be a part of a research staff. I did not even know that research existed at my university. Then at the end of my second year of school, I transferred to Boise State University. Boise State University clearly and explicitly explained the importance of research to the field of psychology as well as the benefits I would receive in interacting with professors in conducting research. This was a rude awakening; at that moment I felt I had wasted the first years of my undergraduate education.

Once I realized the time and opportunity I had wasted, I immediately sought after a professor who would accept me as a research assistant. I was fortunate enough to work with Dr. Keli Braitman. The project I was assigned to involved the media's impact on male body image. I initially started the project collecting data, data entry, and data analysis. As the project continued, I found myself in a lead role of the research project. I earned the responsibilities of leading a focus group, participating in a focus group, collaborating on experimental method and design, development of questionnaires, data collection in both large group settings and on an individual basis, debriefing of participants, data entry into statistical analysis program (SPSS), item analysis, and presentation of the research at a local and regional conference. Dr. Braitman excelled in allowing her students to take the lead role in the development of the project, conducting the research, and presenting the results. Not only did I gain knowledge and experience from the research, I became excited about research. I was eager to learn more about research methodology, psychological measurement, and quantitative methods. I elected to enroll in all the classes I could that explored the field of psychological research.

Figure 6.4 *(Continued)*

I graduated the summer after working with Dr. Braitman, but I felt I did not have adequate research experience, especially with my goals of graduate study. I contacted Dr. R. Eric Landrum, a professor who inspired and educated me about the importance of research when I first attended Boise State University. I wanted to complete another research project prior to entering graduate school, in which Dr. Landrum was generous enough to supervise an individual project.

I was interested about the theory of self-efficacy initially proposed by Albert Bandura, particularly in an academic setting. My project is comparing the levels of academic self-efficacy between the different groups of higher education. The groups include associate/technical students, undergraduate students, and graduate students. I am in the process of completing the project and I am anticipating presenting the research at a regional conference.

Dr. Landrum took the role of an advisor very seriously. I am very thankful for the position that he established in our working relationship. Dr. Landrum left all of the decision-making and organization to me, allowing me to learn from the process of completing an individual project. I have truly learned a vast amount from this experience. I have had a direct encounter with an Institutional Review Board, which has taught me the importance of anticipating any risks to human subjects, as well as the need to explore and explain the research design to the smallest detail. I have learned to appreciate the time and energy involved in establishing the logistics of collecting data from large multiple groups. The experience I have received in participating in the research projects has better prepared me for study at graduate school.

I am interested in UAA clinical program for a number of reasons. One reason is the flexibility of the program. My future career goal is to earn a doctorate in clinical psychology with an emphasis in quantitative methodology. The program structure of UAA will help facilitate my goals. If I was given the opportunity to attend the UAA program, I will choose to place my educational emphasis in both the research and clinical tracks. The second reason for my interest in the program is the available resources to the program and the graduate students. The primary resource that attracted me is the large faculty size and relatively few graduate students. The Psychological Services Center seems to be an excellent resource for students in the master's program. Plus, there are definite advantages with having the department located in the same building as the university library.

I do have one relevant piece of information is in regards to my transcript. The summer of 2002 I initially enrolled in Psychology 351 Personality. I never attended the course due to financial reasons, and I expected to be administratively dropped. I have never dropped a course prior to this point in my educational career. However, I was not dropped from the class and received an "F" in the course. I did appeal the outcome with supporting documentation from the professor, Dr. Tedd McDonald, however the Office of Appeals chose to disregard the information and I was forced to accept the grade. I did take the course of my own volition in the spring of 2003 and earned an "A."

The primary interest in my education and my future career is in clinical psychology. The flexibility of the discipline, the scientist-practitioner approach, and the use of applied research is what I find appealing about the field. Attendance to the UAA clinical psychology program would make my goals possible, as well as furthering my knowledge and experience in clinical psychology. Thank you.

A Student's Guide to the Curriculum Vita (CV), with Examples

6.7 Create a curriculum vita

Another component of this arduous graduate school application process involves the preparation of a *curriculum vita* (CV), which literally translates as "academic life." Although related to the resume, the vita chronicles your accomplishments, whereas the resume is a brief introduction to your skills, abilities, and employment history. A goal in resume writing is keeping the resume short, one or two pages. A CV is usually a longer document that tracks your entire history of academic performance, not just a summary of employment positions. In a bit, we will offer some sample student CVs. First, we present some ideas on how to organize your CV (see also Table 6.7).

There is much good advice about preparing a vita, including what to do and what not to do (however, much of the available advice is aimed at faculty members

Table 6.7 Suggestions for Organizing Your Curriculum Vita

- Personal information (address, phone number, e-mail)
- Educational history (degrees earned, when and where)
- Honors and awards (list each, who awarded, and date awarded)
- Association memberships (relevant clubs and societies, student affiliate status)
- Professional experience (beginning with college, list jobs relevant to the major)
- Research interests (if applicable and appropriate)
- Current research and teaching experience (if applicable and appropriate)
- Professional presentations (titles, organizations, in APA format if possible)
- Publications (use APA format, be careful with "in press," "under review")
- References (list names, titles, and addresses of three to four people whom you have asked)

Possible CV Categories

Academic Background	Degrees
Areas of Expertise	Education
Awards	Foreign Language(s)
Books/Book Chapters	Journal Articles
Career Highlights	Professional Memberships
Certification(s)	Professional Studies
Committee Chair(s)	Publications
Committee Service	Service
Computer Skills	Teaching Experience
Conference Presentations	Travel Abroad Experience
Consulting	

SOURCES: Hayes and Hayes (1989); Plous (1998); Hodges, S., & Connelly, A. R. (2010). *A job search manual for counselors and counselor educators: How to navigate and promote your counseling career*. Alexandria, VA: American Counseling Association.

and their CVs). Lord (2004, p. 10) suggests using a beginning CV as an inspirational document:

> At first, you might find it depressing to construct an academic vita, because many of the headings will be followed by blank lines. Do not worry about it. Everyone starts that way. One reason for constructing an academic vita is to remind you that it is empty. Write in your appointment book a time once a month when you will print your vita and think about how you could improve it.

Table 6.8 lists some additional tips offered by Plous (1998) for creating your CV.

In Figure 6.5, you will find two sample student vitae. These vitae represent years of work by these students to build their credentials. *If you are just starting out in psychology,*

Table 6.8 Tips for Preparing Your Curriculum Vita

- Your vita should be a clear and concise summary of your professional qualifications. Take care in every word used.
- Try to obtain copies of vitae from people who are at your stage or slightly ahead of you; although a faculty member's vita might give you some organizational ideas, some sections will be inappropriate due to your entry-level status in the discipline.
- Create an inviting and elegant format. Take the time to add some style, and include white space (but, don't overdo it).
- Make absolutely sure that there are no errors in your vita. Have more than one person proofread it for you—show it to your professors to review. It must be completely error-free.
- Avoid padding your vita because you feel you don't have much to list. Do not list high school accomplishments or excessive details about activities you have completed en route to your bachelor's degree.
- Do not list irrelevant personal information, such as height, weight, or general health. List hobbies only if you think they make you look like a more well-rounded individual.
- Try not to list categories on your vita if you have only one accomplishment in that category (like the outlining rule, you need a B for every A.). The exception to this rule would be if you have only one publication—it is so worthy of note, the category will draw the attention to this accomplishment. Remember, publication credit is the number one secondary selection criterion for graduate admissions committees.
- When using category headings and subheadings, don't get too ambitious. This is where copying the format of a faculty member may be a bad idea; don't have a "Grants and Contracts" section if you have neither grants nor contracts.

Figure 6.5 Sample Student CVs

Anna Holdiman

Curriculum Vitae

456 Elm Street
Boise, ID 83725

Phone: 319-555-7555
E-mail: annahold@unreal-email.com

EDUCATION

Boise State University
B.S. Psychological Science
Certificate in Elementary Spanish
Certificate in American Sign Language
Expected graduation in May 2018
Cumulative GPA 3.81

AWARDS

Spring 2017 Academic All-American Track and Field
Summer 2016 – Spring 2017 Dean's List Highest Honors
Boise State Student Research Travel Award 2016, $500
Fall 2013-Spring 2015 Dean's List High Honors

MANUSCRIPTS SUBMITTED FOR PUBLICATION

Holdiman, A., & Pritchard, M. E. (2017). Eating behaviors, motivations for exercise and attitudes about weight amongst college athletes. Manuscript under review at. *Eating and Weight Disorders - Studies on Anorexia, Bulimia and Obesity.*

MANUSCRIPTS IN PREPARATION

Holdiman, A., & Pritchard, M. E. (Spring 2017). Social media: *The influence of social media on body image and anxiety*. Data analysis underway.

Holdiman, A., & Masarik, A. (Fall 2016- Current). *Resettlement Stress and Family Functioning in Refugees: An illustrative review.*

Holdiman, A., & Masarik, A. (Spring 2017-Present). *Refugee Parenting & Language.*

CONFERENCE PRESENTATIONS

Holdiman, A., & Pritchard, M. E. (2017, April). *Social media: The influence of social media on body image and anxiety*. Oral presentation given at the Boise State Undergraduate Research Symposium, Boise ID.

(continued)

Figure 6.5 *(Continued)*

Holdiman, A., & Masarik, A. (2017, April). *Resettlement stress and family functioning in Refugees: An illustrative review.* Oral presentation given at the Boise State Undergraduate Research Symposium, Boise ID.

Holdiman, A., & Pritchard, M. E. (2017, April). *Social media: The influence of social media on body image and anxiety.* Poster presentation given at the Rocky Mountain Psychological Association Conference, Salt Lake City, UT.

Holdiman, A., & Masarik, A. (2017, April). *Resettlement stress and family functioning in refugees: An illustrative review.* Oral presentation given at the Rocky Mountain Psychological Association Conference, Salt Lake City, UT.

Holdiman, A., McGuire, M. K., & Pritchard, M. E. (2016, April). *Eating behaviors, motivations for exercise and attitudes about weight amongst college athletes.* Oral presentation given at Boise State Undergraduate Research Symposium, Boise, ID.

Holdiman, A., McGuire, M. K., & Pritchard, M.E. (2016, April). *Eating behaviors, motivations for exercise and attitudes about weight amongst college athletes.* Oral presentation given at the Rocky Mountain Psychological Association Conference, Denver, CO.

TEACHING EXPERIENCES

Teaching assistant to Dr. Kimberly Henderson: Spring 2016, Fall 2016, Spring 2017
Course: PSYC 101, General Psychology. Skills Developed:

- Contributed to the development of new material for department courses (e.g. online game, podcast connecting course material)
- Taught a lecture to over 200 students
- Conducted 1-2 hours per week of office hours to respond to students' questions
- Managed administrative tasks including preparation of Power Points, reading guides, and test questions
- Attended weekly T.A. meetings to contribute to the evolution of the course
- Posted materials in "BlackBoard Grade System" and responded to students' questions verbally and electronically
- Attended all lectures and took detailed notes on the course content presented in lecture
- Ensured that students assignments were graded with feedback in a timely manner

RESEARCH EXPERIENCE

Researcher in Dr. Mary Pritchard's Health Psychology Lab Spring 2016 – Present

- Conduct literature reviews of information surrounding research topics
- Participate in IRB application process
- Collect and manage data of 100 - 300 participants
- Perform extensive qualitative data management and analysis
- Use SPSS to conduct statistical analysis and interpret data
- Conduct research, publish & present projects
- Assist with faculty research projects

Figure 6.5 *(Continued)*

Researcher in Dr.April Masarik's Human Ecology & Development Lab Fall 2016 - Present

- Conduct literature review of information surrounding research topics
- Participate in the creation of a data management system for local Boise High School counseling services
- Participate in IRB application process
- Collect and manage data
- Use SPSS to conduct statistical analysis and interpret data
- Publish and present research
- Collaborate with the Boise School district and local non-profits (Agency for New Americans, Idaho Refugee Coalition, and International Rescue Committee) to help the refugee community

INTERNSHIP, VOLUNTEER, & PROFESSIONAL EXPERIENCE

Habilitative Supports Worker May 2015- Present

- Work 1:1 with adolescents with various physical and developmental disabilities in an at-home and community setting
- Reinforce communication, life and coping skills
- Support clients with community engagement
- Provide academic support
- Attend all occupational therapy and speech therapy appointments
- Support clients with supplementary speech activities as assigned by their speech language pathologist
- Observed 55 documented observation hours of ASHA clinically certified speech language pathologist

Community Outreach Counseling Clinical Psychology Intern Fall 2016

- Implemented a pilot study focusing on refugee families
- Managed data from clients
- Created a panel of culturally relevant psychological measurements
- Participated in grant writing
- Interpersonal and cross-cultural collaboration with refugee families
- Volunteered over 100 hours

International Rescue Committee Intern Spring 2015

- Attended case management sessions with social workers
- Applied refugee families for low income housing
- Scheduled English language learning support and language interpretation appointments
- Managed over 30 refugee families housing requests
- Visited refugee families homes to help cultural orientation
- Managed volunteers to help with cultural orientation of refugee families
- Volunteered over 200 hours

(continued)

Figure 6.5 *(Continued)*

PRACTICED SKILL SETS

- Proficiency in data management
- Working knowledge of SPSS
- Descriptive data analysis and interpretation
- Grant writing experience
- Working knowledge of the IRB application process
- Proficient in PC & Mac Systems, Word, PowerPoint, Excel\
- Excellent written and oral communication skills
- Implementation and support of speech therapy activities for clients
- Over 250 volunteer hours with various non-profit agencies
- Experience working with adults and children with various developmental and physical disabilities
- Extensive work with individuals that do not have English as there first language
- Tutoring services to non-native English speakers
- Course administration

REFERENCES

Kimberly Henderson, Ph.D
Professor (Department of Psychological Science)
1910 University Drive
Boise, ID 83725

Eric Landrum, Ph.D
Professor (Department of Psychological Science)
1910 University Drive
Boise, ID 83725

April Masarik, Ph.D
Professor (Department of Psychological Science)
1910 University Drive
Boise, ID 83725

Mary Pritchard, Ph.D
Professor (Department of Psychological Science)
1910 University Drive
Boise, ID 83725

Joan Rigg, MS PT
600 N. Robbins Rd. Suite 101
Boise, Idaho 83702

Figure 6.5 *(Continued)*

MORGAN KAWAMURA

123 Old Mail Avenue, Boise, Idaho 83702

(208) 555-1234 ◆ MKawamura@arealfakeemail.edu

EDUCATION

Boise State University (Boise, Idaho) August 2011 – May 2015

Bachelor of Science – Psychology & Criminal Justice (May 2015)

Degree Honors: Summa Cum Laude

Cumulative GPA: 3.982 / 4.000

Boise State University GPA: 3.987 / 4.000

PROFESSIONAL EXPERIENCE

United States Attorney's Office- District of Idaho July 2012 - Present

Student Clerk/Receptionist - Boise, Idaho

- Responsible for providing support to the administrative division by organizing travel arrangements, assisting in paying bills, acting as the primary receptionist, and upholding security procedures for all office securities.
- Coordinator for Idaho's federal misdemeanor and infraction violations with the responsibility to draft and file motions and proposed orders to the U.S. District Court, work closely with federal law enforcement, and maintain arrest warrants, payment agreements, and delinquent cases.
- Responsible for providing litigation support to attorneys and support staff by performing various projects throughout the office including redacting sensitive case discovery, performing legal assistant work for the First Assistant United States Attorney, and maintaining case files.

Bingham County Courthouse August 2010 - May 2011

Student Intern - Blackfoot, Idaho

- Assisted the Bingham County District and Magistrate Court clerks and judges with maintaining criminal, civil, juvenile, and specialty case files.
- Performed clerical duties including office deliveries, sorting and distributing mail, and assisting with a variety of requested projects.
- Worked with the state computer system to input data into the iStars system for mental, misdemeanor, felony, and juvenile drug courts.

TEACHING & RESEARCH ASSISTANTSHIPS

- Psychology 120: The Psychology Major, Lead Teaching Assistant Fall 2014
- Psychology 101: General Psychology, Teaching Assistant Fall 2014
- Criminal Justice 315: Theories of Crime, Teaching Assistant Fall 2014
- Psychology 321: Research Methods, Teaching Assistant Spring 2014
- Psychology 295: Statistical Methods, Teaching Assistant Fall 2013
- Storytelling as Pedagogy, Research Assistant for Dr. Eric Landrum Fall 2013 – Spring 2015

RESEARCH INTERESTS

- Social and psychological variables that contribute to the negative behaviors of adolescents and adults.
- The effects of judgment, risk perception, and decision-making on behavior.
- Pedagogical instruments and techniques on student learning, memory, and success.

Figure 6.5 *(Continued)*

RESEARCH PRESENTATIONS

Kawamura, M., Landrum, R.E. (2014). What if students remembered course content? Storytelling as pedagogy. Poster presentation at the Western Psychological Association, Portland, OR.

Kawamura, M., Landrum, R.E. (2014). What if students remembered course content? Storytelling as pedagogy. Poster presentation at the Boise State University Undergraduate Research Conference, Boise, ID.

HONORS & AWARDS

- Boise State University Dean, Summa Cum Laude Degree Honors — Fall 2011 – Spring 2015
- Boise State University Dean's List: High and Highest Honors — Fall 2011 – Spring 2015
- Dona Harris Memorial Scholarship: Private Academic Scholarship — Fall 2011 – Spring 2015
- Blackfoot Education Foundation Scholarship: Academic Scholarship — Fall 2011 – Spring 2012
- Junior Miss Scholarship: Interview, Talent, and Fitness Scholarships — Fall 2011 – Spring 2012
- Robert R. Lee Promise Scholarship: Idaho State Board of Education Scholarship — Fall 2011 – Spring 2013
- Stufflebeam Education Foundation Scholarship: Private Academic Scholarship — Fall 2011 – Spring 2012
- Jane Parkinson Excellence Scholarship: Private Academic Scholarship — Fall 2012 – Spring 2015
- Boise State Psychology Department Scholarship: Academic Scholarship — Fall 2013 – Spring 2015
- Anderson Criminal Justice Award: Private Academic Scholarship — Fall 2014 – Spring 2015

PROFESSIONAL AFFILIATIONS & LEADERSHIP POSITIONS

- President of the Boise State University Student Foundation — Spring 2013 – Spring 2015
- Member of Psi Chi, Psychology International Honors Society — Fall 2013 – Spring 2015
- Student Member of the Western Psychological Association — Fall 2013 – Fall 2015
- Member of Alpha Phi Sigma, Criminal Justice National Honors Society — Spring 2014 – Spring 2015

CONFERENCES & CONVENTIONS ATTENDED

- Council for Advancement and Support of Education: Affiliated Student Advancement Programs Convention, New Orleans, LA — August 2013
- Western Psychological Association Annual Convention, Portland, OR — April 2014
- Boise State University Undergraduate Research Conference, Boise, ID — April 2013, 2014, & 2015

REFERENCES

R. Eric Landrum, PhD.
Boise State University
Department of Psychology,
Professor
1910 University Drive
Boise, Idaho 83725

Teresa Taylor, PhD.
Boise State University
Department of Psychology,
Professor
1910 University Drive
Boise, Idaho 83725

Wendy J. Olson
United States Attorney
District of Idaho
800 E. Park Boulevard,
Suite 600
Boise, Idaho 83712

2

your vita will not look like these samples. It takes time to gain experience, so start as early in your career as you can. If you wait to do things like serving as a research assistant or teaching assistant until your last semester of college, those experiences will not be as valuable as they could have been had they occurred earlier. Also, we recommend NOT using faculty CVs as examples for preparing your own CV. A faculty vita is likely to have many more categories that do not apply to undergraduate students. Also, if you compare your student CV to a faculty member's CV, you may become disappointed because it looks as if you have done so little. Remember, you are just getting started, and it has been that faculty member's job to be a psychologist; they have years and years head start on building a vita. Thus, if you want to look at a faculty member's vita, do so after you have created yours.

Success Stories

Mark Wojda
Wright State University

As the son of two teachers, education has always been important to me. College wasn't a dream or a goal for me; it was simply an expectation. I was your typical All-American kid in high school, an academic high achiever who also excelled athletically. When the time came, I applied to colleges that were recruiting me athletically, as well as those that offered academic scholarships. I ultimately accepted a full ride academic scholarship to a mid-sized state school, but after attending for a year I knew I had made a mistake. After another round of applications, I chose to transfer to Albion College. I knew that I was in for a challenge, socially and academically, when I transferred. What I did not expect, though, was how much I would learn from my college experience.

I integrated quickly when I arrived at Albion, joining the football and baseball teams, while declaring a major in psychology. By a stroke of luck, I enrolled in an I/O Psychology course taught by Dr. Andrew Christopher because it sounded interesting. After the first test, Dr. Christopher asked me to stay after and speak with him. I had scored well, so I was confused as to why he would need to speak with me. Dr. Christopher had noticed my score, realized I was new to campus, and asked if I had an advisor. I did not, and we agreed that he would be my advisor moving forward. Although I did not realize it at the time, this small decision would have a profound impact in my life. Dr. Christopher and I shared many research interests and worked extremely well together. Soon, in addition to advising me on classes, we were conducting research together. This led to my first publication, a senior honors thesis, and plans to enroll in a Social Psychology Ph.D. program after my time at Albion was done. All was going according to plan. I was set to graduate with honors, head off to graduate school, and continue like the high achiever I had always been. Then, something strange happened: I didn't get in to graduate school.

After the initial shock wore off, I began to regroup. First among my priorities was to call Dr. Christopher. As always, he calmed me down and encouraged me to look at the bigger picture. I had cultivated a great skillset while at Albion and had many qualifications that graduate programs desire. My time at Albion had given me not only knowledge of psychology, but of statistics,

(continued)

time management, and persistence that other candidates couldn't replicate. More importantly, I had learned that when my first option didn't work out, I could persevere. Months later, after reevaluating my priorities, I applied and was accepted to several terminal master's degree programs. Although this was a different course than I anticipated, I knew that I would be able to succeed.

Graduate school posed its own unique set of challenges, trials, and tribulations. After (yet another) school change and an advisor leaving, I graduated with my master's degree. Looking back, it would be easy to feel cynical and spurned by my educational experience. I choose, however, to view each stop along the way as another learning opportunity. Each experience stands on its own, building on previous stops and contributing to my eventual success. Although my journey was not the one the All-American high school kid envisioned, it was the one that showed me how a passion for learning, adaptability, and perseverance can lead to a successful career in psychology.

Research Experience, and Match and Fit with Your Program of Interest

6.8 Evaluate graduate programs for their individual fit

As alluded to earlier, research experience is important in the admissions process. It still remains important in light of the most recent research findings, and of course research is at the heart of the psychology; basic research is what we do, and basic research informs our applied practice. Serving as a research assistant should allow you to gain valuable knowledge, skills, and abilities, and you will likely have enough meaningful interactions with a faculty member through the research process that he or she will be able to write you a strong letter of recommendation. Much of Chapter 7 is devoted to demonstrating the importance and benefits of participating in research.

Additionally, you need to carefully consider your own personal goals with respect to the goals and orientation of the graduate schools to which you are applying. The "match" or "fit" between you and the school is not to be underestimated. Way back, Landrum et al. (1994) asked graduate admissions committee members to describe the exact procedures and decision-making rules they followed in the selection process. Content analysis of these decision protocols indicated that the most frequent strategy used in selection was the match between the applicant and the school and faculty. Even in the Littleford et al. (2018) results, "student-mentor research match" is of primary importance in graduate admissions decisions today. On another level, although the prospects of gaining admission may be daunting at this point, you do not want to go to any school just for the sake of going to graduate school. You might be admitted, but if the program is not a good match or good fit, you may be miserable and drop out (this chapter started with the acceptance rates into graduate school). A disastrous first experience may impact everything you attempt to do later in psychology. We would encourage you not to underestimate the importance of the match or fit between you and the schools you are applying to. Thus, if you mention in your personal statement that you want to work with a particular faculty member—mean it—because it might happen. In fact, some graduate programs take an additional step to ensure match or fit—they invite applicants for an on-campus interview. If at all possible, attend, even if it costs you money out of your own pocket. Some programs, like clinical and counseling psychology programs, rely on interviews more than other specialty areas. Just like a job interview, although the program is interviewing you, you are also interviewing the program. Table 6.9 presents some possible interview questions for you to use when on-campus—Oudekerk and Bottoms (2007) also provide additional ideas for questions for you to ask during your interview.

According to Appleby (1990), there may be two general types of students in graduate school: (1) students who find the experience unpleasant, to be endured, survived, and eventually forgotten and (2) students who thrive in the system, are respected by the faculty, and end up with the best employment prospects. If you would rather be in the latter group, here are some of the characteristics (Bloom & Bell, 1979) of those individuals who became graduate school superstars:

Visibility—highly motivated, seem to always be in the department at all hours

Willingness to work hard—seen by faculty as hard-working, persevering

Reflection of program values—seen by faculty as having professional values that lead to research and scholarly success

True interest in research—engaged in research projects in addition to the master's thesis and dissertation; curious enough about a problem and wanted to see data on it

Development of a relationship with a mentor—listen, learn, grow, and are productive through a close working relationship with one or two faculty members

As Appleby (1990) alluded to, none of these characteristics mention intellect, GPA, or writing ability. Perhaps those qualities are constants that the faculty member expects to see in all graduate school students. The above list constitutes qualities *over and above* those needed for entrance into the graduate program. Lord (2004) specifically addresses the undergraduate to graduate school transition:

> The transition from undergraduate to graduate study involves a transition from student to scholar and researcher. Many of the skills that guarantee success as an undergraduate (e.g., strong test-taking skills and good grades) can be unrelated to success as a graduate student, where the ability to conduct research—both effectively and prolifically—is the strongest measure of success. For some students, this transition is difficult, and successful graduate students are those who are able to discover research areas they truly enjoy and who are able to translate this interest into publications, the holy grail of graduate work. (p. 15)

Lord's conclusion is probably more applicable to those seeking the Ph.D. than the Psy.D., however.

If you do make it into graduate school, congratulations! Remember the transition between high school and college? Remember how at the beginning of college you wished for the luxury of time (and perhaps money) that you had at the end of high school? It is

Table 6.9 Questions Prospective Graduate Students Might Ask During Their Interview

- How is the training in this program organized?
- What is the typical program of study?
- What kind of opportunities would I have?
- What is the typical success rate for finding jobs for individuals in this program?
- Would I be likely to get financial aid my first year?
- What kinds of teaching and research assistantships or traineeships are available? Can first-year students receive them?
- What is this program's retention rate? How long does it typically take to complete the program successfully?
- [If applicable]. I understand that I will get a master's degree on my way to the doctorate. What are the master's and doctoral requirements?
- When are the comprehensive/preliminary exams typically taken?
- Are faculty members supportive with regard to original ideas for research?
- Is it possible to talk to a few graduate students in this program?

SOURCE: APA (1997a).

likely that another transition like that is in your future. Cox et al. (2010, pp. 327–328) wrote about the transition from undergraduate to graduate education, suggesting that you will likely notice (a) no longer being the smartest person in the class; (b) very high academic standards; (c) increasing reading; (d) balancing classwork with research, teaching, and writing responsibilities; (e) increased personal contact with faculty, staff, and peers; (f) heavy emphasis on honing public speaking skills for professional venues; (g) increased pressure to develop highly refined time-management skills; and (h) increased need for mentoring relative to your professional development (compared to your undergraduate experience). We tell you this not to dissuade you from the experience, but to give you a heads up—as you already know, life is indeed all about a sequence of transitions.

Strategies to Consider if You Do Not Get in

6.9 Summarize followup strategies for unsuccessful applications to graduate school

It is quite a process, but that is what it takes to become a psychologist. If it were easy, many people would do it, and the value of the skills and abilities learned would be lessened. It is difficult for undergraduate students to step back and get the "big picture" when you are in the process of applying to graduate schools and planning for your future. When students are unsuccessful in graduate school admission, they often forget about context. In other words, you are competing with the best and brightest students from around the nation, and often the world. Some students think that because they consistently get the top grades in their classes they will be the top applicants. Adding to the complexity, the pool of applicants changes every year, so one year you might be quite competitive and the next year you might not make the cut. If you are not accepted on your first attempt, what are your options?

We suggest that you seek out honest appraisals of your credentials. The first step might be to consult with your faculty mentor or other psychology department faculty about your application package. With a high GPA, were your GRE scores a bit low? Because you transferred your senior year, were your letters of recommendation not very strong? What types of experiences did your letter writers write about? Did you attend any conferences to present your research? Seek an honest and blunt appraisal of your credentials. If weaknesses can be identified, then try to correct them. It might mean retaking courses to raise your GPA (if you have not graduated), retaking the GRE to increase scores, or adding an extra year of your undergraduate education so that you can acquire additional experiences, such as serving as a research assistant or completing an internship. This last option is known by the dreaded three-word moniker "extend-your-stay"—and it works for some students, and for other students, that is just not an option.

Another strategy to consider is to contact the graduate schools that you applied to. Write to the director of graduate admissions, and ask for a sincere appraisal of your application. Try to obtain a personalized response—this may take a bit of work and persistence. However, your persistence may pay off the next year that you apply—especially if someone on the graduate admissions committee takes time to point out the weaknesses in your application and you take the next year turning those weaknesses into strengths. Be reasonable with yourself, and don't beat up on yourself concerning your weaknesses. However, if multiple opinions converge (faculty advisor, multiple graduate program faculty) concerning an area of concern, then you should consider what you can do to improve in that area. Be sure to tap into the experiences and expertise of your mentors, faculty members, and academic advisors. Persistence and appropriate networking can pay off.

Exercise 6.1 Reasons Checklist: Predicting Graduate School Attendance and Postponement

In two separate studies, researchers examined the variables that are significantly correlated with graduate school attendance (Stoloff et al., 2015) and compiled the reasons to postpose the pursuit of graduate school after completing their undergraduate degree in psychology (Zimak et al., 2011). It should be noted that in this latter study, the focus was students applying to clinical Ph.D. programs, but given that the clinical Ph.D. is the most popular program (highest number of applications) and one of the most competitive, it stands to reason that these explanations for postponing graduate school likely represent the pool of possible reasons.

For the left and right checklists below, check all that apply to you. You might want to circle back to this checklist from time to time to see if your attitudes and opinions have changed. There are no right or wrong answers. You will get the most out of this if you answer honestly and reflect deeply about your answers and what they mean to you. And remember, this is just a checklist for your self-exploration—correlations do not lead to causation! Regardless of how many checkmarks you can place on the left side of this exercise, you still have to do all the work to earn the credentials to be qualified. Don't be disappointed by a low number of checkmarks and do not be overconfident by a high number of checkmarks—your results may vary.

Check ✓	Positive Predictors of Graduate School Attendance	Check ✓	Reasons for Postposing the Pursuit of Graduate School
PERSONAL—you have some control over whether these happen or not			desire to get a job
	field placement or service learning		desire to start a family
	participation in study abroad		did not like schools for which I was accepted
	presentation software practice		not enough motivation
	spreadsheet practice		not interested in a Ph.D. at this time
	statistical software practice		not sure what to do
	student experience on a research team		rejected from all graduate schools
	student participation in student organizations		restricted by financial constraints
	student presenting research at a professional conference		restricted by geographical constraints ("land-locked")
	student presenting research on campus		too much financial debt
	student serving as a teaching assistant		uncertain about succeeding
	word processing practice		waited until it was too late to apply
INSTITUTIONAL—you really don't have much control over these, at least not directly			want to further professional development
	faculty attendance at student organization events		wanted to gain more life experience
	faculty involve students in research collaborations		wanted to gain more research experience
	faculty provide academic advising		wanted to improve GPA
	faculty provide help with classes		wanted to improve GRE scores
	faculty supervision of internships, field placements, and teaching assistantships		wanted to take a break from school
	institution is bachelor's degree only		
	low student–faculty ratio at institution		
	private institution		
	small class size capstone classes		
	small class sizes on advanced content		

SOURCES: Stoloff, M. L., Good, M. R., Smith, K. L., & Brewster, J. (2015). Characteristics of programs that maximize psychology major success. *Teaching of Psychology, 42*, 99–108. doi:10.1177/00986283115569977; Zimak, E. H., Edwards, K. M., Johnson, S. M., & Suhr, J. (2011). Now or later? An empirical investigation of when and why students apply to clinical psychology Ph.D. programs. *Teaching of Psychology, 38*, 118–121. doi:10.1177/0098628311401585

Exercise 6.2 Letter of Recommendation Request Worksheet

In this exercise, use this form to organize the letter of recommendation process. This form can be used for employers as well as graduate school applications. There are lots of details to attend to, so use the checklist to make sure you don't forget everything and that your letter writer has everything he or she needs to write you the strongest letter they can. The checklist has been derived in part from Bates College (2000) and Rewey (2000). Remember, paying attention to details is important; if you can't follow the instructions for applying to graduate school, many graduate schools will figure that you couldn't follow the instructions once you were admitted to graduate school (so why bother?).

Category	Check✓	Details
Initial Contact	______	Discuss the letter of recommendation with each faculty member/letter writer face-to-face.
	______	Ask "Would you be willing to write me a strong letter of recommendation?"
	______	Make this contact as soon as possible; no later than 1 month before the first letter is due.
Demographic Information	______	Provide the letter writer with your name, campus and permanent address, e-mail address, and phone numbers (including cell phone).
Academic Information	______	List your major, minor, GPAs, test scores, academic awards, honor society memberships.
	______	State the nature of the relationship, the length of time they have known you.
Experiences	______	Describe internships, independent study, directed research, senior thesis, work experiences, extracurricular activities (e.g., Psi Chi, Psychology Club).
Accomplishments	______	Give some details about your skills, talents, abilities, personal qualities, and relevant accomplishments.
	______	List relevant accomplishments with details, dates, etc.
	______	List relevant scholarships, recognitions (e.g., Dean's List).
Personal Characteristics	______	Describe academic strengths and weaknesses, why you are qualified for graduate school.
	______	Provide concrete examples of skills, such as dependability, intellect, drive and motivation, written and oral communication skills, interpersonal skills.
Wrap Up	______	State how you can be reached by the letter writer if he or she needs more information.
	______	Thank the letter writer formally with a handwritten card.
	______	Keep the letter writer informed about the progress of your efforts.

Chapter 7

Outside-of-Class Opportunities: Research Assistantships, Teaching Assistantships, Internships, and Organizational Involvement

Learning Objectives

7.1 Explain the value of a research assistantship

7.2 Explain how undergraduates can make the best use of professional conferences

7.3 Summarize the functions of a senior thesis project

7.4 Describe the responsibilities and benefits of being a teaching assistant

7.5 Explain the usefulness of field experiences and internships

7.6 Characterize work as an intern

7.7 Define service learning in a psychology undergraduate context

7.8 Compare opportunities for organizational involvement

If you have carefully read the first few chapters of this book, one theme that emerges is that you need to be involved outside the classroom to obtain the full range of skills and abilities to be successful in psychology. These experiences are invaluable whether you are going to graduate school-bound or workforce psychology-bound. This chapter directly addresses opportunities such as research assistantships, a senior thesis project, teaching assistantships, internships, service learning, and organizational opportunities.

These outside-the-classroom activities give you an opportunity to increase your skills in applying the psychological principles you are learning in the classroom (technically, as a teaching assistant, you are likely "in the classroom," but not in the traditional student role). Also, reading about research results and actually doing research are two very different learning experiences. However, you will likely obtain research experiences in some of your courses (Omarzu, et al., 2006; Perlman & McCann, 2005). Furthermore, by being involved beyond coursework, you give your psychology faculty more opportunities to get to know you and become familiar with your professional abilities and potential. Moreover, these faculty–student collaborations can often lead to strong letters of recommendation. If you are a student (one of many) in a class, the instructor has relatively limited exposure to your skills and abilities. If you are a student in the instructor's class, did research with her or him for a year that resulted in a poster presentation at a regional psychology convention, did an off-campus internship, served as a teaching assistant for another professor, and you were Vice President of your Psi Chi chapter, your instructor will be able to write a stronger letter because you are a more well-rounded student (and because you worked with more than one person, you will have additional sources of letters of recommendation). Whether you are looking for a good job with your bachelor's degree or looking for admission into graduate school, you need to be competitive with regard to skills and abilities. If you can take advantage of some of the opportunities presented in this chapter, you will be well on your way to achieving a competitive edge.

What Is Research Assistantship?

7.1 Explain the value of a research assistantship

In an article by Clay (1998), Eugene Zechmeister, the director of the undergraduate program at Loyola University (Illinois), said, "I know this will sound sacrilegious, but skills are actually more important than course content" (p. 2). We both believe he is correct. Courses lay the foundation for information and knowledge about psychology, but that information and knowledge will do little good without the skills needed to utilize that knowledge. Said another way, gasoline is to content as the engine is to skills. Gas is important for the engine to run; it's necessary, but not sufficient. And different types of gas can make that engine run. But what really gets us anyplace is the engine. In the same fashion, the content, the topics in psychology are indeed interesting. But we believe that it's the skills that you will take away from your undergraduate training—the critical thinking, public speaking skills, thinking ethically, thinking like a psychologist, statistical literacy, hypothesis testing, yes, even practice with APA style and format—these skills are the "engine" that will take you places, no matter what content you pour into the engine (developmental, social, cognitive, personality, experimental, etc.). Since its formal inception in 1879, psychology has been an empirical, research-based discipline. Teaching and research focus on the heart of the matter—we expand our knowledge about psychology through research, and it is this research that gives us the subject matter that we teach. For the discipline of psychology to succeed and thrive, we need a balance between teaching and research.

What is a research assistantship? It is an opportunity for undergraduate students to assist faculty members in a program of research. When you serve as a research assistant (RA), you will actually be involved in *doing* the research rather than reading about it in your textbook or journal article. There are multiple advantages to serving as a research assistant: (a) acquisition of skills and knowledge not easily gained in the classroom; (b) opportunity to work one-on-one with a faculty member; (c) opportunity to contribute to the advancements of the science of psychology; (d) exposure to general research techniques helpful for pursuing later graduate work; (e) opportunity to practice written and oral communication skills by preparing for and attending professional conferences and preparing and submitting manuscripts for publication; and (f) cultivation of a mentoring relationship with a faculty member that will be helpful for acquiring letters of recommendation.

What do you do as a research assistant? This is best answered by asking the faculty member directly. Although the answer will vary from research topic to research topic, the list presented in Table 7.1 describes some of the general tasks and duties that you may be asked to perform—see also Sleigh and Ritzer (2007) and Silvia et al. (2009) for more examples. You might also have the opportunity to work with a faculty member as part of his or her research lab—a collaborative group (perhaps a mixture of undergraduate and graduate students) that typically works on varied projects centered around a theme. Lai et al. (2010, p. 26) offered some potential questions to ask about getting involved in a research lab; here is a sample of some of those questions:

- How many projects is the lab currently undertaking?
- How often will you interact with the faculty associated with the project?
- In what stage of the research project is the lab currently, and how do they see the lab developing in the next few years (collecting and analyzing data)?
- Are the hours flexible or scheduled?
- Are there any opportunities to present at conferences and/or contribute to publications?
- Are there opportunities to learn new techniques (e.g., data analysis, data collection procedures, direct work with participants, the institutional review board process, data programming)?

Your commitment to serve as a research assistant is a weighty one—you have some responsibility to see that several aspects of the research process get done. It is a serious commitment that you should not take lightly. In fact, Roig (2007) suggested guidelines for a student–faculty research agreement, and Landrum (2008) provided sample criteria for evaluating a research assistant's performance. The faculty member you are working with will be counting on you to get things done, and done right; here is the place you want to shine. By watching you complete tasks and by observing you accepting more responsibility, your faculty mentor will have plenty of good things to write about in those letters of recommendation. However, the reverse is also true. If you don't take the commitment seriously, if you make repeated mistakes on important tasks, then the recommendations of the faculty member will be weakened. If you choose to take on this commitment, know what you are getting into. At many schools, research assistants can also earn course credit—with a title such as directed research, independent study, or supervised research—and these credits are often senior-level upper-division credits. Take advantage of this opportunity; these credits make a positive impression on your

Table 7.1 Typical Tasks Performed by Research Assistants

- Administer research sessions with student participants (this procedure is called data collection, or "running subjects").
- Score and/or code the collected data, and enter them into a spreadsheet or statistical analysis program (such as SPSS, R, Minitab, Excel).
- Conduct literature searches using resources such as *PsycINFO*, Google Scholar, and Web of Science. [more information about these sources is presented in Chapter 8]; search your local library database for books and periodicals; make copies of articles available; order unavailable resources through interlibrary loan; organize PDFs; undertake general library research.
- Work with the faculty member to develop new research ideas; often these ideas are developed from research just completed, the need that arises from a particular situation, or reviews of the existing literature.
- Attend lab meetings with other undergraduate research assistants, discuss research ideas, collaborate on projects.
- Use word processing, spreadsheet, scheduling, and statistical analysis programs to complete the research project.
- Work on project outcomes so they can be submitted for presentations at local or regional conferences, prepare abstracts; if accepted, work on poster or oral presentations of the research materials for presentation at professional conferences.
- Collaborate with faculty member to submit work to an appropriate journal to share the results with the broad scientific community.

transcripts. When asked about why they became involved in research, Slattery and Park (2002) found that students' most common responses were to increase probability of graduate school admission and because they were interested in research.

Other researchers have approached this issue from another perspective. For instance, Vittengl et al. (2004) reported that when predicting those students who will have higher interest in research, the key predictors are (a) viewing research as relevant to plans after receiving the bachelor's degree, (b) a personality with high openness to experience, and (c) score higher on the ACT mathematics subscale. Pawlow and Meinz (2017) reported that psychology students who serve as research assistants had higher self-reported scores in the areas of career knowledge, core knowledge, statistics/methodology knowledge, higher critical thinking and writing skills, and higher SPSS skills. Vittengl et al. (2004, p. 94) stated it in this fashion:

> .... undergraduates with relatively low interest in research might be described as (a) less sophisticated, more conventional thinkers with lower intellectual curiosity than their peers; (b) students who struggle with the concepts and application of high-school-level mathematics, which is commonly used in statistical analyses; and (c) students who, accurately or inaccurately, consider research knowledge and skills to be largely irrelevant to their anticipated post undergraduate activities.

Please remember that these are not cause-and-effect relations, however. We encourage all psychology undergraduates, regardless of their career plans, to pursue opportunities such as research and teaching assistantships. The benefits of such participation are highlighted throughout this chapter. Table 7.2 offers some suggestions on how to go about securing a research assistant (RA) position.

In a national survey, Landrum and Nelsen (2002) systematically studied the benefits of serving as an RA from the faculty member perspective. Out of a 40-item survey, faculty members ranked these benefits as most important: (a) an opportunity to enhance critical thinking skills, (b) preparation for graduate school, (c) gains enthusiasm for the research process, (d) participates in the data collection process, and (e) improved writing ability. Although the research assistant–faculty collaboration is often a positive experience, there are times when problems arise. Slattery and Park (2002) described some of the most helpful strategies to avoid problems in research collaboration: (a) meet students regularly, (b) mentor student researchers in whatever way possible, (c) train students carefully for tasks given to them, (d) involve them in faculty research, and (e) choose student researchers carefully. As stated previously, research is a serious commitment by both student and faculty—care should be taken to properly nurture this relationship and monitor progress toward common goals.

Table 7.2 Suggestions for Securing a Research Assistant Position

- Review the listing of the faculty in your psychology department and their research interests. You might find this information available in a pamphlet in the department, as part of advising materials, or perhaps on the department's website. If there is no such list available, encourage your Psi Chi chapter or local psychology club to create one.
- Then, make appointments with faculty members, preferably during their posted office hours, to discuss research possibilities.
- If you want to impress this faculty member, do your homework. Do a PsycINFO search beforehand and be ready to talk about topics that this faculty member has already studied. Do not ask a faculty member "So what is your research area?"
- When you meet with the faculty members, be yourself. Let them know that you are willing to work hard on their program of research. Ask them about the specific requirements that they expect from their research assistants. You'll want to know about the duration of this project, what your responsibilities will be, grading practices, weekly time commitment, etc. Also, what length of commitment is the faculty member looking for? Some faculty may want RA help only for a semester, whereas other faculty will ask for a 1-year or longer commitment.
- If you come to an agreement with a faculty member to serve as an RA, there may be additional online forms that you have to fill out to register for credit.

Success Stories

Meghan Pavelka
Appalachian State University
Alumnus

I discovered a passion for caregiving when I interned at a local nursing home during my senior year of high school. My internship roles involved direct interaction with residents, and I quickly found a love for serving a geriatric population. This realization, combined with my curiosity in science, led me to an interest in medicine. I started college with the goal of medical school in mind, but instead of pursing a typical pre-medical degree, I decided that majoring in psychology would allow me to better understand patients' motivations, behaviors, and experiences. I figured that having a background in psychology would provide me with a broader perspective of the many factors that influence patients' health.

I was able to further my interest in patient care by working at a nursing home and volunteering at a free clinic throughout my college career. These experiences allowed me to utilize the lessons from my psychology coursework to better connect with individuals from backgrounds that are very different from my own. My psychology courses also provided me with a greater appreciation for the social determinants of health, such as environmental influences, health behaviors, and social support. The lessons I learned from this coursework allowed me to develop deeper relationships with patients, as I was able to apply textbook concepts to real scenarios of patient care.

After dealing with my own health problems in college, I decided to take a couple of gap years before applying to medical school. I knew that I wanted to fill those two years with something enjoyable and educational; thus, I decided to continue doing what I love most – working directly with patients in a clinical setting. Upon graduating from college, I decided to pursue a two-year clinical fellowship with MedServe, in partnership with AmeriCorps VISTA. I was drawn to MedServe because of their mission: "connecting medicine with community service." In my position as a MedServe Fellow, I have had the opportunity to serve both clinical and community outreach roles, as I build upon my clinical skillset in preparation to apply to medical school.

I'm extremely thankful for my decision to major in psychology due to the opportunities that I've been provided during and after college. I would advise students to explore careers that may not be in line with a particular major, and if possible, take courses that will help to provide a more unique perspective on an intended career path

What research experience is the most beneficial for students? Are all research experiences of equal value? If you are planning to attend graduate school, it appears that some components of the research assistantship experience are more valuable than others. In an interesting study, Kaiser et al. (2007) surveyed graduate admissions directors to answer this question. The results are consistent with previous research. The four most important types of undergraduate research experiences (from a graduate school admissions director's perspective) were that the student (a) published in a refereed journal,

(b) published a senior thesis, (c) was the first author on a refereed journal article, and (d) made a paper presentation at a national conference. Other research experiences were also valuable, but these four were most important.

Presenting Research at Conferences

7.2 Explain how undergraduates can make the best use of professional conferences

By becoming involved in research, you will give yourself a number of additional opportunities as well. For instance, you may be able to make a presentation at a local or regional professional conference, or at a more student-centered research conference. For a very nice overview of academic conferences (and the creators of the delightful phrase related to conferences—binge thinking), see Silvia et al. (2009; Chapter 8). Two types of "presentations" are typically made at conferences—papers and posters. A paper presentation is usually a 12- to 15-minute talk given to an audience about your research project. You may have handouts for your audience, or use audiovisual aids (such as a PowerPoint presentation), or do both. Table 7.3 offers suggestions for oral paper presentations, and more advice is found in Silvia, Delaney, and Marcovitch (2009).

A poster presentation is substantially different from a paper presentation. In the paper presentation, you present your findings to a large audience in a relatively short time period. The method is somewhat impersonal, but it is an efficient method to present the materials to a large number of people. In a poster presentation, you present your research work in a poster format for a longer period of time (1–1½ hours). You are available to speak personally with "audience members" who are interested in your work. In the poster session, you will probably reach fewer people, but you'll have more personal conversations with people who are genuinely interested in your work. Your poster is displayed on a freestanding bulletin board in a session with other posters, in a room large enough to hold the posters, the presenters, and the people who wander through the session.

Usually, the size of your poster is around 30 inches × 40 inches. As for preparing the text of your poster, Sue and Ritter (2007) recommend these font sizes for different parts of your text:

- Logos and headers—5.5 inches tall
- First headline, main panel—120-point font

Table 7.3 Making an Oral Presentation at a Conference

- Know your audience and prepare and practice for your presentation.
- Consider the big picture. What are the main ideas and findings of your study?
- Decide on a limited number of significant ideas that you want your audience to comprehend and remember.
- Minimize the nitty-gritty details (like procedure, data analysis strategies, etc.) and highlight the main points.
- State clearly, without jargon, the point of your research, what you found, and what it means—try to tell a good story.
- Write out your presentation as a mini-lecture, with a clear outline. You may use these as cues while you make your presentation.
- Practice your presentation out loud, making sure it fits into the time restraints, and have a small audience listen to you to give you constructive feedback.
- Prepare overheads or PowerPoint slides to keep your audience engaged in your presentation.
- Do not read your paper. Talk to your audience about what you did to complete the work. At a professional conference, it is very irritating to be read to—everyone there can already read.
- Try to speak loudly and clearly enough to hold the attention of your audience. There will be distractions—people coming in, others getting up and leaving. Don't be offended. Try to be enthusiastic enough to sustain interest over these distractions.
- State your final conclusions and end on time. Be prepared to answer audience questions if time permits. Offer to answer questions after the session if there is continued interest but your time expires.
- If you have handouts, be sure to include contact information on them—name, conference, and date of presentation.
- Bring copies of your paper to the conference, or provide a sign-up sheet for persons who may want copies to be sent to them.

SOURCES: Karlin (2000); Williams-Nickelson (2007).

- Second headline or large bullet items—72-point font
- Smaller bullet items—48–60-point font
- Text blocks—30–36-point font
- Captions—18–24-point font

Thus, nothing printed on your poster should be smaller than an 18-point font! The audience picks and chooses what posters to read; they can acquire more detailed information from the poster authors in this one-on-one conversation format. Table 7.4 presents tips for preparing and making poster presentations. For more presentations about the effective use of PowerPoint, see McGregor (2011) and Berk (2011). For more tips about poster presentations, see Feldman and Silvia (2010) and Silvia et al. (2009).

Professional conferences provide a wonderful opportunity to network with others. When giving advice to student attendees of conferences, Prohaska (2008) noted that you can get a sneak peek at the future of psychology by attending conferences, because you'll see research results long before they appear in print. Conferences also provide an opportunity to hear distinguished psychologists ("big names") speak in person, such as at Psi Chi Distinguished Lectures (more about Psi Chi later in this chapter). Prohaska also noted that conferences provide important networking opportunities for students, which can be especially helpful to meet graduate faculty members from a program that you intend to apply to. You might also find conference programming specific to your needs, such as how to prepare a curriculum vita or personal statement, or hear the latest admissions data for graduate schools.

If you have the opportunity, try to get involved as a research assistant. If you do not have the opportunity, try to create it. When you work with a faculty member on a research project, it is a mutually beneficial relationship. What does the faculty member get out of this relationship? He or she gets a hard-working, eager student to do some of the labor-intensive portions of a research project. Many faculty members, especially those at institutions that do not have a graduate program in psychology, depend on undergraduate students to help further their own research agenda. If this research culture does not exist at your school, try to develop it. Find that student-friendly faculty member who realizes how important the research opportunity is to you, and chances are you will find a way to collaborate on some sort of research project. Often, faculty members have ideas for studies that they would like to do but don't have the time or the assistance. A talented undergraduate student assisting that faculty member can make that project happen. Davis (1995) clearly articulated the advantages faculty members receive from conducting collaborative research with undergraduate students (see Table 7.5).

Table 7.4 Presenting a Poster at a Conference

- Construct the poster to include the title, authors, affiliations, and a description of the research.
- Minimize the detail that is presented, and try to use jargon-free statements.
- Pictures, tables, and figures are especially useful and helpful in poster presentations. If possible, use color in your poster.
- Make sure the lettering is neatly done and large enough to be read from a distance—poster session attendees will quickly scan the content before stopping to inquire further—use fonts no smaller than 18 points; try to use 24 points or larger if possible.
- During your poster presentation, have your name badge on and placed where conference attendees can see it.
- Categorize onlookers into three types: passive, reflective, and active. Passive onlookers will take a handout and keep moving. Reflective observers will read your poster, stand back and process it, and may or may not ask you a question. Active observers will come up, introduce themselves, and ask the classic question "What did you find?"
- Do not overwhelm the viewer with excessive amounts of information; try to construct a poster display that encourages and enhances conversation.
- Be ready to pin up and take down your poster at the specified times (you may want to bring your own thumbtacks or pushpins); often poster sessions are scheduled back to back, so you want to be on time so the next session can also be on time.
- Bring 30–50 copies of your handouts to provide more information about your study and your contact information.

SOURCES: Karlin (2000); Stambor (2008).

Table 7.5 Benefits to Faculty in Working with Undergraduate Research Assistants

Witnessing student professional growth and development—perhaps the best reward
Facilitating reviews of the current literature in a particular research area, staying current
Keeping analytic skills fine-tuned and active through the design and the completion of research
Generating useful and meaningful empirical data
Maintaining and expanding professional networks through attending conventions, especially for students
Enhancing effectiveness as a teacher through active involvement in research

What Is a Senior Thesis?

7.3 Summarize the functions of a senior thesis project

At many colleges and universities, undergraduate students have the opportunity to complete a senior thesis project (at some schools, a senior thesis project is required). What is the difference between a research assistant position and a senior thesis? Generally speaking, when you agree to become a research assistant, you are going to help the faculty member with her or his research. Although you might make some suggestions and eventually put your own "spin" on the research program, this research essentially "belongs" to the faculty member, and you are truly "assisting." For a senior thesis project, the student is the principal investigator, the student "owns" the research, and the faculty member plays an advisory or consulting role. Often, in a senior thesis project the student gets to test his or her own research ideas, under the supervision and guidance of a faculty member. Note that you will have to find a faculty member willing to supervise your work—so you might be limited to the specialty areas of your faculty. The only way to find out is to consult with faculty members individually. Silvia et al. (2009) provided good advice about senior thesis projects and how students can advance their own research agenda.

The senior thesis typically requires much more responsibility and independence compared to the research assistantship. Faculty members have an inherent self-interest in seeing their own research succeed, for multiple reasons (including promotion and tenure). Note, however, that many faculty members supervise senior thesis projects with little or no compensation—so be sure to be appreciative, keep appointments, and value the opportunity that the faculty member is providing. Of course, faculty members want to see students succeed in their own senior thesis research, but the stakes are lower for faculty members. Unfortunately, there is essentially no research available on the benefits of completing a senior thesis project, and the senior thesis is barely mentioned in the literature. One exception—Wood and Palm (2000) utilized students enrolled in a psychology senior thesis course and examined if anxiety scores would be elevated prior to a required oral presentation; they were. This does not tell us much about the benefits of a senior thesis project, though.

We would assume that the benefits of a senior thesis project would be similar to those experienced by students serving as RAs. When the time comes, talk to faculty members at your school to see if a senior thesis option is available—and note that it could be called something else at your institution (e.g., independent study). In general, you will want to have completed your courses in statistics and experimental design/research methods prior to embarking on such an independent project. With careful planning and the right supervision, you can make this project into something that will help you stand out from the crowd, engage in original research, perhaps lead to a conference presentation, and help build rapport with a faculty member. The potential is huge!

Becoming a Teaching Assistant

7.4 Describe the responsibilities and benefits of being a teaching assistant

What about being a teaching assistant (TA)? Serving as a teaching assistant is usually much less involved and time-consuming than being a research assistant. Usually, a

Table 7.6 Potential Tasks of a Teaching Assistant

- Attend class and take notes so that students have a resource available to get notes when they miss class.
- Hold office hours where you may conduct tutoring sessions, review notes with students, review class assignments before they are due, and answer class-related questions.
- Help to proctor exams, help to grade exams and/or term papers, and help to enter these scores in the instructor's gradebook.
- Hold general review sessions prior to tests where groups of students can receive supplemental instruction over course-related topics.
- Help the instructor in the general administration and completion of the course to provide the best experience possible for enrolled students.

teaching assistant helps a faculty member for one semester (or quarter) in the administration of a specific course, such as Introduction to Psychology or Statistical Methods. You might have a number of different responsibilities as a teaching assistant, depending on the instructor, the course, the history of the institution in utilizing teaching assistants, etc. Table 7.6 presents some of the tasks you might complete.

The teaching assistantship is an excellent way to build a mentoring relationship with a faculty member. Also, serving as a TA is a low-risk activity. Being a TA is usually not as demanding as being an RA, and the typical time commitment for TAs is one semester only. Thus, if you really don't "bond" with that faculty member, there is no harm done (and you earned credits toward graduation).

However, the benefits can be substantial. Almost certainly during the course of the semester, a situation will occur where you can step in and provide some real assistance to a faculty member teaching a course. These are the types of events that faculty members will be thankful for and may write about in a letter of recommendation. Also, many of our students tell us that sitting in on the general psychology course is a great study strategy when they prepare for the GRE Advanced Test in Psychology. You should know, however, that not all schools offer the opportunity for students to serve as undergraduate teaching assistants. If being a teaching assistant is not an opportunity at your school, you may have to be creative in finding this opportunity—perhaps seeking out an instructor who "wants help" in administering his or her course and is willing to give you independent study or internship credit—and don't forget about asking instructors of online courses if they need teaching assistants; often they do. If the formal opportunity does not exist, there are creative ways of gaining the beneficial experience anyway! If you are faced with a choice of serving as a research assistant or as a teaching assistant, try to do both. You will be busy, but you will gain valuable skills, abilities, and knowledge for your future.

Becoming a research assistant or teaching assistant are certainly ways to stand out from the crowd, but they are not the only ways. Here we present the ins and outs of internships, service learning, as well as apprise you of the opportunities to get involved in psychology via organizations.

Field Experiences and Internships

7.5 Explain the usefulness of field experiences and internships

Field experiences and internships are opportunities to learn about and apply psychological principles out of the classroom and in the field. These placements are in agencies that relate to some aspects of human behavior—hence, you can imagine that many places are possible internship sites. They also differ from teaching and research assistantships in that a nonfaculty member at the placement site typically supervises field experiences. A faculty member often serves as the departmental coordinator of the field experience or internship program.

If you do an internship in your community, what might you do? You might be an intern at a social service agency, assisting in intake interviews, psychological testing, report writing, or behavior modification. You might be an intern in a human resources

Table 7.7 Potential Benefits from Completing an Internship

Practical, on-the-job experience
Development of professional and personal confidence, responsibility, and maturity.
Understanding of the realities of the work world and acquiring human relations skills.
Opportunity to examine a career choice closely and make professional contacts.
Opportunity to test the ideas learned in the classroom out in the field.
Opportunity to make contacts with potential employers.
Enhancement of classroom experiences.
Learning what careers *not* to pursue.
Development of skills that are difficult to learn and practice in the classroom.
College credit in some, but not all, circumstances.
Possible earnings to help offset college expenses.

department, where you learn to administer structured interviews, write performance appraisals, and coordinate special projects and programs. The opportunities are endless. In some instances, if an internship opportunity is not available to meet your needs, you may be able to arrange your own specialized internship.

Blanton (2001) developed an internship model for undergraduates based on the Chickering and Reisser (1993) model of college student development. The Chickering and Reisser model generates four primary tasks for undergraduate students: (a) increasing self-awareness, (b) managing emotions, (c) increasing integrity, and (d) developing purpose. In this model, increasing self-awareness is achieved by achieving the latter three tasks. How does this apply to internships?

What are the benefits of participating in an internship? Table 7.7 was compiled from Jessen (1988), Mount Saint Vincent University (1998), and the University of Michigan at Dearborn (1998). Knouse et al. (1999) found that students who had completed an internship were more likely to have a job at graduation than students who did not complete an internship. The internship provided an immediate benefit to graduates. For words of wisdom from the workplace about internships, see Hettich (2012).

How do you find out about field experiences and internships? There is probably a key faculty member in your department who makes sure that internship sites are suitable, establishes the policies and procedures for working with agencies, ensures that grades are submitted on time, handles inquiries from internship supervisors, etc. Find that person. Most departments have some well-established connections with agencies in and around your community; if you want to do something where the relation is not established, you may have to do more of the groundwork yourself. This latter approach gives you the chance to show some initiative and really demonstrate to your internship site your willingness to work hard and persevere at the task. Gardner (2011) discussed the characteristics of a high-stakes internship; that is, one where you have the chance to truly make a difference as well as gain an enhanced skill set. From Gardner's perspective, the high-stakes internship event means that you (a) know your interests and yourself well; (b) seek an internship with a high frequency of contact and practice; and (c) seek an internship experience with adequately high difficulty such that the opportunities to learn and grow are present.

What Interns Do

7.6 Characterize work as an intern

What will you do as an intern? Ideally, you will get a realistic glimpse of the types of tasks necessary for success in a particular office or agency. Where appropriate, you will have the opportunity to acquire new skills and hone those that you already have. Internships are not designed to provide agencies with extra office staff, although you may occasionally be asked to help pitch in when agencies are under time or budget constraints. Although you might not be conducting a group therapy session, you might sit in on such a session and help facilitate that session under the supervision of appropriately trained and licensed personnel. In addition to these tasks, there may be group supervisory sessions if your site has multiple interns, and your on-campus faculty internship coordinator will probably require that you keep a weekly journal of your intern experiences (Jessen, 1988). Although most students have an invigorating internship experience, we have known some students who come back from an internship with the conclusion "I definitely do *not* want to do that for my entire career." This decision is a very valuable outcome of the internship process. Although it is unfortunate that the student did not enjoy the internship process, it is better to have an unsatisfying 16-week internship experience than to go to a graduate program to get a degree to enter a job that leads to a lifetime of misery. Knouse et al. (1999) evaluated an internship program for business majors and found that students with internships had higher GPAs, were a bit younger, and were more apt to be employed after graduation compared to students without internships. Thus, internships were positively related to both college performance and receiving a job offer postgraduation. Kampfe et al. (1999) concluded that students perceived their internships as important, relatively nondisruptive, and that they had control over the circumstances of their internship. Close to half perceived their internship as stressful, however, and about 25% perceived very little control over the internship situation. Blanton (2001) based the evaluation of a successful internship experience on these three criteria: (a) perceiving the supervisor as understanding, (b) feeling supported in the growth process, and (c) satisfaction with the level of supervision. When Peterson and Shackelford (2011) reported on the benefits of internship-like experiences comparing pre- to post-levels, students reported significant gains in occupational information, planning, and problem solving—based on a measure of career decision-making self-efficacy. The benefits of internships can be substantial.

Service Learning

7.7 Define service learning in a psychology undergraduate context

Related to these field experiences and internships are some other options to gain practical, hands-on experiences. You might not have all these opportunities available on your campus, or they might exist under different titles, so look carefully. These other methods of getting involved include service learning, peer advising, and paraprofessional programs. Service learning is typically defined as "a form of experiential education in which students engage in activities that address human and community needs together with structured opportunities intentionally designed to promote student learning and development" (Jacoby, 1996, p. 5). Service learning (in some cases it is called the fourth credit option) involves adding one credit to a three-credit class and providing volunteer services to the community. Supervised by the course instructor, students receive an additional one credit for completing volunteer service.

Simon (2017) makes the case that some of the benefits of service learning accrue because of the action research orientation that service learning projects can take in the community. In fact, multiple researchers are interested (e.g., Geller et al., 2016; Weller et al., 2013) in the mechanisms which lead to the beneficial effects of service learning. In a summary of numerous service learning projects and publications, clear benefits can be identified for student participants, faculty members, and the community (Rutti et al., 2016).

Some psychology departments have a peer-advising program that provides academic advising services to undergraduate majors. This program is an opportunity for undergraduates to become involved in interviewing and conversational skills, and gain professional and personal confidence in dealing with the issues related to undergraduate education. Additionally, some psychology departments that have a counseling center affiliated with them also have a paraprofessional program. In a paraprofessional program, undergraduates receive training in some therapeutic approaches and, under the supervision of counseling faculty, practice these skills by providing workshops to other students. Check with your department to see if any of these types of outside-of-class opportunities are available for you. The bottom line is that internships are a great chance to expand upon your skills outside of the classroom and begin to make valuable connections in the field. Many undergraduate internship and related opportunities turn into job offers after graduation. We highly recommend that you inquire about the possibility of an internship at your school.

Organizational Involvement

7.8 Compare opportunities for organizational involvement

The opportunities discussed in this chapter focus on developing skills and abilities. Organizational involvement also provides the chance to enhance knowledge about the discipline and to find opportunities to network within it. On a regional, national, or international level you can become involved in organizations designed for students, or join organizations (as a student affiliate) designed for psychology professionals. In addition, you may have some opportunities on your own campus to get involved and gain valuable information and skills.

American Psychological Association

On the national level, the oldest organization for psychologists is the American Psychological Association (APA). APA was founded in 1892. APA provides an impressive website that we recommend, www.apa.org. According to the APA website:

> APA is the leading scientific and professional organization representing psychology in the United States, with more than 115,700 researchers, educators, clinicians, consultants and students as its members.
>
> Our mission is to advance the creation, communication and application of psychological knowledge to benefit society and improve people's lives. We do this by:
>
> - Encouraging the development and application of psychology in the broadest manner.
> - Promoting research in psychology, the improvement of research methods and conditions and the application of research findings.
> - Improving the qualifications and usefulness of psychologists by establishing high standards of ethics, conduct, education and achievement.
> - Increasing and disseminating psychological knowledge through meetings, professional contacts, reports, papers, discussions and publications.
>
> **SOURCE:** American Psychological Association. (2018). *About APA*. Retrieved from http://www.apa.org/about/index.aspx

APA offers an undergraduate student affiliate status as a membership category in the organization. For $35 a year (at the time of this writing), the benefits of becoming and undergraduate student affiliate include access to career and professional development tools, a subscription to the organization's flagship journal *American Psychologist* and the *APA Monitor on Psychology* magazine, a $10 credit toward another journal subscription, discounts on APA products, and discounted rates when registering for APA's annual convention. In addition to using its website, one of the best ways to find out about APA is to talk with your faculty. Some of them may be current members of APA; both of your authors are members of APA.

The Association for Psychological Science

Although much younger than APA, the Association for Psychological Science (APS; the original name of this organization was the American Psychological Society) has also become an important source of information for psychological scientists (www.psychologicalscience.org). According to APS:

> APS is the leading international organization dedicated to advancing scientific psychology across disciplinary and geographic borders. Our members provide a richer understanding of the world through their research, teaching, and application of psychological science. We are passionate about supporting psychological scientists in these pursuits, which we do by sharing cutting-edge research across all areas of the field through our journals and conventions; promoting the integration of scientific perspectives within psychological science and with related disciplines; fostering global connections among our members; engaging the public with our research to promote broader understanding and awareness of psychological science; and advocating for increased support for psychological science in the public policy arena.
>
> **SOURCE:** Association for Psychological Science. (2018). *About APS: Who we are*. Retrieved from https://www.psychologicalscience.org/about

And, to be fair, both of your authors are members of APS as well. APS also offers an undergraduate student affiliate program. An undergraduate student affiliate membership is open to any student who is currently enrolled full-time as a psychology major at an accredited institution. Student members receive the same benefits as regular members. For a $41 annual fee for undergraduates (at the time of this writing), student members receive electronic subscriptions to *Psychological Science*, *Current Directions in Psychological Science*, *Psychological Science in the Public Interest*, *Perspectives on Psychological Science*, and *Advances in Methods and Practices in Psychological Science*, and the *Observer* news magazine. Other benefits include a discount on registration rates for the annual convention, award and grant opportunities for students, a student caucus, access to an online membership directory, and discounted subscriptions to psychological journals (APS, 2018).

Psi Chi

The best-known organization explicitly designed for students is Psi Chi, the International Honor Society in Psychology (https://www.psichi.org/); Psi Chi chapters exist at four-year institutions. Psi Chi was founded in 1929 for the purpose of encouraging, stimulating, and maintaining excellence in scholarship, and for the advancement of psychology. Psi Chi membership is conferred on students who have met minimum qualifications at institutions where there is a chapter (there is an application process, and not all students can be members). If you are a student at a community or junior college (and if there is a chapter), you can become a member of Psi Beta (psibeta.org)—see below for more about Psi Beta.

Psi Chi is an impressive organization benefiting students on many levels. Involvement in your local chapter can lead to opportunities to develop leadership skills, and Psi Chi members are often the most involved and well-connected psychology students around. Note however, like other campus organizations, that your Psi Chi chapter (and/or a psychology club) will only be as strong as the student leaders. On the regional, national, and international levels, Psi Chi has various programmatic and scholarship offerings. At major regional and national conferences held each year, Psi Chi has an important presence in promoting the scholarly achievements of undergraduate and graduate psychology students. Psi Chi has a long tradition of providing student-friendly programming at these conferences. Both of your authors were Psi Chi members as undergraduate psychology students! We are also proud to report that both of your authors have also served as President of Psi Chi. If your school does not have a Psi Chi chapter, consult with a faculty member about starting a chapter—the starter kit is here: bit.ly/PsiChiChapter

Even if your institution does not have a Psi Chi chapter, there may be a psychology club on campus. Usually, these clubs are open to anyone with an interest in psychology, and members do not have to be psychology majors. Often, students who are unable to join Psi Chi (perhaps due to a GPA being too low or not yet accumulating enough credit hours in psychology) can be active and involved as members of the local psychology club. On campuses where both groups exist, they often coordinate activities and opportunities for the benefit of all students interested in psychology. Because it is an honor society, not everyone will be able to join Psi Chi. The eligibility requirements include the following:

- Be enrolled as a major or minor in a psychology program or a program psychological in nature
- Have completed at least 3 semesters or equivalent of full-time college coursework
- Have completed at least 9 semester credit hours or equivalent of psychology courses
- Have earned a cumulative GPA that is in the top 35% of their class (sophomore, junior, or senior) compared to their classmates across the entire university or the college that houses psychology (minimum GPA of 3.0 on a 4-point scale)
- Have a minimum 3.0 GPA average for psychology courses

SOURCE: Psi Chi. (2018). *Become a member*. Retrieved from https://www.psichi.org/page/become_member#.W2XM_NVKh9A

We believe that the benefits of Psi Chi are substantial and worth your time and investment. Others have come to the same conclusion. In a study of psychology alumni, Tarsi and Jalbert (1998) compared Psi Chi alumni with non–Psi Chi alumni on a number of measures. For instance, Psi Chi members were significantly more positive about their education than non–Psi Chi members; this may be due to the higher Psi Chi standards leading to a greater self-investment by students. Among Psi Chi members only, Tarsi and Jalbert (1998) found that the more active students were, the more worthwhile they reported their Psi Chi experience. We encourage you to continue this tradition of involvement and contribution.

Psi Beta

Psi Beta is the community college honor society in psychology. Founded in 1981, it is the mission of Psi Beta ". . . to encourage professional development and psychological literacy of all students at two-year colleges through promotion and recognition of excellence in scholarship, leadership, research, and community service" (Psi Beta, 2018a, para. 1). Psi Beta enumerates many potential benefits of membership:

- Members gain recognition for achieving the honor of membership. Among the entities that recognize Psi Beta membership: Psi Chi, APA, APS, psychology departments at colleges and universities, and employers.
- Verification of membership for references throughout the member's lifetime.
- Eligibility for national awards (e.g., the student research paper awards provide cash prizes of $500, $300, and $200 to three winning students).
- Eligibility for these different annual awards: Building Bonds, Chapter Excellence, Chapter Community service, Individual Community Service, College Life Award, and Faculty Advisor.
- Publication of membership and activities in the nationally distributed Psi Beta Newsletter.
- Psi Beta offers the experience of operating a chapter and provides opportunities to acquire leadership skills, interact with faculty outside the classroom, learn more about the professional and educational choices available in psychology, meet outstanding professionals in psychology, participate in community service, meet peers with similar interests, and be involved with Psi Beta on the national level.
- Psi Beta membership contributes to the member's confidence and feelings of self-worth.
- Psi Beta offers the opportunity to participate in national, regional, and local psychological association programs, including paper and poster presentations at professional conferences.
- Psi Beta student members are eligible for student affiliate membership in the American Psychological Association (APA) and the Association for Psychological Science (APS).
- Psi Beta membership meets one of the requirements for entrance at the GS-7 level (2 levels higher) in numerous occupations in Federal service.

SOURCE: Psi Beta. (2018b). *Benefits of membership*. Retrieved from http://psibeta.org/site/students/benefits

Regional Associations

In addition to the national organizations described previously, there are a number of regional psychological associations that host annual conferences in psychology. Often this regional convention is more convenient and accessible for faculty members and students to attend. Each regional convention also encourages student involvement. Students can present oral papers and posters of their research—in fact, Psi Chi often hosts student-centered events at regional conventions. We encourage you to discuss with your faculty members the possibility of attending a regional convention. Even if you are not presenting research, attending a convention can have numerous benefits.

Table 7.8 Regional Psychological Associations and Websites

New England Psychological Association (NEPA) https://www.newenglandpsychological.org/
Eastern Psychological Association (EPA) https://www.easternpsychological.org/
Midwestern Psychological Association (MPA) https://www.midwesternpsych.org/
Rocky Mountain Psychological Association (RMPA) http://www.rockymountainpsych.com/
Southeastern Psychological Association (SEPA) http://www.sepaonline.com/
Southwestern Psychological Association (SWPA) http://www.swpsych.org/
Western Psychological Association (WPA) https://westernpsych.org/

In addition to exposing you to a wide variety of psychological topics and psychologists, conventions allow students to network with other students and faculty members. If you are interested in graduate school, you might be able to meet directly with faculty members from your school of interest who are attending the convention. Making paper or poster presentations also helps build your vita and helps to acculturate you to the way scientists exchange information and present diverging viewpoints. Attending a regional (or national) convention does involve a small financial investment, but if you are serious about psychology and your future, it is money well spent.

There are seven loosely organized "psychological" regions in the United States. We say loosely for a couple of reasons. First, sometimes a state is claimed by more than one region. Second, even though these regions are by definition "regional," many are more national in scope. You do not have to be from a particular region to attend that conference's regional convention. Thus, attendees at the Midwestern Psychological Association meeting (held in Chicago each year for some time now) are from all over the country. The seven regions and their associated websites are presented in Table 7.8. Note that these regions are not exactly the same regional designations as Psi Chi—Psi Chi divides the country into six regions, not seven, and Psi Chi has international chapters too.

One last recommendation is that you get involved in activities in your own department! Often during the academic year your department may sponsor guest speakers, or faculty members may participate in some sort of colloquium series (sometimes held over the lunchtime, these are called "brown bags"). As a student, you want your faculty to be supportive of your efforts—you also need to be supportive of the faculty. Attending such presentations also gives you a chance to hear about faculty research, which might interest you and lead to an opportunity to serve as a research assistant. Perhaps hearing about research being conducted at a homeless shelter in your community might inspire you to think about an internship. Attending these departmental events shows your commitment to psychology and your general interest in the happenings of the department.

Taking advantage of the opportunities highlighted in this chapter should lead to a better education and give you the skills, abilities, and knowledge to make you more marketable with your bachelor's degree or better qualified as a candidate for graduate school. It's up to you to seize the opportunity—now make it happen!

Exercise 7.1 The Undergraduate Research Questionnaire

Created by Taraban and Logue (2012), the Undergraduate Research Questionnaire (URQ) is designed to be an assessment given at the end of an undergraduate research experience. You can use this instrument in many ways; for instance, you could use this instrument

- before you decide to commit to serving as a research assistant, to anticipate whether or not you think you can achieve these goals;
- during your research assistant experience, to assess your progress and growth as a research assistant and then to make any mid-course corrections as needed; and
- after your undergraduate research experience (as the instrument was designed) to assess the experience.

The researchers identified five subsets or subcategories of questions: a research mindset, faculty support, research methods, an academic mindset, and peer support. There are no right or wrong answers to the items below. Answer honestly, and then we encourage you to reflect upon your answers. How was your research assistantship? How is it going? Do you think serving as an RA is for you?

	Amount of Agreement with Statement			
	Not at all	Slightly	Moderately	Extremely
Research Mindset				
Owing to my experience conducting research, I want to pursue a career in science.	○	○	○	○
My motivation to pursue a science career has increased.	○	○	○	○
It is important to be excited about science.	○	○	○	○
I am more interested in research due to my research experience.	○	○	○	○
The academic environment I am in encourages me to consider a research career.	○	○	○	○
My research experience has helped me think more scientifically.	○	○	○	○
Doing research is an important part of my undergraduate experience.	○	○	○	○
My self-confidence has increased due to my involvement in research.	○	○	○	○
Faculty Support				
A faculty member has encouraged me to excel in my coursework.	○	○	○	○
I received academic support from a faculty mentor.	○	○	○	○
A faculty member encouraged me in my academic goals.	○	○	○	○
A faculty member has been a good role model for me.	○	○	○	○
It has been easy to discuss ideas about career options with a faculty member.	○	○	○	○
It is easy to discuss ideas in my area of study with a faculty member.	○	○	○	○
A faculty member has given me useful feedback about my writing.	○	○	○	○
Research Methods				
I can design experiments.	○	○	○	○
I troubleshoot experiments.	○	○	○	○
I understand how to report experimental results.	○	○	○	○
Generating hypotheses is something I can do.	○	○	○	○
Data analysis is something I can do.	○	○	○	○
Carrying out experiments is something I can do.	○	○	○	○
Academic Mindset				
Being efficient in my academic work is something I have learned.	○	○	○	○
Balancing my class schedule with other obligations is something I have learned.	○	○	○	○
I have better time-management skills.	○	○	○	○
I have become more independent academically.	○	○	○	○
I have developed a routine for completing my schoolwork.	○	○	○	○
I have become more academically responsible.	○	○	○	○
Peer Support				
Other students have encouraged me to excel in my coursework.	○	○	○	○
Other students have helped me clarify my professional goals.	○	○	○	○
Other students have been good role models for me.	○	○	○	○
I have received academic support from students in my major.	○	○	○	○
Fellow students gave me useful feedback about my oral presentations.	○	○	○	○

Exercise 7.2 Predictions of College Success after Graduation

Recently, the Gallup organization and Purdue University have been collaborating on an American-based survey of 30,000 college alumni from all majors, asking questions about work engagement, survival, social, physical, financial, and community well-being (Busteed, 2015). Alumni who report long-term success—feeling well-prepared for life after college, frequently experiencing feelings of well-being and engagement at work. As it turns out, there are six key (statistically significant) predictors of alumni success; they are:

Check ✓	Success Factor
	A professor who made them excited about learning.
	Professors who cared about them as a person.
✓	A mentor who encouraged them to pursue their goals and dreams.
	Worked on a long-term project.
	Had a job or internship where they applied what they were learning.
	Were extremely involved in extracurricular activities.

SOURCE: Busteed, B. (2015). Is college worth it? That depends. *Gallup, Inc.* Retrieved from https://news.gallup.com/opinion/gallup/182312/college-worth-depends.aspx

It is important to realize that these are not items that are achieved in a day. Furthermore, this is not a cause and event situation; this is a predictive relationship. That is, the behaviors in the checklist, when checked, go with the pattern or profile of individuals that Busteed (2015) and the Gallup-Purdue researchers found to be statistically related. It's always important to remember that correlation does not equal causation. Please read carefully the six statement presented as success factors. Rate each one to the extent that you could strongly agree with that statement now.

There are no right or wrong answers. Check back in six months or one year and see if your answers have changed. Evaluate and reflect on what may or may not have changed over time.

Chapter 8
Sharpening Your Research Skills

Learning Objectives

8.1 Generate research topics using idea guidelines

8.2 Explain the importance of literature research

8.3 Identify challenges in working with references

8.4 Summarize strategies for narrowing down research topics

8.5 Outline international standards for information literacy

8.6 Summarize how to locate books relevant to a research topic

8.7 Explain how journal articles work in a psychology context

8.8 Evaluate Internet-based materials for credibility

8.9 Describe common literature search strategies

8.10 Determine the use of Google and Wikipedia in research

Beginning with this chapter and continuing throughout the rest of this book, we focus on the skills and abilities needed to navigate the psychology major and strategies to be a successful college student. In this chapter, we focus on how to find research that exists and generate ideas for research; in Chapter 9 we address how to write about research. Before we address how to find research that is complete, you need to know what you are looking for. Sometimes, this task might be a paper or study idea that your instructor assigns, but you may also be asked to generate your own ideas for research projects (such as in an independent study, senior thesis, or perhaps even in a research methods/experimental design course).

Generating Research Ideas

8.1 Generate research topics using idea guidelines

Students are sometimes stumped when faculty ask them about their own ideas for research. How do you get these ideas? How do experimental psychologists get ideas for doing research? The following guidelines, based in part on Martin (1991), should give you some starting points in thinking about topics to study:

Observation. Just look at the world around you and feel free to tap into your own interests. If you enjoy people-watching, go watch and be willing to wonder about their behavior and why people behave the way they do. Remember that better questions to be asked in a research-type format are (a) repeatable, (b) observable, and (c) testable.

Vicarious observation. Vicarious observation is a sophisticated way of saying observe through the observations of others. Simply put, read about research that is complete and then think about follow-up studies that are needed. Find a psychological journal in the library with articles in your favorite subject area, and look for ideas and issues to explore.

Expand on your own previous ideas. Perhaps in other courses you have written a paper, finished a project, studied a topic, or heard a lecture that you found especially interesting. Why not pursue that avenue of interest through a research project?

Focus on a practical problem. Many students select topics that are of practical, everyday concern as opposed to theoretical, basic research. Select a facet of real life that interests you, and study it systematically as your research project.

When you work with a faculty member on a research project, you may not be able to select what you want to study. In fact, that faculty member might want you to generate research ideas specific to her or his research domain. In that case, much of the work is already focused for you—what will be important here (and with every project) is that you have a firm understanding of the literature. Hence, the literature review is a critical component of the research project.

Success Stories

Regan A. R. Gurung

A Bombay Boy Makes Good

I almost did not make it to college. Growing up in Bombay, India, I yearned for an American college education because of the intellectual choice it afforded. I knew I could get to study a variety of subjects and decide what I wanted to do. In India, I was to be slotted into one discipline right after 12th grade. The problem? In those days, there were no scholarships for foreign students. Paying for it myself seemed out of question coming from a poor family. But I persevered and relied on the support of friends and family. One family friend in particular had graduated from an American college and loved her experience. Apply to Carleton College in Northfield, MN, she said. I had already looked it up and decided against it due to the high cost. Fear not she said, apply anyway. Get in and I will help you get there.

I applied to what became my dream school, a liberal arts college that promised intellectual challenges and the springboard to the career of my dreams. I still remember the December I received the notification that I had got in (I had applied early decision). I ran to my friend's house to share the news and hope she could work the promised magic. She did. She got on the phone and contacted friends from her graduating class and within months I had a full scholarship to Carleton courtesy of alumni of the school (thank you Betty and Bill Hulings and Nuvart Mehta!).

If I had just given up and settled for something local I would not have the career I have had. Carleton widened my mind, gave me the skills to me a successful academic, and inspired me to be a passionate teacher. It all came down to not giving up and chasing down options to get where I wanted. Sure, good fortune and chance played a part in that my friend had some good friends. But I have realized that chance favors those prepared to work. Even today, I know that my chances of getting a paper accepted or a grant approved increase with the greater number of papers and proposals I submit. If we do not try and increase our chances of success, good things are less likely to happen.

Follow your passion and do not underestimate the power of your support networks.

The Literature Review

8.2 Explain the importance of literature research

Each author who publishes in a scholarly journal reviews prior, relevant studies and develops the background to the problem of interest. This introductory portion of the journal article is called the literature review. By reviewing previous research, you set the theoretical foundation for your topic. The author also discusses why the present study is valuable and states the hypotheses to be tested. This section organizes the previous research you identified as important.

Sometimes new researchers are so excited about the prospects of doing their own original research that they minimize or overlook the importance of the literature search. If you try to skip this step, it could be very costly in terms of your investment of time and energy to complete a research project. Also, if you have long-term goals of presenting the outcomes of your research at a professional conference or submitting a manuscript for publication, it will be necessary for you to have done your homework; that is, review the literature and place your current work in the context of your particular specialty area within psychology. There are a number of benefits that accrue from reviewing the literature:

- Maybe someone has already done something very similar. Why re-invent the wheel? Although there are a number of areas in psychology that are not well understood (hence ripe for new research), other areas in the field are fairly well understood. You won't know which is which unless you review the literature.
- Depending on the course or the assignment, it might be perfectly appropriate to repeat a study that has been done before—this is called a *replication*. Replication studies are very important in psychology (Earp & Trafimow, 2015; Makel, Plucker, & Hegarty, 2012). If you repeat a study that has been conducted before, but you add a new twist (such as a new variable), the phrase often heard for this is "replication and extension."
- Other investigators might have already identified some of the key challenges to doing research in a particular area. Learn from their efforts and avoid their mistakes. Many publications end with a discussion of where future research should go—you might get an idea for your own research project just by reading and understanding what has already been done.
- New ideas in psychology (in any science) must fit within the framework of existing ideas and theories. New theories can put forward new information, but those theories also must explain why former theories were wrong, inaccurate, or inappropriate. To be able to do the latter, you must be familiar with those former theories—hence the importance of the literature review. By the way, *completely* new and original ideas are fairly rare.

The Special Role of References

8.3 Identify challenges in working with references

The references listed at the conclusion of a research article make the cited literature accessible to the reader. This documentation enables other scholars to locate and explore firsthand the prior research or theoretical sources that constitute the framework for the current research. The reference section is critically important to many readers because it is a demonstration of the scholarly nature of your work. The scientist and the critical thinker examine and use evidence to support ideas and contentions; you provide your evidence in the reference section (as well as in the results section). When you cite a source, be sure you are familiar with the article. It can be a dangerous practice to cite references that you have never seen or read. This type of citation (citing something without having read it) is called a secondary source, and there are specific ways to list such references. Be careful: Your instructor just might be familiar with that reference. You should note that the references list is *not* a bibliography. Bibliographies refer the interested reader to additional sources for further reading that were not necessarily cited in the manuscript through paraphrasing or direct quotation, and are not used in American Psychological Association (APA)-style manuscripts. Remember that the reference section contains *only* the articles directly cited in the text of the paper, and all articles cited in the text of the paper are included in the reference list. At the top of the list of your references, use the word References—and *not* Works Cited.

Research Strategies

8.4 Summarize strategies for narrowing down research topics

At some level you have to choose or select a research topic. Again, your faculty supervisor may dictate this choice, or it could be an assigned class project. Nevertheless, you will probably have some range of topics to select from within your specific areas of interest. The list in Table 8.1 (from University of California–Santa Cruz 1998; Vanderbilt University, 1996) should help in your choice of a topic. Inevitably, this choice also involves the next step, which is finding the background information.

There are numerous research strategies that you can use to find useful information. In the remainder of this section we will cover how to (a) make the best use of books, (b) find journal articles, (c) use the Internet, and (d) use other strategies with which savvy researchers are familiar.

Perhaps one of the best tips we can offer is to be sure to utilize the reference librarians who may be available to you if you are on a physical campus. Not only can they help you determine the library's holdings, but they can also offer additional, specific search strategies for your particular library. Of course, the Internet has become a powerful source of information, but using this resource requires caution. Later in this chapter, we will offer some guidelines concerning the evaluation of Internet information.

Table 8.1 Tips for Selecting a Research Topic

Try not to choose a topic that is too broad.
Choose a topic that is of interest to you—and also choose an additional backup topic.
Choose a topic that will enable you to read and understand the literature.
Choose a topic that has resources available—check this before making a commitment if you can.
Make sure that the resources are available in time for you to meet your deadlines.
Read through the background information.
If there is not enough information available, you may want to go to your backup topic.
State your topic idea as a question—this will help you outline and frame your paper.
Start making a list of key words to use in later searches.

Information Literacy

8.5 Outline international standards for information literacy

An alternative title to this chapter could have been "information literacy," because a person's research skills indeed are a key component of broad idea of information literacy. In fact, there are a cluster of skills often grouped together known as information and communication technology, which comprised information literacy (as in the ability to find and use information), Internet literacy (as a communication form), and computer literacy (as a mode of technology) (Lau and Yuen, 2014). As you can imagine, librarians and others who teach research skills are interested in information literacy standards (Association of College and Research Libraries, 2016) and techniques to assess those skills (Cameron et al., 2007; Whitlock & Ebrahimi, 2016). To begin to appreciate the complex skills involved regarding information literacy, see Table 8.2.

Following this broad overview of information literacy skills, we delve now into some specific strategies that may be useful to you as you review the available literature on a topic of interest.

Table 8.2 The Three International Standards for Information Literacy

I. **Access.** The user accesses information effectively and efficiently
   A. Defines or recognizes the need for information
      1. Decides to do something to find the information
      2. Express and defines the information need
      3. Initiates the search process
   B. Location of information
      1. Identifies and evaluates potential sources of information
      2. Develops search strategies
      3. Accesses the selected information sources
      4. Selects and retrieves the located information

II. **Evaluation.** The user evaluates information critically and competently
   A. Assessment of information
      1. Analyzes, examines, and extracts information
      2. Generalizes and interprets information
      3. Selects and synthesizes information
      4. Evaluates accuracy and relevance of the retrieved information
   B. Organization of information
      1. Arranges and categorizes information
      2. Groups and organizes the retrieved information
      3. Determines which is the best and most useful information

III. **Use**. The user applies/uses information accurately and creatively.
   A. Use of information
      1. Finds new ways to communicate, present, and use information
      2. Applies the retrieved information
      3. Learns or internalizes information as personal knowledge
      4. Presents the information product
   B. Communication and ethical use of information
      1. Understands ethical use of information
      2. Respects the legal use of information
      3. Communicates the learning product with acknowledgment of intellectual property
      4. Uses the relevant acknowledgment style standards

SOURCE: Lau, J. (2006). *Guidelines on information literacy for lifelong learning*. Boca del Rio, Veracruz, Mexico: International Federation of Library Associations and Institutions. Retrieved from http://www.ifla.org/files/assets/information-literacy/publications/ifla-guidelines-en.pdf

Books

8.6 Summarize how to locate books relevant to a research topic

With respect to *books*, there are at least two avenues to pursue. First, there are general reference books that can lead you to other sources, and then there are specific books in psychology that may be written about your topic. To find books in the latter category, you can use the search methods for finding journal articles that we discuss in the next section.

In addition to these resources, your university library has an online database that contains the inventory of the library. Terminals for access to this database are probably located in the library and around campus, but, in most cases, Internet access provides the same level of access as being in the physical library facility. In courses where research is time-dependent, you may want to get a jump-start on your library literature search because some of the books and journal articles that you need may not be available in your library. You can usually obtain these materials through *interlibrary loan*, but depending on where this information has to come from, your request may take some time (and more time than you have). Also, do not overlook other libraries in your community, such as the public library, other college and university libraries in your region, or perhaps even a hospital or law school library. Note that if you attend a state school, you may have borrowing privileges at other state colleges and universities. Most college and university libraries are organized using the Library of Congress Cataloging System, and a quick Google search will give you access to the Library of Congress Classification Codes. To find psychology titles quicker, look for codes starting with BF, HM, or LB.

Journal Articles

8.7 Explain how journal articles work in a psychology context

Although books are an important resource for information, perhaps the most important communication mode of the results of psychological research comes in the form of journal articles. Journals have a timelier publication frequency, can reach large numbers of people, have a rigorous acceptance and publication process, and are a well-established means of information distribution. There are hundreds of journals in psychology that publish 4, 6, or 12 issues per year (i.e., per volume).

As a psychology major, if you have not started reading psychology journal articles on a regular basis yet, you will soon start reading these articles. When you read your first journal article, you immediately notice some important differences in relation to regular magazine articles; it may seem as if a journal article follows a quirky set of rules. The rules that dictate how articles are to be written in psychology are found in the 6th edition of the *Publication Manual of the American Psychological Association* (American Psychological Association, 2010). Knowledge of the APA format rules will help you in reading psychological research and is essential for success in writing your own research papers in psychology—more on this topic in Chapter 9.

How is a journal article different from a magazine article? Perhaps the fundamental difference between a magazine and a journal is how the article is published. Journals in psychology operate under a *peer review system* where several professionals review article submissions before an acceptance decision is made. Let's say that you wanted to publish the results of your research. After selecting a journal to send your manuscript to (not always an easy task—although if you have access to *APA Academic Writer* on your campus, it may be a bit easier), you would send multiple copies to the journal editor. You may submit a manuscript to only one journal at a time. The editor sends copies of your manuscript out for review. Here is where the review process begins. The editor asks your peers in the field (other psychologists or content area experts) to review your manuscript and decide if it is suitable for publication. The peers are also called referees, and sometimes you hear the phrase "refereed journal" (which means the journal follows this peer review process). See an example of the first page of a journal article on p. 126.

How does an individual reviewer evaluate a manuscript? (To be clear about terminology, authors submit a manuscript in hopes that it will be accepted; this accepted manuscript becomes a journal article.) The answer to this question varies across journals and individuals, but in general, scholarship is the key. For the manuscript to be considered scholarly there should be a thorough review of the literature, a keen grasp of the subject matter, concise writing, adequate research skills, demonstrated importance of the work to psychology, and an understanding of the journal readership (the journal subscribers). Often reviewers are individuals with prior success in publishing their own manuscripts. Once the editor has received the reviews, a decision must be made whether to accept the paper, suggest that the author make some revisions and resubmit, or reject the paper. Journals go through this long, tedious, and expensive process to select the articles to be published (by the way, reviewers typically do not get paid for this service, and reviews are often done anonymously). This procedure is as fair and objective as possible. Also, in an effort to keep the process fair, the author of the manuscript typically does not know the identity of the reviewers and sometimes the reviewers may not know the name(s) of the author(s) (i.e., a blind review).

This process also differs from a magazine in that magazines pay people to write articles; authors of journal articles are not paid and sometimes even help defray the cost of journal publishing. Whereas magazine articles may be checked for accuracy, they do not undergo the same scrutiny, examination, and review as journal articles. The majority of journal articles are well documented with supporting references noted as to when an idea has been adopted from another source (academics must avoid plagiarism just as students must avoid plagiarism). A magazine article is rarely as extensive in documenting the academic and scholarly work of the author. Another difference between the two is that journals are typically not available for purchase at a bookstore but must be subscribed to, whereas magazines are typically available at a bookstore. However, magazines can be a great resource if you are trying to *get* some ideas about research topics.

Now that you are familiar with journal articles, where do you find them? The best place to begin your search is the library, either in the brick-and-mortar facility or search it electronically. Academic journals are expensive (and international journals can be *extremely* expensive), and your library likely subscribes to selected journals of particular interest to faculty and students. Care and respect should be given to these resources. Never tear or cut any page out of a journal, and take the journal out of the library only if permissible and if necessary. When you photocopy an article, always copy the entire reference section. Sometimes students try to cut corners by not copying the references, and often regret it later; those references are valuable sources of information on your topic. Libraries often subscribe to journals electronically. That is, you can search your library electronically and may be able to retrieve articles as a PDF or HTML file. Also realize that some of your faculty members may subscribe to particular journals—ask to see if someone in your department already has access to the information you need.

The key component of the database for searching the psychological literature is a product called *PsycINFO.* Although this service provides a great deal of convenience for the user, one additional benefit is that the journal database has been expanded to an index of psychological articles published since the 1800s. In *PsycINFO,* you can print out the bibliographic citation as well as the abstract, and you can use search operators (e.g., "and," "or," "not"). Also, some APA journals also have full-text versions available over the Internet. For more information about the variety of costs and services available to psychology students, check the APA website at www.apa.org. You need to be sure to get the complete article and read it before you write about it in a paper. You *cannot* write a good research paper from a stack of abstracts. But using *PsycINFO* through your school's library may provide some direct links to access certain articles that may be available online.

Journal of Applied Psychology
2016, Vol. 101, No. 2, 190–208

0021-9010/16/$12.00 http://dx.doi.org/10.1037/apl0000047

Intervention Effects on Safety Compliance and Citizenship Behaviors: Evidence From the Work, Family, and Health Study

Leslie B. Hammer
Portland State University

Ryan C. Johnson
Ohio University

Tori L. Crain and Todd Bodner
Portland State University

Ellen Ernst Kossek
Purdue University

Kelly D. Davis
Pennsylvania State University

Erin L. Kelly
University of Minnesota

Orfeu M. Buxton
Pennsylvania State University and Harvard Medical School

Georgia Karuntzos
RTI International, Research Triangle Park, North Carolina

L. Casey Chosewood
Centers for Disease Control and Prevention, Atlanta, Georgia

Lisa Berkman
Harvard University

We tested the effects of a work–family intervention on employee reports of safety compliance and organizational citizenship behaviors in 30 health care facilities using a group-randomized trial. Based on conservation of resources theory and the work–home resources model, we hypothesized that implementing a work–family intervention aimed at increasing contextual resources via supervisor support for work and family, and employee control over work time, would lead to improved personal resources and increased employee performance on the job in the form of self-reported safety compliance and organizational citizenship behaviors. Multilevel analyses used survey data from 1,524 employees at baseline and at 6-month and 12-month postintervention follow-ups. Significant intervention effects were observed for safety compliance at the 6-month, and organizational citizenship behaviors at the 12-month, follow-ups. More specifically, results demonstrate that the intervention protected against declines in employee self-reported safety compliance and organizational citizenship behaviors compared with employees in the control facilities. The hypothesized mediators of perceptions of family-supportive supervisor behaviors, control over work time, and work–family conflict (work-to-family conflict, family-to-work conflict) were not significantly improved by the intervention. However, baseline perceptions of family-supportive supervisor behaviors, control over work time, and work–family climate were significant moderators of

This article was published Online First September 7, 2015.

Leslie B. Hammer, Department of Psychology, Portland State University; Ryan C. Johnson, Department of Psychology, Ohio University; Tori L. Crain and Todd Bodner, Department of Psychology, Portland State University; Ellen Ernst Kossek, Krannert School of Management, Purdue University; Kelly D. Davis, Human Development and Family Studies, Pennsylvania State University; Erin L. Kelly, Department of Sociology, University of Minnesota; Orfeu M. Buxton, Department of Biobehavioral Health, Pennsylvania State University, Division of Sleep Medicine, Harvard Medical School, Boston, Massachusetts; Georgia Karuntzos, RTI International, Research Triangle Park, North Carolina; L. Casey Chosewood, National Institute for Occupational Safety and Health (NIOSH), Centers for Disease Control and Prevention, Atlanta, Georgia; Lisa Berkman, Harvard School of Public Health, Harvard University.

Tori L. Crain is now at the Department of Psychology, Colorado State University. Kelly D. Davis is now at Oregon State University. Erin L. Kelly is now at the MIT Sloan School of Management.

This research was conducted as part of the Work, Family and Health Network (www.WorkFamilyHealthNetwork.org), which is funded by a cooperative agreement through the National Institutes of Health and the Centers for Disease Control and Prevention: Eunice Kennedy Shriver National Institute of Child Health and Human Development (Grant # U01HD051217, U01HD051218, U01HD051256, U01HD051276); National Institute on Aging (Grant # U01AG027669); the National Heart, Lung, and Blood Institute (R01HL107240); Office of Behavioral and Social Sciences Research; and National Institute for Occupational Safety and Health (Grant # U01OH008788, U01HD059773). Grants from the William T. Grant Foundation, Alfred P. Sloan Foundation, and the Administration for Children and Families have provided additional funding. The contents of this publication are solely the responsibility of the authors and do not necessarily represent the official views of these institutes and offices. Special acknowledgment goes to Extramural Staff Science Collaborator, Rosalind Berkowitz King, PhD, and Lynne Casper, PhD, for design of the original Workplace, Family, Health and Well-Being Network Initiative. The findings and conclusions in this manuscript are those of the authors and do not necessarily represent the views of these institutes and offices.

Correspondence concerning this article should be addressed to Leslie B. Hammer, Department of Psychology, Portland State University, 1721 SW Broadway Street, Portland, OR 97207. E-mail: hammerl@pdx.edu

SOURCES: Hammer, L. B., Johnson, R. C., Crain, T. L., Bodner, T., Kossek, E. E., Davis, K. D., et al. (2016). Intervention effects on safety compliance and citizenship behaviors: Evidence from the work, family, and health study. Journal of Applied Psychology, 101(2), 190–208.

The Internet and Evaluating Information

8.8 Evaluate Internet-based materials for credibility

The Internet is an important source of information about psychology and life in general. Caution should be used in interpreting information taken from the Internet. In particular, look for the same signs of scholarship that you would expect to find from a scholarly research article or from a legitimate scientific entity: accuracy, authority, objectivity and reliability, and currency (Brandeis University, 1998). Look for information from reliable sources, such as professional organizations (e.g., APA, Association for Psychological Science [APS], and Psi Chi) or from colleges and universities. Although you should evaluate *any* type of information critically, Internet materials necessitate additional scrutiny. It is easy for anyone to post to the Internet and make it universally accessible—it is not nearly so easy to start your own peer-reviewed scholarly research journal and publish it yourself. It's hard to know where this is originated, but librarians and others who teach about information literacy often refer to the CRAAP Test (e.g., Meriam Library, 2010; University of Iowa, 2011; University of the Fraser Valley, 2009). This stands for currency, relevance, authority, accuracy, and purpose. For more details about the CRAAP test, see Table 8.3.

Table 8.3 The CRAAP Test for Evaluating Information

CURRENCY: the timeliness of the source and the information	• When was the information posted? • When was it last revised? • Are links functional and up-to-date? • Is there evidence of newly added information or links? • Is the information still considered accurate? Has more recent research challenged this information? Don't exclude articles or information because of the publication date; instead think about the currency and relevance of the arguments presented.
RELEVANCE/COVERAGE: the importance and scope of the information	• Does the information relate to your topic or answer your question? • Is the topic covered with sufficient depth and breadth? Is the information comprehensive enough for your needs? Are the complexities of your topic adequately addressed? • Could you find the same or better information in another source? • Is the information relevant to current scholarly discussions on the topic? Do scholars refer to this source?
AUTHORITY: the source of the information	• Is the author/sponsor clearly identified? Is contact information easy to find? • What are the author's credentials? Is the author knowledgeable in his/her field (based on employment, publications, sponsorship by reputable organizations)? • Has the author published works in traditional formats? (Look up the authors in Google Scholar.) • Is the author affiliated with an organization? Does this organization appear to support or sponsor the page? (Google the authors and/or sponsoring organizations.) • What does the sponsoring site (e.g., www.noaa.gov, www.uiowa.edu) and domain name (e.g., .com .edu .gov .org .net) reveal about the source of the information, if anything?
ACCURACY: the reliability, truthfulness, and correctness of the content	• Where does the information come from? Can you verify any of the information in independent sources or from your own knowledge? • Are the original sources of information listed? • longitude • What evidence is presented to support claims made? • Has the information been reviewed or refereed? • Does the language or tone seem objective and unbiased? • Is the information free of spelling, grammar, and typographical errors?
PURPOSE: the reason that the web site exists	• Is the purpose of the page stated? Is the purpose to: inform? teach? entertain? enlighten? sell? persuade? Are possible biases clearly stated? • Is advertising content vs. informational content easily distinguishable? • Are editorials/opinion pieces clearly labeled?

SOURCES: Meriam Library. (2010). *Evaluating information—Applying the CRAAP Test*. Retrieved from https://www.csuchico.edu/lins/handouts/eval_websites.pdf; University of Iowa. (2011). *Evaluate information online: The CRAAP test*. Retrieved from http://www.lib.uiowa.edu/instruction/; University of the Fraser Valley. (2009). *Evaluating information: The CRAAP test*. Retrieved from http://www.ufv.ca/library/tutorials/craaptest.htm

Next time you are asked to retrieve information for an assignment, think about applying one or more of these criteria to the information you retrieved. To be a critical thinker is to be skeptical, not cynical. It is better to ask questions before drawing conclusions than to be apologizing for making mistakes because you misinterpreted misleading or perhaps even patently false information.

More Literature Search Strategies

8.9 Describe common literature search strategies

There are a handful of other strategies that you can use in your search for prior research. *Treeing* is a technique that can be used forward and backward. To tree backward through your references, try to find a great, current article that is right on target with your research idea—then look at that article's reference section. You may find some good leads in the articles you already have. Don't forget about textbooks—they have reference sections that you can use to tree backward. Also remember that you can ask faculty members. If you are at a larger institution, your department may have graduate students who might be quite knowledgeable about your particular topic or just be helpful with information search strategies in general. Other students, including senior-level psychology majors, may also be excellent sources of research tips.

Treeing forward through the references can involve the use of another bibliographic resource, which is called the Web of Science (you should be able to set up a free account at webofknowledge.com). To tree forward, find a classic article that is commonly referenced in your field of study—perhaps a major article that shaped the direction of research since it was published. By using the Web of Science, you can look at all the authors of articles who have cited that classic article since it was published. That is, you can find the more current information related to your area of interest by looking for other researchers who cited that classic article, and then obtain their publications. Web of Science is a valuable resource, and personally, we think undergraduates do not use it as much as they should. Want to set yourself apart from the crowd? Learn how to use this resource and become a major asset to your research supervisor. Here we show a couple of screenshots that of Web of Science at work. In the first screenshot, we show an author search to find the article of interest. In this case, we are interested in who has cited Leon Festinger's 1954 classic regarding cognitive dissonance.

If you look in the left column under 'Analyze Results,' you will find his very popular work. At the time of this search, his 1954 classic article appearing in the journal *Human Relations* had been cited by others 7,114 times. Because one of your authors (REL) did this search logged in as a Boise State University faculty member, you see the logo *B* and **Find It** buttons, as one could go retrieve the article. But that is not the real value of Web of Science. By clicking on the hyperlinked number 7,114, we can see a listing of all the articles that have cited Festinger (1954). The next screenshot shows just an example of what those results would look like.

Just by a cursory examination of the titles and the sheer volume of reference citations, it appears that cognitive dissonance is one of those psychological phenomena that continues to influence researchers today. As we hope you can see, Web of Science is an incredibly powerful information extraction tool.

A less-powerful but more readily available search approach is to use Google Scholar, which is available to everyone, and does not require an institutional affiliation (as Web of Science sometimes does). Google Scholar will identify journal articles, books, and book chapters related to your topic. The Google Scholar is certainly a good and quick way to start a search, and it is more "academic" if you will than a singular Google search. If you were to conduct a Google Scholar search on Leon Festinger, the results screen might look like this:

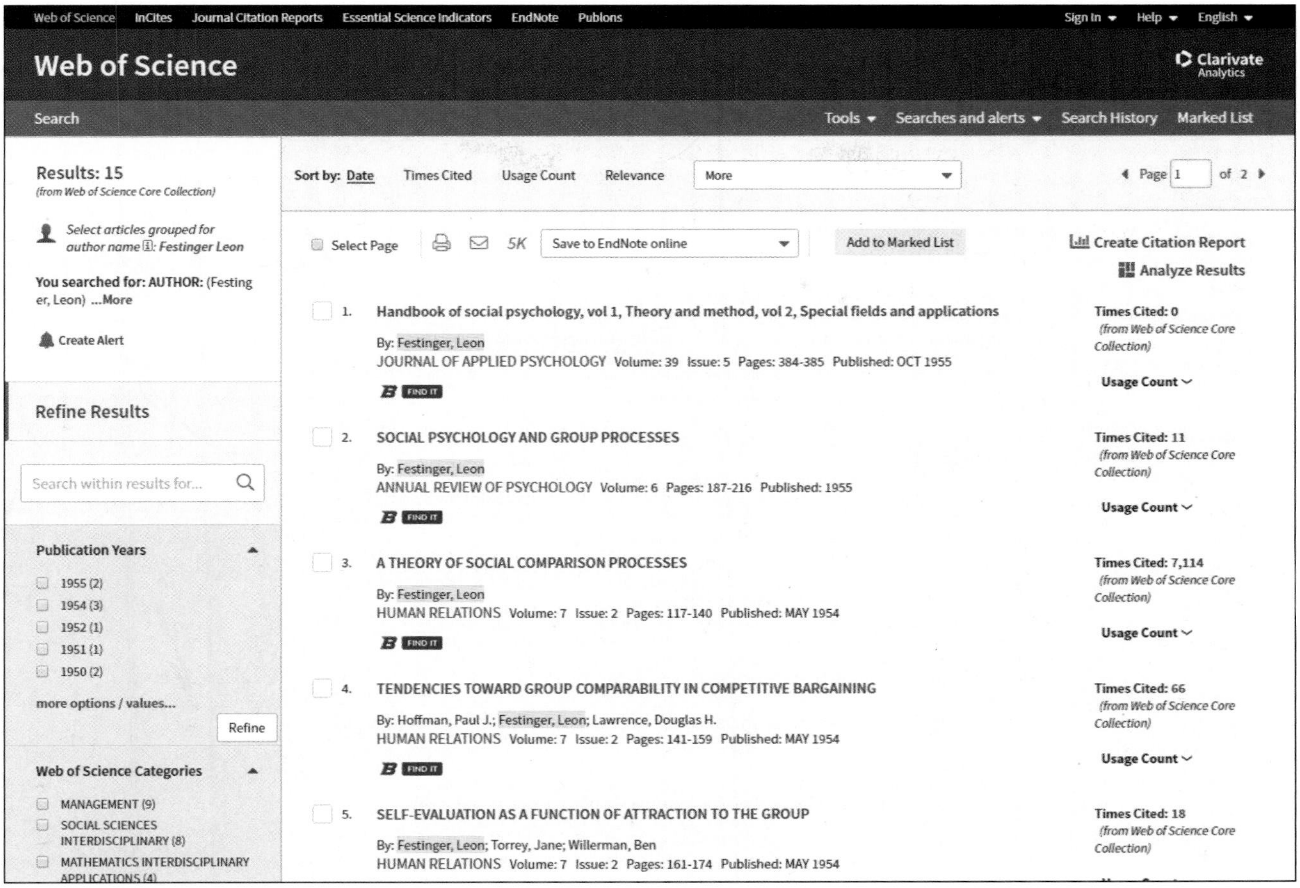
Web of Science InCites Journal Citation Reports Essential Science Indicators EndNote Publons
Sign In Help English
Web of Science
Clarivate Analytics
Search
Tools Searches and alerts Search History Marked List
Results: 15
(from Web of Science Core Collection)
Select articles grouped for author name: Festinger Leon
You searched for: AUTHOR: (Festinger, Leon) ...More
Create Alert
Refine Results
Search within results for...
Publication Years
1955 (2)
1954 (3)
1952 (1)
1951 (1)
1950 (2)
more options / values...
Refine
Web of Science Categories
MANAGEMENT (9)
SOCIAL SCIENCES INTERDISCIPLINARY (8)
MATHEMATICS INTERDISCIPLINARY APPLICATIONS (4)
Sort by: Date Times Cited Usage Count Relevance More
Page 1 of 2
Select Page 5K Save to EndNote online Add to Marked List
Create Citation Report
Analyze Results
1. Handbook of social psychology, vol 1, Theory and method, vol 2, Special fields and applications
By: Festinger, Leon
JOURNAL OF APPLIED PSYCHOLOGY Volume: 39 Issue: 5 Pages: 384-385 Published: OCT 1955
Times Cited: 0 (from Web of Science Core Collection)
Usage Count
2. SOCIAL PSYCHOLOGY AND GROUP PROCESSES
By: Festinger, Leon
ANNUAL REVIEW OF PSYCHOLOGY Volume: 6 Pages: 187-216 Published: 1955
Times Cited: 11 (from Web of Science Core Collection)
Usage Count
3. A THEORY OF SOCIAL COMPARISON PROCESSES
By: Festinger, Leon
HUMAN RELATIONS Volume: 7 Issue: 2 Pages: 117-140 Published: MAY 1954
Times Cited: 7,114 (from Web of Science Core Collection)
Usage Count
4. TENDENCIES TOWARD GROUP COMPARABILITY IN COMPETITIVE BARGAINING
By: Hoffman, Paul J.; Festinger, Leon; Lawrence, Douglas H.
HUMAN RELATIONS Volume: 7 Issue: 2 Pages: 141-159 Published: MAY 1954
Times Cited: 66 (from Web of Science Core Collection)
Usage Count
5. SELF-EVALUATION AS A FUNCTION OF ATTRACTION TO THE GROUP
By: Festinger, Leon; Torrey, Jane; Willerman, Ben
HUMAN RELATIONS Volume: 7 Issue: 2 Pages: 161-174 Published: MAY 1954
Times Cited: 18 (from Web of Science Core Collection)

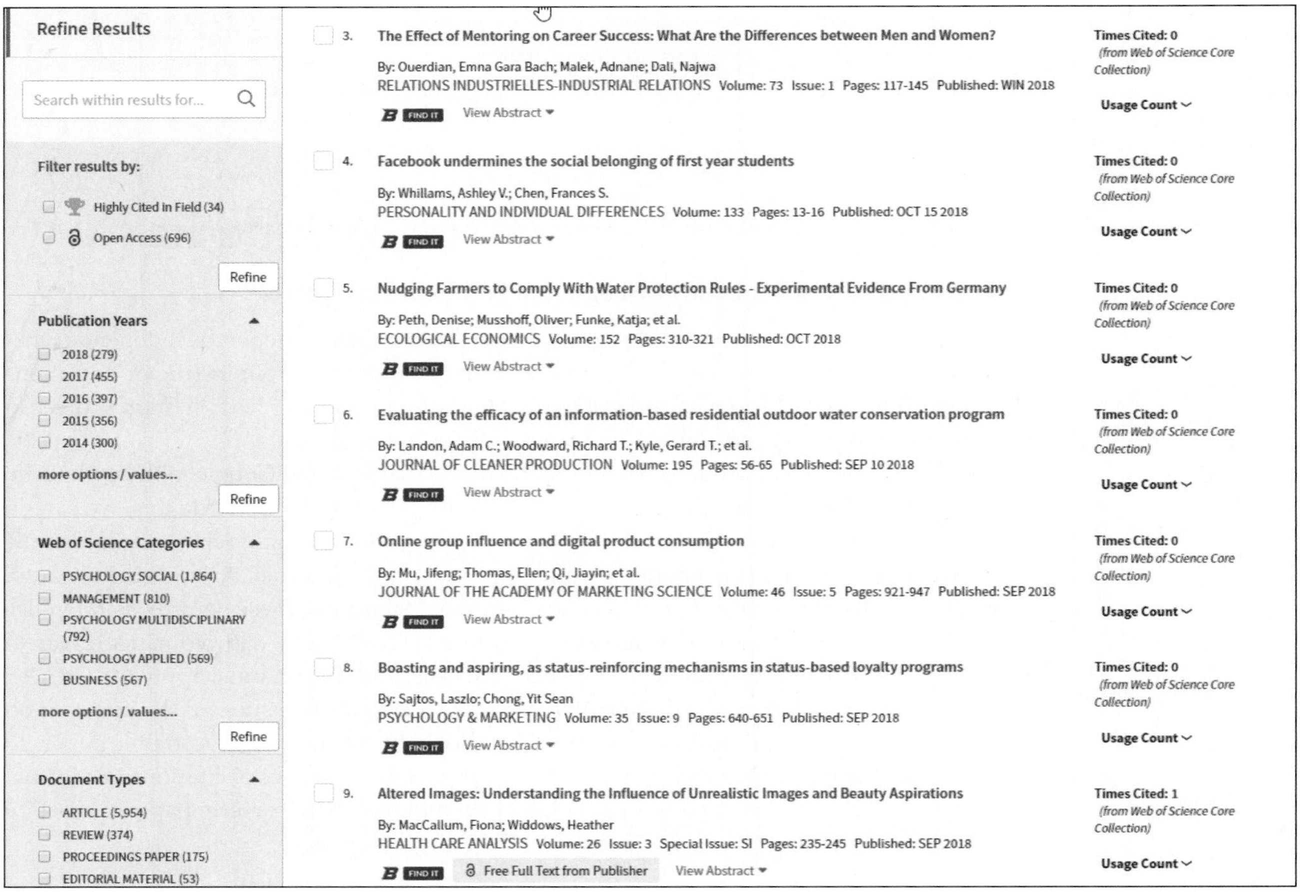
Refine Results
Search within results for...
Filter results by:
Highly Cited in Field (34)
Open Access (696)
Refine
Publication Years
2018 (279)
2017 (455)
2016 (397)
2015 (356)
2014 (300)
more options / values...
Refine
Web of Science Categories
PSYCHOLOGY SOCIAL (1,864)
MANAGEMENT (810)
PSYCHOLOGY MULTIDISCIPLINARY (792)
PSYCHOLOGY APPLIED (569)
BUSINESS (567)
more options / values...
Refine
Document Types
ARTICLE (5,954)
REVIEW (374)
PROCEEDINGS PAPER (175)
EDITORIAL MATERIAL (53)
3. The Effect of Mentoring on Career Success: What Are the Differences between Men and Women?
By: Ouerdian, Emna Gara Bach; Malek, Adnane; Dali, Najwa
RELATIONS INDUSTRIELLES-INDUSTRIAL RELATIONS Volume: 73 Issue: 1 Pages: 117-145 Published: WIN 2018
View Abstract
Times Cited: 0 (from Web of Science Core Collection)
Usage Count
4. Facebook undermines the social belonging of first year students
By: Whillams, Ashley V.; Chen, Frances S.
PERSONALITY AND INDIVIDUAL DIFFERENCES Volume: 133 Pages: 13-16 Published: OCT 15 2018
View Abstract
Times Cited: 0 (from Web of Science Core Collection)
Usage Count
5. Nudging Farmers to Comply With Water Protection Rules - Experimental Evidence From Germany
By: Peth, Denise; Musshoff, Oliver; Funke, Katja; et al.
ECOLOGICAL ECONOMICS Volume: 152 Pages: 310-321 Published: OCT 2018
View Abstract
Times Cited: 0 (from Web of Science Core Collection)
Usage Count
6. Evaluating the efficacy of an information-based residential outdoor water conservation program
By: Landon, Adam C.; Woodward, Richard T.; Kyle, Gerard T.; et al.
JOURNAL OF CLEANER PRODUCTION Volume: 195 Pages: 56-65 Published: SEP 10 2018
View Abstract
Times Cited: 0 (from Web of Science Core Collection)
Usage Count
7. Online group influence and digital product consumption
By: Mu, Jifeng; Thomas, Ellen; Qi, Jiayin; et al.
JOURNAL OF THE ACADEMY OF MARKETING SCIENCE Volume: 46 Issue: 5 Pages: 921-947 Published: SEP 2018
View Abstract
Times Cited: 0 (from Web of Science Core Collection)
Usage Count
8. Boasting and aspiring, as status-reinforcing mechanisms in status-based loyalty programs
By: Sajtos, Laszlo; Chong, Yit Sean
PSYCHOLOGY & MARKETING Volume: 35 Issue: 9 Pages: 640-651 Published: SEP 2018
View Abstract
Times Cited: 0 (from Web of Science Core Collection)
Usage Count
9. Altered Images: Understanding the Influence of Unrealistic Images and Beauty Aspirations
By: MacCallum, Fiona; Widdows, Heather
HEALTH CARE ANALYSIS Volume: 26 Issue: 3 Special Issue: SI Pages: 235-245 Published: SEP 2018
Free Full Text from Publisher View Abstract
Times Cited: 1 (from Web of Science Core Collection)
Usage Count

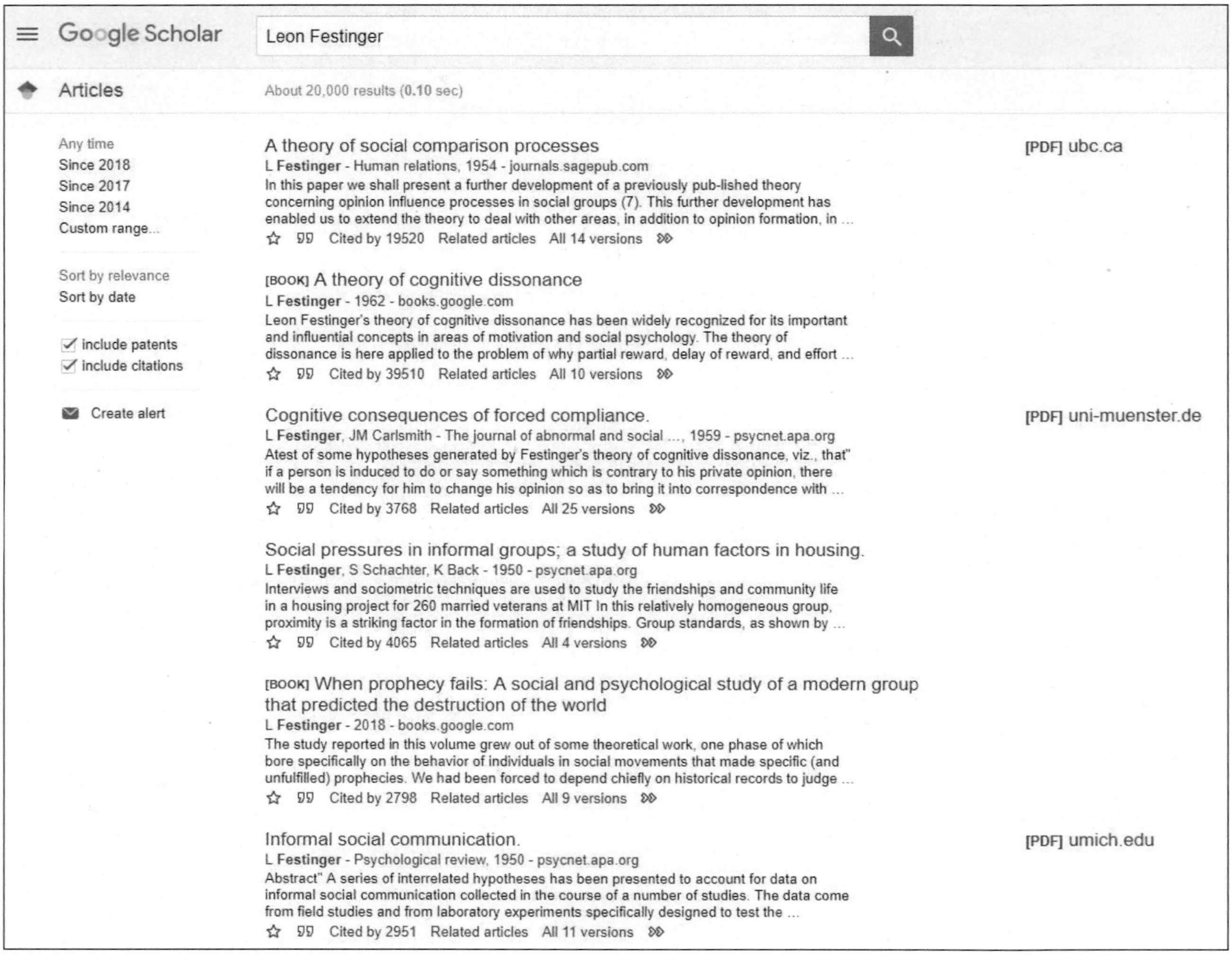

What about Google and Wikipedia?

8.10 Determine the use of Google and Wikipedia in research

The answer to this broad and vague question is, of course, it depends. It depends what you are using these resources for, and it certainly depends on your instructor's opinions and preferences. There are at least two main routes to consider here: citation sources in a research paper, and sources for ideas/topics to write about.

When we talk about "googling" something, that is, using Google in the verb form, this is an Internet search for websites related to the topic. As we write this, we can do a very quick Google search on the topic of depression. Google reports back, in 0.84 seconds, that there are about 496 million results on the Internet. As you click through the results of this search, the question becomes—can I use these sources as reference citations in my paper? Our answer would be (1) first check with your instructor to determine her or his preference for such practices, and (2) you must apply the CRAAP Test (described earlier in this chapter; see Table 8.3) to the website and the information found there in order to determine its suitability to being cited in an academic paper. To be fair, the type of paper you are writing matters too. The types of citations in a formal research methods or capstone paper are likely different than in a term paper or reaction paper—but one of our major points here is do not guess, ask.

The uneasiness of citing a web page as a source comes from the fact that anyone can create a web page and have it go live—which means that you could be citing anything. This is a similar concern that some people have with Wikipedia—that posts and entries are editable, so if you are reading something on Wikipedia, it might have been excellently well-sourced originally, but has the site been tampered with? Again, the CRAAP Test is your litmus test for determining the suitability for citation—keeping in mind the type of paper being prepared and the preferences of your instructor.

To be fair, we think that Google searches and Wikipedia entries can be terrific places to start to get ideas about what to write about or to brainstorm about what hypotheses to test. Reading a Wikipedia post should provide you with citations you could follow up on, and then you can read the original sources. But as you develop your skills as a psychology major, try to practice using the tools of the trade, especially *PsycINFO*. Anyone can do a Google, Google Scholar, or Wikipedia search—develop your specialized expertise at navigating a database of over 4.5 million entries dating back to the 1880s (APA, 2018). That is not a common skill, and something that can set you apart from the crowd. Learning to use and master tools like *PsycINFO* and Web of Science can not only help you now as an undergraduate write better papers and find information more efficiently, but it can help you acquire these specialized skills that can facilitate your role as a researcher, perhaps in a consulting agency, law firm, or in psychology graduate school. Remember, skills will matter throughout your career!

Exercise 8.1 Practice with the *PsycINFO* Author Search Tool

Below is a sample screenshot of how your *PsycINFO* interface might look (this is the interface from Boise State University). See where it says "Select a Field (optional)". If you hit the drop-down arrow, you will find that you can search on a number of different parameters, including journal title, author, etc. For this exercise, search in *PsycINFO* for journal articles written by faculty members at your college or university. If they have an uncommon last name that will probably do in the "Search for": first box (and instead of 'Select a Field (optional)' in the second box, select Author). If they have a common last name, you'll get plenty of hits, so you'll either have to scroll through those or you'll have to add a first name and/or initials to the search. When done, write down some of the details of your search on the lines below.

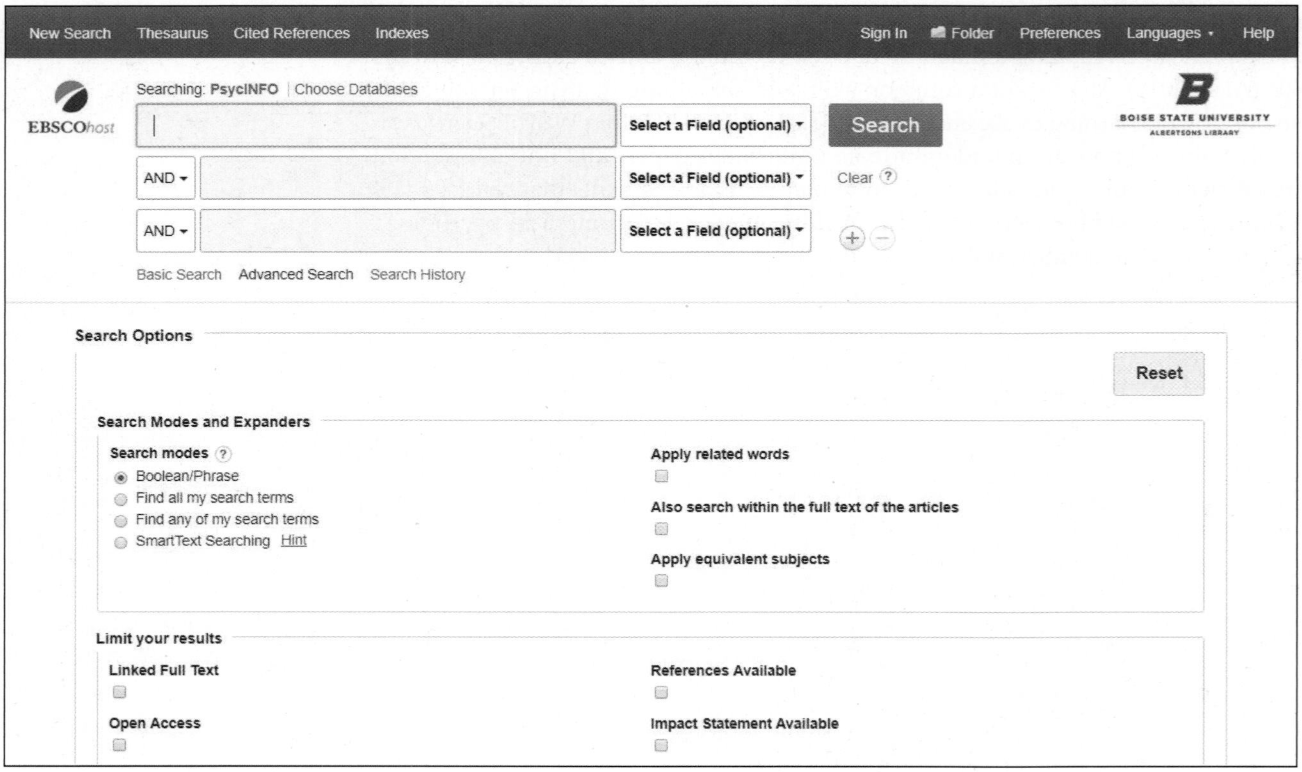

Exercise 8.2 An Information and Communication Technology (ICT) Literacy Scale

The need for computer skills and information literacy is accelerating at a rapid pace. Lau and Yuen (2014) created an Information and Communication Technology (ICT) Literacy Scale to measure these constructs. They began this work during 2011–2012. What is interesting about all of this is that by the time they finished their work and published their scale, information and communication technology had already changed so quickly that some of the questions may feel out-of-date!

The original 17-item ICT Scale is presented below. There are no right or wrong answers.

Items	Strongly Disagree	Disagree	Neither Disagree no Agree	Agree	Strongly Agree
I am able to identify the appropriately needed information from a question.	O	O	O	O	O
I am able to collect/retrieve information in digital environments.	O	O	O	O	O
I am about to use ICT to appropriately process the obtained information.	O	O	O	O	O
I am able to interpret and represent information, such as using ICT to synthesize, summarize, compare, and contrast information from multiple sources.	O	O	O	O	O
I am able to use ICT to design or create new information from information already acquired.	O	O	O	O	O
I am able to use ICT to convey correct information to appropriate targets.	O	O	O	O	O
I am able to judge the degree to which information is practical or satisfies the needs of the task, including determining authority, bias, and timeliness of materials.	O	O	O	O	O
I am able to set a homepage for an Internet browser.	O	O	O	O	O
I am able to search for information on the Internet using a search engine.	O	O	O	O	O
I am able to use e-mail to communicate.	O	O	O	O	O
I am able to use instant messaging software to chat with friends.	O	O	O	O	O
I am able to download files from the Internet.	O	O	O	O	O
I am able to set header/footer in word processor software (e.g., Microsoft Word).	O	O	O	O	O
I am able to plot a graph and chart using spreadsheet software (e.g., Microsoft Excel).	O	O	O	O	O
I am able to insert an animation in presentation software (e.g., Microsoft PowerPoint).	O	O	O	O	O
I am able to edit a photo using image processing software.	O	O	O	O	O
I am able to set up a printer (e.g., installing printer drivers).	O	O	O	O	O

SOURCE: Lau, W. W. F., & Yuen, A. H. K. (2014). Developing and validating of a perceived ICT literacy scale for junior secondary school students: *Pedagogical and educational contributions. Computers & Education, 78*, 1–9. doi:10.1016/j.compedu.2014.04.016

Chapter 9
An APA Format Primer

Learning Objectives

9.1 Describe the basics of writing an effective psychology paper

9.2 Outline strategies for writing the different elements of a psychology paper

9.3 Relate grammar and vocabulary to a successful paper

9.4 Analyze the consequences of plagiarism

9.5 Evaluate a sample psychology paper

As you begin to read more and more journal articles in psychology, you may wonder, "Why APA format?" For years, the American Psychological Association (APA) has published the *Publication Manual of the American Psychological Association*; the 2010 version is the sixth edition. Psychologists all over the world follow these steps and guidelines in the preparation of manuscripts. In fact, a number of scientific disciplines have adopted basic APA format as the *de facto* standard of manuscript preparation. The first formal presentation of manuscript instructions appeared in the *Psychological Bulletin* (an APA journal) in 1929. A six-member panel attending a Conference of Editors and Business Managers of Anthropological and Psychological Periodicals issued a report on manuscript guidelines called "Instructions in Regard to Preparation of Manuscript." This document offered general guidance for authors preparing manuscripts for publication. Although many of the details of page layout and preparation have changed and evolved into the current edition, some of the advice given in 1929 (p. 57) still holds true today. Consider this comment on the general form of the manuscript:

> A safe and useful prescription is to be as brief as possible without sacrificing clarity or pertinent facts. Pressure upon space in the scientific journals and the present heavy demands upon the informed reader both reinforce this prescription. Careless writing is usually diffuse, incoherent, and repetitious. Careful reading by a competent critic will usually suggest means for reduction.

Why the specific format? One of the basic tenets of science and scientific knowledge is communicability (one other basic tenet of scientific knowledge is replication). APA format facilitates communication of scientific, psychological knowledge by the reporting of results in a consistent and predictable format. Any paper written by a psychologist in APA style has information presented in the following order: title page, abstract, introduction, method, results, discussion, and references. Knowing the parts of the manuscript and where they are located gives an advantage to the reader; you may not understand the jargon used, but you know there is a description of how the study was conducted in the Method section, and the statistical findings of the study are recorded in the Results section. When you read enough journal articles over time, you come to expect the story to be told in this order, and this predictability becomes an asset to the reader.

This common format facilitates the communication of ideas in the scientific community. Some students are initially confused by APA format because they have already been taught a paper-writing format, often the style of the Modern Language Association (MLA). APA format is not necessarily superior to any other writing style or format; in fact, APA format can be confusing and tedious at times. However, it is the standard of communication in psychology for authors. Whether you are submitting your work to a journal for publication or writing a paper in a psychology course, you should follow the established standards and use APA format (unless, of course, you are instructed otherwise).

Writing Psychology Papers

9.1 Describe the basics of writing an effective psychology paper

The basic rules for writing in APA format are relatively straightforward. Much of the APA *Publication Manual* is dedicated to contingencies and events that do not occur very often. For example, in using APA format in the reference section of your paper, the *Publication Manual* lists dozens of different methods of referencing; whereas the two basic reference citations are journal articles and books.

Assume that you are eventually going to write a journal-style paper. Perhaps you are writing about your own experiment, a group project, or an experiment proposal. How do you get your notes organized to write the paper? Many authors use the notecard method or their own variation of this method. The notecard method is a technique of conducting library-type research in such a way that it facilitates later writing of the introduction and discussion sections of a manuscript by increasing the synthesis of a paper. By integrating multiple sources from your library research into the paper, it reads better, it flows better, and is one sign of scholarly writing. The notecard method is an organized procedure for collecting research notes when preparing a major term paper. Students are challenged in such papers to not only analyze information from various sources, but also to synthesize the views and reports of these sources. The difference between a good paper and an excellent paper is often the level of synthesis. By using the notecard method, students organize their thoughts and ideas beforehand, rather than at the moment of paper creation/typing/completion. For a more complete description of the notecard method with examples, we recommend Landrum (2012). Also, realize that you do not literally need to use notecards; it could be sticky notes or other types of paper, and there are software versions of the notecard method available if you prefer to work completely electronically. You could use an Excel file or Google spreadsheet to create your own digital versions of paper notecards.

The Parts: Introduction, Method, Results, and Discussion

9.2 Outline strategies for writing the different elements of a psychology paper

There are various details that must be attended to in preparing a manuscript in APA format, and a discussion of each of these sections follows. Note that, in general, APA has moved toward writing in the active voice (as opposed to the passive voice). Examples—

PASSIVE: The breakfast was eaten by me.

ACTIVE: I ate breakfast.

PASSIVE: The survey data were collected by me.

ACTIVE: I collected survey data.

Your instructor can help you to make this writing transition. There are many other tips to offer, such as the word "relationships" is used when referring to people, but use the word relations when presenting information about the association between variables (Beins et al., 2010). One of the most common confusions of all is effect and affect. When writing psychology papers, you will likely use affect as a verb, such as "the independent variable affected the dependent variable," whereas you will likely use the term effect as a noun, such as "the intervention had a relatively small effect on the outcome" (Beins et al., 2010). As for the main parts of an APA manuscript, Table 9.1 provides a quick overview of these sections.

The Introduction and Literature Review

This section is especially frustrating to persons who are unfamiliar with writing in APA format. Authors typically attempt to accomplish three goals in this opening portion of the paper. *First*, introduce the problem. The body of the paper opens with an introduction that presents the specific problem under study and describes the research strategy. Before writing the introduction, consider the following: What is the point of the study? How do the hypotheses and the experimental design relate to the problem? What are the theoretical implications of the study? How does the study relate to previous work in the area? A good introduction answers these questions in a paragraph or two and, by summarizing the relevant arguments and the data, gives the reader a firm sense of what was done in the study and why.

Second, develop the background. Discuss the literature, but do not include an exhaustive historical review. Assume that the reader has knowledge in the field for which you are writing and does not require a complete listing. Although you should acknowledge the contributions of others to the study of the problem, cite only research that is pertinent to the specific issue and avoid references with only general significance. Note: It takes repeated practice in writing APA style papers to become confident in knowing what is pertinent and what is not. Refer the reader to general surveys or

Table 9.1 Major Sections of an APA Manuscript

Title page (Take credit) Author's name, affiliation Other information as your professor requests Page numbering (header) and running head information
Abstract (Quick summary) No more than 120 words Some assignments will not require an abstract
Introduction (What you are studying) Introduce the problem Develop the background State the purpose and rationale for the present study
Method (What you did) Participants, materials, procedure Should be in enough detail to replicate if desired
Results (What happened) Presentation of statistical outcomes; tables and/or figures if necessary Presentation, not interpretation
Discussion (What it means) Was there support for the research idea? Did the study help resolve the original problem? What conclusions can be drawn? Suggest improvements, avenues for further/new research
Reference section (Give credit where credit is due) Starts on its own page Authors listed alphabetically by last name, no first names used, only initials Be sure all citations in the text are referenced Shows your scholarly ability and how you did your homework

reviews of the topic if they are available. A real challenge for writers is to demonstrate the logical continuity between previous research and the present work (your paper). Develop the problem with enough breadth and clarity to make it generally understood by as wide a professional audience as possible. Do not let the goal of brevity mislead you into writing a statement understandable only to the specialist. As you can see in the student sample paper at the end of this chapter, the author takes about four double-spaced paragraphs to develop the idea. You may want to use subheadings in longer papers to better organize your thoughts.

Third, state the purpose and rationale. After you have introduced the problem and developed the background material, you are in a position to tell what you did. Make this statement in the closing paragraphs of the introduction. At this point, a definition of the variables and a formal statement of your hypotheses give clarity to the paper. Often you will see the sentence containing the hypothesis clearly beginning "It is hypothesized that . . . " Clearly develop the rationale for each hypothesis. End the introduction with a brief overview of your own study. This overview provides a smooth transition into the Method section, which immediately follows. Bordens and Abbott (1988) provided a checklist for the introduction and literature review found in Table 9.2.

The Method Section

The goal of this section is to describe your participants, materials or apparatus, and procedures so clearly that another person in your field could replicate or repeat your research. You are inviting others to repeat what you did. This section is conventionally divided under three headings: participants, apparatus or materials, and procedure (a research design heading is sometimes included).

PARTICIPANTS. Describe the major demographic characteristics of the participants, such as age, sex, type of institution they were drawn from, and geographic location. Be sure to be sensitive to individual differences here; the general principle to remember is "put the person first." That is, use the phrase "persons with disabilities" rather than "disabled persons." Describe the procedures by which the participants were available for participation, such as student volunteers or students fulfilling course requirements. Include any criteria you used in determining who could be a participant. Describe the procedures by which you assigned participants to groups. If certain participants were dropped from the study, explain why in this section.

MATERIALS. If specialized equipment is an integral part of your research, describe this equipment and how you used it. If the equipment is standard, cite the manufacturer and any relevant identifying labels or numbers (this section might be labeled apparatus in that case). If standardized test materials were used, briefly describe them under a heading of materials. If the materials were specially designed for your study, describe them in enough detail so that someone experienced in your field could reproduce them for replication or further research purposes.

Table 9.2 Introduction/Literature Review Checklist

Introduction to the topic under study
Brief review of the research findings and theories related to the topic
Statement of the problem to be addressed by the research (identifying an area in which knowledge is incomplete)
Statement of purpose of the present research
Brief description of the method intended to establish the relation between the question being addressed and the method being used to address it
Description of any predictions about the outcome and of the hypotheses used to generate those predictions

PROCEDURE. Describe the research chronologically, step-by-step. In descriptive research, describe the conditions under which you observed or tested the participants as well as specific instructions or tasks presented to them. In experimental research, indicate how the participants in each group were exposed to the independent variable, and describe any control procedures used in the design. Instructions to the participants should be included verbatim if they were a key part of the study. Provide clear details on the measurement of participants' behavior.

The Results Section

Verify that all conditions stipulated in the Method section were accomplished. If any variations occurred, describe them here; then briefly describe the procedures used for data collection and analysis. How were your observations converted into analyzable data? What type of statistical analysis was selected, and how was it conducted? It is now time to present the findings. Briefly describe your results in writing. After doing so, repeat the results in numerical form. When reporting the results of statistical tests, include the following: the name of the test (such as t or F), the degrees of freedom, the results of the specific computation, and the alpha level (or p value), reported to three decimal places. Now, you may elaborate or qualify the overall conclusion if necessary in writing. Be sure to end each section of the results with a summary of where ideas stand. APA format requires that when you report the mean, you also report the standard deviation. For certain analyses, you will need to report the effect size along with the inferential statistic value. If you are not sure what an effect size is or if you need to report it in your paper, be sure to check with your instructor.

As you continue to write more in the psychology major, perhaps in advanced classes or in graduate school (if that is in your future), you will hear about two new set of reporting standards for journal articles: journal article reporting standards for quantitative research (Applebaum et al., 2018), and journal article reporting standards for qualitative, meta-analytic, and mixed method research (Levitt et al., 2018). It's unlikely that as an undergraduate that you will need to dig too deeply into these standards; familiarity with the APA *Publication Manual* is a better investment of time and effort. However, we wanted you to be aware of these new developments in our field.

FIGURES AND TABLES. Unless a set of findings can be stated in one or two numbers, a table or figure may accompany results that are sufficiently important to be stressed. However, you do not want the information presented in a table or figure to be redundant with information already presented in the text. The basic rule of presentation is that a reader should be able to grasp your major findings either by reading the text or by looking at the tables and figures. Be careful in preparing figures and tables: There are very specific APA rules governing their construction, they are time-consuming, and they are often difficult to prepare correctly.

If you need help with the formatting of specific parts of the APA-formatted manuscript, there are many videos available from a number of sources. In fact, one of your authors (REL) has his own YouTube channel that has a Playlist of videos dedicated to showing the step-by-step instructions on how to use Microsoft Word to do the following:

- Citation reference formats for a book, journal article, Internet source, book chapter
- Page formatting help on tables, line spacing, margins, page headers, and using track changes

To access these completely free resources (with no advertising), go to https://www.bit.ly/APA_format_YouTube

The Discussion Section

Begin the discussion by telling the reader what you have learned from the study. Open with a clear statement on the support or nonsupport of the hypotheses or the answers to the questions you first raised in the introduction. Do not simply reformulate and repeat points already summarized in the Results section. Each new statement should contribute something new to the reader's understanding of the problem. What inferences can be drawn from the data? What are the theoretical, practical, or even political implications of the results? Next, compare your results with the results reported by other investigators and discuss possible shortcomings of your study—that is, conditions that might limit the extent of legitimate generalizations. Do not dwell compulsively on flaws in your study. Typically, there is a section included that considers questions that remain unanswered or have been raised by the study itself, along with suggestions for the kinds of research that would help to answer them. You will likely list the limitations of your own study; not to be hypercritical, but to be realistic (every study ever publish has limitations and flaws; no real study will ever be perfect). A good discussion section has a three-part conclusion that re-states the take-home message (that one idea the reader should remember), reminds the reader of the gap your study filled in the literature, and reminds the reader of the overall importance of your general topic.

REFERENCES. List the scholarly works that you used (cited) in your paper in the reference section. List only works that you actually used; the reference section is *not* a bibliography (in a bibliography, you would list all the research that you gathered, regardless of whether or not that information was used in the paper). Also, note that references have their own rules of capitalization, and these rules are counterintuitive to students at first. For example, most students think that every word of a book title or journal article is always capitalized—in APA format in the reference section that is not true. There are many, many different types of reference materials that you can use in an APA format paper. Unfortunately, each type has a slightly different APA format. For the listing of examples on how to format references, see the *Publication Manual* (APA, 2010). Table 9.3 presents the most common reference formats (note that they are not double-spaced as they would be in true APA format). Commenting on the importance of references as an indication of scholarship, Smith (2000) listed three types of major offenses to avoid: (a) no references, (b) references that are out of date, and (c) references that are irrelevant.

Table 9.3 Examples of APA Format References

Periodicals/Journal Articles

Halonen, J. S., Bosack, T., Clay, S., McCarthy, M., Dunn, D. S., Hill, G. W., IV, . . . Whitlock, K. (2003). A rubric for learning, teaching, and assessing scientific inquiry in psychology. *Teaching of Psychology, 30*, 196–208.

Rosenthal, R. (1979). The "file drawer problem" and tolerance for null results. *Psychological Bulletin, 86*, 638–641.

Books

Arum, R., & Roska, J. (2011). *Academically adrift: Limited learning on college campuses*. Chicago, IL: University of Chicago Press.

Festinger, L. A. (1957). *A theory of cognitive dissonance*. Evanston, IL: Harper & Row, Peterson.

Edited Book

Halpern, D. F. (Ed.). (2010). *Undergraduate education in psychology: A blueprint for the future*. Washington, DC: American Psychological Association.

Book Chapters

Apple, K. J., Serdikoff, S. L., Reis-Bergan, M. J., & Barron, K. E. (2008). Programmatic assessment of critical thinking. In D. S. Dunn, J. S. Halonen, & R. A. Smith (Eds.), *Teaching critical thinking in psychology* (pp. 77–88). Malden, MA: Blackwell Publishing.

Lagemann, E. C., & Lewis, H. (2012). Renewing the civic mission of American higher education. In E. C. Lagemann & H. Lewis (Eds.), *What is college for? The public purpose of higher education* (pp. 9–45). New York, NY: Teachers College Press.

Peden, B. F., & VanVoorhis, C. R. (2009). Developing habits of the mind, hand, and heart in psychology undergraduates. In R. A. R. Gurung, N. L. Chick, & A. Haynie (Eds.), *Exploring signature pedagogies: Approaches to teaching disciplinary habits of mind* (pp. 161–182). Sterling, VA: Stylus.

Internet Materials

Green, R. J. (2005, January). What we can do to help undergraduate students not going on for graduate studies. *APS Observer, 18*(1). Retrieved from http://www.psychologicalscience.org/observer/getArticle.cfm?id=1709

Hanneman, L., & Gardner, P. (2010, February). *Under the economic turmoil a skills gap simmers*. Collegiate Employment Research Institute Research Brief 1-2010. Retrieved from http://www.ceri.msu.edu/wp-content/uploads/2009/10/skillsabrief1-2010.pdf

APA format concerning citing information from the Internet is much clearer than it used to be. APA has recommendations available (http://www.apastyle.org). As with all reference materials, the ultimate goal is to provide enough information in the reference so that other researchers are able to follow your path to the same information.

TITLE AND ABSTRACT. The title and abstract of your article permit potential readers to get a quick overview of your study and decide if they wish to read the entire article. Titles and abstracts are also indexed and compiled in reference works and computerized databases (e.g., PsycINFO). For this reason they should accurately reflect the content of the article; write the abstract after you have completed the article and have a firm view of its structure and content. The recommended length for a title is 10–12 words. The title should be fully explanatory when standing alone and identify the theoretical issue(s) or the variable(s) under investigation. A good title is hard to write; plan to spend some time on it. There is a famous article written by Miller (1956) in which he titled "The magical number seven, plus or minus two: Some limits on our capacity for processing information." As Sternberg (2000) rightly stated, this title piqued readers' interest. But consider the "attraction" of an alternative title that Sternberg suggested Miller could have used—"Limitations on information-processing capacity: A review of the literature."

The abstract is a short paragraph that summarizes the entire work—it should not exceed 120–150 words. It should state the problem under investigation, the participants (specifying pertinent characteristics), the experimental method (including apparatus, data-gathering materials, test names), the findings (including statistical significance levels), and the conclusion with the implications or applications. Dunn (2011, pp. 87–88) provided excellent advice by creating a template for crafting the abstract:

- One sentence about the background and purpose of the study, indicating why your study is important
- One sentence with the main hypothesis of the study with key variables included
- One sentence describing the sample of participants studied
- One sentence about the design of the study
- Two sentences about the methodology used, independent variables, control groups, and general design
- Two to three sentences that focus on the results and how they support or refute the main hypothesis
- One to two sentences that offer conclusions about the implications of the research, ending with the takeaway message for the reader.

Following this template should provide a solid start for writing what is often considered the single-most difficult paragraph to write in an APA-format paper.

AN APPENDIX. An appendix contains materials important to the research that are too lengthy or detailed for inclusion in the Method section. These items may include technical materials, listing of a computer program, word lists used as stimuli, or an original survey/questionnaire. Try to minimize the use of appendices; in fact, for most APA-type undergraduate writing assignments, it is likely that you will not even need to include an appendix.

APA FORMAT TYPING INSTRUCTIONS. There are a number of specific details that are followed when preparing a manuscript in APA format. Some of the more basic guidelines are presented here. As always, heed your instructor's modifications to this list.

- Do not use underlining in 6th edition APA format—only italics.
- Double-space everything.
- Use a one-inch margin on *all* sides.

- Do not justify lines if using a word processing program (i.e., you should have a ragged right margin). In Microsoft Word, make sure the leftmost selection (as shown here) stays selected. 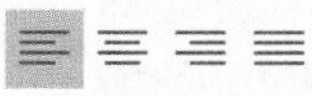
- Use a 12-point font, preferably Times New Roman or equivalent—always make sure the font is absolutely readable.
- Number every page, including the title page (except figures)—upper right-hand corner, inside the one-inch margin.
- Indent the first line of every paragraph using the tab key (usually set at one-half inch indention) or use five to seven spaces to indent.
- Center the title page information on the first page; it should contain the paper's title, the author's name, and the author's affiliation. The running head also appears on the title page—this short description is what would appear at the top of the page if the article were published in a journal. The title is also repeated again on the first page of manuscript text (this is page 3 of the paper if there is an abstract on page 2).
- Place the abstract on a page by itself (page 2 of the paper). The word "Abstract" should be centered at the top of the page. The abstract should be about 120 words in length and must be typed as one blocked (not indented) paragraph. Include keywords at the end of the Abstract paragraph.

SPACING AND PUNCTUATION. APA format requires only *one* space after punctuation in the body of the paper and Reference section. Check with your instructor on his or her preference. Some instructors may want you to follow APA format exactly; others will want two spaces because they believe it improves readability; and others won't care. The Reference section starts on its own page.

Grammar and Vocabulary

9.3 Relate grammar and vocabulary to a successful paper

You can imagine that with all of these sections, the flow of a research paper might be choppy and the text difficult to read. The skilled writer uses transitions between sections and paragraphs to improve the flow and readability. Here are some suggestions for transitions:

- Time links: then, next, after, while, since
- Cause–effect links: therefore, consequently, as a result
- Addition links: in addition, moreover, furthermore, similarly
- Contrast links: but, conversely, nevertheless, however, although, whereas

One of the most confusing aspects to the writer new to the use of APA format regards the use of verbs. The verb tense that is used depends upon the section of the paper (see Table 9.4). As a general note, the *Publication Manual* does a good job

Table 9.4 Verb Use in Sections of an APA Format Paper

Introduction (Literature review)	
	Past tense ("Davis concluded")
	Present perfect tense ("Researchers have concluded")
Method	
	Past tense ("Participants completed the task in 5 minutes")
	Present perfect tense ("The task was completed by the participants in 5 minutes")
Results	
	Past tense ("Scores declined after the intervention")
Discussion (discuss results and present conclusions)	
	Present tense ("Participants take the computer task seriously")

of providing the basics of formatting, and does have helpful examples. You should remember to always consult your instructor to determine his or her particular preferences in the application of APA format rules. At times, instructors may want you to vary from the rules to improve readability or to fulfill a departmental or institutional requirement.

Here are some different types of verb tense and an example of each. When appropriate, use the active voice. Try to increase the frequency of active voice construction—"Davis designed the study." The passive voice is acceptable when you focus on the outcome of the action, rather than who made the action happen. Try to minimize the use of passive voice—that is, try to avoid "the survey was administered by the students." Use past tense to discuss something that happened at a specific, definite time in the past (e.g., writing about another researcher's work or when reporting your results)—"Landrum (1999) found that 63% of students reporting average work expected a grade of B or a grade of A." Use the present perfect tense to discuss a past action that did *not* occur at a specific, definite time in the past—"Since the completion of the study, we have found further evidence to support our conclusions."

Using Direct Quotes versus Paraphrasing

Use a direct quote only if the author has stated the idea so perfectly that any paraphrasing of the original would not do justice to it. In general, you should paraphrase information you take from other sources. To paraphrase means that you read and comprehend the material, but then you write it in your own words, not the author's words (as a direct quote would do). *You still need to give the writer credit for his or her work*, even though you have put it in your own words; if you do not, you have plagiarized.

In general (and this is *our* suggestion, not APA format), use direct quotations sparingly. No more than one or two per paper, and do not use block quotes (quotes longer than 40 words). When instructors see a string of quotations or a bunch of block quotes, they are drawn to the conclusion that the student thought that stringing quotes together would look good and satisfy the requirement. A scholarly paper is *not* a string of direct quotations. Examples of paraphrasing include some sentences that have phrases like these: (a) Landrum (1998) found that . . . ; (b) . . . as reported in a previous study (Landrum, 1998); and (c) In 1998, Landrum concluded that . . .

There are many rules to follow and much attention to detail will be necessary to successfully navigate APA format. Allow us to make two more points here. First, always check with your instructor to see what variations, if any, they wish to make when they "require" APA format. For instance, an instructor might assign an APA format paper, but they want it single-spaced. Well, technically APA format is double-spaced. Of course, do not argue with the instructor. Be flexible and adaptable, and savvy enough ahead of time to ask the instructor about their preferences or variations away from strict APA format. And sometimes, the instructor might not even know their preference (e.g., two spaces after a sentence rather than one space) is not true APA format. If the instructor has a grading rubric, ask her or him if they will share it with the class prior to the assignment being due.

Our second point is to share with you the outcomes of two research studies as presented in Table 9.5. By examining the outcomes of the results of these two studies, you can start to anticipate what might be the most common errors when students are writing APA style papers. You might even think of Table 9.5 as your own checklist to make sure that you do not make these mistakes prior to turning in your own work

Table 9.5 Results to Two Studies About Students' Writing Errors, Including Largest Gaps in Writing Skills

Instructor-Identified Most Frequent Errors* Mandernach et al. (2016)	Largest Gaps Between Faculty Importance Ratings and Faculty Assessments of Average Student Writing Skills** Landrum (2013)
1. Format of in-text citations	1. Claims made with appropriate supporting evidence
2. Use of in-text citations	2. Proofreading ability
3. Format of references on references page	3. Ability to properly revise rough drafts
4. Format of direct quotes	4. Effect sizes properly presented
5. Proper use of headings/subheadings	5. Writing an abstract
6. Precision of writing	6. Direct quotes used appropriately/sparingly
7. Writing style	7. Using terms like significant and correlation properly
8. Format of title page	8. Personal opinions presented with appropriate framing
9. Use of active/passive voice	9. Avoid using phrases like "psychologists prove . . . "
10. Clarity	10. Proper hedging of conclusions

*Most frequent error identified by instructors, starting with the most frequent as #1.

** Largest perceived gap in student skill levels on important skills is listed as #1, second largest as #2, and so on.

SOURCES: Mandernach, B. J., Zafonte, M., & Taylor, C. (2016). Instructional strategies to improve college students' APA style writing. *International Journal of Teaching and Learning in Higher Education*, *27*(3). Retrieved from http://www.isetl.org/ijtlhe/; Landrum, R. E. (2013). Writing in APA style: Faculty perspectives of competence and importance. *Psychology Learning and Teaching*, *12*, 259–264. doi:10.2304/plat.2013.12.3.259

Success Stories

Cierra Abellera

Mentorship played a crucial role in helping me navigate academia. As an underrepresented scholar from Hawaii, I struggled to fit in on-campus. I transferred to a four-year university after graduating from community college with my associate's in liberal arts and taking a semester off. Entering university in a town very different from my home in almost every way possible was the biggest culture shock I've experienced even after traveling throughout Europe, New Zealand, and Ghana.

My first semester of this transition was the most challenging as I started to feel the "imposter phenomenon" and significantly doubted if I belonged in academia at all. My grades began slipping in a class I was passionate about and was hoping to be a teaching assistant for. Worried about my low-grades, I reached out to the professor for advice on the next test. I didn't realize it until this meeting, but I seemed to struggle more with the hidden curriculum of academics more than my classes. I felt unprepared and intimidated in approaching my professors, especially those I admired. Thankfully, my professor advised me on successfully approaching critical questions in the class and also gave me an opportunity to work as a research assistant in their lab at the end of the semester.

Though I felt supported by my professor, I still could not understand the other feelings and experiences I was going through. As an underrepresented individual at a predominately white institution, I often experienced unnecessarily long stares when walking through campus and was frequently asked questions like "What are you?" and "Where are you from?" referring to my mixed-race background while my peers were asked

(continued)

about their research interests and career goals. By the end of my first semester, I was overwhelmed by these questions and experiences. Naturally an introvert, it was hard for me to seek out help when I needed it. Because of my experiences on-campus, my professors grew from academic advisors and became life mentors. I was encouraged out of my normal comfort zone as I joined clubs and organizations that opened opportunities to visit different universities and work with others across the nation. Slowly, my overwhelming experiences became less and less as I became more connected to the academic community. By surrounding myself with supportive mentors, I made the most of my university experience as an engaged and connected learner.

A Brief Note on Plagiarism

9.4 Analyze the consequences of plagiarism

In Chapter 12, we address plagiarism more thoroughly, but it is important to mention it here while presenting information about writing. You need to avoid plagiarism at all costs. What is plagiarism? According to Landau (2003), "Plagiarism occurs when people take credit for thoughts, words, images, musical passages, or ideas originally created by someone else" (p. 3). Landau suggested that there are two main types of plagiarism—intentional and unintentional plagiarism. Regarding unintentional plagiarism, Landau suggested two types: (a) students inadvertently present someone else's work as their own (source memory error) or (b) misapprehension, or that students do not know what they were doing was wrong.

There are serious consequences for students who are caught plagiarizing; these vary from instructor to instructor as well as institution to institution. You should be able to find detailed information about this in your student handbook. The consequences could be receiving an F on the assignment, an F in the course, and worse punishments in some cases. In the real world, plagiarism has its consequences too. Read this excerpt by Margulies (2002, pp 1–2, 4) about what happened in one case of plagiarism:

> Less than two weeks after he was called to task for borrowing liberally from others in his welcome address to the freshman class, the president of Hamilton College resigned on Tuesday. Although some faculty members had criticized Eugene M. Tobin, many people on the campus expressed surprise and disappointment at his resignation. Mr. Tobin stepped down after nine years at the helm of the Clinton, NY, college. He spoke to his colleagues at an afternoon faculty meeting after having consulted with a circle of advisors and constituents almost continuously from the time his act of plagiarism was exposed last month. In a convocation address that focused on the books he had read over the summer, Mr. Tobin used phrases and passages, without citation, from a number of book reviews and descriptions posted on Amazon.com.

A college president lost his job because of plagiarism.

Writing an APA-formatted paper well is a complicated enterprise, and a cottage industry of books has emerged to help student writers interpret the *Publication Manual* for their own needs. In Table 9.6, we provide a brief listing of the guides available to help you. Although this chapter should give you a good jump-start as to what is expected, these book-length guides can give you more nuanced details about writing like a psychologist.

Writing is a skill that can serve you well no matter what direction your career path take you. Our ability to write is an indicator of our thoughts, our

Table 9.6 Writing Resources for Students

Beins, B. C. (2012). *APA style simplified: Writing in psychology, education, nursing, and sociology*. Malden, MA: Blackwell.
Beins, B. C., & Beins, A. M. (2008). *Effective writing in psychology: Papers, posters, and presentations*. Malden, MA: Blackwell Publishing.
Dunn, D. S. (2011). *A short guide to writing about psychology* (3rd ed.). Boston, MA: Longman/Pearson.
Hacker, D., & Sommers, N. (2013). *A pocket style manual, sixth edition, APA version*. Boston, MA: Bedford/St. Martin's.
Kail, R. V. (2015). *Scientific writing for psychology: Lessons in clarity and style*. Thousand Oaks, CA: Sage.
Landrum, R. E. (2012). *Undergraduate writing in psychology: Learning to tell the scientific story* (Revised ed.). Washington, DC: American Psychological Association.
Mitchell, M. L., Jolley, J. M., & O'Shea, R. P. (2013). *Writing for psychology* (4th ed.). Belmont, CA: Wadsworth/Cengage.
Rosnow, R. L., & Rosnow, M. (2009). *Writing papers in psychology* (8th ed.). Belmont, CA: Wadsworth/Cengage.
Schwartz, B. M., Landrum, R. E., & Gurung, R. A. R. (2016). *An easyguide to APA* style (3rd ed.). Thousand Oaks, CA: Sage.
Silvia, P. J. (2007). *How to write a lot: A practical guide to productive academic writing*. Washington, DC: American Psychological Association.
Szuchman, L. T. (2011). *Writing with style: APA style made easy* (5th ed.). Belmont, CA: Wadsworth/Cengage.

intellect, our emotions, and our humanity. Zinsser (1988, p. 49) expresses a similar sentiment:

> Writing is a tool that enables people in every discipline to wrestle with facts and ideas. It's a physical activity, unlike reading. Writing requires us to operate some kind of mechanism—pencil, pen, typewriter, word processor—for getting our thoughts on paper. It compels us by the repeated effort of language to go after those thoughts and to organize them and present them clearly.

Sample Paper

9.5 Evaluate a sample psychology paper

Following the two exercises, we have included a sample student paper. Like actual APA format, each page is contained on one piece of paper, and pages are printed on one side of the page. Writing an APA format paper early in your academic career can be a daunting and frustrating task—try not to be discouraged. It is a skill and it takes time to acquire skills. As with most other things, practice helps; the more papers you write, the better you will become at writing in this style. The conventions used in APA format will become familiar over time, and you will eventually appreciate the organizational structure and logical sequence of thought that a well-prepared APA paper provides. Our thanks go to Carol Pack, a graduate of the Department of Psychological Science at Boise State University, for allowing us permission to use a modified draft of her research paper prepared for a Research Methods course. Note that we have added some illustrative points to help you attend to some of the most important details that students might miss when just starting to learn APA format. For your information—this is not an example of a perfect paper, but a good student paper. The presentation of the formatting details should be quite helpful to you as you prepare your own papers.

Exercise 9.1 Practice Proofreading APA Format

Below is a sample page created by your first author. It can be used at the beginning and ending of a semester to assess the degree to which students acquire competency in APA formatting skills. Your goal is to correctly identify errors, both with regard to formatting and style. What are the mistakes made in this APA format paper assignment? If you wish, get out a red pen and mark up the page with all the mistakes you can find, and make suggestions on how to correct the mistakes. Do not peek ahead to the pages that follow this next page. Not yet.

RUNNING HEAD: Relationships: Quality or Quantity pg. 7

Many couples want a successful relationship that is also satisfying. Partners who are satisfied with their interactions tend to be satisfied with other non-romantic relationships (Emmers-Sommer, 514). As a response to ongoing interaction between partners, loving attitudes are formed, things that are shaped by personality type and past and existing relationship interactions (Meeks, Hendrick and Hendrick, '98). That is what my paper is about.

So which aspect of interaction in a relationship is more important; the amount or quality of interaction? Arguments 4 both sides exist.. Self-disclosure defined as face—to—face communication of information is often reciprocal, and related to the development of close personal ties (Arliss 1991). Another aspect to examine is if males and females view interaction and relationship quality differently, as suggested by Galliher, Walsh, Rostosky & Kawaguchi (2004): "**the domains of couple interaction that predict global relationship quality were different for males and females.**" (214). Tucker and Anders and et al (1999) report that women have been found to be more satisfied when their partner shows concern with emotional intimacy, but the same has not been found true of men.

A *t* test was used to examine differences on the agreement scale item "Sharing personal thoughts, feelings and experiences with my partner improves our relationship," and answers to the **yes/no** item "Over the duration of my relationship, our physical interaction has increased". A significant relationship exists between "yes" (M=4.43, SD = 0.562) and "no" (M = 3.9, SD =.65) participants on self-disclosure scores, t(4,5) = 2.693, p < .05. This data is significant

This research done by me stresses the importance of the willingness to self-disclose and encourages positive interaction to achieve relationship satisfaction. LAC issues are proved to be important to consider when pursuing a romantic relationship. Like we talked about in lecture, men and women sometimes want different things out of relationships. Sometimes quality, sometiems quantity. According to John Gottman's website, relationship quality is important.

Galliher, RV, Welsh, DP, Rostosky, SS and MC Kawaguchi. (2004) Interaction and Relationship Quality in Late Adolescent Romantic Couples. Journal of Social and personal Relationships, *21*(2), 203-16. DOI: 10.1177/0265407504041383.

As you already understand, skills develop with practice. If you are new to APA format, you found some errors in Exercise 9.1, but it is unlikely that you found all the errors. And here's the thing—maybe even your authors did not find all the errors, and your instructor looking at this exercise might find something that we did not find as an error. This exercise, after you complete it, might make for a good discussion topic with your instructor—it might give you a way to gauge how "picky" a grader he/she is without having to find out the "hard" way—by getting your first low grade.

By our estimation, we count a total of 87 errors on that single page, including APA style and format errors, punctuation errors, grammar errors, and so on. To see how your authors marked it up (one version of the "answer key," we suppose), now turn to the next page.

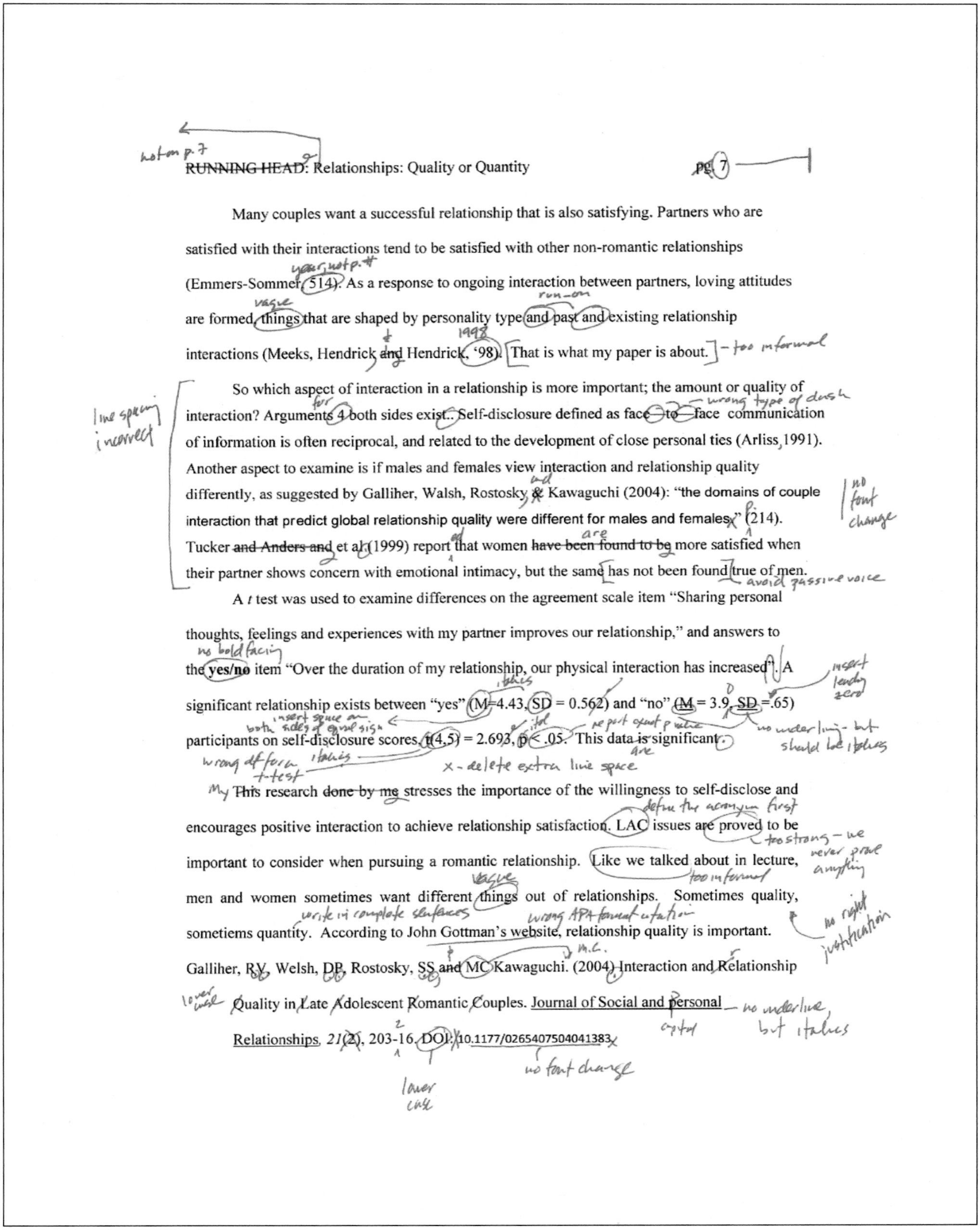

RUNNING HEAD: Relationships: Quality or Quantity pg. 7

Many couples want a successful relationship that is also satisfying. Partners who are satisfied with their interactions tend to be satisfied with other non-romantic relationships (Emmers-Sommer, 514). As a response to ongoing interaction between partners, loving attitudes are formed, things that are shaped by personality type and past and existing relationship interactions (Meeks, Hendrick and Hendrick, '98). That is what my paper is about.

So which aspect of interaction in a relationship is more important; the amount or quality of interaction? Arguments 4 both sides exist.. Self-disclosure defined as face—to—face communication of information is often reciprocal, and related to the development of close personal ties (Arliss 1991). Another aspect to examine is if males and females view interaction and relationship quality differently, as suggested by Galliher, Walsh, Rostosky & Kawaguchi (2004): "the domains of couple interaction that predict global relationship quality were different for males and females." (214). Tucker and Anders and et al (1999) report that women have been found to be more satisfied when their partner shows concern with emotional intimacy, but the same has not been found true of men.

A *t* test was used to examine differences on the agreement scale item "Sharing personal thoughts, feelings and experiences with my partner improves our relationship," and answers to the **yes/no** item "Over the duration of my relationship, our physical interaction has increased". A significant relationship exists between "yes" (M=4.43, SD = 0.562) and "no" (M = 3.9, SD =.65) participants on self-disclosure scores, t(4,5) = 2.693, p < .05. This data is significant.

This research done by me stresses the importance of the willingness to self-disclose and encourages positive interaction to achieve relationship satisfaction. LAC issues are proved to be important to consider when pursuing a romantic relationship. Like we talked about in lecture, men and women sometimes want different things out of relationships. Sometimes quality, sometiems quantity. According to John Gottman's website, relationship quality is important.

Galliher, RV, Welsh, DP, Rostosky, SS and MC Kawaguchi. (2004) Interaction and Relationship Quality in Late Adolescent Romantic Couples. Journal of Social and Personal Relationships, *21*(2), 203-16. DOI: 10.1177/0265407504041383

Exercise 9.2 Honing Specific Writing Skills—Avoiding Passive Voice Errors and Pathetic Fallacy Errors

Instructors, when grading students' papers long enough, tend to develop pet peeves, that is, certain errors start to bother or bug the instructor more than other errors. It would be very prudent every semester/quarter for you to get to know your instructor, and try to detect her/his pet peeves.

We don't know how common or widespread these two errors are, but they certainly bubble to the top of our lists. Let us define and explain each a bit, then give you a chance to read some sentences that may or may not have these errors, and start to practice recognizing the errors and also practice correcting the errors.

Passive Voice

The passive voice involves making the object of an action into the subject of a sentence. Technically, using the passive voice is not an error, but it is not the preferred method of writing for APA style. Some examples of passive voice sentences (in italics) include *Why was the road crossed by the chicken?* and *The breakfast was eaten by me*. A clearer and more direct approach is to write in the active voice, which involves the removal of the "to be" verb form.

You can recognize passive-voice expressions because the verb phrase will always include a form of be, such as **am, is, was, were, are**, or **been**. The presence of a be verb, however, does not necessarily mean that the sentence is in passive voice. Another way to recognize passive-voice sentences is that they may include a "by the . . . " phrase after the verb; the agent performing the action, if named, is the object of the preposition in this phrase (Purdue Owl, 2018).

Still confused about what's the difference between passive and active voice? *If you can add the phrase "by zombies" after the verb, your sentence has passive voice.* For example:

Passive Voice = She was chased [by zombies].

Active Voice = Zombies chased [by zombies] her.

And voila! Now there's a simple and fun way to identify when you're using passive voice (The Writing Center at American University, 2012).

Pathetic Fallacy

A pathetic fallacy error is a misattribution of human qualities (e.g., emotions, feelings, thoughts, traits) to an inanimate object (sometimes called an anthropomorphism error). Some examples of pathetic fallacy errors (in italics) include *Air hates to be crowded* and *Studies often find no significant results*. Pathetic fallacy is attributing human feelings to inhuman things. If you describe a storm cloud as "angry" or a strong wind as "vengeful," that's pathetic fallacy.

It is better to attribute the action of the sentence to someone who can perform such action rather than an inanimate object which can "do" nothing. That is, people perform actions, but inanimate objects do not perform actions. The pathetic fallacy is the illogical act of saying that inanimate object is performing some action. Studies cannot find, results cannot indicate, research cannot suggest, and so on.

SOURCES: Purdue Owl. (2018). *More about passive voice*. Retrieved from https://owl.purdue.edu/owl/general_writing/academic_writing/active_and_passive_voice/more_about_passive_voice.html; The Writing Center at American University. (2012, October). *Identify passive voice (with zombies!)*. Retrieved from http://auwritingcenter.blogspot.com/2012/10/identify-passive-voice-with-zombies.html

For the following sentences, some will have a passive voice error, some will have a pathetic fallacy error, some will have both errors, and some will have no errors at all. There is no answer key. Review the sentences and see if you can detect the errors. When you detect an error, use the space provided to provide an APA-appropriate re-write of the sentence.

1. Research has shown alcohol consumption to peak at the end of the freshman year.
2. It is hypothesized that alcohol use increases from freshman year to senior year.
3. This study will focus on the relationships between adolescent males and females.
4. Average sleep times for college students have been found to range between 6.6 hours per night and 8.2 hours per night.
5. Over one-third of college students surveyed reported being tired for most of the day.
6. Many studies examine the viewpoint of potential sexual abuse in heterosexual couples.
7. Researchers have conducted many different studies about how teenagers obtain information about sexuality.
8. This study found that most people do not take birth control seriously when having sex.
9. If there are ways to increase the use of birth control, it could reduce the spread of disease and reduce teen pregnancy rates.
10. Regular exercise has been show to help decrease the risks of developing a variety of physical disorders.

11. Students are realizing that it is much more difficult to find a job after gaining an undergraduate degree.
12. My first hypothesis states there is not a significant difference between males and females on stereotypically masculine characteristics.
13. International research has been conducted with rural communities and their struggle with interference from government entities.
14. It has also been predicted that being in a successful committed relationship requires a person to have qualities such as reliability and impulse control.
15. This data indicates that individuals who have experienced childhood abuse do not display poorer academic performance.
16. I hypothesize that childhood abuse has a distressing effect on cognitive functioning.
17. Researchers have indicated that stress and anxiety disorders are often predecessors to eating disorders.
18. The research on college student's degree choice shows individual studies on parental influence, lifelong goals, and potential earnings tied to career choices.
19. Hopefully, this study will give the student and the university knowledge about how the traditionally aged student is changing.

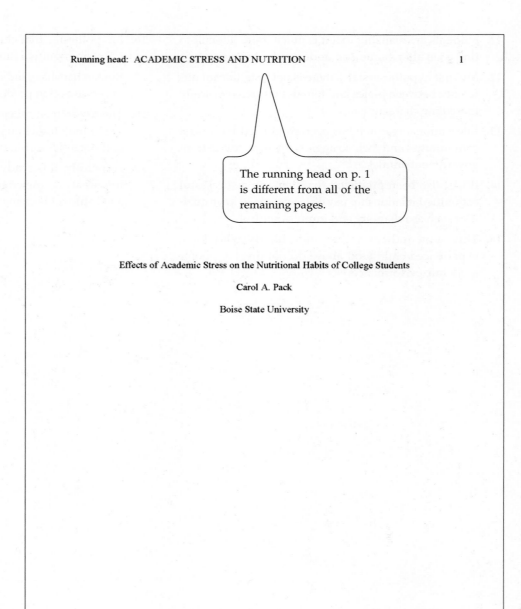

Running head: ACADEMIC STRESS AND NUTRITION 1

The running head on p. 1 is different from all of the remaining pages.

Effects of Academic Stress on the Nutritional Habits of College Students

Carol A. Pack

Boise State University

ACADEMIC STRESS AND NUTRITION 2

Abstract

I examined the effects of academic stress on the nutritional habits of college students. Sixty-two participants responded to a 6-question survey. Perceived levels of stress significantly affected a student's desire to prepare healthy meals for themselves, the way they viewed their overall state of health, and their overall ability to cope with stress. There was a significant negative relationship between fast food consumption and perceived states of health, indicating that as fast food consumption increased, one's view of their state of health decreased. Stress has a significant effect on the dietary practices of college students.

Keywords: college students, eating habits, health, stress

The abstract is not indented, and should typically be limited to 120 words.

The title is repeated from p. 1.

Effects of Academic Stress on the Nutritional Habits of College Students

In the competitive and stressful world of today's college student that not only carries a full academic load but works part to full-time, perhaps one of the first behaviors to be sacrificed is that of a healthy and nutritious diet. Nutritional habits bear strongly upon one's ability to optimally perform in the world. Unfortunately, many find it easier to take the course of least resistance and allow healthy behaviors, such as healthy eating habits, to be modified by the level of stress being experienced. According to the Bureau of Labor Statistics (1999), missed work days due to occupational stress were more than four times the median absence for all occupational injuries and illnesses. Stress is an issue in all areas of endeavor, and subsequently, when everyday stressors lay claim to already hectic schedules it is not unreasonable to expect repercussions in other areas of life.

Previous research exists regarding college student stress and a variety of behaviors impacted, including the specific underlying causes of the inability to maintain a healthy diet during stressful times. What are the stress factors at play within the lives of college students that keep them from fulfilling this very basic and vital need? Verplanken and Faes (1999) examined this issue in light of what they termed "implementation intentions," which are concrete plans of action that specify when, where, and how actions should be taken to accomplish a specific goal. They investigated whether implementation intentions would help students to counteract the effects of stress upon dietary habits and practices. Oaten and Cheng (2005) examined the idea that exertions of self-control will be followed by periods of diminished capacity, where placing additional demands on students would potentially produce regulatory failures in other areas where lack of control had not previously been an issue. They hypothesized that many forms of self-control break down under stress, and that the stress of college could potentially cause an

Notice the even (1 inch) margin on all four sides. Note that it won't be 1 inch on the page you are looking at because of the printing of the book, but you can see that it is proportional.

exertion of self-control that depletes an inner resource that allows regulation of other behaviors, such as healthy nutritional practices.

In a study conducted by Soweid, El Kak, Major, Karam, and Rouhana (2003), students who attended a health awareness class were studied to see if the health information they received in the class would cause improved health attitudes and behaviors. The stress management abilities of the students attending this class showed significant improvement. Understanding the attitudes and behaviors of students during stressful times would provide a starting point for the development of an approach to educating students about working through times of stress while continuing to maintain a healthy diet.

The goal of my study was to expand upon previous research regarding the attitudes and behaviors of college students under stress and how this stress affects their desire and ability to practice healthy nutritional habits. Participants were drawn from a pool of Boise State University general psychology students who elected to participate in four experiments for which they received class credit. They were asked to complete a questionnaire regarding their perceived stress levels and their subsequent nutritional habits. I hypothesize that academic stress interferes with a student's ability and desire to regulate behaviors such as healthy dietary habits and practices.

First person voice is acceptable in APA style.

Method

Participants

Participants in this study were recruited from a pool of general psychology students who self-selected via Experimetrix, an Internet-based subject pool management program. There were 62 student participants, 39 women and 23 men. The participants ranged in age from 18 to 33 years (M = 19.67, SD = 2.61). Just over 93% of participants indicated never being married, 1.7%

When a mean is presented, so is a measure of variability; in this case, a standard deviation.

Notice the boldfacing of the subheadings on this page.

The words that represent the anchor points of a scale are italicized.

indicated they were married, and 5.0% indicated they were divorced. When participants were questioned regarding whether they were responsible for preparing meals for others, 73.8% responded 'no' and 26.2% responded 'yes.'

Materials

The participants were presented with a series of six questions relating to perceived stress and nutritional habits. These six questions were created by the author and pilot-tested before their final presentation. Please see Table 1 for a list of the questions presented.

Procedure

The six questions presented by this study were part of a greater omnibus survey consisting of 181 total questions. Participants were tested in two groups. They were given 60 min to complete the survey, but finished on average within 30 min. After the survey was completed, the participants were debriefed, thanked for their contributions, and given class credit for their participation.

Results

Please see Table 1 for a complete list of all means and standard deviations for the survey questions. Significant relations were found between answers to the question, rated on an evaluative scale ranging from 1 = *low* to 3 = *high* "how would you rate your overall stress level during an average semester," and the answers to the questions, rated on a frequency scale ranging from 0 = *never* to 3 = *always* "how often do you feel unable to cope with the level of stress you are experiencing during an average semester," $r(60) = .63$, $p = .008$, and "how often does your stress level interfere with your desire to prepare a healthy meal for yourself," $r(59) = .50$, $p = .012$; as well as the question, rated on an evaluative scale ranging from 1 = *poor* to 4 =

excellent "how do you perceive your overall state of health during an average semester," $r(60) = -.56, p = .010$.

A significant relation was shown to exist between the question, rated on a frequency scale ranging from 0 = *never* to 3 = *always*, "how frequently do you eat fast food" and the question, rated on an evaluative scale ranging from 1 = *poor* to 4 = *excellent* "how do you perceive your overall state of health during an average semester," $r(60) = -.31, p = .034$.

The r for correlation is italicized, and all p values are reported to 3 decimal places.

Discussion

In my opinion, the results of this study support the idea that stress has an effect upon the desire and ability of college students to regulate a healthy diet. Anecdotally, from my own personal experience it appears that the stress of college plays a major role in the inability and lack of desire to practice healthy nutritional habits. Therefore, it was not surprising to discover that the findings of this study supported that hypothesis, as well as confirmed previous studies conducted on this topic.

I hypothesized that academic stress would interfere with a student's desire and ability to regulate behaviors such as healthy dietary habits and practices. The most important outcome of this study was the participants' perceived stress levels and how they related to other areas affected by stress, such as the desire to prepare healthy meals for oneself, perceived states of health, frequency of fast food consumption, and inability to cope with stress. When someone perceives the stressors in their life as approaching levels which they view as excessive, or with which they feel they cannot cope, their desire to cook meals for themselves or others will be affected. The negative correlation between perceived stress levels and perceived states of health demonstrates that when one observes their level of stress rising, the perception of their overall state of health decreases. Furthermore, when fast food consumption increases, one's health is perceived more negatively due to the increase in fast food consumption. Stress is clearly a hindering factor in healthy nutritional practices. Stress not only affects the desire and ability to practice healthy nutritional habits, but also influences the perception of one's state of health.

In light of previous research on this topic, it is confirmed that stress plays a role in our ability or inability to maintain and function properly in life. Glass and Singer (1972) concluded that there is a "psychic cost" for adapting to stress in our lives, and that dealing with this stress results in a reduced capacity to deal with other stressors, which could simply be meeting basic and healthy dietary needs. According to Muraven and Baumeister (2000), controlling behavior costs something and exhausts inner resources that if not replenished or strengthened in some way, will cause regulatory failures in other areas. They note that coping with stress is likely to lead to dietary failure and relapses in smoking.

Results reported by Oaten and Cheng (2005) coincided with the significant relationships found in this study between perceived stress levels and their effects upon a student's ability and desire to regulate a healthy diet. Their study examined the idea that the stress of college potentially creates adverse exertions of self control in which a student's capacity to deal with other stressors is diminished. This diminished capacity affects them in several ways, one potentially being an inability and lack of desire to regulate a healthy diet. Hudd, Dumlao, Erdman-Sager, Murray, Phan, and Soukas (2000) reported that 52.1% of students who participated in their study indicated relatively high levels of stress during the course of a typical semester. These levels of stress appeared in the students' consumption patterns, food choices, lack of exercise, and lower levels of overall health satisfaction.

The college atmosphere is not the only arena in life where stress can cause major havoc. The results of studies such as this could be generalized to other areas of life where stress plays a major role, such as the corporate world. The need for a greater understanding of the effects of academic stress, as well as effective coping strategies, should be a continuing focus of study. The limitations of this study were predominately the small sample size and the limited number of questions. It would be advantageous to continue studies such as this, but be more specific and directed in the questions asked, as well as having a greater number of questions and a larger sample size.

The importance of this research cannot be overemphasized, since stress affects the ability to function in the world in which one lives, studies, and works. It is clear from multiple informational sources that academic stress effects the dietary practices of college students. Human beings cannot exist without eating and will not be healthy if the correct foods are not consumed. If stress is the cause of dietary neglect then students are, in essence, contributing to their own demise. It would be of great benefit to students to understand the causes and effects of academic stress more thoroughly, so that this very crucial time in their lives would not be hindered by unhealthy dietary habits and practices.

Note that the References section starts at the top of its own page, and "References" is not boldfaced.

ACADEMIC STRESS AND NUTRITION 9

References

Bureau of Labor Statistics (1999). *Occupational stress and time away from work.* Retrieved September 27, 2005, from http://stats.bls.gov/opub/ted/1999/Oct/wk3/art03.htm

Glass, D. C., & Singer, J. E. (1972). *Urban stress: Experiments on noise and social stressors.* New York, NY: Academic Press.

Hudd, S. S., Dumlao, J., Erdman-Sager, D., Murray, D., Phan, E., & Soukas, N. (2000). Stress at college: Effects on health habits, health status, and self-esteem. *College Student Journal, 34*, 217-228.

Muraven, M., & Baumeister, R. F. (2000). Self-regulation and depletion of limited resources: Does self-control resemble a muscle? *Psychological Bulletin, 126*, 247-259.

Oaten, M., & Cheng, K. (2005). Academic examination stress impairs self-control. *Journal of Social and Clinical Psychology, 24*, 254-279.

Soweid, R. A. A., El Kak, F., Major, S. C., Karam, D. K., & Rouhana, A. (2003). Changes in health-related attitude and self-reported behavior of undergraduate students of the American University of Beirut following a health awareness course. *Education for Health, 16*, 265-278.

Verplanken, B., & Faes, S. (1999). Good intentions, bad habits, and effects of forming implementation intentions on healthy eating. *European Journal of Social Psychology, 29*, 591-604.

References are presented with hanging indent style, meaning that the first line is flush left and all other lines indented. The trick for doing this in Microsoft Word is to highlight the entire reference and hit "Ctrl-T" on the keyboard. Try it.

ACADEMIC STRESS AND NUTRITION 10

Table 1

Overall Means and Standard Deviations for Survey Items

Survey Item	*M*	*SD*
1. How would you rate your overall stress level during an average semester?	1.96	0.72
2. How often do you feel unable to cope with the level of stress you are experiencing during an average semester?	0.87	0.77
3. How often does your stress level interfere with your desire to prepare a healthy meal for yourself?	1.00	0.83
4. How do you perceive your overall state of health during an average semester?	3.04	0.63
5. How frequently do you eat fast food?	1.29	0.73

Note. Items 2, 3, and 5 were measured on a scale ranging from 0 = *never* to 3 = *always.* Item 1 was measured on a scale ranging from 1 = *low* to 3 = *high.* Item 4 was measured on a scale ranging from 1 = *poor* to 4 = *excellent.*

Note the spacing of the table (entirely double-spaced) as well as there are only three horizontal lines in this table, as per APA format.

Chapter 10

Doing Well in Psychology Classes: Study Tips

Learning Objectives

10.1 Summarize basic college study tips

10.2 Outline strategies for creating effective study habit

10.3 Describe successful note-taking strategies

10.4 Explain how to use tests effectively

10.5 Relate metacognition research to undergraduate learning

10.6 Explain how and why tackling math anxiety can help psychology majors

When giving study tips, there are overlapping goals such as time management, test preparation, avoiding study distractions—they all seem to relate to one another. And to be honest, study tips for doing well in psychology classes are also study tips for doing well in *all* classes. So be sure to review this chapter for any tips you can add to your current student repertoire of study strategies.

It also is important to note that some of the study strategies that were successful for you in high school may no longer work in college. Our advice—start each course as if you expect it to be the hardest course you will ever encounter in college. Once you understand the course and instructor expectations, then you can adjust your study strategies accordingly. If the course turns out to be easier or less time consuming than expected, then you can "ease up a bit." It is difficult, however, to start a semester with a lackluster performance and then have to scramble at the end with perfect execution. Instructors are all too familiar with the end-of-semester/quarter "what can I do to raise my grade" pleas, and many instructors wish that the student had cared as much about the grade since the beginning of the course. So, be that student—start the course fully engaged, and hopefully you will be able to avoid that uncomfortable, end-of-course panic.

General Study Tips

10.1 Summarize basic college study tips

Many students enter college unprepared or underprepared for the academic challenges ahead (Gabriel, 2008). The strategies that worked for you previously may not be effective now. In fact, you may find that different college classes, even different psychology classes, may require different study strategies. Broekkamp and Van Hout-Wolters (2007) outlined three types of study strategies:

1. Learning strategies, which are directed at the acquisition of knowledge and skills.
2. Resource-management strategies that include time management, help-seeking behaviors, study environment selection, and self-motivation.
3. Metacognitive strategies, including planning and other processes such as self-monitoring and revising.

The following information is designed to give you some tips on how to improve your study habits, improve your reading, get more out of lectures, and improve your test-taking skills. You need to concentrate on what you know, and you need to discover what works and does not work for you. The studying process involves a complicated sequence of behaviors.

Fight-Delaying Tactics

Delaying tactics are strategies that you use when you know the task is boring, long, or difficult (Wahlstrom & Williams, 2004). Three strategies for avoiding delaying tactics include (a) facing boring assignments with short concentrations of effort, (b) conquering long assignments by breaking them down into smaller tasks, and (c) fighting difficult tasks by tackling them first and by making sure you understand them. Delaying tactics differ from procrastination because procrastination is defined as intentionally putting things off. Delaying tactics are typically viewed as unintentional (Wahlstrom & Williams, 2004).

Get the Most from Faculty

In many cases, you may have access to nationally known or even world-class experts in a particular field of study. Why not take advantage of that opportunity when you have the chance? Gould (2012) offered good advice about making the most of the opportunity, including (a) attend class, (b) be prepared, (c) participate regularly, (d) confess your confusion, (e) utilize office hours, and (f) don't be a grade grubber. Typically, there are two different learning approaches that students take: students can be grade-oriented or learning-oriented. It's not that students are either one or the other, but there is typically a preference, such as a handwriting preference (righty or lefty). If you are grade-oriented, you might occasionally win your point with the professor, but at what cost overall? The faculty member that you bicker with over a point will probably not be writing you a strong letter of recommendations, or will not be keeping you posted on outside-of-class opportunities. Ultimately, we advise following the tenets of the Golden Rule: Treat others the way you wish to be treated. The high road is not always the easy road, but it is the high road.

Utilize Office Hours

Another important tip is this: meet your instructor outside of the classroom during office hours. Getting to know a faculty member a bit better can help you connect to your college or university (Foss, 2013), and that connection can be important in many ways. It could lead to gaining great advice, finding a mentor, starting a research project, or just gaining a better understanding of the course material. Busteed (2015) reports from the Gallup-Purdue alumni research that connecting with a faculty member who cares about you as an individual is a significant predictor of alumni perceptions of satisfaction with college and career success. Guerrero and Rod (2013) found that office hours visits were positively correlated with academic performance.

You might be interested to know what faculty expect from their students; sometimes, faculty are not very clear about this. For example, a faculty member might want to be called "Dr.," but that faculty member never tells her or his students this information. It is difficult to guess what faculty members expect, especially if the faculty member is not articulate about this.

Developing Effective Study Habits

10.2 Outline strategies for creating effective study habit

Studying is probably not one of your most enjoyable tasks. Studying is hard work. However, by being efficient, organized, and consistent you can make it easier. Here are some tips.

Create a Regular Schedule for Studying

You probably have more obligations now than before college; hence, finding time to study may be difficult. Set aside times during the week that are specifically used for studying (*and only studying*). Choose times when you are at your mental peak—wide awake and alert. Some people are "morning" people, some are "night" people; choose your time to study accordingly. You probably already know when your "prime time" is for studying. When scheduling study time, write it down or use an app. You can then schedule certain hours for specific activities. Be realistic; don't plan to study for 6 hours if you know that you can't really do that. Also, think in the long term. Use a calendar program that allows you to see the entire semester/quarter. This way, assignment due dates are less likely to sneak up on you if you can see your entire semester at a glance.

Writing your schedule down/recording it in an app helps to make it concrete and allows for time management. Elegant paper products and fancy digital interfaces for your calendaring program do you no good if you fail to use the resource. *Time management* is even more important if you have many other responsibilities (like working, family, sports). Here are some tips for time management:

- Set aside times and places for work.
- Set priorities; then do things in priority order.
- Break large tasks into smaller ones.
- Plan to do a reasonable number of tasks for the day.
- Work on one important task at a time.
- Define all tasks specifically (e.g., not "write paper").
- Check your progress often.

Once you develop your basic schedule, add school events (exams, papers, presentations). Sticking to a schedule can help you to avoid cramming and procrastination. Cramming isn't a good study idea (especially for long-term retention, such as a course with a cumulative final exam), because it strains your memory processes, drains you of energy, and exacerbates test anxiety. When people are faced with a number of tasks, most of us do the easy things first, saving the harder tasks for later. Unfortunately, by the time you get to the harder ones, you are tired and not at your best. To avoid this situation, break difficult tasks into smaller tasks. To emphasize this aspect even further, Hopper (1998) offered the 10 principles of scheduling shown in Table 10.1.

Reward Your Studying

Try to reward your *successful* study sessions with something you like (watching Netflix, eating a healthy snack, or texting a friend). Many of the traditional rewards of studying (good grades, a college degree) take time, so give yourself some immediate rewards. Take breaks and be realistic about what you can accomplish in one study session.

Table 10.1 Ideas for Better Scheduling and Time Management

Make use of daylight hours.
Study before a class that requires discussion or frequently has pop quizzes.
Study immediately after lecture classes (this is why it is best not to schedule back-to-back classes).
Study at the same time every day to establish a study habit.
Plan enough time to study.
Space your study periods.
List your study activities according to priorities, and tackle the most difficult task first.
Study during your own prime time, paying attention to your own daily cycles and levels of alertness.
Leave time for flexibility—if you don't do this, you probably won't get much use out of your schedule.
Analyze your use of time—keep a log every once in a while to see how you are using your time and where you might make improvements.
Avoid TV, YouTube, Netflix, iTunes, or listening to conversations (as in the library). Find your special nook somewhere that is *your* study place.

Getting More Out of Lectures

10.3 Describe successful note-taking strategies

Lectures can be tedious; however, poor class attendance is associated with poor grades. Even if the instructor is disorganized, going to class helps you understand how the instructor thinks, which may help with exam questions or assignment expectations. Most lectures are coherent and understandable, and accurate note-taking is related to better test performance. Here are some *tips on improving your note-taking skills*:

- You need to listen actively to extract what is important. Focus all attention on the speaker, and try to anticipate meanings and what is coming up.
- If the lecture material is particularly difficult, review the material in the text ahead of time.
- Don't try to be a human tape recorder. Try to write down the lecturer's thoughts *in your own words* (as much as you can). Be organized even if the lecture is not. Practice determining what is important and what is not (sometimes instructors give verbal or nonverbal cues).
- Ask questions during lecture. You can clarify points you missed and catch up in your notes. Most lecturers welcome questions and often wish students weren't so bashful.
- If the lecture is fast-paced (or if you are a slow note-taker), try to review your notes right after class if possible. Consult with a fellow classmate to make sure you didn't miss anything important. You may want to form a study group to regularly review lecture materials and textbook readings.

You should note that instructors are often integrating the use of technology into course instruction. Your professor may make additional materials available through a Learning Management System (LMS)—some examples include Blackboard, Canvas, or Desire2Learn. Many textbooks now come with online support, dedicated websites, customized YouTube video, and all kinds of support. Be sure to consult with your instructor to know what support materials are available for your particular course.

Improving Test-Taking Strategies

10.4 Explain how to use tests effectively

Your strategy should relate to the type of test you are taking. Most students study differently for a multiple-choice test compared with an essay exam. One myth about multiple-choice tests is that you should go with your first answer and not go back and change answers. Researchers long ago determined that this idea is *wrong*, and that 58% of the time students changed wrong answers to right ones; 20% of the time students changed right answers to wrong; and 22% of the time students changed a wrong answer to another wrong answer (Benjamin et al., 1984). Some of the items in the lists below are from Wahlstrom and Williams (2004); other sources are noted as well.

Here are some **general tips for test-taking situations**:

- When you first receive your test, preview the test (Gould, 2012), as in " . . . flip the examination sheet over and simply unload. Unloading means taking two or three minutes to jot down on the back of the exam sheet any key words, concepts, and ideas that are in your mind" (Wahlstrom & Williams, 2004, p. 176). This helps to relieve anxiety, as well as to prevent forgetting.
- Pace yourself. Make sure that when half your time is up, you are halfway through the test.
- Don't waste lots of time by pondering difficult questions. If you have no idea, guess (don't leave a question blank). If you think you can answer a question but need more time, skip it and come back later.
- Don't make the test more difficult than it is. Often simple questions are just that—simple.
- Ask a question if you need clarification.
- If you finish all the questions and still have time, review your test. Check for careless mistakes, such as double-checking earlier questions that you may have skipped.

Here are some tips for **multiple-choice exams**:

- As you read the question, anticipate the answer without looking. You may recall it on your own.
- Even if you anticipated the answer, read all the options. A choice further down may incorporate your answer. Read each question completely.
- Eliminate implausible options. Often questions have a right answer, a close answer, and two fillers. Eliminating filler items makes for an easier choice. In other words, you'd like to be able to bet on a sure thing (McKeachie, 2002).
- Often tests give away relevant information for one question in another question. Be on the lookout.
- Return to questions that are difficult.
- There are exceptions, but alternatives that are detailed tend to be correct. Pay extra attention to options that are extra long.
- Options that create sweeping generalizations tend to be incorrect. Watch out for words such as *always, never, necessarily, only, must, completely*, and *totally*.
- Items with carefully qualified statements are often correct. Well-qualified statements tend to include words such as *often, sometimes, perhaps, may*, and *generally*.
- Look for opposite choices. One of the two opposites is likely the correct answer.

If you can guess without penalty, then use these options with your multiple-choice items: (a) choose between similar sounding options; (b) if options are numbers, pick in the middle; (c) consider that the first option is often not correct; and (d) pick a familiar term over an unfamiliar one. Be sure to clarify with the instructor first to make sure there is not a penalty for guessing.

Here are some tips for **essay exams**:

- Time is usually a critical factor in essay exams. When reviewing questions, consider what you know, the time you think it will take to answer, and the point value. Answer questions that you know first, but don't neglect questions with high point values.
- Organize your thoughts so you can write them down coherently. Take one or two minutes (i.e., unload) and plan your essay (make an outline) (McKeachie, 2002).

Then make your answer easier to read by numbering your points—organizational cues and signposts will help the grader find the points you are making.

- The challenge with essays is to be both complete and concise. Avoid the "kitchen-sink" method (you don't know the exact answer, so you write all you know hoping the answer is in there somewhere).
- You have probably learned a great deal of jargon and terminology in the course, so demonstrate what you've learned in your essay (but make sure that you use the jargon correctly!).

Depending on the instructor's goals, an essay question or exam may be attempting to gauge a student's performance along a particular cognitive dimension. In Table 10.2, adapted from Gould (2012), we present commonly accepted cognitive levels with tips for how students may determine what instructors are asking for.

If possible, try to get your graded test back from your instructor, or at least specific feedback about your test performance. Use the strategies presented in Table 10.3 to make the most from **returned tests** (University of California–Berkeley, 1998).

Study skills, reading, understanding lectures, and test-taking skills are all important to achieving academic success. You cannot develop these skills overnight; however, they will emerge with practice. The rewards can be worth the effort—knowledge gained, a feeling of accomplishment, improved grades, and progress toward your degree.

Metacognition and Leveraging Learning Science

10.5 Relate metacognition research to undergraduate learning

The ideas of metacognition have existed for quite some time in the realm of cognitive psychology. What is exciting is that in the past 10 years or so, a number of cognitive

Table 10.2 Possible Cognitive Levels in Essay Exams

Cognitive Level	Student Task	Terms You May See in an Essay Question
Remembering	recalling facts, terms, concepts, definitions, principles	define, identify, label, list, name, state
Understanding	explaining or interpreting the meaning of the material	account for, convert, explain, give an example, infer, interpret, paraphrase, predict, summarize, translate
Applying	using a concept or principle to solve a problem	apply, compute, demonstrate, make use of, modify, show, solve
Analyzing	recognizing how parts relate to each other and the overall structure	break down, connect, correlate, dissect, explore, relate, link
Evaluating	making a judgment based on a pre-established set of criteria	appraise, critique, evaluate, judge, justify, recommend, which would be better
Creating	producing something new or original from component parts	change, construct, create, design, develop, formulate, imagine, write a dialogue or short story

SOURCE: Gould (2012).

Table 10.3 Making the Most of Returned Tests

If you receive your test back to keep, rework your errors trying to reason out why the correct answer was correct and yours was not.
If you do not receive your test back, visit your instructor's office to take a look at your answer sheet and the questions you missed.
Look for the origin of each question—textbook, class notes, labs, Web information, etc.
Identify the reason you missed a question. Did you read it incorrectly? Was it something that you were not prepared for? Did you run out of time?
Check the level of detail and skill of the test. Were most of the questions over precise details and facts, or over main ideas and principles (the big picture)?
Did questions come straight from the text, from lecture and class discussion, or from both?
Did you have any problems with anxiety or blocking during the test?

SOURCE: Gould (2012).

psychologists and others have been conducting the translational science from the laboratory to the elementary, secondary, and postsecondary classrooms. College students (among others) are now the beneficiaries of such work, with information about how to make the best use of your energies while studying, and what strategies to avoid because they are known to be relatively in effective.

Metacognition is typically defined as our thoughts about our own thoughts (Dunlosky & Metcalfe, 2009), that is, our thinking about our thinking. This in and of itself is a fascinating idea to think about for cognitive psychologists and philosophers alike. The scientists who study these methods often think about three stages or levels with regard to metacognition and learning:

1. Metacognitive knowledge: what you know about your own learning and what you know about how to improve your own learning
2. Metacognitive monitoring: assessing whether you are understanding what you are reading and judging whether you are approaching the correct solution to a problem you are attempting to solve
3. Metacognitive control: deciding to allocate time and energy to a particular problem-solving solution or deciding to switch to a new tactic.

Although all three of these metacognitive processes are relevant to learning, our brief focus here in this chapter is on the notion of metacognitive control, that is, the regulation of current study activity, and making the decision—do I keep studying? Have I studied enough? Do I need to study differently? Self-regulated learning is clearly related to student achievement (Panadero et al., 2017), and it involves so many different metacognitive processes, such as rehearsal, effort regulation (a.k.a. termination of effort), and help-seeking.

Not only has there been a rapid expansion of metacognitive research in the past decade that is applicable to the college classroom, but researchers are also providing user-friendly advice which distils and summarizes the complex accumulation of research studies (Dunlosky et al., 2013; Miyatsu et al., 2018; Weinstein et al., 2018). For example, Dunlosky et al. (2013) were very clear in their summary of what worked best, what worked OK, and what techniques don't work. Curious? Check out Table 10.4.

As for general instructions and tips, the information provided in Table 10.4 is top-notch. However, research efforts continue to increase our knowledge about college student learning, translated from laboratory studies to the actual classroom. Check out

Table 10.4 The Effectiveness of Learning Strategies from an Evidence-Based Perspective

Top Learning Strategies—Robust, Reliable Results Across Situations, Long-Lasting Improvements in Knowledge and Comprehension
• Self-Testing: Students create their own tests outside of class and take their own tests. Can be flash cards, answering sample questions at end of chapter.
• Distributed Practice: Rather than cram, distribute time spent learning over spans of time. Longer intervals are typically more effective. "To remember something for one week, learning episodes should be 12 to 24 hours apart; to remember something for five years, they should be spaced six to 12 months apart" (p. 50).
Learning Strategies that Show Promise—Not Enough Evidence Yet, Too Little Classroom Testing
• Elaborative Interrogation: Students create "why" questions as study prompts, and their studying involves providing the answers to the 'why' questions. Appears to work better when applied to building on prior knowledge rather than acquisition of completely new concepts.
• Self-Explanation: A student creates an explanation for what they have just learned. It capitalizes on repetition, seems easy to implement, but the long-term learning benefits are unknown.
• Interleaved Practice: Rather than study one topic or one type of problem in a block, interleaving suggests mixing up the problems to be studied. Laboratory studies have not always shown a positive outcome for interleaving, or it may be that it is not being used as it was designed to be used.
Inefficient Learning Strategies—Ineffective, Only Useful for Short-Term Learning, More Distracting, Inefficient/Too Time Consuming
• Highlighting: Although simple and quick, highlighting does little to improve performance, and there is evidence that it can hurt performance.
• Re-reading: The evidence is mixed that re-reading improves text comprehension.

SOURCE: Dunlosky, J., Rawson, K. A., Marsh, E. J., Nathan, M. J., & Willingham, D. T. (2013). *Scientific American Mind*, *24*(4), 46–53.

the advice that Miyatsu et al. (2018) provide in their comprehensive review of the study strategies of re-reading, marking the text, taking notes, outlining, and using flash cards. Notice the sophistication of the advice these researchers provide—the type of study strategy suggested can vary based on the testing scenario—note the last two columns of Table 10.5.

Math Anxiety

10.6 Explain how and why tackling math anxiety can help psychology majors

According to Conners et al. (1998), "Math anxiety is an emotional state of dread of future math-related activities. It interferes with statistics learning by making students so nervous they cannot concentrate and by lowering motivation, which, in turn, lowers effort and achievement" (p. 40). Throughout this book, we have emphasized the skills and abilities that are necessary to be successful in psychology. Math skills (especially statistics) are going to be an important part of your undergraduate career, and also your career in psychology. Math anxiety is not insurmountable, and to be successful in your undergraduate and graduate careers, you have to tackle and confront it.

Dealing with this type of anxiety is not something that you can wave your hand at and make go away, and it's not the type of situation where you wake up one morning and your math anxiety is gone. One method of dealing with this anxiety is to shape your behavior using successive approximations. Success in a math course also helps. If you have a problem in this area, try to schedule your math classes during a semester in which you can give math your best level of attention. Do not wait until the end of your career to take all of your required math classes! You'll do better in statistics and research methods, and be a more useful research assistant (and, as this sequence progresses, get better letters of recommendation, score better on the quantitative GRE section, etc.)

Table 10.5 Study Strategies to Use (with Optimization Tips and Mistakes to Avoid) by Type of Test

			Type of Testing Situation	
Study Strategy	How to Make the Most of the Strategy	Common Mistakes Using this Strategy	Multiple-Choice Type Factual Question Test	Recall-type Test to Remember Term and Apply (Essay, Short Answer)
Re-reading	• Space out the readings • Test yourself in between the readings	• Mistaking the fluency of a second reading meaning that the material is now learned	Recommended	Not recommended
Marking	• Read through the text first before marking • Pay attention to the text structure when identifying important information to mark	• Marking too little; marking non-critical information • Mindless marking	Recommended	Not recommended
Taking notes	• Make sure to review notes before an exam	• Copying lecture notes verbatim and not reviewing them	Recommended	Recommended
Outlining	• Identify the main points after reading through the whole section • Pay attention to the text structure • Use skeletal outline as a guide	• Outline from scratch without paying attention to text structure	Recommended	Recommended
Flash cards	• Retrieve an item correctly at least three times before dropping it from study	• Dropping flash cards from study after one successful retrieval	Recommended	Not recommended

SOURCE: Miyatsu, T., Nguyen, K., & McDaniel, M. A. (2018). Five popular study strategies: Their pitfalls and optimal implementations. *Perspectives on Psychological Science*, *13*, 390–407. doi:10.1177/1745691617710510

Success Stories

Liza Veliz
South Texas College

Growing up I never realized that I was poor, a minority, and a cost to my family. My parents were exceptional at shielding me from the realization that we lived in poverty, that our culture was not a universal, and that my success would require many sacrifices for them. I remember one such instance when, during middle school, I came home and asked my mom if I could be a cheerleader and needed one hundred dollars to pay for the gear. Without hesitation, my mom said yes! Over 20 years passed, and my mom finally confessed to me the great lengths she had to endure to obtain that money with such short notice because they never had a savings; there wasn't any money left to save. My family did not live paycheck to paycheck, but rather day to day. At that moment I began to cry, as feelings of guilt came over me, and I gave her a hug thanking her for her sacrifice. In hindsight, I suppose she saw how excited I was and didn't want to limit my opportunities in that way. I am sure there are many more similar recollections, and there is no doubt in my mind that my success is their success.

My ethnic identity is not one I ever thought of, much less established, as an adolescent. It wasn't until I attended college that I realized how "brown" I was, and the implications that carried in terms of my mindset, belief—system, language, and the exclusion I continue to experience in professional settings and familial context. Ironically enough, my culture and ethnicity have not always helped buffer against struggles but have manifested intrapersonal obstacles such as the perception that "I think I'm better than my family" as a result of my success. To many members, outside my immediate family and in the larger scope of the culture, my attendance and success in college is a luxury, and not even a privilege that they would be grateful I had. And with that mindset, I am seen as a traitor to my culture and have even been told that I should stop trying to be "white". My parents have also received demeaning comments to the cost of my success because it is as if I betrayed my macrosystem, especially because I was the first in my extended and immediate family to graduate college and earn a post-secondary degree. Despite their unspoken feelings of failure aimed at my success, I matriculated and hold an academic position at a Hispanic Serving Institution where I mentor students, with similar challenges to mine, and guide them toward a future that makes their entire family proud as I have.

No matter the challenges life presents us with, we must persevere and push forward. Even though my parents were never exposed to the college-going culture, they tried to understand the level of commitment and dedication required to succeed. I remember my dad walking into my bedroom and seeing me sitting in the middle of my bed with journal articles all around me as I prepared my thesis. All he would do was grin at me, as I looked up at him with a dreadful face, and say "¡Échale ganas!" then walk away. There is no direct translation in English, I can only compare it to something coaches tell their players when facing defeat but with time remaining on the clock: "Keep going" or "Give it your all." That is my message to you, "¡Échenle ganas!".

if you take the math and statistics courses early. If you are serious about graduate school, try to take an advanced statistics course if one is available. Do not be afraid to look outside your department—sociology, political science, economics, and math departments might also offer useful upper-division advanced-level statistics courses.

Study skills will be beneficial to you not only in college, but throughout the rest of your life, because we are all truly life-long learners. At your college or university, there are tremendous resources available to you to help you learn—they may be available for your specific course, in your specific major and department/program, or campus-wide. Just as you want to take advantage of the recreational centers for your physical health and counseling services for your mental health on your campus (more on these topics in the next chapter), take advantage of workshops about test anxiety, teaching assistants, instructor office hours, and so much more to keep improving your academic health. We firmly believe that help-seeking behaviors are a sign of strength, and for more on the overall topic of student self-care, keep reading.

Exercise 10.1 Locations for Studying

In using the table below, think of the three most common places that you study, and give each an arbitrary label (Place A, Place B, Place C). Answer the true–false questions for each of the locations. *The location that has the most "false" responses may be the least distracting place to study*. Try to plan your day so that the bulk of your studying is done in the most favorable place.

Study Distractions Analysis

Place A		Place B		Place C		
True	**False**	**True**	**False**	**True**	**False**	**Questions**
						1. Other people often interrupt me when I study here.
						2. Much of what I can see here reminds me of things that don't have anything to do with studying.
						3. I can often hear radio/TV/Internet when I study here.
						4. I can often hear a cell phone ringing when I study here.
						5. I think I take too many breaks when I study here.
						6. I seem to be especially bothered by distractions here.
						7. I usually don't study here at regular times each week.
						8. My breaks tend to be too long when I study here.
						9. I tend to start conversations with people when I study here.
						10. I spend time on my cell phone here that I should be using for study.
						11. There are many things here that don't have anything to do with study or schoolwork.
						12. Temperature conditions here are not very good for studying.
						13. The chair, table, and lighting arrangements here are not very helpful for studying.
						14. When I study here I am often distracted by certain individuals.
						15. I don't enjoy studying here.
						TOTALS

SOURCE: Hopper (1998).

Exercise 10.2 The Need for Achievement Scale

The psychological concept of need for achievement, sometimes abbreviated as n-Ach, is the general notion about a person's internal (intrinsic) drive to achieve or excel. A high or low need for achievement scale score is neither good nor bad. Theorists suggests that low n-Ach scorers like very easy tasks (to avoid failing) or incredibly hard tasks (something that everybody would fail). High scorers on the n-Ach scale, in theory, like a task in-between easy and hard, a task that is challenging but doable.

Here are the items on the Need for Achievement Scale. The scoring instructions follow the scale items. Answer the 20 items using the scale provided, and answer as honestly and openly as possible. Write your score in the box to the left of each statement.

Select the Score That Best Represents Your Opinion.								
Almost Never	1	2	3	4	5	6	7	Almost Always

Response	Statement
4	1. I finish my work before I relax.
3	2. "People before work," that is what I say.
3	3. I like to tell people what to do.
6	4. I have obtainable goals and I am sure I will reach them.
6	5. I prefer to avoid competitive situations.
3	6. People think I am a bit lazy.
7	7. I can be very happy just sitting at home and relaxing.
3	8. I believe problems work themselves out if you don't think too much.
5	9. I am not very independent.
6	10. I am an effective leader.
6	11. I will stay up very late if it will help me get ready for an exam.
3	12. I love solving difficult problems.
7	13. I want people to notice what I have accomplished.
5	14. I hate to compete.
7	15. I commune with nature whenever I can.
7	16. I tend to worry about things.
5	17. I feel that life is too short to worry about what we get done.
4	18. I am basically a very intense person.
7	19. I usually avoid head-to-head conflicts.
4	20. I tend to be a busy person.

Scoring Instructions

First, total the scores from Statements 1, 3, 4, 10, 11, 12, 13, 16, 18, and 20. Add here: 50

Second, total the scores from Statements 2, 5, 6, 7, 8, 9, 12, 14, 15, 17, and 19. Add here: 54

Take the First Score 50 and subtract the Second Score 54 = -4

Take the answer to the subtraction problem directly above, and add 70 = 66

Now, use that final score with the table below:

Level of Need for Achievement	Score Range
High Need for Achievement	Above 90
Intermediate Need for Achievement	50–90
Low Need for Achievement	Below 50

SOURCE: McClelland, D. (1961). *The achieving society*. Princeton, NJ: Van Nostrand.

Chapter 11
Student Self-Care

Learning Objectives

11.1 Summarize the elements of self-care

11.2 Describe stressors undergraduates experience

11.3 Explain how to practice effective self-care

Let's face it, the life of a college student is not always easy and care-free. Movies and television shows from decades past rarely depicted the complexities and stressors of college life. During Fall 2017, the American College Health Association (2018) administered a survey that examined campus health trends nationally. There were 52 participating undergraduate institutions of all types from all different parts of the country. The overall response rate to the assessment was 18%, resulting in 26,139 respondents. As you can imagine, this type of methodological approach can provide an accurate approximation of what is likely occurring on college campuses throughout the nation.

What impacts academic performance? In the survey, undergraduates were asked to indicate factors that negatively impacted academic performance, such as earning a lower exam grade, lower project grade, lower course grade; earning an incomplete or dropping a course; or if there was a substantial interruption in a senior thesis, internship, or research project-type of work (American College Health Association, 2017). In Table 11.1, we present the percentage of students reporting which events negatively impacted academic performance.

As a college student, do you see any recent life events you have experienced on this list? The question really should be how many did you see? Life is stressful as it is, and college brings its own challenges and stressors, and the college context and environment can compound the stress. That is why we think a chapter devoted to student self-care is vital to this book.

What Is Self-Care?

11.1 Summarize the elements of self-care

Self-care is an elusive concept to define; there may be nearly 140 definitions of the term in the literature (Godfrey et al., 2010; Greene et al., 2017). Self-care depictions often include activities such as physical activity, healthy choices, nutrition, spirituality, stress management, positive coping skills, professional support, life balance, and more (Ayala & Almond, 2018). When a person is engaging in self-caring, health-promoting behaviors, the benefits that accrue include life satisfaction, improved health status, and well-being. Living a healthy lifestyle, in turn, not only can lead to a productive life and fulfillment, but also be protective against burnout and some stress-related illnesses (Stark et al., 2012).

The overall goal, of course, is positive mental health, which is also may be difficult to define. Roulston et al. (2018) follow the World Health Organization (WHO) definition, which we paraphrase as a person's ability to maintain a state of well-being such

Table 11.1 Types and Prevalence of Factors Negatively Impacting Academic Performance

Percent Reporting	Event or Situation
33.5%	Stress
26.2%	Anxiety
22.9%	Sleep difficulties
17.6%	Depression
14.7%	Cold/Flu/Sore throat
13.2%	Work
11.2%	Concern for a troubled friend or family member
11.0%	Participation in extracurricular activities
9.7%	Internet use/computer games
9.1%	Relationship difficulties
6.8%	Finances
6.5%	Attention Deficit/Hyperactivity Disorder
6.2%	Death of a friend or family member
5.5%	Roommate difficulties
5.1%	Sinus infection/Ear infection/Bronchitis/Sore throat
4.6%	Homesickness
4.3%	Chronic health problem or serious illness
3.9%	Learning disability
3.5%	Chronic pain
3.3%	Alcohol use
2.6%	Allergies
2.4%	Injury
1.8%	Sexual assault
1.7%	Drug use
1.6%	Eating disorder/problem
1.3%	Discrimination
0.8%	Physical assault
0.6%	Pregnancy (yours or partner's)
0.4%	Sexually transmitted disease/infection (STD/I)
0.3%	Gambling

SOURCE: American College Health Association. (2017). *American College Health Association-National College Health Assessment II: Reference group, executive summary, fall 2017*. Hanover, MD: Author.

that they can reach their potential, be able to cope with the normal stressors of life, and are able to be productive and contribute to their own community. Well-being is not just the absence of illness, but it implies a complete state of mental, physical, and social well-being (Moses et al., 2016). Greene et al. (2017) categorized self-care strategies into four domains: physical/biological, emotional/psychological, social/leisure, and spiritual. Some examples of self-care strategies would include:

- physical/biological: appropriate nutrition, adequate sleep, and regular exercise
- emotional/psychological: journaling, reflection, engaging in psychotherapy
- social/leisure: spending time with friends/family, creative activities, vacations
- spiritual: meditation, yoga, attending church, spending time in nature

Nowack et al. (1985) reported very similar dimensions of health habits presented in five areas: diet and eating, sleep and rest, personal hygiene, substance use/abuse, and exercise and fitness. Myers et al. (2012) defined self-care practices as behaviors promoting physical and emotional well-being, with a particular emphasis on how each of the five following areas are related to the reduction of stress: sleep, exercise, social support, emotion regulation, and mindfulness. Mindfulness is a technique by which a person can actively pay attention in the moment and process feelings without labeling those feelings as good or bad. The goal of mindfulness is to bring awareness to the present moment and for the person practicing mindfulness to disengage from the types of thoughts that are detrimental to well-being, such as ruminations and anxiety (Roulston et al., 2018).

We have known for some time about the importance of social support and how that support not only helps us cope with ongoing stress, but also that social support is directly beneficial to our physical and psychological well-being (Nowack et al., 1985). A straightforward measure of social support can be the number of others that a student can turn to for support as well as the student's sense of satisfaction with his or her own support system. Without that support system (and when other indicators of self-care and positive mental health are absent), college students are at risk for stress and all of the negative effects that accompany stress.

Success Stories

Therese Losardo
D'Youville College

As a young girl, I realized that psychology was a field of study that truly interested me. I always had a knack to want to listen to people's struggles and allow them to feel heard. I knew how much it meant to people to have someone effectively listen to their concerns and feel validated.

Despite this ability to empathize and help others, I was never quite as good in helping myself. During my youth I developed significant body image issues. I felt grossly obese even though I was quite thin, and became obsessed with working out, eating in moderation, and my overall appearance. I was bullied about this by a friend and it significantly contributed to the destruction of my self-esteem. Those close to me only perpetuated my situation by constantly commenting on my appearance, as well. At the age of 14, my body image issues became even worse when I began developing cystic acne. I loathed my appearance so much that I began slipping into a deep depression and truly believed that there was no place in this world for such an ugly person. The only person I truly could rely on for support was my boyfriend. He tried his absolute best to reassure me that my thoughts were not true, but I ultimately needed professional help to deal with my internal demons and ways of thinking.

My situation worsened once I began college. My family made me feel guilty about moving out and growing into an independent adult. They had such high expectations of me, and I felt pressured to conform to their ideas of who I should be. I felt rejected by the people who were supposed to love me the most. This contributed to further self-loathing and feelings of insecurity that hampered my ability to make new friends in college. So, I was left with no new close relationships my first two years of college. I constantly thought that if I can't even help myself, how could I expect to help other people? I came to a point in my life where I almost committed suicide on two separate occasions.

Through the help of psychotherapy and a small support system, I was able to improve. The inner part of me that desperately wanted to live overcame the destructive thinking that controlled my life. The Psychology faculty where I studied truly believed in my abilities as a student and helped me more than they realize. I was able to get more involved on campus by joining the Psychology Club and eventually become an officer, which only grew my love for the field. It was through my own struggles that I realized the suffering I went through made me grow as a person – one who could better empathize and help others who are dealing with similar pain. To help just one person overcome their struggles would make everything that I endured worth it. As I continue my path towards my degree in Psychology, I know my true purpose in this field is to produce goodness.

College Student Stressors and Detrimental Effects

11.2 Describe stressors undergraduates experience

Based on the latest data available from the National Center for Education Statistics (2017), 16,869,212 undergraduate students are enrolled either full-time or part-time at either 2-year or 4-year higher education institutions in the United States. Given that sizeable number, think about how the percentages in Table 11.2 would generalize from the National College Health Assessment II (American College Health Association, 2017) to all college campuses in the United States.

These results may confirm an experience(s) that you have had. We wanted to mention two additional stressors for college students before presenting some of the research-based outcomes about evidence-informed practices involving student self-care.

When students experience test anxiety, this manifests as increased arousal, worrying, negative/self-denigrating thoughts, increased tension, and often loss of sleep or reduced quality of sleep (Damer & Melendres, 2011). There are many different measures of test anxiety available, including some measures specific to mathematics and statistics

Table 11.2 Data About College Student Experiences

Violence, Abusive Relationships, and Personal Safety

Within the last 12 months, college students reported experiencing:

	Percent Reporting	
Situation	**Male**	**Female**
A physical fight	9.8%	2.6%
A physical assault (not sexual assault)	3.8%	2.9%
A verbal threat	25.8%	17.9%
Sexual touching without their consent	3.8%	13.3%
Sexual penetration attempt without their consent	1.0%	5.5%
Sexual penetration without their consent	0.6%	3.6%
Stalking	2.6%	7.7%
An emotionally abusive intimate relationship	6.2%	11.5%
A physically abusive intimate relationship	1.4%	1.9%
A sexually abusive intimate relationship	1.0%	3.3%

Table 11.2 Data About College Student Experiences *(Continued)*

Mental Health

This is the percentage of males and females reporting experiencing the stated conditions in the past 12 months:

Situation	Percent Reporting	
	Male	Female
Felt things were hopeless	43.5%	57.0%
Felt overwhelmed by all you had to do	76.7%	91.9%
Felt exhausted (not from physical activity)	73.5%	88.2%
Felt very lonely	55.2%	64.4%
Felt very sad	56.5%	73.4%
Felt so depressed that it was difficult to function	31.6%	43.3%
Felt overwhelming anxiety	45.6%	68.6%
Felt overwhelming anger	35.9%	44.1%
Seriously considered suicide	10.9%	13.1%
Attempted suicide	1.7%	2.0%
Intentionally cut, burned, bruised, or otherwise injured yourself	5.2%	9.2%

Within the last 12 months, diagnosed or treated by a professional for the following:

Situation	Percent Reporting	
	Male	Female
Anorexia	0.7%	1.9%
Anxiety	10.4%	26.3%
Attention Deficit and Hyperactivity Disorder	7.9%	6.4%
Bipolar Disorder	1.2%	2.0%
Bulimia	0.7%	1.4%
Depression	10.1%	20.8%
Insomnia	3.5%	5.9%
Other sleep disorder	2.3%	2.6%
Obsessive Compulsive Disorder	2.1%	3.7%
Panic attacks	4.0%	14.1%
Phobia	0.9%	1.4%
Schizophrenia	0.5%	0.2%
Substance abuse or addiction	1.6%	0.9%
Other addiction	1.0%	0.4%
Other mental health condition	2.7%	3.8%
Student reporting none of the above	79.9%	65.6%
Students reporting only one of the above	8.7%	9.6%
Students reporting both depression and anxiety	6.9%	17.3%
Students reporting any two or more of the above excluding the combination of depression and anxiety	5.5%	10.9%

Within the last 12 months, any of the following been traumatic or very difficult to handle:

Situation	Percent Reporting	
	Male	Female
Academics	39.3%	51.7%
Career-related issue	20.0%	26.0%
Death of family member or friend	13.1%	18.7%
Family problems	19.1%	34.8%
Intimate relationships	26.7%	32.9%
Other social relationships	22.0%	32.5%
Finances	25.7%	37.4%
Health problem of family member or partner	13.8%	23.4%

(continued)

Table 11.2 Data About College Student Experiences *(Continued)*

Situation	Percent Reporting Male	Percent Reporting Female
Personal appearance	18.5%	35.0%
Personal health issue	14.2%	27.3%
Sleep difficulties	25.8%	34.0%
Other	8.2%	11.0%
Students reporting none of the above	33.7%	19.8%
Students reporting only one of the above	14.9%	10.8%
Students reporting two of the above	12.5%	11.8%
Students reporting three or more of the above	38.8%	57.6%

SOURCE: American College Health Association. (2017). *American College Health Association-National College Health Assessment II: Reference group, executive summary, fall 2017*. Hanover, MD: Author.

test anxiety. Researchers work to make these assessment instruments as useful as possible. For example, Taylor and Deane (2002) worked to make an existing Test Anxiety Inventory (Spielberger et al., 1980) which contains 20 items into a short form that only contains five items so that the research tool would be more useful under conditions of time constraints. Here are the five items—if you had to agree or disagree, what would your answer be:

- During tests, I feel very tense.
- I wish examinations did not bother me so much.
- I seem to defeat myself while working on important tests.
- I feel very panicky when I take an important test.
- During examinations, I get so nervous that I forget facts I really know.

Even though there are many sources of stress for college students, there are also multiple strategic methods by which to provide self-care (details forthcoming). However, we would be remiss if we did not mention an additional stressor that affects many college students: "research exploring stress in Asian American, African American, and Latino undergraduate students attending a predominately white university found stress specifically related to one's minority status to be distinct from global perceived stress and significantly related to college persistence" (Myers et al., 2012, p. 56).

Engaging in Effective Self-Care

11.3 Explain how to practice effective self-care

Typical studies about the effectiveness of self-care are often conducted with specialized, narrow populations of interest, such as medical school students, social work majors, nursing school majors, or even graduate students in psychology programs. Thus, our recommendations for undergraduates about how to engage in effective self-care come from studies based on different populations—in other words, your individual results may vary. For example, reporting on the results of a previous study with nearly 500 clinical psychology graduate students, Moses et al. (2016) summarized the outcomes of eight self-care practices and students perceived stress levels. Five of the eight practices were linked to reductions in stress levels: healthy sleep, social support, mindful acceptance, expressive suppression, and cognitive reappraisals. However, this means that three strategies were not significantly related to stress reduction levels: exercising, mindful awareness, and frequency of mindfulness practice.

In a different, slightly more recent study, mindfulness practices may have multiple, positive benefits. Roulston et al. (2018) reported the following:

- "Increase physical and emotional well-being, confidence, resilience, focus, concentration and ability to stay in the present moment, ability to cultivate self-compassion and kindness, emotional intelligence, attention and awareness.
- Improve responses to stress, the ability to make effective and balanced decisions and the ability to problem solve.
- Improve creativity, interpersonal relationships and skillfulness in communication" (p. 158).

Ayala and Almond (2018) presented a comprehensive array of possible self-care behaviors in the areas of self-compassion, relaxation and stress management, interpersonal relations, hobbies, physical wellness, and outdoor recreation. Now you should know that the participants in this study were all women pursuing their doctoral degree in health service psychology programs, so the results may not widely generalize, but what is intriguing about this study is that the researchers asked participants to rate the importance of the self-care behaviors. In Table 11.3, the six arrays are presented, and all of those presented above the shaded area were rated on average at or above 4.0 on a scale ranging from 1.0 = *not at all important* to 5 = *extremely important*.

Table 11.3 Ranked Self-Care Behaviors by Category with High Importance Indicator

Self-Compassion
Forgive myself for not being productive
Focus on not being so hard on myself
Advocate for myself as much as I can
Express gratitude to those I care about
Practice positive thinking
Mindfulness
Deep breathing
Give myself a break from dissertation guilt
Say "no" to projects that are asking too much
Therapy
Meditation
Participate in areas where I feel masterful
Relaxation and Stress Management
Take a break from doing work
Sleep
Try to stay organized
Get work done in advance to alleviate stress
Incorporate things I enjoy into daily life
Protect free time with boundaries
Stay on top of work
Take time for relaxation
Get at least 8 hours of sleep
Follow a routine
Time for quiet activities
Rest
"Me" time
Down time every night
Leisure time
Maintain appearance
Days or weekends off (no school-related work)
Take time at end of day to decompress
Solitude
Take an hour a day to do something mindless
Lazy days to lounge around
Take a day to do absolutely nothing

Table 11.3 Ranked Self-Care Behaviors by Category with High Importance Indicator *(Continued)*

Relaxation and Stress Management
Use a bedtime
Decide not to look at email for a while
Dress nicely
Interpersonal Relations
Communicate
Laugh with others
Time for friendship
Quality time with partner
Social support
Time with significant other
Eat dinner with significant other
Time with friends
Talk to friends outside of psychology
Visit significant other
Go out with friends
Process difficulties
Time with family
Talk to family
Call family
Drinks with friends
Have sex
Vent to friends and family
Time with pets
Talk to mentors
Text friends and family
Travel home
Try new restaurants with loved ones
Visit family
Date night
Play with pets
Have a glass of wine with classmate
Enjoy time outside as a family
"Girls" night
Time at home
Go to the dog park with my dog
Plan monthly outings with school friends
Hobbies
Listen to music
Cook
Hobbies
Recreational activities
Read for fun or leisure
Clean
Physical Wellness
Exercise
Workout
Eat a well-balanced diet
Be health conscious
Cook balanced meals
Running
Eat three meals per day
Cook myself a good meal after a long day
Shop for healthy foods
Yoga
Regular medical check-ups
Cycling
Take vitamins or supplements

Table 11.3 Ranked Self-Care Behaviors by Category with High Importance Indicator *(Continued)*

Outdoor Recreation
Go outside
Leisure activities during the weekend
Make the most of breaks in academic year
Fun on weekends
Engage in outside interests (e.g., art shows)
Go away for the weekend
Go on walks
Plan fun future
Experience nature
Go on trips
Spend time outdoors
Eat out
Experience new restaurants and activities
Outdoor activities
Travel to feed my soul
Explore my city
Go to the park
Spend time in nature
Sit outside
Plan activities
Take day trips where I do not bring work
Go out to listen to music
Hike

SOURCE: Ayala, E. E., & Almond, A. L. (2018). Self-care of women enrolled in health service psychology programs: A concept mapping approach. *Professional Psychology: Research and Practice*, *49*, 177–184. doi:10.1037/pro0000190

As you think about your own strategies for self-care, let Table 11.3 show you both possibilities and starting points for effective stress-reduction approaches. Remember, the stressors of college are real stressors.

Of course, every individual is different, and it will take you some trial and error to determine what works best for you to minimize stress and maximize feelings of well-being in your life. However, these are valuable life skills to learn in college, because stressors will continue with your college-to-career workforce launch, no matter what the pathway or ultimate destination.

Exercise 11.1 The Mindful Attention Awareness Scale

Below is a collection of statements about your everyday experience. Using the scale provided, please indicate how frequently or infrequently you currently have each experience. Please answer according to what *really reflects* your experience rather than what you think your experience should be.

	Please Circle the Number that Corresponds to your Answer.					
Scale Item	**Almost Always**	**Very Frequently**	**Somewhat Frequently**	**Somewhat Infrequently**	**Very Infrequently**	**Almost Never**
I could be experiencing some emotion and not be conscious of it until some time later.	1	2	3	4	5	6
I break or spill things because of carelessness, not paying attention, or thinking of something else.	1	2	3	4	5	6
I find it difficult to stay focused on what's happening in the present.	1	2	3	4	5	6
I tend to walk quickly to get where I'm going without paying attention to what I experience along the way.	1	2	3	4	5	6
I tend not to notice feelings of physical tension or discomfort until they really grab my attention.	1	2	3	4	5	6
I forget a person's name almost as soon as I've been told it for the first time.	1	2	3	4	5	6
It seems I am "running on automatic" without much awareness of what I'm doing.	1	2	3	4	5	6
I rush through activities without being really attentive to them.	1	2	3	4	5	6
I get so focused on the goal I want to achieve that I lose touch with what I am doing right now to get there.	1	2	3	4	5	6
I do jobs or tasks automatically, without being aware of what I'm doing.	1	2	3	4	5	6
I find myself listening to someone with one ear, doing something else at the same time.	1	2	3	4	5	6
I drive places on "automatic pilot" and then wonder why I went there.	1	2	3	4	5	6
I find myself preoccupied with the future or the past.	1	2	3	4	5	6
I find myself doing things without paying attention.	1	2	3	4	5	6
I snack without being aware that I'm eating.	1	2	3	4	5	6

When finished, add the scores for the numbers you circled/selected for each of the scale items. The higher the score, the greater your mindfulness according to Brown and Ryan (2003).

SOURCE: Brown, K. W., & Ryan, R. M. (2003). The benefits of being present: Mindfulness and its role in psychological well-being. *Journal of Personality and Social Psychology, 84*, 822–848. doi:10.1037/0022-3514.84.4.822

Exercise 11.2 The Epworth Sleepiness Scale

How likely are you to doze off or fall asleep in the following situations, in contrast to just feeling tired? This refers to your usual way of life in recent times. Even if you have not done some of these things recently, try to work out how they would have affected you. Use the following scale to choose the most appropriate number for each situation:

0 = would never doze

1 = slight chance of dozing

2 = moderate chance of dozing

3 = high chance of dozing

Response?	Situation
1	Sitting and reading
1	Watching TV
0	Sitting, inactive in a public place (e.g., a theater or a meeting)
0	As a passenger in a car for an hour without a break
3	Lying down to rest in the afternoon when circumstances permit
0	Sitting and talking to someone
0	Sitting quietly after a lunch without alcohol
0	In a car, while stopped for a few minutes in the traffic

Scoring: Add your responses together, then use the system below to interpret your scores (Ball & Bax, 2002):

0–5 = desirable 5

5–10 = mild sleepiness

11–15 = moderate sleepiness

16–24 = severe sleepiness, usually associated with impaired performance

NOTE: A clinical intervention is often suggested for scores 11 and higher.

SOURCES: Johns, M. W. (1991). A new method for measuring daytime sleepiness: The Epworth Sleepiness Scale. *Sleep, 14*, 540–545; Ball, S., & Bax, A. (2002). Self-care in medical education: Effectiveness of health-habits interventions for first-year medical students. *Academic Medicine, 77*, 911–917.

Chapter 12
Ethical Issues for Psychology Majors

Learning Objectives

12.1 Determine the consequences of poor student ethics

12.2 Relate ethics to psychology research

12.3 Explain why and how the APA developed its code of ethics

12.4 Summarize current standards and applications of APA ethics

12.5 Analyze the relationship between ethics and activism

In this chapter, we present ethical issues from two different perspectives: ethics as a student enrolled in a college or university (whether you are a psychology major or not), and ethics from the perspective of an undergraduate researcher. As discussed earlier, serving as a research assistant for a professor allows you to gain valuable skills/abilities and a potentially strong letter of recommendation. However, the opportunity to serve as a research assistant carries additional responsibilities, such as the guarantee of ethical interactions with your research participants and the assurance of confidentiality (Handelsman, 2012). The latter portion of this chapter reviews the general principles for ethical behavior as a psychologist.

Before we address those principles specific to psychology, however, a broader topic involves your ethical behavior as a person. How do you treat other people? Do you treat everyone you encounter with dignity and respect? Do you show respect for the laws of the land and the rules that your institution imposes on the student body? It is clearly difficult to legislate ethical behavior among people—in fact, some people walk a fine line between actions and behavior that are probably unethical but not technically illegal. This is indeed a larger societal challenge. Ayal et al. (2015) reported the following in U.S. annual losses: $1 billion paid out in bribes, $270 billion lost to the nation through taxes due to unreported income, and $42 billion lost in the retail sector because of shoplifting and employee theft. Of course, we would encourage you to seek the higher moral and ethical plane—some people behave in a certain way because they don't think they'll be caught, whereas others know the difference between right and wrong and do what's right, even if they could get away with what's wrong. As an undergraduate psychology major, you should have exposure to ethical concepts and ideas, hopefully in a number of different classes. It is clear from the literature that education in ethics is valuable for undergraduate students (Lamb, 1991; Mathiasen, 1998) and that students can learn ethical behavior and beliefs (LaCour & Lewis, 1998). For instance, student researchers who worked with Institutional Review Boards (more on this topic later in this chapter) became more serious about the research process (Kallgren & Tauber, 1996).

The Ethics of Being a Student

12.1 Determine the consequences of poor student ethics

What are the ethical responsibilities of being a college student? Most colleges and universities address this topic with respect to cheating and academic dishonesty. Much of the work in this area is credited to one of the authors of this book, Stephen Davis (Davis, 1997; Davis & Ludvigson, 1995; Davis et al., 1992; Davis et al., 1995; Davis et al., 2009). In a series of studies conducted across the nation, 40–60% of college students self-report that they have cheated at least once during their college career, and over 50% of that number report cheating on a regular basis. Although many colleges and universities have academic dishonesty policies (and some have honor codes), students still cheat—again, it is hard to legislate ethical behavior.

It is fair to ask "So what if a student cheats on an exam?" As discussed in earlier chapters, if you have a career in psychology, at some point someone is going to expect you to know about your major and the discipline. Cheating is a short-term solution that leads to bigger problems—it will probably become apparent at some point after graduation that you did not "know your stuff," and that lack of knowledge may create some significant employment issues for someone who has cheated. Additionally, it makes your institution look bad because faculty members graduated students who did not "know their stuff." This perception lowers the value of a degree of other graduates from your institution, and specifically those graduates in your major. Think of it this way—do you want a surgeon operating on you who cheated his or her way through medical school? Do you want a lawyer protecting your legal interests who cheated her or his way through law school? Do you want someone who is having serious psychological problems (perhaps a loved one of yours) to see a psychologist who cheated his or her way through graduate school? The bottom line is that someone someday is going to expect you to know about and understand the principles of psychology and be able to demonstrate the skills we except college graduates to have (e.g., critical thinking skills, communication skills, sociocultural, and interpersonal awareness)—why not just learn the material, complete the projects, and acquire the skills rather than spending an enormous amount of time and effort cheating?

The consequences of academic dishonesty can be serious, including failure on the assignment, failure in the class, and suspension or expulsion from the university. Be sure you are familiar with the particular policies of your institution. It is clear there are ethical responsibilities to being a student, but what about the special responsibilities of being a student researcher? The remainder of this chapter is devoted to that topic.

The Ethics of Research

12.2 Relate ethics to psychology research

Ethics is a commonly used term that has broad applications in psychology. For example, we might question the ethics of a particular researcher, whether or not a procedure is ethical, or if measuring a participant's behavior can be done in an ethically prudent way. Ethics generally refers to a code of honor in science that researchers follow proper procedures and treat the research participants (whether they be human or animal) properly. As you might expect, psychologists trained in research methods occasionally disagree as to what is proper. And these issues are just as complicated (if not more so) for clinicians and practitioners.

Fortunately, the APA has developed a set of rules and regulations of ethical behavior (first adopted in 1953, with major revisions in 1982, 1992, 2002), with amendments to the 2002 code in 2010 and 2016. For the most current version of the code, see www.apa.org/ethics/code/index.aspx. Portions of this code are presented near the end of this chapter. As an overview, Handelsman (2011a) describes the seven "Cs" of ethics, which include:

- competence, which can be seen as providing significant value or as not doing harm;
- confidentiality, or disclosing to others what is only necessary;
- conflict of interest, such as avoiding harmful dual-role relationships;
- consent, that is, the provision of adequate information such that informed decisions are possible;
- character, to develop virtuous traits in addition to "following the rules";
- consultation, meaning to seek out help from others when needed, thus being truly humble; and
- codes, which are our ethical principles that guide and inspire our behavior in the psychological community.

> In doing psychological research, the overriding consideration is the analysis of cost versus benefit. The researcher must weigh this decision carefully in any situation involving the participation of humans. Do the potential benefits that might be derived from a research study outweigh the potential harms (or costs) to the participant? Researchers do not take this decision lightly. One method to minimize the costs or harms to a human participant is to fully inform the person about the nature of the research. Thus, if there are potential harms from placing the participant at risk, then the participant can make an informed judgment about whether to participate or not. This judgment is typically called *informed consent*. According to Jones (1985), informed consent is the process by which potential research participants must be given enough information in advance to make an informed decision about whether or not they want to participate in the research. Informed consent should always include both the risks and the benefits of participating in a research study.

The Development and Use of APA Ethical Principles

12.3 Explain why and how the APA developed its code of ethics

Although psychologists were self-motivated to generate a code of ethics on their own, events made public after World War II hastened the need for a written ethical code. In many of the Nazi concentration camps in Europe, prisoners were experimented on under horrible conditions and without regard for the sanctity of human life. Out of those events came the Nuremberg Code (Trials of War Criminals Before the Nuremberg Military Tribunals Under Control Council Law No. 10, 1949), from which much of the APA ethical guidelines are based. The 10-point Nuremburg Code is presented in Table 12.1.

As early as 1935, the American Psychological Association (APA) formed a special committee to discuss ethical matters and make recommendations on how to resolve complaints. By 1948, this committee recommended that the informal procedure they had used for years be formalized into a code of ethics for psychologists. The Committee on Ethical Standards for Psychology was formed and used a unique method of forming and organizing the formal code of ethics. This committee surveyed thousands of members of the APA and asked them to describe any situation in which a psychologist would need to make an ethical decision. Based on the responses, the committee developed a code designed to encompass a large variety of ethics-type situations, which at that time condensed into six general categories: responsibility to the public, the relationship between therapist and client, teaching, research, publishing, and professional

Table 12.1 The Nuremberg Code

1. Participation of subjects must be totally voluntary and the subject should have the capacity to give consent to participate. Further, the subject should be fully informed of the purposes, nature, and duration of the experiment.
2. The research should yield results that are useful to society and that cannot be obtained in any other way.
3. The research should have a sound footing in animal research and be based on the natural history of the problem under study.
4. Steps should be taken in the research to avoid unnecessary physical or psychological harm to subjects.
5. Research should not be conducted if there is reason to believe that death or disability will occur to the subjects.
6. The risk involved in the research should be proportional to the benefits to be obtained from the results.
7. Proper plans should be made and facilities provided to protect the subject against harm.
8. Research should be conducted by highly qualified scientists only.
9. The subject should have the freedom to withdraw from the experiment at any time if he (or she) has reached the conclusion that continuing in the experiment is not possible.
10. The researcher must be prepared to discontinue the experiment if it becomes evident to the researcher that continuing the research will be harmful to the subjects.

relationships (Crawford, 1992). After input was received from the membership, this code was published as the *Ethical Standards of Psychology* by the APA in 1953. This basic code has been revised several times, and the general principles are presented in Table 12.2. Handelsman (2011b) reminded us that the two overarching reasons for an ethics code are to "(a) inspire professionals to act according to important principles and high ideals, and (b) provide specific and useful guidance for how to behave" (p. 12).

Table 12.2 General Principles from Ethical Principles of Psychologists and Code of Conduct (APA, 2010)

General Principles
This section consists of General Principles. General Principles, as opposed to Ethical Standards, are aspirational in nature. Their intent is to guide and inspire psychologists toward the very highest ethical ideals of the profession. General Principles, in contrast to Ethical Standards, do not represent obligations and should not form the basis for imposing sanctions. Relying upon General Principles for either of these reasons distorts both their meaning and purpose.

Principle A: Beneficence and Nonmaleficence
Psychologists strive to benefit those with whom they work and take care to do no harm. In their professional actions, psychologists seek to safeguard the welfare and rights of those with whom they interact professionally and other affected persons, and the welfare of animal subjects of research. When conflicts occur among psychologists' obligations or concerns, they attempt to resolve these conflicts in a responsible fashion that avoids or minimizes harm. Because psychologists' scientific and professional judgments and actions may affect the lives of others, they are alert to and guard against personal, financial, social, organizational, or political factors that might lead to misuse of their influence. Psychologists strive to be aware of the possible effect of their own physical and mental health on their ability to help those with whom they work.

Principle B: Fidelity and Responsibility
Psychologists establish relationships of trust with those with whom they work. They are aware of their professional and scientific responsibilities to society and to the specific communities in which they work. Psychologists uphold professional standards of conduct, clarify their professional roles and obligations, accept appropriate responsibility for their behavior, and seek to manage conflicts of interest that could lead to exploitation or harm. Psychologists consult with, refer to, or cooperate with other professionals and institutions to the extent needed to serve the best interests of those with whom they work. They are concerned about the ethical compliance of their colleagues' scientific and professional conduct. Psychologists strive to contribute a portion of their professional time for little or no compensation or personal advantage.

Principle C: Integrity
Psychologists seek to promote accuracy, honesty, and truthfulness in the science, teaching, and practice of psychology. In these activities psychologists do not steal, cheat, or engage in fraud, subterfuge, or intentional misrepresentation of fact. Psychologists strive to keep their promises and to avoid unwise or unclear commitments. In situations in which deception may be ethically justifiable to maximize benefits and minimize harm, psychologists have a serious obligation to consider the need for, the possible consequences of, and their responsibility to correct any resulting mistrust or other harmful effects that arise from the use of such techniques.

Principle D: Justice
Psychologists recognize that fairness and justice entitle all persons to access to and benefit from the contributions of psychology and to equal quality in the processes, procedures, and services being conducted by psychologists. Psychologists exercise reasonable judgment and take precautions to ensure that their potential biases, the boundaries of their competence, and the limitations of their expertise do not lead to or condone unjust practices.

Principle E: Respect for People's Rights and Dignity
Psychologists respect the dignity and worth of all people, and the rights of individuals to privacy, confidentiality, and self-determination. Psychologists are aware that special safeguards may be necessary to protect the rights and welfare of persons or communities whose vulnerabilities impair autonomous decision-making. Psychologists are aware of and respect cultural, individual, and role differences, including those based on age, gender, gender identity, race, ethnicity, culture, national origin, religion, sexual orientation, disability, language, and socioeconomic status and consider these factors when working with members of such groups. Psychologists try to eliminate the effect on their work of biases based on those factors, and they do not knowingly participate in or condone activities of others based upon such prejudices.

The Role of Informed Consent and the Institutional Review Board

12.4 Summarize current standards and applications of APA ethics

In terms of ethical behavior, one of the fundamental concepts that emerge from examining both the Nuremburg Code and the *Ethical Principles* of the American Psychological Association is that participants must be told, at some time or another, about the nature of the research project. In most cases, it is preferable to accomplish this objective prior to the onset of the research. Why? First, it allows participants to make a judgment (i.e., informed consent) about whether they want to participate. Second, it gives the participants more information about the general nature of the required tasks. Third, telling participants about the general nature of the research prior to onset allows the researcher to obtain informed consent. Informed consent means that participants have some idea about the research study and have given their permission not only to participate, but also that the researcher may collect data.

Although we may think about informed consent in the traditional face-to-face experiment (where the researchers and participants are located in the same room), a great deal of research is now conducted on the Internet. As you can imagine, data collection via the Internet presents its own challenges, including that of securing informed consent for participants. Although beyond the scope of our chapter here, Buchanan and Williams (2010) thoroughly described 16 different challenges to data collection on the Internet. To provide some brief examples, think about how you might solve these challenges: (1) How do you secure and guarantee informed consent prior to online research participation? (2) What do you do with participants who do not complete participation; how do they receive debriefing materials, and what type of credit might they receive (if enrolled in a course where research participation is part of course credit)? (3) How would you prevent minors from participating in your Internet survey if you are asking for volunteer participants? These are examples of just a few of the challenges to conducting research on the Internet.

Who decides whether an experiment (minimal risk, informed consent, or deception) meets the ethical standards of the APA? Although researchers are required always to consider the ethical practices in their research, most colleges and universities also have a standing committee called the Institutional Review Board (IRB; this committee is sometimes called the Human Subjects Committee). The IRB is typically composed of faculty members from various disciplines and individuals from the community; it is charged with one major function: to protect the rights of persons and animals who participate in research. Any college or university that receives federal funding for research is required to have such a committee. Gone are the days when a researcher might design a new experiment in the morning and actually administer that experiment to participants (i.e., "run subjects") that afternoon. The hypotheses, research methodology, and participant recruitment and treatment all come under scrutiny of the IRB. Only after the approval of this board may researchers go forward with their research. The IRB screens research projects so that no or minimal harm occurs to persons who participate. If minimal harm may occur, the IRB certifies that the proper informed consent procedures are in place. Experiments involving deception come under the close scrutiny of the IRB, especially in weighing the risk of the deception against the potential benefits of the outcomes.

Although the chief function of the IRB is the protection of the participant population, other advantages occur from its use. The IRB also serves as a screening device for the college or university in knowing what kinds of research activities are taking place on campus (and on the Internet). If the IRB feels that a particular research project may involve too much risk (risk to the participant or risk to the university), it may reject a project. Another advantage of the IRB is for the protection of the researchers. Often the IRB may have procedural suggestions to make and offer improvements.

The decision to conduct psychologically sound research is not a light one. There are a number of factors that must be carefully considered in making this decision—only a handful of those factors have been discussed here. In Table 12.3, we present a listing of the rights and responsibilities of research participants; and for some great resources for both students and faculty members, see Barber and Bagsby (2012). This listing echoes the sentiments of the Nuremburg Code and the APA *Ethical Principles*. Although we have focused on your responsibilities as a researcher, the participant also has responsibilities in this process. The dual benefit that accrues from student participation in research is that it allows psychologists to study human behavior and collect data to further the human condition; this opportunity gives students a firsthand learning experience with the research process. To read about research in a textbook or journal article is one way to learn it; you gain a very different experience by being an active participant in actual "real" research.

There are times when the research enterprise goes wrong; sometimes there are accidents, and at other times there is purposeful misconduct. Because of the importance of ethical principles and protecting human and animal subjects, it is also worth the effort to be proactive in our research practices and attempt to prevent scientific misconduct. In Table 12.4, we present a few specific strategies that scholars have suggested toward this end.

Table 12.3 Rights and Responsibilities of Research Participants

Rights of Research Participants

1. Participants need to be told what to generally expect, just like anyone would like to know what is about to happen.
2. A participant can withdraw from a research study at any time, and if they do withdraw, they are entitled to the full benefits of the study as originally promised.
3. The potential gains or insights from study participation must outweigh the potential losses or drawbacks from participating. If participants do not receive what they were promised, they may withhold their data from further analysis by the researchers.
4. What happens during the study session is to remain confidential, unless the participant otherwise gives their permission.
5. Participants, especially college students, cannot be forced or coerced into participation in research; equitable alternatives must be available when exposure to research is a course requirement.
6. Deception in research should be avoided when possible; if necessary, participants should be told about the deception as soon as possible. If the participants are displeased with the procedures used, they have the right to withhold data.
7. If something goes wrong during a research study, a participant needs to inform all relevant parties, including the Department Chair as well as the Institutional Review Board or similar body.

Responsibilities of Research Participants

1. Participants need to listen to instructions and inquire if there are questions.
2. Participants should be on time for their research appointment, or complete the task in the agreed upon time frame.
3. Participants need to provide their best and honest efforts in completing the research tasks.
4. Participants need to work to understand the purpose of the study and why events unfolded as they did.
5. If asked not to disclose to others, participants should honor this request from researchers.

SOURCE: Adapted from Korn (1988).

Table 12.4 Methods to Help Prevent Scientific Misconduct

- Whistle-Blowing—laboratory colleagues familiar with the work making the accusation of misconduct
- Completing a Responsible Conduct of Research (RCR) course—this is in addition to the typical social and behavioral researchers/Institutional Review Board (IRB) ethics training researchers complete
- Reducing the Emphasis on Number of Publications and Impact Number on Judging a Researcher's Productivity—would then in theory reduce the lure of misconduct and misrepresentation
- Data Recording and Data Sharing—storing and sharing all of the original data and data analysis tools in a reproducible fashion for access by others

SOURCE: Gross, C. (2016). Scientific misconduct. *Annual Review of Psychology, 67*, 693–711. doi:10.1146/annurev-psych-122414-033437

Success Stories

Taylor Cook

I attended Catholic school my entire elementary and high school career because the schools in my inner-city, Saint Louis district held dangerous, unsuccessful reputations, even lacking proper accreditation. College never existed as an option; both parents and teachers insisted college remain a requirement. However, most of my classmates came from affluent backgrounds with college-educated parents, while my only exposure to upper-level education developed from what I watched on basic cable. School was never about enriching knowledge, but getting straight As in order to receive acceptance letters. I prioritized college in order to make my parents proud and eventually reimburse them for all they sacrificed for my future. I looked at the future as a benefit to them and a burden on myself. My motivation remained almost entirely extrinsic, even into my initial semester. Being a first-generation college student provided a small sense of pride, but it was not until my second semester of my freshman year that I discovered and embraced the true meaning of higher education. Thus, I began a crusade for social justice.

One bitter January afternoon, I entered the classroom of Dr. Beloso, a Gender, Women and Sexuality Studies professor at Butler University. Enrolling in her class changed my life quite literally. The course titled "Intersections of Identities" aimed to expose students to the experiences of people with different backgrounds and illustrate how various cultural identifiers (race, gender, sexual orientation, etc.) affect daily experiences. As someone with an extensive private school, Catholic education and limited exposure to diverse demographics, I tell you confidently that the concepts of inclusivity and equality expressed in this class were mostly overlooked or presented with bias during my previous years of education. After a couple weeks of this course, I realized how much knowledge I lacked about certain social issues. Quite frankly, I felt misled by the education system I trusted. I value my schooling for instilling in me the discipline required to succeed in any academic environment, but Dr. Beloso's class taught me that straight As are not the most important aspect when getting a degree. This course opened my mind and sparked my desire for accruing knowledge. Dr. Beloso showed me knowledge truly is power and, especially with technology today, I possess all the tools I need to campaign for progress.

In alignment with my desire to thrive in my chosen field, I aimed to acquire as much experience as possible. I applied and accepted a position as an Undergraduate Learning Assistant in the psychology department. Although the idea of joining a research team intimidated me, I examined a list of active teams and stumbled upon the Educational Psychology lab of Dr. Young-Jones. Excitement arose within me as I imagined exploring my newfound passion of diversity and inclusion by the side of others sharing my academic interests. I felt this lab was a perfect match and my interest in conducting research became more intrinsic. My enthusiasm only grew as we began to construct studies on micro-aggressions and perceptions of diverse populations. Eventually, social justice enlightened my understanding. Today, research operates as my weapon against a lack of knowledge. Participating in research promoted development of leadership, organization, and critical thinking skills. Understanding proper procedures and measurements increased confidence in my career path. Excitement ensues knowing I am and will continue to contribute to a pool of public knowledge. Participating in Dr. Young-Jones research lab challenged me like never before. I desire to challenge others to strengthen their own knowledge so they, too, possess a weapon in the battle toward social justice.

Once again within a higher academic environment, a professor helped me realize my passions and potential. Dr. Young-Jones awakened me to new opportunities perfectly aligned with my interest and skill set. After the team concluded a diversity workshop presentation for a local middle school class, she approached me eagerly expressing how well I commanded the room, while holding students attention and leading a fresh, interactive discussion. She asked if I ever considered School Psychology, a field I never heard of prior to this experience, but quickly researched after discovery. Following this enlightenment, I imagined no better way to support others than by providing knowledge to our youth. Education evolved into a weapon in my battle toward social justice.

Actually, conducting research is a complicated enterprise, not only from the methodological perspective, but also from an ethical perspective. As undergraduate student researchers, you have a responsibility to protect the health and welfare of your research participants, and at the same time pursue research that enables you to test worthy hypotheses. A psychologist must never take lightly the consideration of using humans or animals for research purposes, and the potential benefits from such research enterprises must always outweigh any potential costs or harm to the participant.

Becoming a Psychologist-Activist

12.5 Analyze the relationship between ethics and activism

Nadal (2017) recently revived the phrase 'psychologist-activist' in his 2017 *American Psychologist* article. A psychologist-activist attempts to balance the roles of psychologist (which are usually well-defined by the time a person earns his or her master's degree or doctorate) and the role of activist (which is often ill-defined for many academics). Although Nadal was addressing primarily practitioners (clinical and counseling psychologists), we believe that this message to engage, to be an advocate for social justice while simultaneously respecting the boundaries of the APA Ethics code is just as vital and relevant for undergraduate psychology majors.

In the profession, there is a long history of social activism, including social movements concerning racial segregation, a woman's right to vote, the legalization of same-sex marriages, Native American people's rights, LGBTQ rights, and more (Nadal, 2017). Many psychologists have been hesitant to engage in social justice/activism efforts, and Nadal highlights five key dilemmas:

- There is a concern that the ethical boundary/expectation is that psychologists are to remain neutral with regard to politics.
- There is the belief that the psychology will be the most effective if they stay neutral by not becoming politically active.

- There is a hesitation to get involved because of the expected additional stressors and burdens social activism would cause in addition to already feeling overworked.
- There is an avoidance due to the lack of advocacy training, that is, how to effectively achieve social justice goals.
- There is a level of disinterest because some psychologists feel no activism is needed because the status quo represents their personal feelings and beliefs.

It is certainly easy to understand why so many psychologists would choose not to take a psychologist-activist position in their lives. The drawbacks are palpable and real. But without the pressures and progress of psychologist-activists from the past, the United States would not have made progress in areas such as public opinion about social stigma, government policies and laws, and changes to how practices/policies are formed and implemented regarding physical and mental health (Nadal, 2017). The two main strategies to continue to be an effective psychologist-activist are (a) utilizing organizational and institution-wide approaches to fighting oppression, and (b) taking an individual/interpersonal approach to fighting oppression.

The balancing act between ethics and activism may be difficult at times, but we believe it is vital to embrace the challenge. We really cannot be any more poignant on this topic than Nadal (2017, p. 944)

> Finally, as individuals, psychologist-activists realize that personal growth and learning are lifelong processes. They challenge themselves by exploring how their power and privileges influence the ways that they see the world and how the world sees them. When they belong to historically marginalized groups, they identify the ways they enact oppression, too, and the intersectional dynamics they participate in. When they have power or privilege, they use those identities to advance social justice, while constantly checking how their identities affect their biases, attitudes, and behaviors. They acknowledge that people are genuinely "allies" when they know they do not need to be identified as such; they also are comfortable with the notion that some people will never, or will be hesitant to, view them as allies at all. They work on their defensiveness. They thrive on learning. They integrate justice into every aspect of their lives, while always staying gracious, because they know injustice anywhere is injustice everywhere.

Exercise 12.1 A Test of Psychological Ethics

This is a test designed to measure your current content knowledge about ethics. Please carefully read the following 10 items about ethics in psychology. Circle the item that you believe is the best, most ethical, answer.

The answer key is provided at the conclusion of the test.

1. It is unethical for research psychologists to:

- **a.** Offer excessive compensation for research participation.
- **b.** Offer no compensation for research participation.
- **c.** Have a restricted research sample.
- **d.** All of the above.

2. Serious relationships (dating, etc.) between psychology instructors and students are:

- **a.** Always ethical.
- **b.** Always unethical.
- **c.** Sometimes unethical.
- **d.** Are prohibited in circumstances in which the professor has evaluative authority over the student.

3. A competent psychologist:

- **a.** Ignores differences between him/herself and his/her clients.
- **b.** Seeks consultation and supervision when developing new areas of practice.
- **c.** Does not serve populations with which he/she has little or no experience.
- **d.** Is able to serve all client populations.

4. A psychologist is required to be confidential about information. But under which of the following circumstances can a psychologist break confidentiality?

- **a.** Under no circumstances.
- **b.** In order to be reimbursed by an insurance company for services rendered.
- **c.** Only when a client says, "I could just kill somebody," but does not identify a specific person.
- **d.** Only with written consent of client.

5. An ethical requirement for research psychologists is to get approval for the research they are performing. The research proposal is reviewed by an Institutional Review Board whose primary purpose is to:

- **a.** Review projects for scientific merit.
- **b.** Protect the public from harm.
- **c.** Establish standards governing the conduct of psychologists in research.
- **d.** All of the above.

6. For psychologists in clinical practice, dual relationships (i.e., having a relationship with a client as a psychologist and in another role like a teacher, supervisor)

- **a.** Are not prohibited unless they are harmful or exploitative.
- **b.** Are always prohibited
- **c.** Are restricted to small or rural community settings.
- **d.** Are always harmful.

7. In obtaining informed consent for participation in a psychology experiment, a psychologist

- **a.** Allows potential subjects the freedom to decline participation.
- **b.** Is required to have written consent for every experiment.
- **c.** Discusses every implication of withdrawing and continuing in the experiment.
- **d.** Does not give the prospective participants the opportunity to ask questions.

8. In the clinical practice of psychology, informed consent includes:

- **a.** Information about the limits of confidentiality.
- **b.** Dialogue about financial arrangements and fees.
- **c.** Respect for the client's autonomy.
- **d.** All of the above.

9. In underserved areas, or areas where there are few psychologists, a psychologist

- **a.** May routinely provide services to a client, even if he/she is not fully competent to provide the services.
- **b.** Provides services to a client population only if he/she is fully competent to do so.
- **c.** Provides services to anyone in case of an emergency.
- **d.** Can choose to work with any population and refer those persons with whom he/she does not want to work.

10. It is difficult to draw a clear line between those student–faculty relationships that are ethical and those that are unethical. We may do so by assessing:

- **a.** The extent the relationship includes coercion (a faculty member intimidating students).
- **b.** The extent of exploitation (a faculty member taking advantage of students).
- **c.** Neither A nor B.
- **d.** Both A and B.

Answer Key:

1. a
2. d
3. b
4. b
5. b
6. a
7. a
8. d
9. c
10. d

SOURCE: Zucchero, R. A. (2011). Psychology ethics in introductory psychology textbooks. *Teaching of Psychology, 38*, 110–113. doi:10.1177/0098628311401583

Exercise 12.2 Making Moral Decisions

Making moral and ethical decisions can be more complex than it might originally appear. On the one hand, it might seem like there are a set of rules, so all a person has to do is just follow the rules. Well, on the other hand, social psychologists tell us that context of the situation can often interfere with the "simplicity" of a situation.

We have adapted a seemingly straightforward ethical dilemma used in a study by Stanley et al. (2018). Read the scenario in the top box, but cover up the two side-by-side gray boxes for now. After reading the top box, stop—before going any further, think about what you would naturally do.

Now flip a coin—heads right box, tails left box. Go to either gray box as indicated by the result of the coin flip. Out of the seven reasons provided, which one is closest to how you really feel? When complete, uncover the remaining c box and read those seven reasons, and make the same selection (which one is closest to how you really feel).

Now, review all three of your responses. How much in sync are they? Did this ethical scenario turn out to be more complicated that you first expected? Evaluate your answer to that question, and why you think that is so.

You were almost finished with your weekly trip to the grocery store. The grocery store you are shopping at is part of a large chain of grocery stores with locations throughout the United States. You had been waiting in line at the grocery store to pay for your groceries for quite some time. Once you finally reach the front of the line to check out, the clerk ignores you for a moment while she sends a text on her phone. Once she finishes sending her text, she checks you out. You pay with cash. The clerk accidentally gives you an extra $40 in change. You just lost your job, so the extra $40 would be helpful while you search for a new job. You have two possible courses of action. You can return the money to the clerk, or you can just walk out of the grocery store with the extra money.

The seven reasons provided for returning the extra money to the clerk:

1. If the manager learns about the missing money, the clerk might lose her job.
2. The missing $40 make be taken out of the clerk's paycheck.
3. If I were in the position of the clerk, I would want customers to return the money.
4. Being honest is always the best course of action.
5. You might feel particularly guilty for keeping the extra money.
6. The clerk could have given me the extra money intentionally to test my character.
7. My friends and family might be disappointed in me for not returning the money.

The seven reasons provided for not returning the extra money to the clerk:

1. This will teach the grocery store clerk to be more responsible.
2. It is not my fault that the clerk gave me extra change.
3. It may help reveal to the store administrators that the clerk is an unprofessional employee.
4. The clerk was being rude by texting on the job anyways.
5. The extra $40 will help me make ends meet while I search for a new job.
6. The grocery store is part of a large corporation that would not suffer from losing $40.
7. The extra money will make up for the inconvenience of waiting in line for so long.

SOURCE: Stanley, M. L., Dougherty, A. M., Yang, B. W., Henne, P., & De Brigand, F. (2018). Reasons probably won't change your mind: The role of reasons in revising moral decisions. *Journal of Experimental Psychology: General, 147*, 962–987. doi:10.1037/xge.0000368

Chapter 13

The Psychology Major: Nurturing Your Career

Learning Objectives

13.1 Summarize personal actions of students that benefit undergraduates

13.2 Relate diversity to the study and practice of psychology

13.3 Identify disciplines that have commonalities with psychology

13.4 Evaluate your vocational alignment using a Self-Directed Search

13.5 Describe resources useful for a psychology student

If you have read the whole book, you know that we have covered a variety of topics. We opened with details about majoring in psychology and what psychology majors can do with a bachelor's degree and higher degrees. Opportunities outside the classroom play a considerable role in your success during your undergraduate years of study. We then focused on some of the skills and abilities that you will need for success in almost any major, but particularly in psychology: locating prior research, tips for writing in APA format, tips for doing well in classes, the ethics of being a college student, and doing research in psychology. We now try to bring this journey full circle by addressing issues related to the psychology major, and other disciplines related to psychology that you might not have considered, and by directing you toward some self-reflection and assessment. Think of this as the "capstone" chapter if you will—attempting to put all of the pieces of the picture together in one place, stepping back, and taking a broad view of the discipline and where you fit within it.

Most of our readers are either psychology majors or students seriously considering the major. You may not yet know your exact career path, and you don't have to. Even if you think you know, it is likely to change, and you can change that path any time along the way. Making a choice about a job or career is not a one-time singular decision that lasts the rest of your life. Sometimes students (and new graduates) place this type of pressure upon themselves, and they think that first career/job choice has to be perfect, else they are doomed. Who makes the absolutely perfect choice the first time they attempt anything important or complex? Hardly anyone! Make the best decision you can with the information available, take some risks, and believe in yourself—see how far you can go. Regardless of the pathway or career route, Goodman et al. (2006) suggested that resilience or career adaptability will be key for you. Career adaptability focuses on the balance between work and life, with special emphasis on your ability to "go with the flow" regarding changing world conditions. Goodman et al. offered these dimensions that comprise the components of career adaptability: (1) work values,

(2) autonomy/sense of urgency, (3) one's perspective on the future, (4) career exploration, (5) workplace information, (6) decision-making skills, and (7) reflections on one's work experiences. We'll return to the theme of self-reflection later in this chapter.

The Psychology Major, with Purpose

13.1 Summarize personal actions of students that benefit undergraduates

In our combined experience over two careers, trends begin to emerge. Given the privilege of having this textbook as an outlet to help students succeed in whatever professional pathway they choose, we are afforded the opportunity to share our observations, even when they are not fully backed by empirical evidence yet. We organize this around three areas of advice, followed by an educational climate goal. Hang on.

Focus on Your Skills

Psychology educators love the content of the discipline, and so do the students. Let's face it, the ideas that you heard about in Introductory Psychology or Abnormal Psychology or Social Psychology likely hooked you into the major. We all love the content of psychology, because, what could be more fascinating than the study of ourselves? We believe what will set you apart is your ability to apply that content in real-world settings, that is, to have skills in which your knowledge of human behavior gives you an advantage over others who do not have that knowledge. We like to think of it this way; content is the fuel and the skills are the engine. Of course we need fuel to get anywhere; but fuel without an engine also is useless. As for employers, they tell us over and over about the skills gaps and how vital real-world application abilities are (e.g., AAC&U, 2018). We encourage all psychology majors to focus on your skills, because you have them, whether you recognize this or not.

Tell Your Skills Story on Your Resume

Actually, that part about "recognizing your skills or not" is really a problem/issue for many psychology majors (and hence psychology faculty). We have noticed (again, anecdotally) that many psychology majors "undersell" their skill sets and accomplishments on their resumes/curriculum vita. That is, they fail to state that they have statistical analysis experience but they worked on a Research Methods project for two semesters using SPSS to analyze their own data, or they forget to mention their study abroad experiences, or how they were the team captain (leadership skills) for a co-curricular organization. Although skills are practiced and honed through experiences such as research assistantships and internships, a well-designed curriculum should lead to skill development for all psychology majors who successfully complete the coursework.

When students fail to tell the complete story on their resumes, they are placed at a disadvantage when competing for jobs in the future. This is especially relevant for those with intentions for the workforce psychology route, for as we have stressed earlier in this book, the challenge is this: there are plenty of jobs available for workforce psychology graduates, but none of those jobs are exclusive to psychology graduates. So the best jobs will have high competition—meaning that the resumes will have to be top-notch—which in turn means that a student will be disadvantaged if they leave anything (especially a marketable skill!) omitted from their resume. This is as much a concern for faculty advisors and department chairs, because the success of our alumni reflects upon the success of our faculty, department, college, and institution. A related corollary to being able to tell the skills story on your resume is this—be able to tell your own story, persuasively, during a job interview, graduate school interview, or professional school (law school, medical school, occupational therapy school, etc.) interview.

Have the 3-minute "elevator pitch" ready at all times. Practice answering interview questions by conducting mock interviews before the actual interviews. Be prepared to set yourself apart from the crowd in a positive way and be primed for success.

Avoid the Imposter Phenomenon

Have you accomplished something truly wonderful, but inside you feel like you just got lucky and if someone examines the situation very closely, you feel like you will be discovered as a fake (or an imposter)? This set of feelings is known as the imposter phenomenon (Clance & Imes, 1978). In higher education, this phenomenon occurs all too often, and we see it not only in our undergraduate psychology majors, but also in graduate students as well as our faculty member colleagues. Rather than taking credit for their hard work and their success, the person will give credit for their success to being lucky or having the right connections (Kumar & Jagacinski, 2006).

That might not seem like a problem, but it is a problem. First, imposters are unsure about their own abilities—do I apply for that scholarship or that grant? If I think that only luck is at play, I might not bother to apply. Researchers tell us that imposters have lower self-perceptions, greater anxiety, and less well-being (Kumar & Jagacinski, 2006). From both the literature and from our personal experiences, our female colleagues, mentees, advisees, and students tend to exhibit imposter phenomenon characteristics far too often. Thus, a female student can undercut or self-handicap her own chances at success in that job application or graduate school application even without knowing it. It is up to advisors and mentors to notice these trends and alert our students to not only focus on skills but tell the skills story, loudly and proudly.

A Bonus and an Extra—Make the Educational Climate a Disruptive Climate

To be sure, please read everything we mean here. What we do not mean here is to go into a classroom and be disruptive—we are not encouraging discourteous or disrespectful behavior. But what we do mean is that students, collectively, can be agents of change and agents of control in their own educational pathways. What does that mean, exactly?

Since higher education began in the United States, the system has been largely a system of faculty design and faculty delivery of a curriculum, and students consume that curriculum as offered. If students did not like the curriculum, they typically had little recourse, although students "vote with their feet"—they leave the major or they leave the institution when they don't like something. This option has been around, and will always exist for students. But what we mean by disruptive climate is the notion of trying to change the educational system/climate by staying at the institution and changing from within. How, exactly? At the Western Psychological Association meeting in 2018, your first author gave a talk about this very topic, where a dream scenario was shared (Landrum, 2018, Slide 31):

> Students shop for courses that have the highest levels of active learning. Instructors who chronically lecture have empty sections, and students drive the type of education they want. Students raise the bar on instructor expectations, because higher expectations of student performance in college can lead to superior knowledge and skill development, leading to a better future.

Students do not need to be passive receptacles of their education; they can be activists and help to shape, in a positive fashion, an educational system that benefits all, including our most important stakeholders, our psychology majors.

Beginning the Journey, After the Journey

Throughout this book, we have emphasized strategies for success—so much so that it's part of the title of the book! If you have been following along chapter by chapter, you can now understand the complexity of majoring in psychology and being successful. If available to you at your college or university, you might be able to take a course that helps you launch into the psychology major. There are a number of universities now (Green et al., 2008; Roscoe & Strapp, 2009) that offer "Introduction to the Psychology Major"-type courses (Dillinger & Landrum, 2002; Landrum et al., 2003; Macera & Cohen, 2006; Mulcock & Landrum, 2002). In an evaluation of the effectiveness of such courses, Thomas and McDaniel (2004) developed a Career Information Survey for psychology majors (see Table 13.1). Students rated each item on a scale from 1 = *strongly disagree* to 5 = *strongly agree*. More recent efforts (Roscoe & McMahan, 2014) also confirm the benefits of such courses. Not only do these types of research studies highlight the information necessary for psychology majors, but it also helps demonstrate the beneficial effects of completing the coursework.

We have some information about a successful launch into the major with major-specific orientation courses, but what about students' attitudes and opinions after all the coursework is complete? If they had it to do all over again, would psychology graduates (i.e., alumni) select the same major? Kressel (1990) conducted a survey of social science (including psychology) alumni and asked a series of questions about degree satisfaction and job satisfaction (see also Braskamp et al., 1979; Finney, Snell, & Sebby, 1989; Keyes & Hogberg, 1990; McGovern & Carr, 1989). Kressel found that 39% of the respondents said they would probably select the same major. The strongest predictor of degree satisfaction was the job-relatedness to the major. The factors that lead to higher satisfaction with the psychology degree include having a higher degree, being female, more course enjoyment, more course difficulty, income satisfaction, and job satisfaction. In more recent work, Landrum and Elison-Bowers (2009) conducted a national study of psychology alumni from seven different Departments of Psychology and the top findings that emerged include:

- older alumni report that previous psychology coursework was more helpful as compared to the opinions of younger alumni;
- current salary was positively correlated with happiness levels in one's career choice; and
- alumni with lower GPAs believed more strongly that the Psychology Department could have been more proactive in assisting students with pursuing career goals.

It is important to remember that the results from this study are correlational, and not cause-and-effect. However, there are some nuggets of advice embedded. First, it may take a while for alumni to see the direct benefit of their undergraduate education and training. Second, it may be that when a person is more satisfied with their career choice, they are motived to work harder, which may result in a better salary. Third (and perhaps most important), be proactive in seeking opportunities that will allow you to maximize your chances at career success. Do not end up being a student who will reflect on their

Table 13.1 Psychology Major Career Information Survey Items

1.	I have a clear understanding of the kinds of work done by different types of psychologists (e.g., clinical, social, experimental, organizational).
2.	If I decide to become a psychologist, I know what steps I will have to take to accomplish this goal.
3.	I know how to go about preparing for, selecting, and getting admitted into graduate school.
4.	I can identify several different fields of study that would allow me to do counseling/therapy and I understand what each of them involves.
5.	I can identify a number of "people helping" careers outside of psychology and I have some understanding of the preparation required for each of these careers.
6.	I can identify several areas within the business world in which a psychology major may be valuable and I know how to pursue a career in business if I should decide to do so.

SOURCE: Thomas & McDaniel (2004).

undergraduate career saying "I wish I did this" or "I wish I did that." Seize the opportunities that you have available to you while an undergraduate; for some students (especially those that realize this late in their academic careers), this sometimes means adding a year of coursework and "extending your stay."

Diversity in Psychology

13.2 Relate diversity to the study and practice of psychology

You can think about diversity in many ways. A person can have number of diverse experiences, or receive her or his education at a diverse collection of schools. Typically, however, we think of diversity as in cultural diversity or ethnic diversity. This type of diversity—racial diversity and ethnic diversity—is extremely important and relevant. However, the world of diversity is much broader and more inclusive; when we think of diversity, we should think about the diversity of gender identity, sexual orientation, and social class. We should strive to consider the full range of diverse peoples, including ages, differing abilities, different nationalities, different religious practices, and many other dimensions not mentioned here.

Diversity is an important component of higher education. Why? In a civilized society, the qualities to which we aspire sometimes are hard to pinpoint, and for some, hard to justify. In February 1999, 67 learned societies banded together to publish a statement about the importance of diversity in higher education. Many learned societies adopted this sentiment as their own view/stance concerning diversity. One such example comes from the American Council on Education, and their publication of a document titled "*On the Importance of Diversity in Higher Education*" in June 2012. The statement is eloquent and on point; some of the key points are that ". . . many colleges and universities share a common belief, born of experience, that diversity in their student bodies, faculties, and staff is important for them to fulfill their primary mission: providing a high-quality education. The public is entitled to know why these institutions believe so strongly that racial and ethnic diversity should be one factor among the many considered in admissions and hiring. The reasons include:

- Diversity enriches the educational experience. We learn from those whose experiences, beliefs, and perspectives are different from our own, and these lessons can be taught best in a richly diverse intellectual and social environment.
- It promotes personal growth—and a healthy society. Diversity challenges stereotyped preconceptions; it encourages critical thinking; and it helps students learn to communicate effectively with people of varied backgrounds.
- It strengthens communities and the workplace. Education within a diverse setting prepares students to become good citizens in an increasingly complex, pluralistic society; it fosters mutual respect and teamwork; and it helps build communities whose members are judged by the quality of their character and their contributions.
- It enhances America's economic competitiveness. Sustaining the nation's prosperity in the 21st century will require us to make effective use of the talents and abilities of all our citizens, in work settings that bring together individuals from diverse backgrounds and cultures" (para. 3–7)

If you believe in the values of diversity as outlined above, then you can be confident that psychology as a profession seems to be headed in a good direction. Given the emphasis of understanding human beings and the study of individual differences, it is hard to think of someone who would not value diversity *but* be truly interested in understanding human behavior.

Success Stories

Daniela Cruz

Throughout all my childhood and adolescent years, my parents always worked hard but even with them working countless hours a week they still barely earned a minimum wage. The circumstances constrained my family to live in impoverished circumstances. We experienced hot summers and freezing winters and even though the money that entered the house could have been used for other matters my mother always reserved enough money to buy my school supplies. She used to wake me up every morning and send me to school always reminding me that I could do better, live better, but in order for me to achieve that goal I had to continue going to school. Only educational excellence could open the doors that would allow me to pursue a future where I and possibly my future children would not lack happiness and comfort. Since the moment I was old enough to comprehend the importance of education I have committed my time and focus to not only attend school but to pursue higher education and exceed at it, not just for me but also for my parents, to repay their hard work and wise counsel and to ensure the bright future, happiness, and success they have always thought me capable of. This, of course, has not been an easy goal to achieve, because of the financial limitations my family endures attending college was a worrisome venture. I did not obtain financial aid for my classes; therefore, my parents and I had to work even harder to raise the money necessary to cover the total cost of tuition and textbooks semester after semester. Nevertheless, I persisted on obtaining the best possible grades and understanding. Achieving the vice president honor roll during the spring semester in 2017 and the president honor role in the fall of 2017. Fortunately, I found wonderful mentors among my professors who continued to encourage me to pursue my dreams and new opportunities. Thanks to my hard work and dedicated mentors I was invited to join a national honor society in psychology and participate in research, which consequently provided me with the skills to enter an abstract proposals competition for undergraduates where my submission to the Southwestern Psychological Association's student research competition was selected as a finalist. I was then finally able to graduate with an associate of arts in social sciences/psychology and immediately commenced my bachelor of science in psychology. Unfortunately, hardship and obstacles persist amongst my new path yet the key character traits such as determination, perseverance, and self-discipline that have brought me thus far prevail. As a consequence, new opportunities have begun to arise reinforcing my commitment and dedication to my studies and to my future.

Other Related Options

13.3 Identify disciplines that have commonalities with psychology

The bulk of our efforts have been to address psychology and students choosing to major in it. There are a number of related disciplines that we want to discuss briefly to make the picture complete. A common response that students give when they are asked,

"Why are you majoring in psychology?" is "Because I want to help people." Although this is a noble reason, it is also broad and vague. Many disciplines also strive to help people—in this section we will focus on anthropology, criminal justice, political science, social work, and sociology. We do not present this information to try to talk you out of psychology but to make you aware of the full palette of possibilities available within the social sciences. Even though you may feel *strongly* that psychology is the major for you, we would be remiss if we did not mention that there are other opportunities for careers that help people. Our ultimate goal is for *you* to be satisfied in your choice of major and career. Below we present some brief descriptions of the disciplines mentioned. Note that it is impossible to convey the essence of any discipline in a single paragraph.

Anthropology

Anthropology is the study of humans, past and present. To understand the full sweep and complexity of cultures across all of human history, anthropology draws and builds upon knowledge from the social and biological sciences as well as the humanities and physical sciences. A central concern of anthropologists is the application of knowledge to the solution of human problems. Historically, anthropologists in the United States have been trained in one of four areas: sociocultural anthropology, biological/physical anthropology, archaeology, and linguistic anthropology. Anthropologists often integrate the perspectives of several of these areas into their research, teaching, and professional lives (American Anthropology Association, 2018, para 3).

Criminal Justice

The field of criminal justice refers to the system of law enforcement, courts and corrections in the United States. It includes the governmental institutions that aim to uphold social control, lessen the occurrence of crime and implement consequences for those who violate laws. Unlike criminology, criminal justice is concerned with directly addressing criminal behavior and crime in society. The study of criminal justice involves learning about the administration side of crime-related careers. Students will learn about criminal investigation, criminal justice reform, criminal profiling, judicial process and constitutional law, among other topics. To be successful in this field, individuals should have strong judgment and analytical skills, along with being observant, responsible and honest (Concordia University, 2014, para 6).

Political Science

Political science is the study of politics and power from domestic, international, and comparative perspectives. It entails understanding political ideas, ideologies, institutions, policies, processes, and behavior, as well as groups, classes, government, diplomacy, law, strategy, and war. A background in political science is valuable for citizenship and political action, as well as for future careers in government, law, business, media, or public service (Northwestern University, 2018, para 1).

Social Work

The profession of social work seeks to improve the quality of life for individuals and to effect system-wide change through the pursuit of social justice. Just like any helping profession, such as nursing and teaching, social work seeks to help people overcome some of life's most difficult challenges. What separates social work from other helping professions is its focus on the person-in-environment model and its emphasis on social justice. Social workers not only consider individuals' internal struggles, as a counselor might, they also work with people to examine their relationships, family structure, community environment, and the systems and policies that impact them in order to identify ways to help address challenges.

Social work also emphasizes a strengths-based approach in which all individuals have strengths and resources and the social worker's role is to help build upon a person's skills and support systems. The profession of social work is varied serving people young and old, from every walk of life, in a number of settings such as hospitals, schools, neighborhoods, and community organizations. It involves work with families, couples, groups, organizations, and communities. Social work is dedicated to the pursuit of social justice through direct service and through advocacy on the local, national, and global levels (Social Work Guide, 2018, paras 3,4).

Sociology

Sociology is the study of human social relationships and institutions. Sociology's subject matter is diverse, ranging from crime to religion, from the family to the state, from the divisions of race and social class to the shared beliefs of a common culture, and from social stability to radical change in whole societies. Unifying the study of these diverse subjects of study is sociology's purpose of understanding how human action and consciousness both shape and are shaped by surrounding cultural and social structures (University of North Carolina, 2018, para 1).

Clearly, there are a variety of methods that you can use to help people—these are just samples of some of the disciplines related to psychology. In addition, the undergraduate degree is good preparation for graduate work in many of the disciplines mentioned above—a career path that students sometimes overlook. Don't limit your horizons and career choices.

Self-Reflection, Self-Assessment, and Career Development

13.4 Evaluate your vocational alignment using a Self-Directed Search

Our focus is to provide information that we believe is critical for you to be a successful psychology major. That goal rests on the notion that you want to be a successful psychology major. In the previous section, we reviewed several options that share some similarity with psychology. In this section we explore career interest tools as well as life development ideas. In particular, we focus on the Self-Directed Search (SDS), a career-planning tool developed by Holland (1994). The SDS developed out of Holland's theories of vocational choice (1958, 1959). According to Holland (1973), four working assumptions drive the theory:

1. In this culture, most persons can be categorized as one of six types: realistic, investigative, artistic, social, enterprising, or conventional.
2. There are six kinds of environments: realistic, investigative, artistic, social, enterprising, and conventional.
3. People search for environments that will let them exercise their skills and abilities, express their attitudes and values, and tackle agreeable problems and roles.
4. A person's behavior is determined by an interaction between his or her personality and the characteristics of his or her environment.

The basic notion of this theory is that people are happier and more successful in a job that matches their interests, values, and skills. Scoring of the SDS is linked to occupational codes and titles. Thus, by determining your preferences for styles or types, the SDS gives you some indication of the jobs that you might like and would make the most of your skills and interests. The fundamental idea is that people and work environments can be classified according to Holland's six types; thus, if you know your own type and understand the types that are associated with particular careers, you can find a match.

Holland's SDS (1994) is a relatively straightforward inventory. There is an Internet version (http://www.self-directed-search.com/), which, for $9.95 (at the time of this writing), you can take on your computer and receive a personalized report with your results. Individuals answer questions about their aspirations, activities, competencies, occupations, and other self-estimates. These scores yield a three-letter Summary Code that designates the three personality types an individual most closely resembles. With this code, test-takers are provided an occupational list where you can explore occupations based on the SDS code, think about daydream occupations, the education that it would take to achieve certain occupations, the career outlook (including wages), and how to leverage the knowledge of your SDS code with other resources such as O*NET (presented in Chapter 3), CareerOneStop, the Occupational Outlook Handbook, and others. Although it is not possible for you to take the SDS here, we describe the six personality types and examples of corresponding careers in Table 13.2. If you are interested in taking the SDS, you might want to contact your campus Counseling and Testing Center or Career Center. There may be a small fee for this service, but the insight and self-reflection gained from the SDS is worth it.

The SDS presents some interesting options for persons thinking about a career. Although you haven't taken the SDS, you can look at the six different types and realize that perhaps one or two of them fit you very well. The idea here is to not be afraid of some self-exploration; it is important for you to figure out what you would like to do for a career. College is a great time for career exploration; if you put some work into it, you will enjoy the rewards you reap.

Self-awareness and self-reflection are critical components to your short-term decision-making and your long-term success with career choices. Thinking deeply about what you want, and what you want to become is a great investment in you and

Table 13.2 Personality Types and Occupations of the Self-Directed Search

Realistic		***Investigative***	
Personality Type	**Occupations**	**Personality Type**	**Occupations**
• Have mechanical ability and athletic ability? • Like to work outdoors? • Like to work with machines and tools? • Genuine, humble, modest, natural, practical, realistic?	• Aircraft controller • Electrician • Carpenter • Auto mechanic • Surveyor • Rancher	• Have math and science abilities? • Like to explore and understand things and events? • Like to work alone and solve problems? • Analytical, curious, intellectual, rational?	• Biologist • Geologist • Anthropologist • Chemist • Medical technologist • Physicist
Artistic		***Social***	
Personality Type	**Occupations**	**Personality Type**	**Occupations**
• Have artistic skills and a good imagination? • Like reading, music, or art? • Enjoy creating original work? • Expressive, original, idealistic, independent, open?	• Musician • Writer • Decorator • Composer • Stage director • Sculptor	• Like to be around other people? • Like to cooperate with other people? • Like to help other people? • Friendly, understanding, cooperative, sociable, warm?	• Teacher • Counselor • Speech therapist • Clergy member • Social worker • Clinical psychologist
Enterprising		***Conventional***	
Personality Type	**Occupations**	**Personality Type**	**Occupations**
• Have leadership and public speaking ability? • Like to influence other people? • Like to assume responsibility? • Ambitious, extroverted, adventurous, self-confident?	• Manager • Salesperson • Business executive • Buyer • Promoter • Lawyer	• Have clerical and math abilities? • Like to work indoors? • Like organizing things and meeting clear standards? • Efficient, practical, orderly, conscientious?	• Banker • Financial analyst • Tax expert • Stenographer • Production editor • Cost estimator

SOURCE: Holland, J. L. (1994). *Self-Directed Search® (SDS®) Form R* (4th ed.). [Instrument]. Odessa, FL: Psychological Assessment Resources.

in your future. Self-awareness can be thought of as a construct that is comprised of self-insight, self-knowledge, self-monitoring, self-regulation, and self-assessment (Klimoski & Hu, 2011), and is believed to be directly linked to one's interpersonal awareness and effectiveness. Thus, self-awareness will be important not only for success as a student but also for success in the workplace and beyond. Just as one example of one technique that can lead to the enhancement of self-assessment, consider the practice of journaling.

Journaling is influential because answering important questions can sometimes yield meaningful and clear answers for your own self-reflection. When you write in a journal regularly, you become the type of person who can define what they want, has definite plans, and can articulate your desires. Combs (2000) suggested the following journalizing questions:

- What are the most important things in your life?
- What are the activities that you love and enjoy most today?
- What would be your ideal work environment today?
- How would your ideal work day go today?
- How would you define success today?
- What might be your purpose or destiny?
- How do you want to be perceived by your friends? Coworkers? Parents? Significant other?
- What magazine would you most like to be featured in for your tremendous accomplishments in 10 years?
- What would you like to be the best in the world at?
- Who are your heroes and what is it about them that you most want to be like?
- What do you really think should be changed in the world?
- What do you most want to be remembered for at the end of your life?
- Whom do you envy and what is it about them that you envy?

As you can see, these are powerful questions and should provoke thoughtful responses. Not only is college a good time for career exploration, but a good time for life exploration as well. There are many different types of self-assessments available that can help you explore career options (McKay, 2010); this includes value inventories, interest inventories, personality inventories, skills assessments, and computer-aided career guidance programs. You might think about exploring the Character Strengths survey (free) from the VIA Institute on Character (https://www.viacharacter.org/www/Character-Strengths-Survey) or perhaps the CliftonStrengths34 (formerly StrengthsFinder), ranging in price from $19.99 to $49.99 at the time of this writing (https://www.gallupstrengthscenter.com/home/en-us/strengthsfinder). Regardless of the method chosen, we strongly encourage you to self-reflect about who you are, where you are, and what you want to be, and then to map out a plan that can help you realize your goals.

More Resources

13.5 Describe resources useful for a psychology student

We designed this entire book to provide you with valuable resources. Be sure to take advantage of the references section (which lists everything we have referenced). As you can tell from our citations, the Internet is a valuable resource for information about psychology. For more information, especially about careers, check out some of the resources listed in Table 13.3.

Table 13.3 Recommended Resources

American Psychological Association. (2007). *Getting in: A step-by-step plan for gaining admission to graduate school in psychology* (2nd ed.). Washington, DC: Author.

Appleby, D. (2007). *The savvy psychology major*. Dubuque, IA: Kendall-Hunt.

Davis, S. F., Giordano, P. J., & Licht, C. A. (2009). *Your career in psychology: Putting your graduate degree to work*. Malden, MA: Blackwell.

Dunn, D. S., & Halonen, J. S. (2016). *The psychology major's companion: Everything you need to know to get you where you want to go*. New York, NY: Worth.

Helms, J. L., & Rogers, D. T. (2015). *Majoring in psychology: Achieving your educational and career goals* (2nd ed.). Malden, MA: Blackwell.

Hettich, P. I., & Landrum, R. E. (2013). *Your undergraduate degree in psychology: From college to career*. Thousand Oaks, CA: Sage.

Kuther, T. L. (2015). *The psychology major's handbook* (4th ed.). Belmont, CA: Wadsworth.

Kuther, T. L., & Morgan, R. D. (2012). *Careers in psychology: Opportunities in a changing world* (2nd ed). Belmont, CA: Thomson Higher Education.

Landrum, R. E. (2009). *Finding jobs with a psychology bachelor's degree: Expert advice for launching your career*. Washington, DC: American Psychological Association.

Landrum, R. E. (2012). *Undergraduate writing in psychology: Learning to tell the scientific story* (2nd ed.). Washington, DC: American Psychological Association.

Morgan, B. L., & Korschgen, A. J. (2013). *Majoring in psych? Career options for psychology undergraduates* (5th ed.). Needham Heights, MA: Allyn & Bacon.

Schultheiss, D. E. P. (2008). *Psychology as a major: Is it right for me and what can I do with my degree?* Washington, DC: American Psychological Association.

Silvia, P. J., Delaney, P. F., & Marcovitch, S. (2016). *What psychology majors could (and should) be doing: An informal guide to research experience and professional skills* (2nd ed.). Washington, DC: American Psychological Association.

Sternberg, R. J. (Ed.). (2006). *Career paths in psychology: Where your degree can take you* (2nd ed.). Washington, DC: American Psychological Association.

Wegenek, A. R., & Buskist, W. (2010). *The insider's guide to the psychology major: Everything you need to know about the degree and profession*. Washington, DC: American Psychological Association.

We have previously mentioned many of these resources. Keep them in mind as you make your career plans. Knowledge is power, so we hope you will gather all the information you can and then make intelligent decisions.

Psychology is an exciting profession with a positive and growing future. The complications of current lifestyles and choices make understanding behavior even more important and imperative. Behavioral problems and difficulties are all the more commonplace nowadays. Compared to other sciences, psychology is relatively young, with many frontiers still to be blazed and a number of behavioral phenomena yet to be explored or understood. We do have a bias, however—we think that psychology is inherently fascinating, and when you are passionate about a topic such as this, it's natural to want to share that feeling and hope it is infectious. Speaking of passion, we particularly like this recent depiction offered by Wallace (2011, para 15):

> So when we urge graduates to pursue dreams and passions, we are not telling them to satisfy selfish desires and neglect everyone else. We are challenging them to go explore the world and find something so compelling that they will dedicate their best energies to pursuing it. We do this knowing that the passionate roads are far from the easiest paths that they could take in life. Far easier to pursue a "steady" predetermined path or career that they will spend judging their accomplishments in dollars and counting the days until retirement. So why pursue the more challenging roads that are build and inspired by passion? Because that *is* how you save communities and transform the world. It's also the strongest weapon you can have for surviving tough times and standing out from the crowd. (emphasis in original)

We hope that you come away from this book feeling more positive and more informed about what psychology has to offer, and how you can succeed by majoring in psychology. As we discussed from the beginning, the choice of psychology as a discipline to study and as a career can take many different directions and occur in many different settings. We hope that your use of this book will continue as you journey through the major—at different times you may need to refer to different sections.

What can be more interesting than understanding human behavior? Many psychologists have found that attempting to answer that question can make for a pleasant and rewarding career choice. May your journey be as rewarding as it can be—now just make it happen!

Exercise 13.1 Your Future Work-Self

For each of the items below, answer honestly using the scale provided.

Item	Strongly Disagree	Disagree	Neutral	Agree	Strongly Agree
1. I am planning what I want to do in the next few years of my career.	O	O	O	O	O
2. I am thinking ahead to the next few years and plan what I need to do for my career.	O	O	O	O	O
3. I engage in career path planning.	O	O	O	O	O
4. I have recently begun to think more about what I would like to accomplish in my work during the next year or two.	O	O	O	O	O
5. I develop skills which may not be needed so much now, but in future positions.	O	O	O	O	O
6. I gain experience in a variety of areas to increase my knowledge and skills.	O	O	O	O	O
7. I develop knowledge and skill in tasks critical to my future work life.	O	O	O	O	O
8. I seek advice from my supervisor(s) or colleagues about additional training or experience I need in order to improve my future work prospects.	O	O	O	O	O
9. I initiate talks with my supervisor about training or work assignments I need to develop skills that will help my future work chances.	O	O	O	O	O
10. I make my supervisor aware of my work aspirations and goals.	O	O	O	O	O
11. I am building a network of contacts or friendships with colleagues to obtain information about how to do my work or to determine what is expected of me.	O	O	O	O	O
12. I am building a network of contacts or friendships to provide me with help or advice that will further my work chances.	O	O	O	O	O
13. I am building a network of colleagues I can call on for support.	O	O	O	O	O

This is a scale about proactive career behaviors. There are four different factors or subscales to this overall scale. In general, the more you agree with the items, the better you are situated with respect to the scale

Career Planning (Items 1–4)

Proactive Skill Development (Items 5–7)

Career Consultation (Items 8–10)

Network Building (Items 11–13)

The ultimate results are yours to interpret. Are you pleased with your results? Are there areas where you might like to improve?

SOURCE: Strauss, K., Griffin, M. A., & Parker, S. K. (2012). Future work selves: How salient hoped-for identities motivate proactive career behaviors. *Journal of Applied Psychology, 97*, 580–598. doi:10.1037/a0026423

Exercise 13.2 A Sample Scale of the Imposter Phenomenon

For the items below, answer honestly using the scale provided.

	Agree						Disagree
	1	2	3	4	5	6	7
I feel I deserve whatever honors, recognition, or praise I receive.							
In general, people tend to believe I am more competent than I really am.							
I often feel I am concealing secrets about myself from others.							
I often achieve success on a project or task when I have anticipated I would fail.							
I feel confident that I will succeed in the future.							
My personality or charm often makes a strong impression on people in authority.							
I consider my accomplishments adequate for this stage in my life.							
I feel confident that I will succeed in the future.							
At times, I have felt I am in my present career position through some kind of mistake.							
Sometimes I am afraid I will be discovered for who I really am.							
I tend to feel like a phony.							
I am certain my present level of achievement results from true ability.							
I find it easy to accept compliments about my intelligence.							

NOTE: This is Harvey's (1982) Imposter Phenomenon Scale, sourced from Fried-Buchalter (1992).

SOURCE: Fried-Buchalter, S. (1992). Fear of success, fear of failure, and the imposter phenomenon: A factor analytic approach to convergent and discriminant validity. *Journal of Personality Assessment*, *58*, 368–379.

References

Actkinson, T. R. (2000, Winter). Masters & myth: Little-known information about a popular degree. *Eye on Psi Chi, 4*(2), 19–21, 23, 25.

Allan, B. (2018, July). Important, worthwhile, and valuable employment: How helping others makes work more meaningful. *Psychological Science Agenda*. American Psychological Association. Retrieved from http://www.apa.org/science/about/psa/2018/07/valuable-employment.aspx

American College Health Association. (2017). *American College Health Association-National College Health Assessment II: Reference group, executive summary, fall 2017*. Hanover, MD: Author.

American Council on Education. (2012, June). *On the importance of diversity in higher education*. Retrieved from https://www.acenet.edu/news-room/Documents/BoardDiversityStatement-June2012.pdf

American Anthropology Association. (2012). *What is anthropology?* Retrieved from http://www.aaanet.org/about/whatisanthropology.cfm

American Anthropology Association. (2018). *What is anthropology?* Retrieved from http://www.americananthro.org/

American Psychological Association. (1986). *Careers in psychology*. Washington, DC: Author.

American Psychological Association. (1996). *Psychology: Careers for the twenty-first century*. Washington, DC: Author.

American Psychological Association. (1997a). *A guide to getting in to graduate school*. Retrieved from http://www.apa.org/ed/getin.html

American Psychological Association. (1997b). *Getting in: A step-by-step guide for gaining admission to graduate school in psychology*. Washington, DC: Author.

American Psychological Association. (1998). *Data on education and employment–doctorate*. Retrieved from http://research.apa.org/doc1.html

American Psychological Association. (2003). Applications, acceptances, and new enrollments in Graduate Departments of Psychology, by degree and subfield area, 2001–2002 [Table]. Source: *Graduate study in psychology 2003*. Washington, DC: Author.

American Psychological Association. (2004). *About APA*. Retrieved from http://www.apa.org/about/

American Psychological Association Research Office. (2003). *Work settings for baccalaureate degree recipients in psychology: 1999*. Washington, DC: American Psychological Association.

American Psychological Association. (2007). *APA guidelines for the undergraduate psychology major*. Washington, DC: Author. Retrieved from http://www.apa.org/ed/precollege/about/psymajor-guidelines.pdf

American Psychological Association. (2007). *Getting in: A step-by-step plan for gaining admission to graduate school in psychology* (2nd ed.). Washington, DC: Author.

American Psychological Association. (2010). *Publication manual of the American Psychological Association* (6th ed.). Washington, DC: Author.

American Psychological Association. (2010). *Ethical principles of psychologists and code of conduct*. Washington, DC: Author. Retrieved from http://www.apa.org/ethics/code/index.aspx?item=1

American Psychological Association. (2012). *Graduate study in psychology*. Washington, DC: Author.

American Psychological Association. (2012). *PsycINFO*. Retrieved from http://www.apa.org/pubs/databases/psycinfo/index.aspx

American Psychological Association. (2012). *APA and affiliated journals*. Retrieved from http://www.apa.org/pubs/journals/index.aspx

American Psychological Association. (2013). *APA Guidelines for the Undergraduate Psychology Major, Version 2.0*. Washington, DC. Author. Retrieved from http://www.apa.org/ed/precollege/undergrad/index.aspx

American Psychological Association. (2017a). *Careers in psychology*. [Interactive data tool]. Retrieved from http://www.apa.org/workforce/data-tools/careers-psychology.aspx

American Psychological Association. (2017b). *Careers in psychology*. [Interactive data tool]. Retrieved from http://www.apa.org/workforce/data-tools/careers-psychology.aspx

American Psychological Association. (2018a). *PsycINFO highlights*. From http://www.apa.org/pubs/databases/psycinfo/index.aspx&tab=3

American Psychological Association. (2018b). *Graduate study in psychology 2018*. [Online]. Washington, DC: Author: Retrieved from http://gradstudy.apa.org/index.cfm?action=browseprogram

American Psychological Association. (2018c). *About APA*. Retrieved from http://www.apa.org/about/index.aspx

Anton, W. D., & Reed, J. R. (1991). *College Adjustment Scales*. Lutz, FL: Psychological Assessment Resources, Inc.

Applebaum, M., Cooper, H., Kline, R. B., Mayo-Wilson, E., Nezu, A. M., & Rao, S. M. (2018). Journal article reporting standards for quantitative research in psychology: The APA Publications and Communications Board Task Force Report. *American Psychologist, 73*, 3–25. doi:10.1037/amp0000191

Appleby, D. (2007). *The savvy psychology major*. Dubuque, IA: Kendall/Hunt.

Appleby, D. (1998, August). *The teaching-advising connection: Tomes, tools, and tales*. G. Stanley Hall lecture, American Psychological Association meeting, San Francisco, CA.

Appleby, D. (1998, August). *Professional planning portfolio for psychology majors*. Indianapolis, IN: Marian College.

Appleby, D. (2000, Spring). Job skills valued by employers who interview psychology majors. *Eye on Psi Chi, 4*(3), 17.

Appleby, D. C. (1990). *Characteristics of graduate school superstars*. Retrieved from http://www.psychwww.com/careers/suprstar.htm

Appleby, D. C. (2001, Spring). The covert curriculum: The lifelong learning skills you can learn in college. *Eye on Psi Chi, 5*(3), 28–31, 34.

Appleby, D. C., & Appleby, K. M. (2006). Kisses of death in the graduate school application process. *Teaching of Psychology, 33*, 19–24.

Appleby, D. C., Millspaugh, B. S., Hammersley, M. J. (2011). An online resource to enable undergraduate psychology majors to identify and investigate 172 psychology and psychology-related careers. *Office of Teaching Resources in Psychology*. Retrieved from http://teachpsych.org/otrp/resources/index.php?category=Advising

Appleby, D. C. (2015). An online career-exploration resource for psychology majors. Office of Teaching Resources in Psychology. *Society for the Teaching of Psychology*. Retrieved from teachpsych.org/Resources/Documents/otrp/resources/appleby15students.docx

Arnold, K. L., & Horrigan, K. L. (2002). Gaining admission into the graduate program of your choice. *Eye on Psi Chi, 7*(1), 30–33.

Association of American Colleges and Universities (AAC&U). (2002). *Greater expectations: A new vision for learning as a nation goes to college.* Washington, DC: Author.

Association of American Colleges and Universities. (2018, July). *Fulfilling the American dream: Liberal education and the future of work.* [White paper]. Washington, DC: Author. Retrieved from https://www.aacu.org/sites/default/files/files/LEAP/2018EmployerResearchReport.pdf

Association of College and Research Libraries. (2016). *Framework for Information Literacy for Higher Education.* Retrieved from http://www.ala.orgt/acrl/standards/ilframework

Association for Psychological Science. (2008). *History of APS.* Retrieved from http://www.psychologicalscience.org/about/history.cfm

Association for Psychological Science. (2008). *Join APS – student member benefits.* Retrieved from http://www.psychologicalscience.org/join/stu_benefits.cfm

Association for Psychological Science. (2018). *About APS: Who we are.* Retrieved from https://www.psychologicalscience.org/about

Atchley, P., Hooker, E., Kroska, E., & Gilmour, A. (2012). Validation of an online orientation seminar to improve career and major preparedness. *Teaching of Psychology, 39,* 146–151. doi:10.1177/0098628312437719

Ayal, S., Gino, F., Barkan, R., & Ariely, D. (2015). Three principles to REVISE people's unethical behavior. *Perspectives on Psychological Science, 10,* 738–741. doi:10.1177/1745691615598512

Ayala, E. E., & Almond, A. L. (2018). Self-care of women enrolled in health service psychology programs: A concept mapping approach. *Professional Psychology: Research and Practice, 49,* 177–184. doi:10.1037/pro0000190

Ball, S., & Bax, A. (2002). Self-care in medical education: Effectiveness of health-habits interventions for first-year medical students. *Academic Medicine, 77,* 911–917.

Barber, L. K., & Bagsby, P. G. (2012). Beyond Milgram: Expanding research ethics education to participant responsibilities. *Society for the Teaching of Psychology, Office of Teaching Resources in Psychology.* Retrieved from http://teachpsych.org/otrp/resources/barber12.pdf

Bates College. (2000). *Letter of recommendation worksheet.* Retrieved from http://www.bates.edu/fellowships/applying/letters-of-recommendation/

Baum, S., Ma, J., & Payea, K. (2010). Education pays 2010: The benefits of higher education for individuals and society. *The College Board.* Retrieved from http://advocacy.collegeboard.org/sites/default/files/Education_Pays_2010.pdf

Beins, B. C. (2012). *APA style simplified: Writing in psychology education, nursing, and sociology.* Malden, MA: Blackwell.

Beins, B. C., & Beins, A. M. (2008). *Effective writing in psychology: Papers, posters, and presentations.* Malden, MA: Blackwell Publishing.

Beins, B. C., Smith, R. A., & Dunn, D. S. (2010). Writing for psychology majors as a developmental process. In D. S. Dunn, B. C. Beins, M. A. McCarthy, & G. W. Hill, IV (Eds.), *Best practices for teaching beginnings and endings in the psychology major: Research, cases, and recommendations* (pp. 253–278). New York, NY: Oxford University Press.

Bendersky, K., Isaac, W. L., Stover, J. H., & Zook, J. M. (2008). Psychology students and online graduate programs: A need to reexamine undergraduate advisement. *Teaching of Psychology, 35,* 38–41.

Benjamin, L. T., Jr., Cavell, T. A., & Shallenberger, W. R., III. (1984). Staying with initial answers on objective tests: Is it a myth? *Teaching of Psychology, 11,* 133–141.

Berk, R. A. (2011). Research on PowerPoint: From basic features to multimedia. *International Journal of Technology in Teaching and Learning, 7,* 24–35.

Bikos, L. H., DePaul Chism, N. F., Forman, R. L., & King, D. R. (2013). Internationalizing the U.S. undergraduate psychology curriculum: A qualitative investigation of faculty perspectives. *International Perspectives in Psychology: Research, Practice, Consultation, 2,* 116–131.

Blanton, P. G. (2001). A model of supervising undergraduate internships. *Teaching of Psychology, 28,* 217–219.

Bloom, L. J., & Bell, P. A. (1979). Making it in graduate school: Some reflections about the superstars. *Teaching of Psychology, 6,* 231–232.

Borden, V. M. H., & Rajecki, D. W. (2000). First-year employment outcomes of psychology baccalaureates: Relatedness, preparedness, and prospects. *Teaching of Psychology, 27,* 164–168.

Bordens, K. S., & Abbott, B. B. (1988). *Research design and methods: A process approach.* Mountain View, CA: Mayfield Publishing Co.

Borysek, M. (2011, March). Six tips for writing an effective resume. *American Society of Mechanical Engineers.* Retrieved from https://www.asme.org/career-education/articles/job-hunting/6-tips-for-writing-an-effective-resume

Bottoms, B. L., & Nysse, K. L. (1999). Applying to graduate school: Writing a compelling personal statement. *Eye on Psi Chi, 4*(1), 20–22.

Brandeis University. (1998). *Library research guides—psychology.* Retrieved from http://lts.brandeis.edu/research/help/featured2.html

Braskamp, L. A., Wise, S. L., & Hengstler, D. D. (1979). Student satisfaction as a measure of departmental quality. *Journal of Educational Psychology, 71,* 494–498.

Briihl, D. S., Stanny, C. J., Jarvis, K. A., Darcy, M., & Belter, R. W. (2008). Thinking critically about careers in psychology. In D. S. Dunn, J. S. Halonen, & R. A. Smith (Eds.), *Teaching critical thinking in psychology: A handbook of best practices* (pp. 225–234). Malden, MA: Blackwell Publishing.

Bringle, R. G., Reeb, R. N., Brown, M. A., & Ruiz, A. I. (2016). Integrating service learning into the curriculum: Cognition, learning, and behavioral neuroscience. In R. G. Bringle, R. N. Reeb, M. A. Brown, & A. I. Ruiz (Eds.), *Service learning in psychology: Enhancing undergraduate education for the public good* (pp. 129–138). Washington, DC: American Psychological Association.

Broekkamp, H., & van Hout-Wolters, B. (2007). The gap between educational research and practice: A literature review, symposium, and questionnaire. *Educational Research and Evaluation, 13,* 203–230. doi:10.1080/13803610701626127

Brown, K. W., & Ryan, R. M. (2003). The benefits of being present: Mindfulness and its role in psychological well-being. *Journal of Personality and Social Psychology, 84,* 822–848. doi:10.1037/0022-3514.84.4.822

Brown, A., & Zefo, B. (2007). *Grad to great.* Chicago, IL: Dalidaze Press.

Buchanan, T., & Williams, J. E. (2010). Ethical issues in psychological research on the Internet. In S. D. Gosling & J. A. Johnson (Eds.), *Advanced methods for conducting online behavioral research* (pp. 255–271). Washington, DC: American Psychological Association.

Buckalew, L. W., & Lewis, H. H. (1982). Curriculum needs: Life preparation for undergraduate psychology majors. *Psychological Reports, 51,* 77–78.

Budnick, C. J., & Barber, L. K. (2018). Developing and enhancing students' job search skills and motivation: An online job search intervention training module. *Society for the Teaching of Psychology.* Office of Teaching Resources in Psychology. Retrieved from https://teachpsych.org/page-1603066

Bureau of Labor Statistics. (2012). Psychologists. *U.S. Department of Labor, Occupational Outlook Handbook, 2012–2013 edition.* Retrieved from http://www.bls.gov/ooh/Life-Physical-and-Social-Science/Psychologists.htm

Burrus, J., Jackson, T., Xi, N., & Steinberg, J. (2013, November). *Identifying the most important 21st century workforce competencies: An analysis of the Occupational Information Network (O*NET)*. Research Report ETS R-13-21. Princeton, NJ: Educational Testing Service. Retrieved from https://www.ets.org/Media/Research/pdf/RR-13-21.pdf

Buskist, W. (2002, Spring). Seven tips for preparing a successful application to graduate school in psychology. *Eye on Psi Chi, 5*(3), 32–34.

Busteed, B. (2015). Is college worth it? That depends. *Gallup, Inc.* Retrieved from https://news.gallup.com/opinion/gallup/182312/college-worth-depends.aspx

Busteed, B. (2017, June 6). 5 ways to make college a success. *Gallup, Inc.* Retrieved from https://news.gallup.com/opinion/gallup/211796/ways-college-success.aspx

Cameron, L., Wise, S. L., & Lottridge, S. M. (2007). The development and validation of the Information Literacy Test. *College & Research Libraries, 68*, 229–236. doi:10.5860/crl.68.3.229

Careercast.com. (2012). *20 great jobs without a college degree*. Retrieved from http://www.careercast.com/print/17321

CareerMosaic. (1997). *Resume writing tips*. Retrieved from http://www.careermosaic.com/cm/rwc/rwc3.html

Carnevale, A. P., & Cheah, B. (2015). From hard times to better times: College majors, unemployment, and earnings. *Center on Education and the Workforce*. Washington, DC: Georgetown University. Retrieved from https://cew.georgetown.edu/wp-content/uploads/HardTimes2015-Report.pdf

Carnevale, A. P., Rose, S. J., & Cheah, B. (2011). *The college payoff: Education, occupations, lifetime earnings (Executive summary)*. Georgetown University Center on Education and the Workforce. Retrieved from http://www9.georgetown.edu/grad/gppi/hpi/cew/pdfs/collegepayoff-summary.pdf

Carnevale, A. P., Strohl, J., & Melton, M. (2011). *What's it worth? The economic value of college majors*. Washington, DC: Georgetown University Center on Education and the Workforce.

Carnevale, A. P., Garcia, T. I., & Gulish, A. (2017). *Career pathways: Five ways to connect college and careers*. Georgetown University Center on Education and the Workforce. Washington, DC: Georgetown University. Retrieved from https://cew.georgetown.edu/wp-content/uploads/LEE-final.pdf

Cashin, J. R., & Landrum, R. E. (1991). Undergraduate students' perceptions of graduate admissions criteria in psychology. *Psychological Reports, 69*, 1107–1110.

Chastain, G., & Landrum, R. E. (Eds.). (1999). *Protecting human subjects: Departmental subject pools and institutional review boards*. Washington, DC: APA Books.

Chen, E. K. Y. (2004). What price liberal arts education. In Siena College (Ed.), *Liberal education and the new economy*. Loudonville, NY: Siena College.

Cheeseman, J. (2012, May 28). Job opportunities: Get a good job without a college degree. *The New England Job Show*. Retrieved from http://nejs.org/2012/05/28/job-opportunities-get-a-good-job-without-a-college-degree/

Chew, S L., Halonen, J. S., McCarthy, M. A., Gurung, R. A. R., Beers, M. J., McEntarffer, R., & Landrum, R. E. (2018). Practice what we teach: Improving teaching and learning in psychology. *Teaching of Psychology, 45*, 239–245. doi:10.1177/0098628318779264

Chickering, A. W., & Reisser, L. (1993). *Education and identity* (2nd ed.). San Francisco, CA: Jossey-Bass.

Chronicle of Higher Education. (1999, February 12). On the importance of diversity in higher education [Advertisement]. *Chronicle of Higher Education*, p. A42.

Ciarocco, N. J., & Strohmetz, D. B. (2017). The Employable Skills Self-Efficacy Survey: An assessment of and resource for fostering skill development. *Office of Teaching Resources in Psychology*, Society for the Teaching of Psychology. Retrieved from http://teachpsych.org/page-1603066

Clance, P. R., & Imes, S. A. (1978). The imposter phenomenon in high achieving women: Dynamics and therapeutic interventions. *Psychotherapy: Theory, Research, and Practice, 15*, 241–247.

Clay, R. A. (1996, September). Is a psychology diploma worth the price of tuition? *APA Monitor*, p. 33.

Clay, R. A. (1998). *Is a psychology diploma worth the price of tuition?* Retrieved from http://www.apa.org/monitor/sep96/tuition.html

Clay, R. A. (2000, May). The postdoc trap [Electronic version]. *Monitor on Psychology, 31*(5). Retrieved from http://www.apa.org/monitor/may00/postdoc.html

CollegeGrad. (2001). *The simple key to interview success*. Retrieved from http://www.collegegrad.com/ezine/20simkey.shtml

Combs, P. (2000). *Major in success: Make college easier, fire up your dreams, and get a very cool job*. Berkeley, CA: Ten Speed Press.

Committee for Economic Development of the Conference Board. (2015). *What are essential competencies on the job?* Retrieved from https://www.insidehighered.com/sites/default/server_files/files/151007%20CED%20Survey%20Results%203.pdf

Concordia University. (2014, February 12). *The differences between criminal justice and criminology: Which degree is right for you?* Retrieved from https://online.csp.edu/blog/criminal-justice-online/the-differences-between-criminal-justice-and-criminology-which-degree-is-right-for-you

Conners, F. A., Mccown, S. M., & Roskos-Ewoldsen, B. (1998). Unique challenges in teaching undergraduate statistics. *Teaching of Psychology, 25*, 40–42.

Cooney, E. (2008, March 11). *Better education translates into longer life expectancy, study finds*. Retrieved from http://www.boston.com/news/health/blog/2008/03/life_expectancy.html

Council of Graduate Schools. (1989). *Why graduate school?* Washington, DC: Author.

Cox, B. D., Cullen, K. L., Buskist, W., & Benassi, V. A. (2010). Helping undergraduates make the transition to graduate school. In D. S. Dunn, B. C. Beins, M. A. McCarthy, & G. W. Hill, IV (Eds.), *Best practices for teaching beginnings and endings in the psychology major: Research, cases, and recommendations* (pp. 319–329). New York, NY: Oxford University Press

Coxford, L. M. (1998). *How to write a resume*. Retrieved from http://www.aboutwork.com/rescov/resinfo/cosford.html

Crawford, M. P. (1992). Rapid growth and change at the American Psychological Association: 1945 to 1970. In R. B. Evans, V. S. Sexton, & T. C. Cadwallader (Eds.), *The American Psychological Association: A historical perspective* (Chapter 7, pp. 177–232). Washington, DC: American Psychological Association.

Dahlman, K. A., & Geisinger, K. F. (2015). The prevalence of measurement in undergraduate psychology curricula across the United States. *Scholarship of Teaching and Learning in Psychology, 1*, 189–199. doi:10.1037/stl0000030

Damer, D. E., & Melendres, L. T. (2011). "Tackling test anxiety": A group for college students. *Journal for Specialists in Group Work, 36*, 163–177. doi:10.1080/01933922.2011.586016

Davis, S. F. (1995). The value of collaborative scholarship with undergraduates. *Psi Chi Newsletter, 21*(1), 12–13.

Davis, S. F., & Ludvigson, H. W. (1995). Additional data on academic dishonesty and a proposal for remediation. *Teaching of Psychology, 22*, 119–121.

Davis, S. F. (1997). "Cheating in high school is for grades, cheating in college is for a career": Academic dishonesty in the 1990s. *Kansas Biology Teacher, 6*, 79–81.

Davis, S. F., Drinan, P. F., & Bertram Gallant, T. (2009). *Cheating in school: What we know and what we can do*. Malden, MA: Wiley-Blackwell.

Davis, S. F., Giordano, P. J., & Licht, C. A. (2009). *Your career in psychology: Putting your graduate degree to work*. Malden, MA: Blackwell.

Davis, S. F., & Ludvigson, H. W. (1995). Additional data on academic dishonesty and a proposal for remediation. *Teaching of Psychology, 22*, 119–122.

Davis, S. F., Grover, C. A., Becker, A. H., & McGregor, L. N. (1992). Academic dishonesty: Prevalence, determinants, techniques, and punishments. *Teaching of Psychology, 19*, 16–20.

Davis, S. F., Pierce, M. C., Yandell, L. R., Arnow, P. S., & Loree, A. (1995). Cheating in college and the Type A personality: A reevaluation. *College Student Journal, 29*, 493–497.

Day, J. C., & Newburger, E. C. (2002). *The big payoff: Educational attainment and synthetic estimates of work-life earnings* (Publication P23-210). Washington, DC: U.S. Census Bureau.

DeAngelo, L., Franke, R., Hurtado, S., Pryor, J. H., & Tran, S. (2011). Completing college: Assessing graduation rates at four-year institutions. *Higher Education Research Institute at UCLA*. Retrieved from http://heri.ucla.edu/DARCU/CompletingCollege2011.pdf

DeGalan, J., & Lambert, S. (1995). *Great jobs for psychology majors*. Lincolnwood, IL: VGM Career Horizons.

DeLuca, M. J. (1997). *Best answers to the 201 most frequently asked interview questions*. New York, NY: McGraw-Hill.

Descutner, C. J., & Thelen, M. H. (1989). Graduate school and faculty perspective about graduate school. *Teaching of Psychology, 16*, 58–61.

Desjardins, J. (2018, July). Which college degrees get the highest salaries. *Visual Capitalist*. Retrieved from http://www.visualcapitalist.com/visualizing-salaries-college-degrees/

Diehl, J., & Sullivan, M. (1998). *Suggestions for application for graduate study in psychology*. Retrieved from http://psych.hanover.edu/handbook/gradapp2.html

Digest of Education Statistics. (2017). Employment outcomes of bachelor's degree recipients. *The Condition of Education*. Retrieved from https://nces.ed.gov/programs/coe/pdf/coe_sbc.pdf

Dillinger, R. J., & Landrum, R. E. (2002). An information course for the beginning psychology major. *Teaching of Psychology, 29*, 230–232.

Dodson, J. P., Chastain, G., & Landrum, R. E. (1996). Psychology seminar: Careers and graduate study in psychology. *Teaching of Psychology, 23*, 238–240.

Doran, J. M., Kraha, A., Marks, L. R., Ameen, E. J., & El-Ghoroury, N. H. (2016). Graduate debt in psychology: A quantitative analysis. *Training and Education in Professional Psychology, 10*, 3–13. doi:10.1037/tep0000112

Dunlosky, J., & Metcalfe, J. (2009). *Metacognition*. Thousand Oaks, CA: Sage.

Dunlosky, J., Rawson, K. A., Marsh, E. J., Nathan, M. J., & Willingham, D. T. (2013). What works, what doesn't. *Scientific American Mind, 24*(4), 46–53

Dunn, D. S., Brewer, C. L., Cautin, R. L., Gurung, R. A. R., Keith, K. D., McGregor, L. N., Nida, S. A., Puccio, P., & Voigt, M. J. (2010). The undergraduate psychology curriculum: Call for a core. In D. F. Halpern (Ed.), *Undergraduate education in psychology: A blueprint for the future of the discipline* (pp. 47–61). Washington, DC: American Psychological Association.

Dunn, D. S. (2011). *A short guide to writing about psychology* (3rd ed.). Boston, MA: Longman/Pearson.

Dunn, D. S., Cautin, R. L., & Gurung, R. A. R. (2011). Curriculum matters: Structure, content, and psychological literacy. In J. Cranney & D. S. Dunn (Eds.), *The psychologically literate citizen: Foundations and global perspectives* (pp. 15–26). Oxford, England: Oxford University Press.

Dunn, D. S., & Halonen, J. S. (2016). *The psychology major's companion: Everything you need to know to get you where you want to go*. New York, NY: Worth.

Earp, B. D., & Trafimow, D. (2015). Replication, falsification, and the crisis of confidence in social psychology. *Frontiers in Psychology, 6*, 621. doi:10.3389/fpsyg.2015.00621

Educational Testing Service. (1998). *Graduate Record Examinations®: Guide to the use of scores*. Princeton, NJ: Author.

Educational Testing Service. (2001). *Coming in October 2002: A new GRE General Test*. [Pamphlet]. Princeton, NJ: Author.

Educational Testing Service. (2012). *About the GRE revised general test*. Retrieved from https://www.ets.org/gre/revised_general/about

Ellis, D. (1997). *Becoming a master student* (8th ed.). Boston, MA: Houghton Mifflin.

English, C. (2011). Most Americans see college as essential to getting a good job. *Gallup, Inc*. Retrieved from http://www.gallup.com/poll/149045/americans-college-essential-getting-good-job.aspx

Ernst, H., Burns, M., & Ritzer, D. (2011). *If I knew then what I know now: Students' expectations before and after entering college*. Poster presented at the National Institute for the Teaching of Psychology, St. Petersburg Beach, FL.

Feldman, D. B., & Silvia, P. J. (2010). *Public speaking for psychologists: A lighthearted guide to research presentations, job talks, and other opportunities to embarrass yourself*. Washington, DC: American Psychological Association.

Festinger, L. (1954). A theory of social comparison processes. *Human Relations, 7*, 117–140. doi:10.1177/001872675400700202

Finney, P., Snell, W., Jr., & Sebby, R. (1989). Assessment of academic, personal, and career development of alumni from Southeast Missouri State University. *Teaching of Psychology, 16*, 173–177.

Fishman, R. (2015, May). *Deciding to go to college: 2015 college decisions survey: Part I*. Washington, DC: New America. Retrieved from https://www.luminafoundation.org/files/resources/deciding-to-go-to-college.pdf

Fister, B. (2010, November 1). Undergraduates in the library, trying not to drown. *Inside Higher Ed*. Retrieved from http://www.insidehighered.com/blogs/library_babel_fish/undergraduates_in_the_library_trying_not_to_drown

Foss, D. J. (2013). *Your complete guide to college success: How to study smart, achieve your goals, and enjoy campus life*. Washington, DC: American Psychological Association.

Foushee, R. D. (2008, March). Academic advising and teachable moments: Making the most of the advising experience. *APS Observer, 21*(3), 33–36.

Fried-Buchalter, S. (1992). Fear of success, fear of failure, and the imposter phenomenon: A factor analytic approach to convergent and discriminant validity. *Journal of Personality Assessment, 58*, 368–379.

Fretz, B. R., & Stang, D. J. (1988). *Preparing for graduate study in psychology: Not for seniors only!* Washington, DC: American Psychological Association.

Gabriel, K. F. (2008). *Teaching unprepared students: Strategies for promoting success and retention in higher education*. Sterling, VA: Stylus.

Gallucci, N. T. (1997). An evaluation of the characteristics of undergraduate psychology majors. *Psychological Reports, 81*, 879–889.

Gallup, Inc. (2014). *Great jobs, great lives: The 2014 Gallup-Purdue Index Report: A study of more than 30,000 college graduates across the U.S.* Washington, DC: Author. Retrieved from https://www.luminafoundation.org/files/resources/galluppurdueindex-report-2014.pdf.

Gallup. (2017a). 2017 college student survey: A nationally representative survey of currently enrolled students. *Strada Education Network and Gallup*. Washington, DC: Gallup. Retrieved from https://news.gallup.com/reports/225161/2017-strada-gallup-college-student-survey.aspx

Garavalia, L. S., & Gredler, M. E. (1998, August). *Planning ahead: Improved academic achievement?* Presented at the American Psychological Association, San Francisco, CA.

Gardner, P. (2007). *Moving up or moving out of the company? Factors that influence the promoting or firing of new college hires.* Collegiate Employment Research Institute (Research Brief 1-2007). East Lansing, MI: Michigan State University.

Gardner, P. (2011). Internships as high stakes events. *Collegiate Employers Research Institute* (CERI), Michigan State University. Retrieved from http://www.ceri.msu.edu/wp-content/uploads/2010/01/High-Stakes-Internships.pdf

Geller, J. D., Zuckerman, N., & Seider, A. (2016). Service-learning as a catalyst for community development: How do community partners benefit from service-learning? *Education and Urban Society, 48,* 151–175. doi:10.1177/0013124513514773

Giordano, P. (2004, April). *Deciding if graduate school is right for you.* Paper presented at the Midwestern Psychological Association meeting, Chicago, IL.

Godfrey, C. M., Harrison, M. B., Lysaight, R., Lamb, M., Grahm, I. A., & Oakley, P. (2010). Care of self-care by other: The meaning of self-care from research practice, policy and industry perspectives. *International Journal of Evidence-based Healthcare, 9,* 3–24. doi:10.1111/j.1744-1609.2010.00196.x

Goodman, J., Schlossberg, N. K., & Anderson, M. L. (2006). *Counseling adults in transition: Linking practice with theory* (3rd ed.). New York, NY: Springer.

Gould, J. B. (2012). *How to succeed in college (while really trying): A professor's inside advice.* Chicago, IL: University of Chicago Press.

Grayson, J. (n.d.). *Principles for successful psychology field placement.* [Handout]. Harrisonburg, VA: James Madison University.

Green, R. J., Allbritten, A., & Park, A. (2008). Prevalence of careers in psychology courses at American universities. *College Student Journal, 42,* 238–240.

Green, R. J., McCord, M., & Westbrooks, T. (2005). Student awareness of education requirements for desired careers and the utility of a careers in psychology course. *College Student Journal, 39,* 218–222.

Greene, D., Mullins, M., Baggett, P., & Cherry, D. (2017). Self-care for helping professionals: Students' perceived stress, coping self-efficacy, and subjective experiences. *Journal of Baccalaureate Social Work, 22,* 1–15.

Gross, C. (2016). Scientific misconduct. *Annual Review of Psychology, 67,* 693–711. doi:10.1146/annurev-psych-122414-033437

Gross, D., Abrams, K., & Enns, C. Z. (2016). The case for internationalizing the undergraduate psychology curriculum. In D. Gross, K. Abrams, & C. Z. Enns (Eds.), *Internationalizing the undergraduate psychology curriculum: Practical lessons learned at home and abroad* (pp. 3–18). Washington, DC: American Psychological Association.

Guerrero, M., & Rod, A. B. (2013). Engaging in office hours: A study of student-faculty interaction and academic performance. *Journal of Political Science Education, 9,* 403–416. doi:10:1080/15512169.2013.835554

Hacker, D., & Sommers, N. (2013). *A pocket style manual, sixth edition, APA version.* Boston, MA: Bedford/St. Martin's.

Halpern, D. F. (Ed.). (2010). *Undergraduate education in psychology: A blueprint for the discipline.* Washington, DC: American Psychological Association.

Halonen, J. S., & Dunn, D. S. (2018). Embedding career issues in advanced psychology major courses. *Teaching of Psychology, 45,* 41–49. doi:10.1177/0098628317744967

Hammer, E. Y. (2003). The importance of being mentored. *Eye on Psi Chi, 7*(3), 4–5.

Handelsman, M. M. (2011a, Winter). Sailing the "seven C's" of ethics. *Eye on Psi Chi, 15*(2), 8–9.

Handelsman, M. M. (2011b, Fall). The ABCs of the APA ethics code. *Eye on Psi Chi, 15*(4), 12–13.

Handelsman, M. M. (2012, Winter). How important is confidentiality? *Eye on Psi Chi, 16*(2), 10–11.

Harvard University. (1998). *Sociology*. Retrieved from http://www.wjh.harvard.edu/soc/

Harvey, J. C. (1982). The imposter phenomenon and achievement: A failure to internalize success (Doctoral dissertation, Temple University, 1981). *Dissertation Abstracts International, 42,* 4969B-4970B.

Hayes, L. J., & Hayes, S. C. (1989, September). *How to apply to graduate school.* Retrieved from http://psych.hanover.edu/handbook/applic2.html

Helms, J. L., & Rogers, D. T. (2011). *Majoring in psychology: Achieving your educational and career goals.* Malden, MA: Blackwell.

Hettich, P. (1998). *Learning skills for college and career* (2nd ed.). Pacific Grove, CA: Brooks/Cole Publishing Company.

Hettich, P. (2012, Winter). Internships! *Eye on Psi Chi, 16*(2), 8–9.

Hettich, P. I. (2004, April). *From college to corporate culture: You're a freshman again.* Paper presented at the Midwestern Psychological Association meeting, Chicago, IL.

Hettich, P. I., & Landrum, R. E. (2013). *Your undergraduate degree in psychology: From college to career.* Thousand Oaks, CA: Sage.

Holder, W. B., Leavitt, G. S., & McKenna, F. S. (1958). Undergraduate training for psychologists. *American Psychologist, 13,* 585–588.

Hodges, S., & Connelly, A. R. (2010). *A job search manual for counselors and counselor educators: How to navigate and promote your counseling career.* Alexandria, VA: American Counseling Association.

Holland, J. L. (1958). A personality inventory employing occupational titles. *Journal of Applied Psychology, 42,* 336–342.

Holland, J. L. (1959). A theory of vocational choice. *Journal of Counseling Psychology, 6,* 35–45.

Holland, J. L. (1973). *Making vocational choices: A theory of careers.* Englewood Cliffs, NJ: Prentice Hall.

Holland, J. L. (1994). *Self-Directed Search® (SDS®) Form R* (4th ed.). [Instrument]. Odessa, FL: Psychological Assessment Resources.

Holton, E. F., III. (1998). Preparing students for life beyond the classroom. In J. N. Garnder, G. Van der Veer & Associates, *The senior year experience: Facilitating integration, reflection, closure and transition* (pp. 95–115). San Francisco, CA: Jossey-Bass.

Hopper, C. (1998). *Ten tips you need to survive college.* Retrieved from http://capone.mtsu.edu/studskl/10tips.html

Hopper, C. (1998). *Time management.* Retrieved from http://capone.mtsu.edu/studskl/

Horn, C. (2015, December 22). Certificates, credentials, and college degrees: Time to shift our thinking. *Forbes.com.* Retrieved from https://www.forbes.com/sites/uhenergy/2015/12/22/certificates-credentials-and-college-degrees-time-to-shift-our-thinking/#2293d7424cdd

Hunt, I., Taylor, R., & Oberman, W. (2017). Advisory board engagement: Assisting undergraduates with resume development. *Journal of Education for Business, 92*, 288–295. doi:10.1080/08832323.2017.1362680

Idaho Department of Labor. (1998, October). *Job application tips*. Meridian, ID: Author.

Institute for Scientific Information. (1998). *Social sciences citation index*. Philadelphia, PA: Author.

Instructions in regard to preparation of manuscript. (1929). *Psychological Bulletin, 26*, 57–63.

Jacoby, B. (1996). Service learning in today's higher education. In B. Jacoby (Ed.), *Service learning in higher education: Concepts and practices* (pp. 3–25). San Francisco, CA: Jossey-Bass.

Jaschik, S. (2008). Non-cognitive qualities join the GRE. *Inside Higher Ed*. Retrieved from http://www.insidehighered.com/news/2008/05/22/ets

Jessen, B. C. (1988). Field experience for undergraduate psychology students. In P. J. Wood (Ed.), *Is psychology for them? A guide to undergraduate advising*. Washington, DC: American Psychological Association.

Jessop, N., & Adams, G. (2016). Internationalising the psychology curriculum: Preliminary notes on conception and assessment of anticipated benefits. *Psychology Teaching Review, 22*, 41–52.

JobWeb. (2001). *How to prepare an effective resume*. Retrieved from http://www.jobweb.com/catapult/guenov/how_to.html

Johns, M. W. (1991). A new method for measuring daytime sleepiness: The Epworth Sleepiness Scale. *Sleep, 14*, 540–545.

Johnson, W. B., Behling, L. L., Miller, P., & Vandermaas-Peeler, M. (2015). Undergraduate research mentoring: Obstacles and opportunities. *Mentoring & Tutoring: Partnership in Learning, 23*, 441–453. doi:10.1080/13611267.2015.1126167

Jones, R. A. (1985). *Research methods in the social and behavioral sciences*. Sunderland, MA: Sinauer Associates.

Julian, T. (2012, October). Work-life earnings by field of degree and occupation for people with a bachelor's degree: 2011. *U.S. Census Bureau*. Washington, DC: U.S. Department of Commerce. Retrieved from https://www.census.gov/prod/2012pubs/acsbr11-04.pdf

Kail, R. V. (2015). *Scientific writing for psychology: Lessons in clarity and style*. Thousand Oaks, CA: Sage.

Kaiser, J. C., Kaiser, A. J., Richardson, N. J., & Fox, E. J. (2007, Winter). Perceptions of graduate admissions directors: Undergraduate student research experiences: "Are all research experiences rated equally?" *Eye on Psi Chi, 11*(2), 22–24.

Kallgren, C. A., & Tauber, R. T. (1996). Undergraduate research and the institutional review board: A mismatch or happy marriage? *Teaching of Psychology, 23*, 20–25.

Kampfe, C. M., Mitchell, M. M., Boyless, J. A., & Sauers, G. O. (1999). Undergraduate students' perceptions of the internship: An exploratory study. *Rehabilitation Education, 13*, 359–367.

Kanchier, C. (2002, April 12–14). Does your attitude limit your options? *USA Weekend Magazine*, p. 9.

Karlin, N. J. (2000). Creating an effective conference presentation. *Eye on Psi Chi, 4*(2), 26–27.

Keith-Spiegel, P. (1991). *The complete guide to graduate school admission: Psychology and related fields*. Hillsdale, NJ: Erlbaum.

Keith-Spiegel, P., & Wiederman, M. W. (2000). *The complete guide to graduate school admission: Psychology, counseling, and related professions* (2nd ed.). Mahwah, NJ: Erlbaum.

Kennedy, J. H., & Lloyd, M. A. (1998, August). *Effectiveness of a careers in psychology course for majors*. Poster presented at the meeting of the American Psychological Association, San Francisco, CA.

Kerckhoff, A. C., & Bell, L. (1998). Hidden capital: Vocational credentials and attainment in the United States. *Sociology of Education, 71*, 152–174.

Keyes, B. J., & Hogberg, D. K. (1990). Undergraduate psychology alumni: Gender and cohort differences in course usefulness, postbaccalaureate education, and career paths. *Teaching of Psychology, 17*, 101–105.

Kirk, E. E. (1996). *Evaluating information found on the Internet*. Johns Hopkins University. Retrieved from http://guides.library.jhu.edu/evaluatinginformation

Klein, M. B., & Pierce, J. D., Jr. (2009). Parental care aids, but parental overprotection hinders, college adjustment. *Journal of College Student Retention, 11*, 167–181. doi:10.2190/CS.11.2.a

Klimoski, R., & Hu, X. (2011). Improving self-awareness and self-insight. In M. London (Ed.), *The Oxford handbook of lifelong learning* (pp. 52–69). New York, NY: Oxford University Press.

Knouse, S. B., Tanner, J. R., & Harris, E. W. (1999). The relation of college internships, college performance, and subsequent job opportunity. *Journal of Employment Counseling, 36*, 35–43.

Korn, J. H. (1988). Students' roles, responsibilities, and rights as research participants. *Teaching of Psychology, 15*, 74–78.

Kressel, N. J. (1990). Job and degree satisfaction among social science graduates. *Teaching of Psychology, 17*, 222–227.

Kumar, S., & Jagacinski, C. M. (2006). Imposters have goals too: The imposter phenomenon and its relationship to achievement goal theory. *Personality and Individual Differences, 40*, 147–157. doi:10.1016/j.paid.2005.05.014

Kuther, T. L. (2006). *The psychology major's handbook* (2nd ed.). Belmont, CA: Wadsworth.

Kuther, T. L., & Morgan, R. D. (2009). *Careers in psychology: Opportunities in a changing world* (3rd ed). Belmont, CA: Thomson Higher Education.

Kuther, T. L. (2013). What employers seek in job applicants: You've got the skills they want. *Psychology Student Network*. Retrieved from http://www.apa.org/ed/precollege/psn/2013/09/job-applicants.aspx

La Sierra University. (2000). *Resumes, letters and interviews*. Retrieved from www.lasierra.edu/departments/psychology/careers/resumes.html

Laber-Warren, E. (2009). What kind of perfectionist are you? *Scientific American Mind*, July/August, 50. Retrieved from https://www.scientificamerican.com/article/can-you-be-too-perfect/

LaCour, J., & Lewis, D. M. (1998). Effects of a course in ethics on self-rated and actual knowledge of undergraduate psychology majors. *Psychological Reports, 82*, 499–504.

Lai, B. S., Margol, A., & Landoll, R. R. (2010, Summer). Doing your research: How to make the most out of research experiences. *Eye on Psi Chi, 14*(4), 24–27.

Lamb, C. S. (1991). Teaching professional ethics to undergraduate counseling students. *Psychological Reports, 69*, 1215–1223.

Landau, J. D. (2003). *Understanding and preventing plagiarism*. Retrieved from http://www.psychologicalscience.org/teaching/tips/tips_0403.html

Landrum, R. E. (1999). Student expectations of grade inflation. *Journal of Research and Development in Education, 32*, 124–128.

Landrum, R. E. (2003). Graduate admission in psychology: Transcripts and the effect of withdrawals. *Teaching of Psychology, 30*, 323–325.

Landrum, R. E. (2004). New odds for graduate admissions in psychology. *Eye on Psi Chi, 8*(3), 20–21, 32.

Landrum, R. E. (2005, Winter). The curriculum vita: A student's guide to preparation. *Eye on Psi Chi, 9*(2), 28–29, 42.

Landrum, R. E. (2008, Spring). Evaluating the undergraduate research assistantship experience. *Eye on Psi Chi, 12*(3), 32–33.

Landrum, R. E. (2009). *Finding jobs with a psychology bachelor's degree: Expert advice for launching your career*. Washington, DC: American Psychological Association.

Landrum, R. E. (2011). Faculty perceptions concerning the frequency and appropriateness of student behavior. *Teaching of Psychology, 38*, 269–272. doi:10.1177/0098628311421328

Landrum, R. E. (2012). *Undergraduate writing in psychology: Learning to tell the scientific story* (Revised ed.). Washington, DC: American Psychological Association.

Landrum, R. E. (2013). Writing in APA style: Faculty perspectives of competence and importance. *Psychology Learning and Teaching, 12*, 259–264. doi:10.2304/plat.2013.12.3.259

Landrum, R. E. (2016, January). Resume at work: Your opportunity to tell your professional story. *Psychology Student Network*. American Psychological Association. Retrieved from http://www.apa.org/ed/precollege/psn/2016/01/resume-work.aspx

Landrum, R. E. (2018a). Affordances and alignments: Continuing challenges in advising undergraduate psychology majors. *Teaching of Psychology, 45*, 84–90. doi:10.1177/0098628317745462

Landrum, R. E. (2018b, April). *More disruption in higher education: Students, skills, and competencies (oh my!)*. Western Psychological Association Psi Chi Career Speaker address, Portland, OR.

Landrum, R. E., & Clark, J. (2005). Graduate admissions criteria in psychology: An update. *Psychological Reports, 97*, 481–484.

Landrum, R. E., & Elison-Bowers, P. (2009). The post-baccalaureate perceptions of psychology alumni. *College Student Journal, 43*, 676–681.

Landrum, R. E., & Harrold, R. (2003). What employers want from psychology graduates. *Teaching of Psychology, 30*, 131–133.

Landrum, R. E., Hettich, P. I., & Wilner, A. (2010). Alumni perceptions of workforce readiness. *Teaching of Psychology, 37*, 97–106. doi:10.1080/00986281003626912

Landrum, R. E., & Nelsen, L. R. (2002). The undergraduate research assistantship: An analysis of the benefits. *Teaching of Psychology, 29*, 15–19.

Landrum, R. E., Jeglum, E. B., & Cashin, J. R. (1994). The decision-making processes of graduate admissions committees in psychology. *Journal of Social Behavior and Personality, 9*, 239–248.

Landrum, R. E., Shoemaker, C. S., & Davis, S. F. (2003). Important topics in an "Introduction to the Psychology Major" course. *Teaching of Psychology, 30*, 48–51.

Lau, J. (2006). *Guidelines on information literacy for lifelong learning*. Boca del Rio, Veracruz, Mexico: International Federation of Library Associations and Institutions. Retrieved from http://www.ifla.org/files/assets/information-literacy/publications/ifla-guidelines-en.pdf

Lau, W. W. F., & Yuen, A. H. K. (2014). Developing and validating of a perceived ICT literacy scale for junior secondary school students: *Pedagogical and educational contributions. Computers & Education, 78*, 1–9. doi:10.1016/j.compedu.2014.04.016

Lefton, L. A. (1997). *Psychology* (6th ed.). Boston, MA: Allyn & Bacon.

Levine, M. (2005, February 18). College graduates aren't ready for the real world. *The Chronicle of Higher Education, Section B*, B11–B12.

Levitt, H. M., Bamberg, M., Creswell, J. W., Frost, D. M., Josselson, R., & Suarez-Orozco, C. (2018). Journal article reporting standards for qualitative primary, qualitative meta-analytic, and mixed method research in psychology: The APA Publications and Communications Board Task Force Report. *American Psychologist, 73*, 26–46. doi:10.1037/amp0000151

Library of Congress. (1990). *LC classification outline*. Washington, DC: Author.

Light, J. (2010, October 11). Psych majors aren't happy with options. *Wall Street Journal*. Retrieved from http://online.wsj.com/article/SB10001424052748704011904575538561813341020.html

Lindgren, A. (2003, August 11). Research the key to successful interviews, CEO says. *Idaho Statesman*, p. CB2.

Littleford, L. N., Buxton, K., Bucher, M. A., Simon-Dack, S. L., & Yang, K. L. (2018). Psychology doctoral program admissions: What master's and undergraduate-level students need to know. *Teaching of Psychology, 45*, 75-83. doi:1177/0098628317745453

Loose, T. (2012). *What are the most effective degrees?* Retrieved from http://education.yahoo.net/articles/most_effective_degrees.htm

Lord, C. G. (2004). A guide to PhD graduate school: How they keep score in the big leagues. In J. M. Darley, M. P. Zanna, & H. L. Roediger, III (Eds.), *The complete academic: A career guide* (2nd ed., pp. 3–15). Washington, DC: American Psychological Association.

Lore, N. (1997). *How to write a masterpiece of a resume*. Retrieved from http://www.rockportinstitute.com/resumes

Lozon, V. (2018, June 30). Didn't graduate college? Here are the highest-paying jobs. *clickondetroit.com*. Retrieved from https://www.clickondetroit.com/money/jobs/didnt-graduate-college-here-are-the-highest-paying-jobs-without-needing-a-college-degree

Lu, S. (2016, April). Median salaries for new psychologists are static. *gradPSYCH Magazine, 14*(2), 22. Retrieved from http://www.apa.org/gradpsych/2016/04/salaries.aspx

Lumina Foundation. (2011). *New study finds that earning power is increasingly tied to education: The data is clear: A college degree is critical to economic opportunity*. Retrieved from http://www9.georgetown.edu/grad/gppi/hpi/cew/pdfs/collegepayoff-release.pdf

Lutsky, N. (2016). Beyond borders: Faculty development to enhance internationalization of the psychology curriculum. In D. Gross, K. Abrams, & C. Z. Enns (Eds.), *Internationalizing the undergraduate psychology curriculum: Practical lessons learned at home and abroad* (pp. 19–34). Washington, DC: American Psychological Association.

Macera, M. H., & Cohen, S. H. (2006). Psychology as a profession: An effective career exploration and orientation course for undergraduate psychology majors. *Career Development Quarterly, 54*, 367–371.

Makel, M. C., Plucker, J. A., & Hegarty, B. (2012). Replications in psychology research: How often do they really occur? *Perspectives in Psychological Science, 7*, 537–542. doi:10.1177/1745691612460688

Mandernach, B. J., Zafonte, M., & Taylor, C. (2016). Instructional strategies to improve college students' APA style writing. *International Journal of Teaching and Learning in Higher Education, 27*(3). Retrieved from http://www.isetl.org/ijtlhe/

Margulies, J. (2002). President of N.Y.'s Hamilton College steps down amid controversy over speech. *The Chronicle of Higher Education*, Retrieved from http://chronicle.com/article/President-of-NYs-Hamilton/116644/

Marietta College. (1998). *Political science*. Retrieved from http://www.marietta.edu/~poli/index.html

Martin, D. W. (1991). *Doing psychology experiments* (3rd ed.). Pacific Grove, CA: Brooks/Cole.

Mathiasen, R. E. (1998). Moral education of college students: Faculty and staff perspectives. *College Student Journal, 32*, 374–377.

McClelland, D. (1961). *The achieving society*. Princeton, NJ: Van Nostrand.

McConnell, K. (1998). *Study skill checklist*. Retrieved from http://cwx.prenhall.com/bookbind/pubbooks/davis2/medialib/part8.html

McGovern, T. V., & Carr, K. F. (1989). Carving out the niche: A review of alumni surveys on undergraduate psychology majors. *Teaching of Psychology*, *16*, 52–57.

McGregor, L. N. (2011, August). *Enhancing instruction through the effective use of PowerPoint*. Poster presented at the American Psychological Association convention, Washington, DC.

McGovern, T. V., Corey, L., Cranney, J., Dixon, W. E., Jr., Holmes, J. D., Kuebli, J. E., Ritchey, K. A., Smith, R. A., & Walker, S. J. (2010). Psychologically literate citizens. In D. F. Halpern (Ed.). *Undergraduate education in psychology: A blueprint for the future of the discipline* (pp. 9–27). Washington, DC: American Psychological Association.

McGovern, T. V., Furumoto, L., Halpern, D. F., Kimble, G. A., & McKeachie, W. J. (1991). Liberal education, study in depth, and the arts and sciences major—psychology. *American Psychologist*, *46*, 598–605.

McKay, D. R. (2010). *Career decisions: Self assessment*. Retrieved from http://www.bamaol.cc/Article/Career/4852.html

McKeachie, W. J. (2002). *McKeachie's teaching tips: Strategies, research, and theory for college and university teachers* (11th ed.). Boston, MA: Houghton Mifflin.

Meara, E. R., Richards, S., & Cutler, D. M. (2008). The gap gets bigger: Changes in mortality and life expectancy, by education, 1981–2000. *Health Affairs*, *27*, 350–360. doi:10.1377/hlthaff.27.2.350

Meeker, F., Fox, D., & Whitley, Jr., B. E. (1994). Predictors of academic success in the undergraduate psychology major. *Teaching of Psychology*, *21*, 238–241.

Menand, L. (2011, June 6). Live and learn: Why we have college. *The New Yorker*. Retrieved from http://www.newyorker.com/arts/critics/atlarge/2011/06/06/110606crat_atlarge_menand

Menges, R. J., & Trumpeter, P. W. (1972). Toward an empirical definition of relevance in undergraduate instruction. *American Psychologist*, *27*, 213–217.

Meriam Library. (2010). *Evaluating information—Applying the CRAAP Test*. Retrieved from https://www.csuchico.edu/lins/handouts/eval_websites.pdf

Merriam, J., LaBaugh, R. T., & Butterfield, N. E. (1992). Library instruction for psychology majors: Minimum training guidelines. *Teaching of Psychology*, *19*, 34–36.

Messer, W. S., Griggs, R. A., & Jackson, S. L. (1999). A national survey of undergraduate psychology degree options and major requirements. *Teaching of Psychology*, *26*, 164–171.

Michalski, D. S., Cope, C, & Fowler, G. A. (2017). Graduate study in psychology 2018: Summary report: Admissions, applications, and acceptances. *Education Directorate*. American Psychological Association. Retrieved from http://www.apa.org/education/grad/survey-data/2018-admissions-applications.pdf

Michalski, D. S., Cope, C., & Fowler, G. A. (2017d, December). Summary report: Admissions, applications, and acceptances. *Education Directorate*. American Psychological Association. Retrieved from https://www.apa.org/education/grad/survey-data/2018-admissions-applications.pdf

Michalski, D., Kohout, J., Wicherski, M., & Hart, B. (2011, May). 2009 doctorate employment survey. *Center for Workforce Studies, Science Directorate*. Washington, DC: American Psychological Association.

Miller, G. A. (1956). The magical number seven, plus or minus two: Some limits on our capacity for processing Information. *Psychological Review*, *63*, 81–97. http://dx.doi.org/10.1037/h0043158

Mitchell, M. L., Jolley, J. M., & O'Shea, R. P. (2013). *Writing for psychology* (4th ed.). Belmont, CA: Wadsworth/Cengage.

Miyatsu, T., Nguyen, K., & McDaniel, M. A. (2018). Five popular study strategies: Their pitfalls and optimal implementations. *Perspectives on Psychological Science*, *13*, 390–407. doi:10.1177/1745691617710510

Montag, A. (2018, August). *This is Jeff Bezos' 3-question test for new Amazon employees*. Retrieved from cnbc/2018/08/01/jeff-bezos-questions-amazon-used-to-hire-employees.html

Morgan, B. L., & Korschgen, A. J. (2009). *Majoring in psych? Career options for psychology undergraduates* (4th ed.). Needham Heights, MA: Allyn & Bacon.

Moses, J., Bradley, G. L., & O'Callaghan, F. V. (2016). When college students look after themselves: Self-care practices and well-being. *Journal of Student Affairs Research and Practice*, *53*, 346–359. doi:10.1080/19496591.2016.1157488

Mount Saint Vincent University. (1998). *Benefits to the co-op student*. Retrieved from http://www.msvu.ca/en/home/programsdepartments/cooperativeeducation/default.aspx

Mulcock, S. D., & Landrum, R. E. (2002, May). *The academic path of students that complete an "Introduction to the Psychology Major"-type course*. Midwestern Psychological Association, Chicago, IL.

Mulvey, T. A., Michalski, D. S., & Wicherski, M. (2010). 2010 graduate study in psychology snapshot: Applications, acceptances, enrollments, and degrees awarded to master's- and doctoral-level students in U.S. and Canadian graduate departments of psychology: 2008–2009. *Center for Workforce Studies*. Washington, DC: American Psychological Association.

Murphy, K. A., Blustein, D. L., Bohlig, A. J., & Platt, M. G. (2010). The college-to-career transition: An exploration of emerging adulthood. *Journal of Counseling & Development*, *88*, 174–181.

Murray, B. (2002, June). Good news for bachelor's grads. *Monitor on Psychology*, *33*(6), 30–32.

Myers, S. B., Sweeney, A. C., Popick, V., Wesley, K., Bordfeld, A., & Fingerhut, R. (2012). Self-care practices and perceived stress levels among psychology graduate students. *Training and Education in Professional Psychology*, *6*, 55–66. doi:10.1037/a0026534

MyPlan.com. (2009). *Highest paying jobs without college*. Retrieved from http://www.myplan.com/careers/top-ten/highest-paying-without-college.php

Nadal, K. L. (2017). "Let's get in formation": On becoming a psychologist-activist in the 21st century. *American Psychologist*, *72*, 935–946. doi:10.1037/amp0000212

Natavi Guides. (2002). *Fishing for a major*. New York, NY: Author.

National Association of Colleges and Employers [NACE]. (2015, May). *First destinations for the college class of 2014*. Bethlehem, PA: Author. Retrieved from http://www.naceweb.org/job-market/graduate-outcomes/first-destination/class-of-2014/

National Association of Colleges and Employers [NACE]. (2017). *Salary survey: Preliminary starting salaries for Class of 2017 new college graduates data reported by colleges and universities*. Retrieved from https://www.naceweb.org/job-market/compensation/class-of-2017s-overall-starting-salary-shows-little-gain/

National Center for Education Statistics. (2017). Historical summary of faculty, enrollment, degrees conferred, and finances in degree-granting postsecondary institutions: Selected years, 1869-70 through 2014-15 [Table 301.20]. *Digest of Education Statistics*. Washington, DC: U.S. Department of Education. Retrieved from https://nces.ed.gov/programs/digest/d16/tables/dt16_301.10.asp?current=yes

National Center for Education Statistics. (2017k). Total fall enrollment in degree-granting post-secondary institutions, by level of enrollment, sex of student, and other selected characteristics: 2016 [Table 303.60]. *Digest of Education Statistics*. Washington, DC: U.S. Department of Education. Retrieved from https://nces.ed.gov/programs/digest/d17/tables/dt17_303.60.asp?current=yes

National Center for Education Statistics. (2017a). Bachelor's degrees conferred by postsecondary institutions, by field of study: Selected years, 1970-71 through 2015-16 [Table 322.10]. *Digest of Education Statistics*. Washington, DC. U.S. Department of Education.

Retrieved from https://nces.ed.gov/programs/digest/d16/tables/dt16_322.10.asp

National Center for Education Statistics. (2017b). Associate's degrees conferred by postsecondary institutions, by race/ethnicity and field of study: 2014-15 and 2015-16 [Table 321.30]. *Digest of Education Statistics*. Washington, DC. U.S. Department of Education. Retrieved from https://nces.ed.gov/programs/digest/d17/tables/dt17_321.30.asp

National Center for Education Statistics. (2017c). Degrees in psychology conferred by postsecondary institutions, by level of degree and sex of student: Selected years, 1949-50 through 2015-16 [Table 325.80]. *Digest of Education Statistics*. Washington, DC: U.S. Department of Education. Retrieved from https://nces.ed.gov/programs/digest/d17/tables/dt17_325.80.asp

National Centre for Vocational Education Research. (2004). Generic skills for the new economy. In Siena College (Ed.), *Liberal education and the new economy*. Loudonville, NY: Siena College.

National O*NET™ Consortium. (2001, May). *O*NET occupational listings*. Raleigh, NC: Author.

Nelson, E. S., & Johnson, K. A. (1997). A senior exit survey and its implications for advising and related services. *Teaching of Psychology, 24*, 101–105.

Newman, J. H. (1852/1960). *The idea of a university* (Edited by M. J. Svaglic). New York, NY: Rinehart Press.

Newport, F., & Busteed, B. (2013, December 17). Americans still see college education as very important. *Gallup, Inc*. Retrieved from https://news.gallup.com/poll/166490/americans-college-education-important.aspx

Norcross, J. C., & Castle, P. H. (2002). Appreciating the PsyD: The facts. *Eye on Psi Chi, 7*(1), 22–26.

Norcross, J. C., Hailstorks, R., Aiken, L. S., Pfund, R. A., Stamm, K. E., & Christidis, P. (2016). Undergraduate study in psychology: Curriculum and assessment. *American Psychologist, 71*, 89–101. doi:10.1037/a0040095

Norcross, J. C. & Hogan, T. P. (n.d.). *Preparing and applying for graduate school in psychology*. [Video series]. Retrieved from http://www.apa.org/education/grad/application-video-series.aspx

Northwestern University. (2018). *What is political science?* Retrieved from https://www.polisci.northwestern.edu/undergraduate/

Nowack, K. M., Gibbons, J. M., & Hanson, A. L. (1985). Factors affecting burnout and job performance of resident assistants. *Journal of College Student Personnel, 26*, 137–142.

O'Hare, L., & McGuinness, C. (2004). Skills and attributes developed by psychology undergraduates: Ratings by undergraduates, postgraduates, academic psychologists and professional practitioners. *Psychology Learning and Teaching, 4*, 35–42.

Occupational Outlook Handbook. (1998). *Social workers*. Retrieved from http://www.bls.gov/oco/ocos060.htm

Occupational Outlook Handbook. (2004). *Psychologists*. Washington, DC: U.S. Bureau of Labor Statistics.

Omarzu, J., Hennessey, E. P., & Rys, L. E. (2006, Winter). Undergraduate research in psychology at four-year institutions. *Eye on Psi Chi, 10*(2), 38–39, 46–48.

O*NET OnLine. (2018). *Summary report for 21-1092.00 – Probation officers and correctional treatment specialists*. Retrieved from https://www.onetonline.org/link/summary/21-1092.00

Osborne, R. E. (1996, Fall). The "personal" side of graduate school personal statements. *Eye on Psi Chi, 1*(1), 14–15.

Oudekerk, B. A., & Bottoms, B. L. (2007, Fall). Applying to graduate school: The interview process. *Eye on Psi Chi, 12*(1), 25–27.

Panadero, E., Jonsson, A, & Botella, J. (2017). Effects of self-assessment on self-regulated learning and self-efficacy: Four meta-analyses. *Educational Research Review, 22*, 74–98. doi:10.1016/j.edurev.2017.08.004

Pawlow, L. A., & Meinz, E. J. (2017). Characteristics of psychology students who serve as research assistants. *College Student Journal, 51*, 77-80.

Payscale. (2018). *Bachelor of Arts (BA), psychology median salary by years experience*. Retrieved from https://www.payscale.com/research/US/Degree=Bachelor_of_Arts_(BA)%2C_Psychology/Salary

Perlman, B., & McCann, L. I. (2005). Undergraduate research experiences in psychology: A national study of courses and curricula. *Teaching of Psychology, 32*, 5–14.

Perlman, B., & McCann, L. I. (1999). The structure of the psychology undergraduate curriculum. *Teaching of Psychology, 26*, 171–176.

Peterson, D. R. (2003). Unintended consequences: Ventures and misadventures in the education of professional psychologists. *American Psychologist, 58*, 791–800.

Peterson, J. J., & Shackelford, C. T. (2011, August). *Pursuing a purpose: Enlightening students through service-internships*. Presented at the annual convention of the American Psychological Association, Washington, DC.

Plous, S. (1998a). *Advice on letters of recommendation*. Retrieved from http://www.socialpsychology.org/rectips.htm

Plous, S. (1998b). *Sample template for creating a vita*. Retrieved from http://www.socialpsychology.org/vitatemplate.htm

Prickett, T. J., Gada-Jain, N., & Bernieri, F. J. (2000, May). *The importance of first impressions in a job interview*. Presented at the Midwestern Psychological Association, Chicago, IL.

Privitera, G. J. (2015). *Getting into graduate school: A comprehensive guide for psychology and the behavioral sciences*. Thousand Oaks, CA: Sage.

Prohaska, V. (2008, Spring). It's conference time. *Eye on Psi Chi, 12*(3), 4.

Pryor, J. H., DeAngelo, L., Blake, L. P., Hurtado, S., & Tran, S. (2011). *The American freshman: National norms fall 2011*. Los Angeles, CA: Higher Education Research Institute, UCLA.

Psi Beta. (2018a). *Welcome to Psi Beta*. Retrieved from http://psibeta.org/site/

Psi Beta. (2018b). *Benefits of membership*. Retrieved from http://psibeta.org/site/students/benefits

Psi Chi. (2012a). *Becoming a member*. Retrieved from http://www.psichi.org/about/becomember.aspx

Psi Chi. (2012b). *Benefits of membership*. Retrieved from http://www.psichi.org/About/benefits.aspx

Psi Chi. (2012c). *What is Psi Chi?* Retrieved from http://www.psichi.org/About/

Psi Chi. (2018). *Become a member*. Retrieved from https://www.psichi.org/page/become_member#.W2XM_NVKh9A

Psi Beta. (2018a). *Welcome to Psi Beta*. Retrieved from http://psibeta.org/site/

Psi Beta. (2018b). *Benefits of membership*. Retrieved from http://psibeta.org/site/students/benefits

Purdue Owl. (2018). *More about passive voice*. Retrieved from https://owl.purdue.edu/owl/general_writing/academic_writing/active_and_passive_voice/more_about_passive_voice.html

Rajecki, D. W. (2008). Job lists for entry-level psychology baccalaureates: Occupational recommendations that mismatch qualifications. *Teaching of Psychology, 35*, 33–37.

Rajecki, D. W., Williams, C. C., Appleby, D. C., Jeschke, M. P., & Johnson, K. E. (2005). Sources of students' interest in the psychology major: Refining the Rajecki-Metzner model. *Individual Differences Research, 3*, 128–135.

Rewey, K. (2000, Fall). Getting a good letter of recommendation. *Eye on Psi Chi*, *5*(1), 27–29.

Robinson, F. P. (1970). *Effective study* (4th ed.). New York, NY: Harper & Row.

Roediger, R. (2004). Vita voyeur. *APS Observer*, *17*(1). Retrieved from http://www.psychologicalscience.org/index.php/publications/observer/2004/january-04/vita-voyeur.html

Roig, M. (2007). *A student-faculty research agreement*. Department of Psychology, St. John's University [posted on OTRP online]. Staten Island, NY: Author.

Roscoe, L. J., & McMahan, E. A. (2014). Outcomes of Introduction to the Psychology Major: Careers and opportunities course. *Teaching of Psychology*, *41*, 110–114. doi:1177/0098628314530340

Roscoe, L. J., & Strapp, C. M. (2009). Increasing psychology students' satisfaction with preparedness through a professional issues course. *Teaching of Psychology*, *36*, 18–23. doi:10.1080/00986280802529426

Rose, J. (2010, May 28). Study: College grads unprepared for workplace. *NPR*. Retrieved from http://www.npr.org/templates/story/story.php?storyId=127230009

Rose, J. (2011, November 28). *Is college overrated? The top 18 highest paying jobs with no college degree*. Retrieved from http://www.goodfinancialcents.com/12-highest-paying-jobs-careers-without-no-college-degree-diploma/

Rosnow, R. L., & Rosnow, M. (2009). *Writing papers in psychology* (8th ed.). Belmont, CA: Wadsworth/Cengage.

Rosnow, R. L., Rotheram-Borus, M. J., Ceci, S. J., Blanck, P. D., & Koocher, G. P. (1993). The institutional review board as a mirror of scientific and ethical standards. *American Psychologist*, *48*, 821–826.

Roulston, A., Montgomery, L., Campbell, A., & Davidson, G. (2018). Exploring the impact of mindfulness on mental wellbeing, stress and resilience of undergraduate social work students. *Social Work Education*, *37*, 157–172. doi:10.1080/02615479.2017.1388776

Rutti, R. M., LaBonte, J., Helms, M. M., Hervani, A. A., & Sarkarat, S. (2016). The service learning projects: Stakeholder benefits and potential class topics. *Education + Training*, *58*, 422-438. doi:10.1108/ET-06-2015-0050

San Diego State University. (1998). *SDSU criminal justice program*. Retrieved from http:/www.sdsu.edu/academicprog/crimjust.html

Schoeneman, K. A., & Schoeneman, T. J. (2006, Winter). Applying to graduate school in clinical psychology: Advice for the aspiring applicant. *Eye on Psi Chi*, *10*(2), 34–35, 45.

Schultheiss, D. E. P. (2008). *Psychology as a major: Is it right for me and what can I do with my degree?* Washington, DC: American Psychological Association.

Schultz, J. R. (2001, December). The transformational process of mentoring. *Council on Undergraduate Research Quarterly*, 72–73.

Schwartz, B. M., Landrum, R. E., & Gurung, R. A. R. (2012). *An easyguide to APA style*. Thousand Oaks, CA: Sage.

Schwartz, B. M., Landrum, R. E., & Gurung, R. A. R. (2016). *An easyguide to APA style* (3rd ed.). Thousand Oaks, CA: Sage.

Seymour, S., & Lopez, S. (2015, April 8). "Big six" college experiences linked to life preparedness. *Gallup, Inc*. Retrieved from https://news.gallup.com/poll/182306/big-six-college-experiences-linked-life-preparedness.aspx

Shen, W. (2010, November). Building your marketability throughout your graduate school career. *Psychological Science Agenda, American Psychological Association*. Retrieved from http://www.apa.org/science/about/psa/2010/11/marketability.aspx

Silvia, P. J. (2007). *How to write a lot: A practical guide to productive academic writing*. Washington, DC: American Psychological Association.

Silvia, P. J., Delaney, P. F., & Marcovitch, S. (2009). *What psychology majors could (and should) be doing: An informal guide to research experience and professional skills*. Washington, DC: American Psychological Association.

Simon, A. F. (2017). Integrating action research into the psychology curriculum: Extending the service learning approach. *Scholarship of Teaching and Learning in Psychology*, *3*, 304–315.

Singleton, D., Tate, A. C., & Kohout, J. L. (2003). *2002 master's, specialist's, and related degrees employment survey*. Washington, DC: American Psychological Association.

Sittser, J. (2004). *The will of God as a way of life: How to make every decision with peace and confidence*. Grand Rapids, MI: Zondervan.

Slattery, J. M., & Park, C. L. (2002, Spring). Predictors of successful supervision of undergraduate researchers by faculty. *Eye on Psi Chi*, *6*(3), 29–33.

Sleigh, M. J., & Ritzer, D. R. (2007, Spring). Undergraduate research experience: Preparation for the job market. *Eye on Psi Chi*, *11*(3), 27–30.

Smith, R. A. (2000). Documenting your scholarship: Citations and references. In R. J. Sternberg (Ed.), *Guide to publishing in psychology journals* (pp. 146–157). Cambridge, United Kingdom: Cambridge University Press.

Smith, T. W. (2007). *Job satisfaction in the United States*. Chicago, IL: National Opinion Research Center, University of Chicago.

Snyder, T. D., & Dillow, S. A. (2011). *Digest of education statistics 2010* (NCES 2011-015). National Center for Education Statistics, Institute of Education Sciences. Washington, DC: U.S. Department of Education.

Social Work Guide. (2018). *What is social work?* Retrieved from https://www.socialworkguide.org/

Spielberger, C. D., Gonzalez, H. P., Taylor, C. J., Anton, E. D., Algaze, B., Ross, G. R., & Westberry, L. G. (1980). *Manual for the test anxiety inventory*. Redwood City, CA: Consulting Psychologists Press.

Stambor, Z. (2008, July/August). Make the most of your post. *Monitor on Psychology*, *39*(7), 80–81.

Stanley, M. L., Dougherty, A. M., Yang, B. W., Henne, P., & De Brigand, F. (2018). Reasons probably won't change your mind: The role of reasons in revising moral decisions. *Journal of Experimental Psychology: General*, *147*, 962–987. doi:10.1037/xge.0000368

Stark, M. A., Hoekstra, T., Hazel, D. L., & Barton, B. (2012). Caring for self and others: Increasing health care for students' healthy behaviors. *Work*, *42*, 393–401. doi:10.3233/WOR-2012-1428

Stead, G. B. (1991). *The Career Myths Scale*. Unpublished manuscript, Vista University, Port Elizabeth, South Africa.

Sternberg, R. J. (Ed.). (2006). *Career paths in psychology: Where your degree can take you* (2nd ed.). Washington, DC: American Psychological Association.

Sternberg, R. J. (2000). Titles and abstracts: They only sound unimportant. In R. J. Sternberg (Ed.), *Guide to publishing in psychology journals* (pp. 37–40). Cambridge, United Kingdom: Cambridge University Press.

Strada Education Network and Gallup. (2018, May). *From college to life: Relevance and the value of higher education*. Retrieved from http://www.stradaeducation.org/consumer-insights/relevance-and-higher-education/

Strapp, C. M., Drapela, D. J., Henderson, C. I., Nasciemento, E., & Roscoe, L. J. (2018). Psychology students' expectations regarding educational requirements and salary for desired careers. *Teaching of Psychology*, *45*, 6–13. doi:10.1177/0098628317744943

Strauss, K. (2017). Job hunting tips for 2017. *Forbes*. Retrieved from https://www.forbes.com/sites/karstenstrauss/2017/03/07/job-hunting-tips-for-2017/#23f719895c12

Strauss, K., Griffin, M. A., & Parker, S. K. (2012). Future work selves: How salient hoped-for identities motivate proactive career behaviors. *Journal of Applied Psychology, 97*, 580–598. doi:10.1037/a0026423

Stoloff, M. L., Good, M. R., Smith, K. L., & Brewster, J. (2015). Characteristics of programs that maximize psychology major success. *Teaching of Psychology, 42*, 99–108. doi:10.1177/00986283115569977

Sue, V. M., & Ritter, L. A. (2007). *Conducting online surveys*. Los Angeles, CA: Sage.

Szuchman, L. T. (2011). *Writing with style: APA style made easy* (5th ed.). Belmont, CA: Wadsworth/Cengage.

Takooshian, H., Gielen, U. P., Plous, S., Rich, G. J., & Velayo, R. S. (2016). Internationalizing undergraduate psychology education: Trends, techniques, and technologies. *American Psychologist, 71*, 136–147.

Taraban, R., & Logue, E. (2012). Academic factors that affect undergraduate research experiences. *Journal of Educational Psychology, 104*, 499-514. doi:10.1037/a0026851

Tarsi, M., & Jalbert, N. (1998). *An examination of the career paths of a matched sample of Psi Chi and Non-Psi Chi psychology majors*. 1997–98 Hunt Award Research Report. Retrieved from http://www.psichi.org/awards/winners/hunt_reports/jalbert.asp

Task Force on Strengthening the Teaching and Learning of Undergraduate Psychological Sciences. (2006). *Teaching, learning, and assessing in a developmentally coherent curriculum*. Report for the Board of Educational Affairs. Washington, DC: American Psychological Association.

Taylor, J., & Deane, F. P. (2002). Development of a short form of the Test Anxiety Inventory (TAI). *Journal of General Psychology, 129*, 127–136.

Taylor, R. D., & Hardy, C. A. (1996). Careers in psychology at the associate's, bachelor's, master's, and doctoral levels. *Psychological Reports, 79*, 960–962.

The Writing Center at American University. (2012, October). *Identify passive voice (with zombies!)*. Retrieved from http://auwritingcenter.blogspot.com/2012/10/identify-passive-voice-with-zombies.html

Thomas, J. H., & McDaniel, C. R. (2004). Effectiveness of a required course in career planning for psychology majors. *Teaching of Psychology, 31*, 22–27.

TMP Worldwide. (1998). *Action verbs to enhance our resume*. Retrieved from http://www.aboutwork.com/rescov/resinfo/verbs.html

Torstel, P. (2015, October 14). It's not just the money: The benefits of college education to individuals and to society. *Lumina Issue Papers*. Indianapolis, IN: Lumina Foundation. Retrieved from https://www.luminafoundation.org/files/resources/its-not-just-the-money.pdf

Toorenburg, M. V., Oostrom, J. K., & Pollet, T. V. (2015). What a difference your e-mail makes: Effects of informal e-mail addresses in online resume screening. *Cyberpsychology, Behavior, and Social Networking, 18*, 135–140. doi:10.1089/cyber.2014.0542

U.S. Chamber of Commerce Foundation. (2017). Learning to work, working to learn. *Center for Education and Workforce*. Washington, DC: Author. Retrieved from https://www.uschamberfoundation.org/sites/default/files/Learning%20to%20Work%20Working%20to%20Learn.pdf

United States Department of Labor. (1991). *Tips for finding the right job*. Employment and Training Administration. Washington, DC: Author.

University of California–Berkeley. (1998). *Taking tests—general tips*. Retrieved from http://slc.berkeley.edu/studystrategies/calren/testsgeneral.html

University of California–Santa Cruz. (1998). *Choosing a topic*. Retrieved from http://library.ucsc.edu/help/howto/choose-a-research-topic

University of Iowa. (2011). *Evaluate information online: The CRAAP test*. Retrieved from http://www.lib.uiowa.edu/instruction/

University of the Fraser Valley. (2009). *Evaluating information: The CRAAP test*. Retrieved from http://www.ufv.ca/library/tutorials/craaptest.htm

University of Michigan at Dearborn (1998). *Benefits to the student*. Retrieved from http://www-personal.umd.umich.edu/~pdjones/benef_s.html

University of North Carolina. (2018). What is sociology? *Department of Sociology*. Retrieved from https://sociology.unc.edu/undergraduate-program/sociology-major/what-is-sociology/

University of Oregon. (2010). *Policy on academic dishonesty*. Retrieved http://oregonstate.edu/studentconduct/faculty/facacdis.php

U.S. Census Bureau. (2011). Table 228. Mean earnings by highest degree earned: 2008. *Statistical Abstract of the United States*. Retrieved from http://www.census.gov/compendia/statab/2011/tables/11s0228.pdf

Vanderbilt University. (1996). *How to select a research topic*. Retrieved from http://www.library.vanderbilt.edu/peabody/research/reshelp/topic.html

Vespia, K. M., Freis, S. D., & Arrowood, R. M. (2018). Faculty and career advising: Challenges, opportunities, and outcome assessment. *Teaching of Psychology, 45*, 24–31. doi:10.1177.0098628317744962

Vittengl, J. R., Bosley, C. Y., Brescia, S. A., Eckardt, E. A., Neidig, J. M., Shelver, K. S., Sapenoff, L. A. (2004). Why are some undergraduates more (and others less) interested in psychological research? *Teaching of Psychology, 31*, 91–97.

Wahlstrom, C., & Williams, B. K. (2004). *College to career: Your road to personal success*. Mason, OH: South-Western.

Walfish, S. (2001). Developing a career in psychology. In S. Walfish & A. K. Hess (Eds.), *Succeeding in graduate school: The career guide for psychology students* (pp. 385–397). Mahwah, NJ: Erlbaum.

Walfish, S., & Turner, K. (2006, Summer). Relative weighting of admission variables in developmental psychology doctoral programs. *Eye on Psi Chi, 10*(4), 20–21.

Wallace, L. (2011, June). The value of following passion in a jobless world. *The Atlantic*. Retrieved from http://www.theatlantic.com/business/print/2011/06/the-value-of-following-passion-in-a-jobless-world/239899/

Walsh, L. L. (2006, Fall). Alternative master's degree programs for psychology majors. *Eye on Psi Chi, 11*(1), 21–23.

Ware, M. E. (2001). Pursuing a career with a bachelor's degree in psychology. In S. Walfish & A. K. Hess (Eds.), *Succeeding in graduate school: The career guide for psychology students* (pp. 11–30). Mahwah, NJ: Erlbaum.

Waters, M. (1998, July). Naps could replace coffee as workers' favorite break. *American Psychological Association Monitor*, p. 6.

Webb, A. R., & Speer, J. R. (1986). Prototype of a profession: Psychology's public image. *Professional Psychology: Research and Practice, 17*, 5–9.

Wegenek, A. R., & Buskist, W. (2010). *The insider's guide to the psychology major: Everything you need to know about the degree and profession*. Washington, DC: American Psychological Association.

Weinstein, C. E., Palmer, D. R., & Schulte, A. C. (1987). *Learning and study strategies inventory*. Clearwater, FL: H&H Publishing Co.

Weinstein, Y., Madan, C. R., & Sumeracki, M. A. (2018). Teaching the science of learning. *Cognitive Research: Principles and Implications, 3*. doi:10.1186/s41235-017-0087-y

Weller, L., Haddock, S., Zimmerman, T. S., Krafchick, J., Henry, K., & Rudisill, S. (2013). Benefits derived by college students from mentoring at-risk youth in a service-learning course. *American*

Journal of Community Psychology, *52*, 236–248. doi:10.1007/s10464-013-9589-z

Whitlock, B., & Ebrahimi, N. (2016). Beyond the library: Using multiple mixed measures simultaneously in a college-wide assessment of information literacy. *College & Research Libraries*, *77*, 236–262. doi:10.5860/crl.77.2.236

Williams-Nickelson, C. (2007, September). Presenting well. *gradPSYCH*, *5*(3), 11.

Wolfle, D. L. (1947). The sensible organization of courses in psychology. *American Psychologist*, *2*, 437–445.

Wood, G. (1981). *Fundamentals of psychological research* (3rd ed.). Boston, MA: Little, Brown.

Wood, M. R., & Palm, L. J. (2000). Students' anxiety in a senior thesis course. *Psychological Reports*, *86*, 935–936.

Yancey, G. B., Clarkson, C. P., Baxa, J. D., & Clarkson, R. N. (2003). Examples of good and bad interpersonal skills at work. *Eye on Psi Chi*, *7*(3), 40–41.

Zimak, E. H., Edwards, K. M., Johnson, S. M., & Suhr, J. (2011). Now or later? An empirical investigation of when and why students apply to clinical psychology PhD programs. *Teaching of Psychology*, *38*, 118–121. doi:10.1177/0098628311401585

Zinsser, W. (1988). *Writing to learn*. New York, NY: Harper & Row.

Zucchero, R. A. (2011). Psychology ethics in introductory psychology textbooks. *Teaching of Psychology*, *38*, 110–113. doi:10.1177/0098628311401583

Zuckerman, R. A. (1995). *Doc Whiz's 40 ways to P.O. the prof.* Retrieved from http://cwx.prenhall.com/bookbind/pubbooks/davis2/medialib/part14.html

Index

D

E

F

G

Q

R

S

T